GW01090309

www.ealing.gov.uk

91400000409427

ABDULLAH GÜL

& the Making of the New Turkey

ABDULLAH GÜL

& the Making of the New Turkey

Gerald MacLean

A Oneworld Book

First published by Oneworld Publications, 2014

Copyright © Gerald MacLean 2014

The moral right of Gerald MacLean to be identified as the Author of
this work has been asserted by him in accordance with the Copyright,
Designs, and Patents Act 1988

ISBN 978-1-78074-562-6
eBook ISBN 978-1-78074-563-3

Typesetting and ebook by Tetragon, London
Printed and bound in Great Britain by
TJ International Ltd, Padstow, Cornwall

Oneworld Publications
10 Bloomsbury Street
London WC1B 3SR
England

Stay up to date with the latest books,
special offers, and exclusive content from
Oneworld with our monthly newsletter

Sign up on our website
www.oneworld-publications.com

CONTENTS

A NOTE ON PRONUNCIATION

In the modern Turkish alphabet, introduced in 1928, words are pronounced phonetically and most letters are pronounced as in English with the following exceptions:

a is always short, as in 'cat'

c 'j' as 'jazz'

ç 'ch' as in 'charity'

ş 'sh' as in 'shell'

ı without a dot as the final vowel in 'Cyril'

i with a dot as in 'bit'; for English readers I have avoided the ungainly looking but strictly correct dotted capital İ

ö as in German

ü as in German

ğ unvoiced, silently lengthens the preceding vowel

ABBREVIATIONS

AKP	*Adalet ve Kalkınma Partisi* or 'Justice and Development Party'
ANAP	*Anavatan Partisi* or 'Motherland Party'
AP	*Adalet Partisi* or 'Justice Party'
BDP	*Barış ve Demokrasi Partisi* or 'Peace and Democracy Party'
CHP	*Cumhuriyet Halk Partisi* or 'Republican People's Party'
CUP	Committee of Union and Progress
DEP	*Demokrasi Partisi* or 'Democracy Party'
DGM	*Devlet Güvenlik Mahkemeleri* or 'State Security Courts'
DP	*Demokrat Parti* or 'Democrat Party'
DSP	*Demokratik Sol Parti* or 'Democratic Left Party'
DTP	*Demokratik Toplum Partisi* or 'Democratic Society Party'
DYP	*Doğru Yol Partisi* or 'True Path Party'
EU	European Union
FOSIS	Federation of Student Islamic Societies
FP	*Fazilet Partisi* or 'Virtue Party'
HEP	*Halkın Emek Partisi* or 'People's Labour Party'
IHH	*Insan Hak ve Hürriyetleri ve Insani Yardım Vakfı* or 'Foundation for Human Rights and Freedoms and Humanitarian Relief'
IMF	International Monetary Fund
JITEM	*Jandarma Istihbarat ve Terörle Mücadele Grup Komutanlığı* or 'Gendarmerie Intelligence and Counter-Terrorism Centre'
KAYSO	*Kayseri Sanayi Odası* or 'Kayseri Chamber of Industry'
KCK	*Koma Civaken Kurdistan* or 'Union of Communities of Kurdistan'
MÇP	*Miliyetçi Çalışma Partisi* or 'Nationalist Working Party'
MHP	*Milliyetçi Hareket Partisi* or 'Nationalist Action Party'

MIT	*Milli Istihbarat Teşkilatı* or 'National Intelligence Organization'
MNP	*Milli Nizam Partisi* or 'National Order Party'
MSP	*Milli Selâmet Partisi* or 'National Salvation Party'
MTTB	*Milli Türk Talebe Birliği* or 'National Turkish Student Association'
MÜSIAD	*Müstakil Sanayici ve Iş Adamları Derneği* or 'Independent Industrialists and Businessmen's Association'
NATO	North Atlantic Treaty Organization
NGO	Non-governmental organization
OECD	Organization of Economic Co-operation and Development
OIC	Organization of the Islamic Conference
OYAK	*Ordu Yardımlaşma Kurumu* or 'Army Mutual Assistance Association'
PACE	Parliamentary Assembly of the Council of Europe
PKK	*Parti Karkerani Kurdistan* or 'Kurdistan Workers' Party'
SHP	*Sosyaldemokrat Halkçı Parti* or 'Social Democratic Populist Party'
SODEP	*Sosyal Demokrasi Partisi* or 'Social Democracy Party'
SP	*Saadet Partisi* or 'Felicity Party'
TIP	*Türkiye Işçi Partisi* or 'Turkish Workers Party'
TRT	Türkiye Radyo Televizyon

ILLUSTRATIONS

Unless otherwise indicated, all illustrations are courtesy of the Office of the Presidency of the Republic of Turkey and Madame Hayrünnisa Gül.

FOREWORD

T his book is an attempt to explore what has been happening in Turkey since the end of the Second World War by focusing on the life and career of Abdullah Gül, the eleventh president. Although it is not an official biography, it could not have been written if President Gül had not been willing to talk to me, and for his time and the support of his staff I am grateful. But before I say anything more about the curious circumstances that led me to undertake this work, it will be useful to indicate in the most general way something of what was going on in Turkey in the period leading up to the story of Abdullah Gül's life and career. Since it is written in English, this book also needs to offer some preliminary account of itself, not least because there are two well-known English-language biographies of Mustafa Kemal Atatürk, the founder and first president of the Republic of Turkey, by Patrick Balfour and Andrew Mango.[1] These are massive, stylishly written tomes that have rightly achieved status as examples of political biography. So the first observation I need to make is that my aims in writing this book are as different from theirs as is my subject. This is not the story of a military leader who forged from the remains of a defeated empire a revolutionary republic of which he became the iconic first president, but the story of an academic banker who founded a political party that achieved democratically elected power by challenging Atatürk's political legacy, and who became Turkey's first president from a background in Islamic politics. Abdullah Gül is as different from Mustafa Kemal Atatürk as this book is from those of Balfour and Mango.

If I have a model before me, it is rather Geoffrey Lewis's *Haci Ömer Sabancı: The Turkish Village Boy Who Built an Industrial Empire* (1988), a translation from Sadun Tanju's Turkish biography of 1983. It is perhaps no coincidence that Sabancı and Gül both come from the central Anatolian region of Kayseri. In the opening sections of this study, I have offered a detailed history of Kayseri since for understanding Turkey's current political scene, the background of politics in this ancient but provincial capital provides important and seldom explored insights not only into President Gül's personality and intellectual development, but also the political movement that his party represents. Though differing in most other respects, the stories of Sabancı's and Gül's careers offer distinctive versions of achievement and success against the disadvantages of their shared provincial background, and illuminate the mixed history of Atatürk's republican revolution. While Sabancı pursued business opportunities newly available under the republican state to found one of the nation's wealthiest dynasties, Gül set out to challenge the democratic inadequacies of that state and the much-revised Constitution of 1924 on which it has been legitimated. So first, a brief recollection of Atatürk and his political legacy might prove useful since they have obvious and direct bearing on the Turkish political scene in which Abdullah Gül developed his views, and will help indicate what has come to be meant by the 'new Turkey.'[2]

In 1923 Turkey, formerly the Ottoman Empire, became a republic. Twelve years later the first president, Mustafa Kemal, assumed a new name, 'Atatürk', that declared him to be the 'Father of the Turks'.[3] Atatürk has since entered the list of the world's most famous political leaders, while the legacy of his new name continues to inspire admiration bordering on adoration among many Turks who are still referred to as 'Kemalists'. Born in 1881, Mustafa Kemal was a career soldier from Salonica who twice became a national hero for defeating foreign invaders: first, for his victory against the Allies in 1916 at Gallipoli in a campaign that saved the capital Constantinople, and the second time in 1922 for turning back the invading Greek armies that had penetrated deeply into central Anatolia. But the man who became a legend was more than a gifted and fortunate military leader. From the beginnings of his career, Mustafa Kemal had been a fierce political opponent of the Ottoman sultanate with its autocratic rule and dubious claims to power over Muslims throughout the entire Islamic world. Before the First World War brought him fame, Kemal had become a leading figure in a revolutionary nationalist movement, the covert *Vatan ve Hürriyet* ('Fatherland and Freedom Society').[4] Amid the political shambles that followed the war while the Sultan and allied powers squabbled over the breakup of the Ottoman Empire, Kemal emerged as the leading figure of a nationalist movement that would replace the centuries-old Islamic empire with a secular republic.

Mustafa Kemal's big chance came on 11 April 1920, when the Ottoman Sultan Vahdettin, known as Mehmed VI, threw a temper tantrum and dissolved the Chamber of Deputies – a body of elected delegates set up in 1877 following attempts to make the Ottoman state appear more democratic. The Sultan wanted uncontested authority so he could cut the best deal with the Allies and disdained interference in his plans. Two weeks later, on 23 April, the nationalist majority of the dismissed but elected delegates gathered together in Ankara for the first meeting of the *Türkiye Büyük Millet Meclisi*, the 'Grand National Assembly of Turkey', now familiarly called the *Meclis*. They declared that sovereignty belongs to the nation, and that the Grand National Assembly held executive and administrative power over the Turkish state under signature of a president elected by the Assembly. They promptly elected Mustafa Kemal the first president of this new state.[5]

From this moment on, Mustafa Kemal's nationalist revolution continued to take shape heroically, confronting frantic opposition from the sultan in Constantinople, and disbelief on the part of interested foreign governments who were still contesting who would get which former Ottoman ports. With invading Greek armies approaching Ankara in September 1921, Kemal boldly assumed control of military tactics. Within a year, he had turned back the Greek forces and become for the second time a monumentally revered figure of national pride. In Ankara, the Grand National Assembly formally declared the Turkish state to be a 'republic' on 29 October 1923. They adopted a new constitution on 20 April 1924 that was designed to protect their authority with indications of future democratic reforms once the time was ready. The constitution gave the Grand National Assembly direct legislative authority and executive powers, which it exercised through a president – elected by the assembly – and a Cabinet of ministers to be chosen by the president. Although the assembly reserved the right to check and even overthrow any government judged to be acting against the constitution, Mustafa Kemal's power appeared to be guaranteed for life. And not everyone was happy about it. Early on, Kemal faced opposition among delegates who split to form their own parties, but Prime Minister Ismet Inönü rallied supporters and the republic adopted new laws in March 1925 that silenced all opposition to the government. For the next twenty-five years, the Republic of Turkey would be governed by one, unopposed political party, Mustafa Kemal's party, the *Cumhuriyet Halk Partisi* ('Republican People's Party', hereafter CHP). Until his death in 1938, Atatürk presided over a one-party state governed by the CHP, which would continue in office and uphold his ideals until 1950 when the first multiparty elections in the history of the republic brought Adnan Menderes and the *Demokrat Parti* ('Democrat Party,' or DP) to power.

Briefly remembering Atatürk will, I hope, indicate that any grounds for comparison between Abdullah Gül and the iconic hero who turned the Ottoman Empire into a secular republic would be futile even if the two men were not entirely different in background, experience, and political outlook. Coincidentally, Gül was born on 29 October 1950, the anniversary of the republic in the year Atatürk's party first lost power. In one sense, that year and the political changes it marked constitute when this book begins. But coincidence does not account for this book's origins or why and how I came to write it.

One origin must be my first visit to Istanbul during the winter of 1975 when I was teaching English across the border in Kavala, Greece. I immediately realized that the Turks were quite different from how I had grown up to think of them, and were most certainly not the villains against whom my Greek students sternly warned me. I began visiting Turkey regularly again in the late 1980s, travelling with my partner Donna Landry on buses throughout central Anatolia and beyond. I have written elsewhere of journeys with our equestrian friend Rosemary Hooley to Urfa and Diyarbakır and along the Syrian border areas in search of horses during the middle to late 1990s.[6] We met other tourists along the way; by the early 1990s I frequently found myself trying to explain what was going on in Turkey – most notably the apparent wealth of the west alongside seeming impoverishment in the rural areas – and what it meant. I began research for a book about the earliest English travellers to the Ottoman Empire, and we re-traced the routes described by several seventeenth-century travel writers throughout Turkey and beyond into Syria and North Africa.[7] In 1999, or thereabouts, Donna and I started plans with Caroline Finkel for an equestrian trip across Turkey following the route of the seventeenth-century Ottoman traveller, Evliya Çelebi. After some years of route planning and seeking sponsors, we met Ercihan Dilari, horseman extraordinaire, who instantly understood the project. In 2009 the team set out on Ercihan's horses from the southern shores of the Sea of Marmara to follow Evliya's route for the legendary forty days and nights, camping in villages along the way.[8] On all such trips, we like to think we make new friends, as we had done on visits further afield in villages and cities throughout the South East. But even so, how did I come to write this book?

*

I first registered Abdullah Gül by name in 2003, a year after his party had come to power, when there was considerable media attention to a new piece of legislation, Article 301, that was being introduced by the *Adalet ve Kalkınma Partisi* ('Justice and Development Party', or AKP). This is the law that brought a number of famous and less well-known Turkish writers to trial on accusations of being disrespectful of the state: Orhan Pamuk, Elif Shafak, Perihan Mağden and numerous other writers and journalists were all indicted under provision of this new law. But I recall Gül being quoted in the UK press for saying that 301 was a law, and that like all laws, it could be changed. Although my scholarly interests belong to the early-modern Ottoman period, I had followed political life in Turkey since the 1980s and was surprised at hearing what was clearly a new voice in Turkish politics. That a senior government minister of the very party that had introduced a piece of legislation should acknowledge how it might need changing seemed truly remarkable. There were many more surprises to come.

Like others, I was taken aback by the energy with which the party Abdullah Gül represented, the AKP, on arrival in government in 2002 went from strength to strength at bringing about social reforms in pursuit of entry to the EU that no previous government had achieved. At the same time, the AKP had emerged from the Islamic and conservative nationalist right wing of the political spectrum. How could it be that such a party could be proving more reformist, more democratic, more enlightened in a European way, than any previous Turkish government?

And Abdullah Gül was a great surprise to many, as response to his nomination for the presidency in 2007 quickly proved. Massive protests in Izmir and other western cities against his nomination – almost entirely because his wife, Hayrünnisa, wears a headscarf – were swiftly accompanied by an almost hysterical interest in who he was, where he came from, who were his ancestors, and how he had come to be even considered for the job first held by Mustafa Kemal Atatürk – still a personal hero of intense imaginative power for the secular and urban middle classes. To many it was a shock that someone with Abdullah Gül's background could have risen so far, while Hayrünnisa was already a target for the secularists. What, many asked in horror, could be going on? Were the Islamists finally taking over? But there was more than simply religion at stake. Since Atatürk, most presidents had come from elite metropolitan families, but Gül was both provincial and from the *esnaf*, the artisanal class that had, since educational reforms of the 1960s, began sending some of its sons and daughters to university. Journalists were quick to follow the scent of this intruder from outside the traditional political classes. They researched, debated and disputed Gül's ancestry in ways that recall scrutiny of Barack Obama's credentials as a US citizen. Along with class and even racial issues in the headlines, it is hardly surprising that Hayrünnisa's headscarf would attract the spotlight for closing the circle of gender and religion: how, the horrified secular middle-class women of Turkey demanded, could the secular republic even consider having a presidential wife wearing a headscarf inside the hallowed halls of Atatürk's presidential palace at Çankaya?

Even as Abdullah and Hayrünnisa Gül were being scrutinized in the Turkish press, I was planning a move to the University of Exeter, where Gül had been a language student back in the early 1970s, at about the same time that I first visited Turkey. In 2005, Exeter had honoured its internationally prominent former student with an honorary doctoral diploma. I had first learned of these surprising links in 2006 from Mehmet Ali Birand, probably Turkey's pre-eminent investigative reporter, who had energetically covered the international scene for the last forty years, right up until his untimely death on 17 January 2013.[9] Indeed, it was Mehmet Ali Birand who originally suggested that we should collaborate on a 'political biography' of Gül but of a higher order than those rapidly generated by Turkish journalists during the presidential elections in 2007.[10] We agreed that Prime Minister Tayyip Erdoğan deserved to be the focus of the media spotlight. But we also agreed that Gül's personal and political development – from his origins in the nationalist right-wing student movements of the 1970s to something closer to the social democrats of Europe – was perhaps more fascinating in terms of Turkish history, party politics and future directions for the country. Gül, after all, had been the primary designer of the Programme which brought the AKP to power in 2002. That Programme is clearly aimed at bringing Turkey as rapidly as possible into conformity with the democratic standards being developed in Europe. Gül, moreover, had overseen managing the country's economic and diplomatic rise since 2002 on the basis of that Programme. Erdoğan made the headlines, but Gül had set the political agenda and was quietly steering Turkey into the larger world of globalized economies and strategic alliances. 'And don't forget,' I recall Mehmet Ali Birand saying with a characteristic grin, 'this book would sell because this is the Turkish politician who everyone agrees looks just like George Clooney!'[11]

I had forgotten these discussions with Mehmet Ali Birand until, in 2007, I found myself at a reception for 29 October, Turkey's Independence Day, held at the Turkish ambassador's residence in London. When I mentioned that

I taught at Exeter, Gül's name quickly came up and I recalled how Mehmet Ali had proposed we work together on an English-language biography for the American and European market. Someone, I don't recall who, told me the next surprising thing, which was that Turkish Independence Day – 29 October – was also Gül's birthday. More than that, he had been born that day in 1950, the very year that multiparty democracy arrived in Turkey. Abdullah Gül, like the protagonists of Salman Rushdie's postmodern fiction, *Midnight's Children*, was born on Independence Day. At a subsequent gathering at the Turkish ambassador's residence, Sadık Arslan – at the time first counsellor to Ambassador Yiğit Alpogan – asked if there were still plans for a book about President Gül. I reported that Mehmet Ali Birand's boss wouldn't let him put his name to such a work, but that he had promised to help if I took on such a project; and indeed he was an invaluable source and inspiration. This must have been a crucial conversation, since some months later I found myself accepting an invitation from the embassy to meet President Gül when he visited London to receive the Chatham House Prize for diplomacy in November 2010. I was impressed by his manner and inclined to like him. Over breakfast, he spoke in flawless English without notes to a group of UK business leaders, and later had a sudden moment of shyness when we were first introduced and his language skills seemed to retreat. A man of about my age, from the lower middle-classes who had won a place at university and confounded traditional expectations, moving ever leftward yet retaining his religious faith even while assuming public office – this seemed like an interesting story not so unlike my own, although I have never entered public service and remain entirely sceptical of all organized religions.

The prospect of writing about Turkey from the focus of a living president became an appealing challenge. With research in the humanities being what it is in the UK, I promptly put in for a research grant – which I didn't get – but I was greatly encouraged in pursuing the project by the readiness of a number of eminent scholars who thought it a good idea. In January 2011 I met Professor Mustafa Isen, the general secretary of the president's office, in Ankara. That meeting was principally concerning a different project, involving a regrettably abandoned equestrian 'friendship ride' from Turkey into Syria as part of the Evliya Çelebi Way Project. But Professor Isen is also a scholar of biography who has published extensive archival research on traditions of life-writing in the Ottoman period, and we found a lot to talk about while discussing my plans for what has become this book. At the end of our meeting, Professor Isen told me that President Gül was happy to meet for an interview, and that the presidential office would assist with contacting family and friends, personal and political. Shortly afterwards, when Dr Mehmet Kalpaklı was able to offer me rooms and a library card to spend the 2011–12 academic year as a visiting professor at Bilkent University in Ankara, it became impossible to resist and the rest of the story is, as it were, to be found in the pages of this book. News that I was writing this book first appeared in the Turkish press in 2011, generating amusing errors and one fairly serious misconception worth sorting out right away. On 18 November the front page of the national daily *Hürriyet* carried a short piece, announcing that a biography of President Gül was being written in English by a professor from an English university. The article appeared alongside a portrait of Prime Minister Recep Tayyip Erdoğan reproduced from the cover of that week's *Time* magazine, but was nevertheless picked up and repeated, in various ways, by editors of provincial newspapers. I had met the *Hürriyet* journalist, Sefa Kaplan, months before in a friend's flat in Istanbul. He had contacted me after hearing about my project and learning that I had met Professor Isen in Ankara to discuss it. For Sefa Kaplan and readers of *Hürriyet*, the story was not really of very much interest until later that year in November when I held the first of several lengthy interviews with President Gül. With the story of Erdoğan appearing on the cover of *Time* magazine as a lead, editors clearly thought that this might be the moment for a word or two about a planned book about President Gül.

As these things often happen, Sefa's notes and write-up quickly appeared in a much-edited and garbled form, telling readers that the President and I had first met in 1974 at the University of Exeter. Evidently there had been a collapsing of 1974, the year in which I had visited Turkey for the first time, Gül becoming a student at Exeter, and 2007, when I joined the Exeter faculty. Several other newspapers throughout the country relayed the story of our 1974 meeting, sometimes adding elaborations. More serious, certainly for careful readers, was the term used to designate President Gül's relationship to the person writing his biography in English: '*görevlendirdi*'. Formed from the noun '*görev*' meaning 'duty' or 'obligation', the term here suggests that Gül 'commissioned' or 'appointed' the biography: in other terms, the President of Turkey had instructed a foreign citizen that it was his duty to write this book. The next day, *Hürriyet* reported that Ahmet Sever, the presidential press officer, had telephoned the paper's editors demanding a correction since the president had not 'commissioned' anything. 'On the contrary,' Sever is reported as saying, 'MacLean had said that he was working on a new research project about Turkey's recent history and wanted to include the president's life and career. Our president positively answered this request.'[12] And such was the case. Errors are frequent in the Turkish press and can be hard to correct; this one still pops up from time to time. 'Probably anti-AKP people created it,' a (secular) Turkish colleague remarked. 'It sounds great for them: Gül ordered a biography from an English professor! So these Islamists are always in cooperation with western spies!'[13]

Published in the president's home city, *Kayseri Haber* was among several provincial newspapers that picked up and developed Sefa Kaplan's initial report. On 5 December 2011, Yusuf Yerli reported that I had recently visited Kayseri and recorded the names of the political and local notables, business leaders and members of President Gül's family whom I visited there.[14] The fantasy report of my first meeting with the president at Exeter back in 1974 now also involved Gül's good friend – the journalist Fehmi Koru – who was indeed studying in London but never in Exeter. The piece also claims that the future president of Turkey was working on his PhD at the University of Exeter, when he was enrolled at Istanbul University; though Exeter did indeed present him with an honorary PhD in 2005. From what he was able to find out, Yerli clearly liked the idea of my projected study – and the Evliya Çelebi Project – so my point is not to correct him over errors that only a biographer might worry over, but he unfortunately missed *Hürriyet*'s published correction, and even used that verb – '*görevlendirmek*' – indicating that I had been commissioned or appointed to write this book. Since then, I have often seen myself directly quoted for saying things that do not quite sound like anything I have ever said; but misquoting is no privilege of the Turkish press. However, the point that does need making once again here is that this book is not in any way an official biography, and might be said to be authorized only insofar as President and Madame Gül both agreed to sometimes quite lengthy interviews, always accompanied by translators and advisers. Members of the president's office have also been more than helpful in arranging meetings and discussing political life in Turkey. That said, both President and Madame Gül have read and agreed on the language of all direct quotations from our interviews.

SOURCES AND
ACKNOWLEDGEMENTS

I have relied largely, but not exclusively, on English-language materials, of which the academic and scholarly production has become truly remarkable, plentiful, and informative since the 1990s. Like other readers of English interested in Turkey, my early understanding was dominated by the biographies of Atatürk by Patrick Kinross and Andrew Mango, and by Bernard Lewis's formative *Emergence of Modern Turkey*, which takes the story of the Turkish Republic up to the end of the Second World War. For the twentieth century, I have greatly relied on Erik Zürcher's *Turkey: A Modern History* for reliable updates through the 1980s, along with works by Feroz Ahmad, Carter Vaughn Findlay and others for challenges and alternatives to Lewis's paradigms. Without William Hale's numerous studies of Turkey's economy and foreign policy, this book would stumble far more often than it does. In addressing two key aspects of Turkish foreign policy – Cyprus and relations with the European Union – I have arguably devoted less attention than these mighty topics might otherwise seem to deserve. These are, however, matters that have been particularly well covered in recent scholarship, and I would advise interested readers to begin with Clement Dodd's excellent *The History and Politics of the Cyprus Conflict* (2010), and with William Hale's summary chapter on 'Turkey and the European Union' in his *Turkish Foreign Policy since 1774* (third edition, 2013) together with the extensive list of studies catalogued by these scholars in their footnotes.

For news and other media coverage, especially in later sections, I have kept an eye on the US and UK media coverage of Turkey alongside the English-language Turkish press – most notably *Hürriyet Daily News*, formerly *Turkish*

Daily News until December 2008 – and *Today's Zaman*. I have occasionally consulted blogsites, but ignored extreme sites, and mostly avoided social media. Thanks to energetic and prompt help from Dr Alaadin Paksoy of the Department of Media Studies at Anadolu University in Eskişehir, I have also been able to keep a watchful eye on the Turkish press and media in recent years. Since 2007, the presidential website provides chronological lists of state visits and protocol meetings, as well as providing English-language versions of many of President Gül's speeches.

During my stay in Ankara, 2011–12, and at other times in other places, I recorded interviews with numerous politicians, businessmen, mayors, civil servants, journalists, academics, and diplomats, as well as personal friends and members of Abdullah Gül's family. Many, but not all, of these meetings were assisted through the president's office; some were attended by journalists, others by a variety of helpful translators. Some of those I spoke with have asked to be left 'off-record' for all or part of our discussions. A few of those I contacted either refused to meet or wished to remain anonymous.

My first thanks, then, must be to President and Madame Gül who have opened their homes, families and lives to me, and to those working in the presidential office who have assisted with logistical support. Madame Gül kindly supplied a number of family photographs that have not previously been made public. Without constant help from Sadık Arslan and support from Professor Mustafa Isen, this book would not have been possible. Presidential advisers Yusuf Müftüoğlu and Mehmet Çarıkçı, and Ayşe Yılmaz and Arzu Aygan from Madame Gül's office have all gone out of their way to be helpful. Mehmet Demirci from the presidency media office has helped with the illustrations. Dr Mehmet Kalpaklı arranged a comfortable home conducive to work at Bilkent University courtesy of the History Department. At Bilkent, I owe thanks to Dr Fahri Dikkaya for giving so valuably of his time helping me organize meetings and by readily coming along to translate; and my thanks to Seda Erkoç for checking some Turkish-language sources for me. Mustafa Boydak deserves special thanks for hosting my visit to Kayseri in November 2011 on behalf of the Kayseri Chamber of Industry (KAYSO).

I am indebted to the following for interviews, conversations, advice, encouragement, inspiration and help along the way: Yiğit Alpogan, Akin Alptuna, Kasım Akçil, Beşir Atalay, Ezgi Başaran, the late Mehmet Ali Birand, Ayşe Böhürler, Ünal Çeviköz, Mehmet Ali Dikerdem, Ercihan Dilari, Işın Eliçin, Dilşen Erdoğan, Seda Erkoç, Andrew Finkel, Caroline Finkel, Sami Güçlü, Ahmet Hamdi Gül, Macit Gül, Mehmet Kalpaklı, Sefa Kaplan, Şükrü

Karatepe, Birgül Koçak, Fehmi Koru, Sinem Köseoğlu, Mesude Nursuna Memecan, Murat Mercan, Nihet Molu, Erik Mortenson, Mahmut Mutman, Leyla Neyzi, Kerem Öktem, Nurşen Özdamar, Mehmet Özhaseki, Alaadin Paksoy, Hugh Pope, Süleyman Sağlam, Abdullah Satoğlu, Dilek Şendil, Norman Stone, Mehmet Tekelioğlu, Ece Temelkuran, Tolga Temuge, Gürcan Türkoğlu, Metin Unver, Yaşar Yakış, Meyda Yeğenoğlu, Bekir Yıldız, Amberin Zaman. Professor Tim Dant kindly read an early draft and made invaluable suggestions without which the book would have been much poorer. Professor William Hale read the completed manuscript for Oneworld, catching numerous howlers and offering indispensable suggestions for improvement. And as always, special gratitude to Donna, who still manages to uncover possibilities in my very worst prose.

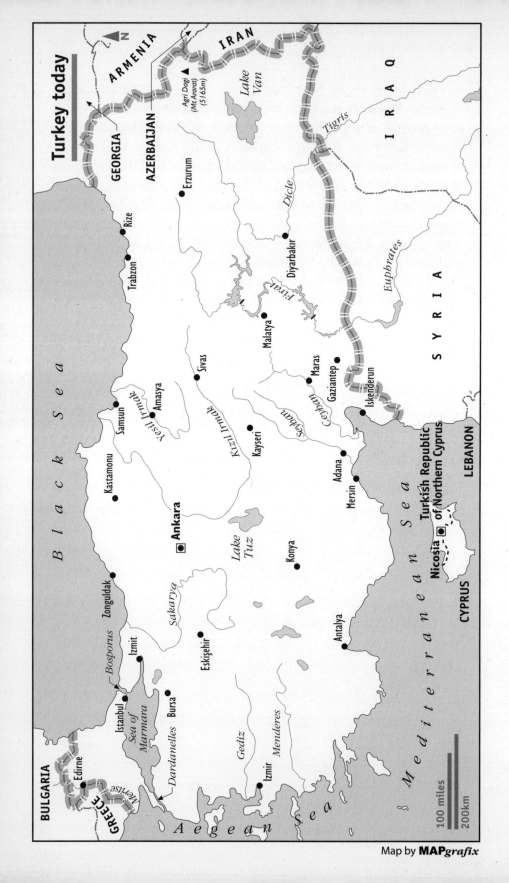

Turkey today

N

BULGARIA
GREECE
ARMENIA
IRAN
GEORGIA
AZERBAIJAN
IRAQ
SYRIA
LEBANON
CYPRUS
Turkish Republic
of Northern Cyprus

Agri Dagi
(Mt Ararat)
(5165m)
Lake
Van
Tigris
Dicle
Euphrates
Erzurum
Rize
Trabzon
Diyarbakir
Fırat
Malatya
Sivas
Amasya
Maras
Yeşil Irmak
Samsun
Gaziantep
Kızıl Irmak
Seyhan
Ceyhan
Iskenderun
Kastamonu
Kayseri
Adana
Mersin
Ankara
Lake
Tuz
Konya
Zonguldak
Sakarya
Izmit
Eskişehir
Antalya
Istanbul
Bursa
Sea of
Marmara
Bosporus
Dardanelles
Gediz
Menderes
Izmir
Edirne
Meriç

Black Sea

Aegean
Sea

Mediterranean Sea

Nicosia

100 miles
200km

Map by **MAP**grafix

1

The Early Years
Kayseri: 1950s and 1960s

Since the start of the twenty-first century, Turkey has proved itself an economic success story amid global financial disasters, and an increasingly powerful political and diplomatic actor amid regional militarized crises. Remarkably, all this has taken place under governments ruled by the *Adalet ve Kalkınma Partisi* ('Justice and Development Party', or AKP), which has origins in Turkish varieties of political Islam. Yet the deep roots of this 'new Turkey' can be traced back to 1950. In that year, Abdullah Gül, one of the AKP's leading founders and President of the Republic since 2007, was born in the central Anatolian city of Kayseri. Coincidentally, the first multiparty elections to be held in the twenty-seven-year history of the Republic of Turkey earlier that year had brought an end to the rule of Mustafa Kemal Atatürk's party. To understand Abdullah Gül and how he came to be elected president requires understanding the importance of Kayseri, not just the strong influence of its history on his character, values and political outlook, but also on the history of what has taken place there, and throughout Turkey, since 1950.

The 1950 elections toppled the *Cumhuriyet Halk Partisi* ('Republican People's Party', or CHP), Mustafa Kemal Atatürk's party, which had ruled unopposed since the foundation of the republic in 1923. Legitimated by a constitution designed to guarantee their authority, CHP governments became increasingly authoritarian in enforcing modernization and secularization policies. These benefited many, but mostly the secular and metropolitan middle classes and bureaucratic elites, while at the same time alienating the religious sensibilities and conservative values of the majority of provincial and rural Turks. Many found Atatürk's republic as oppressive as the former Ottoman Empire, just in different ways. Soviet planners were brought in, and factories began appearing in provincial cities, such as Kayseri, with conservative and traditional populations, such as the Güls. Ahmet Hamdi Gül, Abdullah's father, worked in the newly constructed aircraft factory in Kayseri, where he found his pious Muslim views often in strong accord with socialist talk encouraged among the workers: he became a respected union leader. Modernization was one thing, but secularism another. Religious life under the republic was controlled by a state fiercely devoted to secular principles. Mosques were now run by civil servants while many traditional religious customs became illegal.

Coming to power in 1950, Adnan Menderes and the *Demokrat Parti* ('Democrat Party', or DP) promised to appease religious voters more than they did, but along the way they ignored the constitution rather too often, causing the army to seize power in 1960. They tried and executed Menderes and two of his ministers on charges of treason. Meanwhile, since the early 1950s, Marshall Plan funding from the US had sparked off new forms of economic activity throughout Turkey. In Kayseri, people are famously proud of their city's ancient history as a multi-ethnic city based on business and trade where Muslims and Christians had lived and worked together for centuries. Traumatized by the expulsions of their Armenian and later Greek Orthodox populations in the opening decades of the twentieth century, the Kayseri business community showed how much they had learned from the non-Muslim merchants who had been their earlier colleagues, filling the void they had left in trade and business. Among the 'Anatolian tigers' – the provincial cities which led Turkey's economic development into the twenty-first century – Kayseri has been called the birthplace of 'Islamic Calvinism', an embrace between Islam and neoliberalism. In Kayseri the sons of skilled factory workers, the *esnaf* class, were being educated for higher education: two of Abdullah Gül's uncles attended university and became eminent engineers,[1] while Abdullah himself achieved a PhD in economics from Istanbul University in 1981.

An auspicious birthday

Abdullah Gül was born on 29 October 1950, a doubly auspicious date. As every Turk knows, it was on that day in 1923 that six hundred years of the Ottoman Empire came to an end when the first session of the Grand National

Assembly met in Ankara and voted to approve a resolution proclaiming 'the form of government of the Turkish state is a Republic'. Later that day, Mustafa Kemal was elected first president of the republic and Ankara became capital of the new republic. Until his death in 1938, Atatürk ruled through a single-party system, enforcing – some say autocratically – reforms that aimed to modernize and secularize the new nation state that emerged in Anatolia after the Western powers had attempted to carve up the former Islamic empire at Sèvres, and later succeeded in doing so at Lausanne while acknowledging Atatürk's military victories and territorial claims in Anatolia. Under Atatürk and his 'Republican People's Party', reforms affecting all aspects of life in Turkey were swiftly enacted by the all-powerful state. Factories and railways arrived, new schools were built and new laws encoded obliging everyone to be happy to be a Turk. Regional, ethnic and traditional cultural practices were proscribed by law: men were to wear brimmed hats not turbans or fezzes; local religious orders were closed down; a Department of Religious Affairs (*Diyanet*) was established to control public religion, transforming imams and muezzins into employees of the state; the call to prayer was changed from Arabic to Turkish. The Turkish language was rapidly modernized, dropping Arabic script for a hybridized alphabet based on the Roman alphabet; overnight the minority of literate Turks found themselves no longer able to read a newspaper.

By the end of the Second World War, however, the authoritarian single-party system had come unstuck. On 28 May 1950, multiparty elections brought the recently formed *Demokrat Parti* (DP) into power under Prime Minister Adnan Menderes, ending the twenty-seven-year rule of Atatürk's CHP. Staunch supporters of the new party and government, Abdullah Gül's family debated whether he should be named '*Cumhur*' in recognition of his propitious birthday: the term refers to the 'people' element of *Cumhuriyet*, the Turkish for 'republic' – not the state but the people. He was named Abdullah instead, but the nickname survives in family legend.

Abdullah Gül was born in Kayseri, the central Anatolian city where both sides of his family had lived for generations. His father, Ahmet Hamdi Bey – the term '*bey*' here is a slightly old-fashioned term of respect pitched somewhere below 'sir' but above 'mister' – was employed in a local factory. The *Kayseri Tayyare Fabrikasi* ('Kayseri Aircraft Factory') had been set up in 1926 under Atatürk's reforms to boost the city's development into modernity. Abdullah Gül's mother, Adviye Hanım – the term '*hanım*' here serving as the equivalent of '*bey*' for women – is the daughter of Ismail Hakkı Satoğlu, member of an extended family of teachers, poets and doctors with branches in both Kayseri and the western coastal city of Izmir. At the time of Abdullah Gül's birth, his parents were well regarded in their neighbourhood – the *mahalle* – for being traditional, honest, respectable and conservative. Yet they were also known for being better educated than many of their immediate neighbours, most of them retailers and tradesmen for whom education was deemed only of secondary importance.[2]

Abdullah Gül was born right in the heart of ancient Kayseri in the house of his paternal grandfather Hayrullah Efendi – the term *'efendi'* here serving like *'bey'* but marking respect for members of an even older generation – himself a merchant. For centuries, the family had lived in the Gülük Mahallesi, a neighbourhood dating back to Selçuk times when it had been developed to accommodate the stonemasons and carpenters employed to build the Selçuk Honat Hatun mosque complex. Here, generations of the family had served as imams in the neighbourhood Gülük Mosque, adopting their surname Gül from the neighbourhood in 1934 when the law required.[3] Two generations back, Hayrullah Efendi's father had moved his growing family to a traditional two-storey house built around a courtyard garden on Birlik Sokak, 'Union Street', in an adjacent neighbourhood. Here Abdullah Gül was born and spent his early years surrounded by grandparents, uncles, visiting aunts and cousins. Times were tough; this was the 1950s and central Anatolia remained scarred from decades of supplying men and provisions to wars being fought far away. Prices were high and essentials were most often in short supply. But Ahmet Hamdi Bey was a skilled technician with a stable salary and the Gül clan are a prudent people. Abdullah Gül recalls a childhood spent within the 'large yard of our house, which was in the middle of the city. We used to call the yard "*hayat*" as it is named in Turkish architecture meaning "life". We used to spend all of our time there, grandparents, uncles, aunts. I remember it was like a stadium it was so big and I spent all my time there and spent many happy hours – granddad's house: I was born there.'[4]

Secure within the family but growing up right in the heart of the city, young Abdullah Gül had only to cross what is now Inönü Boulevard to find himself wandering among memorials to Kayseri's glorious past: the walls of the Byzantine citadel, and the magnificent thirteenth-century Selçuk Honat Hatun mosque complex, complete with still-functioning bath-house (*hamam*) spewing steam into the air as it has done for eight centuries. Local historians will proudly tell you that this was the first such mosque complex to be built by the Selçuks, who also established the still active Gülük Mosque.

Kayseri: history and people

For Turks everywhere today, and for generations, coming from Kayseri has special meanings. When Abdullah Gül was born there, Kayseri was a rather dusty provincial backwater that had long fallen on hard times and was struggling to recover. Outwardly at least, it displayed little memory of its important, glorious, and certainly ancient past. Centuries before the sixth century CE when Justinian built the Byzantine fortress here, the early Romans had established their regional capital nearby at Mazarca, which they promptly renamed Caesarea, and from here ruled over the former kingdom of Cappadocia. Even earlier, Mazarca had been a capital of the Hattians until they were displaced by the Bronze Age Hittites at the dawn of the second millennium BC. Before that, since the middle of the third millennium BC, Assyrian traders had maintained a colony just a few miles up the road at Kültepe. It was here, at Kültepe, that archaeologists unearthed the world's oldest trading records in the form of a massive archive of clay tablets dating from over four thousand years ago.

Kayseri has been on the map, as it were, since international trade began, and trade is a key to the well-known stereotype of those who come from the city. Nestled on the slopes of an extinct volcano, Mount Erciyes – at 12,848 feet (3,916 metres), the fifth highest mountain in Anatolia – Kayseri enjoys obvious natural advantages. Commanding, as it does, the crossing over the Kızıl Irmak river – the river Halys of Strabo and the early geographers – Kayseri controls the ancient trade routes linking the Euphrates with the Black Sea, Anatolia's Aegean ports with Syria, and the northern silk road from Iran and beyond. Geographically, the site remains a natural hub for trade.

Because of its distinctive geography and position, Kayseri has prospered and declined for millennia with the flows and vagaries of international trade and with the comings and goings of dynasties and empires. Virtues of necessity, openness to difference, compromise and adaptability are still discernible today and continue to exert an enormous influence on the city's culture and the self-image of its people. Under the Romans, the prehistoric trading centre flourished into a prosperous regional capital of empire and for a time was home to an important metal works where cavalry armour was manufactured. Yet Roman Caesarea is probably better known for becoming a centre of Eastern Christian learning under Eusebius and St Basil until the Arab incursions of the seventh century sacked the city and pretty much put an end to trade for some time. But Christianity survived here and throughout the adjacent region of Cappadocia, whose extraordinary volcanic landscape had been home to fugitive Christian communities for centuries. A large group of Armenian refugees from Ani, accompanied by their king, Gagik II, settled in Kayseri shortly before the Selçuks arrived in 1080 and commanded the city for Islam. In 1097, crusaders failed to recover the city which remained an active Selçuk capital until the Mongols invaded in 1243. For the next century and a half, the city served as a fortified capital for various tribal dynasties until 1397 when it first entered Ottoman hands under Beyazit I, who promptly lost it to Tamerlane in 1402 following his humiliation at the battle of Ankara (Angora). Karamid and Mamluk chiefs ruled here until Yavuz Sultan Selim I (r. 1512–20) recaptured the region for the Ottomans.

Under the Ottomans, trade started up again and sixteenth-century Kayseri found itself recovering some of its former wealth and importance as caravans passed through on the northern route linking Istanbul with Erzurum and Iran. Ottoman Kayseri was also an important stage on the more southerly route from Istanbul to Aleppo, Damascus and Mecca; this included a stretch from Eregli to Sivas by way of Kayseri that was much used during the sixteenth and seventeenth centuries for Ottoman armies setting out for Safavid border-lands.[5] During the sixteenth century, Kayseri grew to become a city of some 33,000 tax payers, making it 'the largest city of Anatolia after Bursa,' a city of the same size as contemporary Amsterdam, Utrecht, Cordoba, Barcelona, Ferrara, and Padua.[6]

Seventeenth-century Kayseri continued to prosper, but during the eighteenth and nineteenth centuries there were no longer Ottoman armies marching this way, and the northern trade route shifted further north to pass from Tokat and Yozgat to Ankara leaving little traffic on the Sivas to Kayseri route. During the final two centuries of Ottoman rule, or more accurately neglect, Kayseri became a provincial crossroads where a long history of trade and migration, warfare and occasional famines, formed communal habits, interfaith customs and beliefs, as well as communal ways of dealing with the imperial authorities in Istanbul.

The stereotype of people from Kayseri, at least a version that is still embraced and elaborated by local people today, began to emerge during the later Ottoman period when Muslims and Christians lived and worked together. It emphasizes a strong business sense amid changing markets combined with a moral commitment to hard work and a patient delight in making deals. It also combines a conviction that religious piety is an essential ingredient of honesty and success, and therefore a quality to be sought in business partners, regardless of whether they are Muslims, Greeks or Armenians. While the pursuit of wealth for its own sake is deeply frowned upon, as it is in both Christianity and Islam, people from Kayseri agreed among themselves long ago that making money for the common good was a virtuous activity. In 2005, a European Stability Initiative report coined the term 'Islamic Calvinists' to describe these characteristics, observing: 'No visitor to Kayseri could fail to notice that this is both a deeply religious society, and one where change and modernization are eagerly embraced ... Islamic charity is a deeply rooted local tradition, and many of the city's educational and cultural establishments were founded with private donations.'[7] These are clearly values generated not only from centuries of passing merchant caravans, but also from an equally long history of international trading communities taking up permanent residence there and legitimating their presence by benefiting the community at large.

Under the Ottomans, Kayseri continued to welcome substantial communities of Armenian and Greek Orthodox merchants and businessmen, many of whom had been there for generations. By the end of the sixteenth century, fewer than eighty percent of the population of tax-paying males show up as Muslims.[8] With a common interest in business matters, Muslims and Christians managed to live and work together in pursuit of good deals; and so the stereotype of the hard-headed, parsimonious, conservative, even cunning businessman from Kayseri came into being. Central to this figure is a strong ethic of making money not for personal gain, but to benefit the community. We can find that stereotype being described in a mid-nineteenth-century account of Kayseri by E. J. Davis, the Episcopal (American) Bishop of Alexandria, who observed how the Greek population of Kayseri at the time was looking elsewhere for business opportunities:

> The 'Roumlis,' or people of Kaisariyeh, have a miserably poor country, and are therefore obliged to emigrate; they are found in every part of Turkey, but they always leave their families at home, and the greater part of the population of Kaisariyeh consists of the wives and families of these men, who are seeking a livelihood away from their native place. They are exceedingly parsimonious, manage to live on astonishingly little, and are beyond measure shrewd and sharp in business; so that (as I was told) 'there are no Jews in Kaisariyeh,' they cannot compete with the natives! I give this statement as it was made to me.[9]

Davis, who reported regular meetings with traders from Kayseri several times in his travels through 'Asiatic Turkey', noted how the Kayseri region is barely recovering from a series of recent famines. Yet people from Kayseri were survivors and widely renowned for driving advantageous bargains. Of one 'Simeon', his host while staying in Maraş, Davis noted that he 'was most attentive, and moreover took admirable care of my horses. Being a Greek of Kaisariyeh, it was but natural that his charge should be somewhat extravagant, but in the end we came to an amicable agreement.'[10]

Coming to an amicable agreement while driving a hard bargain, getting the better of the other guy without alienating him: that is central to the Kayseri skill-set and self-image and it has roots in the religious and ethnic exchanges that had been shaping Kayseri society for centuries. The Muslim population had come to adopt customs of their Greek and Armenian neighbours in ways that were unusual among Ottoman Turkish communities. The American Bishop Davis, understandably, paid special attention to the Greeks since he doubtless spoke some version of the Greek language and he might have believed – as Anglo-Protestant churchmen for some time had commonly believed – that there was a good chance of converting Greek Orthodox congregations to their own brand of Christianity. Yet his observations reveal crucial components of what was special to the Kayseri character – that determination and entrepreneurial spirit common to its people regardless of religious affiliation – and its links to the competitive and long-established multiracial mix of the city. It was that same commercial and enterprising spirit that inspired those 'Roumlis', or Greeks of Kayseri, who, recognizing that business was bad, went looking for opportunities elsewhere.

The exodus of Kayseri's Greeks as a result of commercial difficulties was evidently well underway when Davis was writing in the 1870s, long before the notorious population exchanges of 1923 that would follow the Treaty of Lausanne and the establishment of the new republic in the aftermath of the First World War. It is worth recalling that for Turkey, even after the armistice of October 1918 had been signed, war continued, and was fought on Anatolian soil, until 1922. Turkish armies had, in fact, been more or less continuously at war since 1912, when the Balkan conflicts put an end to 'Turkey in Europe' and populated Istanbul and western Anatolia with hundreds of thousands of refugees. Joining Germany in August 1914 was the last great blunder of the Ottoman state. It opened the way for Britain and France to set about dismantling the Ottoman Empire; and their agreement involved tacit approval of a Greek land-grab in western Anatolia, or 'Asia Minor' as those supporting the project would have called the area. In May 1919, while the 'Great Powers' looked the other way, Greek troops landed on the Aegean coast and set about claiming land they said belonged to Greece.

For those living in Kayseri at the time, the brutal 1919–22 war between Greece and Turkey generated more anguish over the killing and waste than anger at their Greek neighbours. Yet the exchange of Greek Muslims for Turkish Orthodox Christians that resulted in 1923 was, for people in Kayseri, an unexpected disaster that could only recall the all-too-recent horrors of 1915 when the Armenian population of the city had been brutally expelled. The arrival of invading Greek forces in 1919 had certainly alarmed Greek Orthodox families and communities throughout Anatolia, but the fear, panic and bloodshed never reached quite as far east as Cappadocia and Kayseri. By August 1922 under command of Mustafa Kemal, the Turkish army reversed the Greek frontlines hundreds of miles away near Eskişehir and Kütahya. Through the war, Kayseri's Greeks were anxious but relatively safe, unlike those in the Black Sea region where war had created open hostilities between Muslim and Orthodox communities who had lived together for generations. Here, the unprecedented policy of conscripting Christians into the Turkish army from 1915 had led to armed resistance, state reprisals and guerrilla warfare. In the mountains above Samsun, the bloodshed and atrocities reported by both sides only increased after 1919 when the arrival of Greek forces in Izmir emboldened the armed Christian guerrillas.

Throughout the ensuing War of Independence (1919–23), the Greek Orthodox communities of Cappadocia and Kayseri never fell out with their Muslim neighbours. They had lived together for centuries and always proved to be loyal subjects of the Ottoman authorities. During the war with Greece, Kayseri remained renowned for the unity and loyalty of its people, Muslim and Christian, and briefly became once more an important centre in the history of Greek Orthodoxy. In July 1921, even as Greek armies continued to advance eastward and moved dangerously close to Ankara, seat of the republican government, Kayseri and its people were deemed safe, secure and loyal. On 24 July, faced with the approach of invading armies, Prime Minister Fevzi Çakmak announced to the Parliamentary Assembly that Ankara was to be abandoned and that all state papers were to be moved to Kayseri where the government would safely resume its responsibilities. In the event, the Greek armies never reached Ankara; they were turned back at the battle of Sakarya by troops bearing Russian-made weapons under the personal command, despite a cracked rib, of Mustafa Kemal.[11]

Through the years of war, Kayseri maintained its reputation and status as a city welcoming to Christians. On 15 September 1922, less than a week after a victorious Turkish army had pushed the Greeks back to the Aegean coast and reoccupied Izmir, and two days after the start of the fire in the Armenian quarter that was still sweeping across that city, a group of Greek Orthodox clergymen chose Kayseri for an important assembly. Even as the flames continued to consume the houses and warehouses of Izmir, in Kayseri an Orthodox clergyman, Pavlos Karahisaritis, and seventy-two other Orthodox clerics met and founded the Autocephalous (Turkish) Orthodox Patriarchate of Anatolia. Opposing rule by the ancient Patriarchate of Istanbul for being primarily concerned with ethnic Greeks and promoting the interests of the Greek state, Karahisaritis and his colleagues declared their loyalty to the new Turkish Republic, including promises to use Turkish in their liturgy. Doubtless in anticipation of the debates currently raging in Lausanne over management of the population exchange, Karahisaritis – who was appointed Papa Eftim I – declared that Muslims and Christians in Cappadocia had proved they could live together. An ardent supporter of the Kemalist reforms, Papa Eftim declared his congregation was committed to the Turkish language and ideals of the newly founded republic to which it would be loyal. A plan not to uproot the Turkish-speaking Greek communities of Cappadocia and Kayseri had been Ankara's position when the Lausanne meeting convened in November 1922. As late as December the plan remained a possible outcome. But when the pushing and shoving at the bargaining table began in earnest, and with an impossible timetable to reach, terms for exempting central Anatolian Christians could not be agreed in time and were omitted: with the notable exception of a clause exempting Karahisaritis and his immediate family, who promptly moved the headquarters of the Turkish Orthodox Patriarchate to Istanbul in 1924.[12]

Even today, despite the last-minute expulsion, some Greeks who were suddenly expatriated from Kayseri back in 1923 continue to wax nostalgic for that lost but recent age when Armenians, Greeks and Muslims were 'all one' in the shadows of Mount Erciyes. As recently as 2009, Stavros Farasolulos, a ninety-eight-year-old expatriated from Kayseri in 1924, recalled the war of 1919–22: 'Greeks and Turks killed each other, but in my hometown nothing happened. That was because there was nothing that separated Turks from Greeks.'[13] Such testimonials from those who lived at the time are not uncommon and shape the living memory of people from Kayseri today. Such recollections of ruptured community only partly serve to mitigate the sadness and horrors of those years, when neighbourhoods were torn apart, and Turkish families were forcibly removed from their homes, simply because of religious faith, to a foreign and in many ways alien country where they were discriminated against for not speaking the language. And yet such memories also support a firm belief of people who come from Kayseri: that what happened to the Greeks and Armenians was not locally instigated or even approved by the Muslim majority, but resulted from the enforced policies of an authoritarian state. 'I know my Kayseri,' Stavros Farasolulos continued, 'Turks, Greeks and Armenians are the same.' The abandonment of the Christians of Kayseri and Cappadocia in 1923 at Lausanne, however, was not the first time that state authorities had, without support from the local Muslim community, uprooted and displaced local Christian families from the city. However strongly people in Kayseri may have believed that Turks, Greeks and Armenians 'are the same', back in 1915, there were powerful authorities in Ankara who thought otherwise about the city's Armenian population.

On 15 June 1915, eleven Armenians were hanged in the square of Kayseri's *Kömür Pazar*, the coal market. On 13 August 1915, the expulsion of all Armenians from the city and nearby towns of Talas and Derevenk began. Many had already fled, taking little with them and often leaving valuables behind in the care of Muslim friends and neighbours, planning to return. Over forty thousand of Kayseri's Armenians were dispatched: some into the Syrian desert where, in the heat of the summer, many died.[14] The operation was reputedly commanded by a brutal outsider, one Yakub Cemil, a member of a group of young officers known as *fedaiin* ('volunteers') who had, since 1908, supported the 'Young Turk' revolution by volunteering 'for dangerous missions, like political murders … and continued to do [their] dirty work after the revolution'.[15] He would have had no understanding of or interest in where he was or who he was expelling, and only contempt for local opinion. Armenians had lived in Kayseri for centuries. Here it was that, in 1314, St Gregory 'the Illuminator' was appointed first bishop and head of the Armenian Church. During the lean years of the nineteenth century, local Armenian businessmen were central to maintaining the local and regional economy. In 1856, the Hasırcıyan brothers opened a carpet factory employing three hundred weavers and were soon selling Kayseri carpets on international markets. Sarkis Gulbenkian was born and married here, running his petroleum import business before moving to Istanbul where his son, the great oil baron and renowned philanthropist Calouste Gulbenkian, was born in 1869. By the dawn of the twentieth century, there were regular Armenian newspapers, magazines and a theatre group. There were three churches, a nearby monastery and many Armenian schools. In 1906, there were three Armenians on the municipal assembly. As late as 1914, Kayseri was being represented in the Ottoman Parliament by Karabet Tomanyan, a local Armenian teacher.[16]

Whatever else remains to be said about the ethnic cleansing of Armenians in 1915, what took place in Kayseri that summer was neither a locally organized operation nor conducted with local approval or general support. Since Kayseri's Armenian population had been peacefully living there for so long, special efforts had to be made to generate local hostility towards them. Accusations that leading Armenian businessmen were conspiring against the state were spread to generate panic and fear; arbitrary arrests and selective executions seemed to support these accusations. There were local opportunists such as Lutfi Gübgübzade Sureya, a local bandit, who was put in charge of the gendarmerie and organized night-time arrests and provocative executions. In February, after a young Armenian who had returned from the USA blew himself up with a home-made explosive device, one Salih Zeki Bey was appointed to 'whip the Muslim population up against the Armenians'. He seized a European machine for making sugar from an Armenian factory and then put it on display, claiming it was used to manufacture weapons to be used against Muslims.[17] Despite these efforts to induce ethnic and religious antagonisms, in Kayseri the killings and expulsions were not generally approved by the local Muslim community, as was the case in Adana and Van.[18]

There was even active resistance on the part of Kayseri Muslims, who hid their Armenian neighbours and protected their property to await their return. More public resistance than this would have been exceptionally difficult to mobilize. There was a war on and all the able-bodied young men were in the army. Those left in Kayseri and the surrounding towns and villages to confront the Ottoman authorities were soldiers' wives, children and old people. They helped when they could; late in 1919, when some Armenians managed to return after the Mondros Armistice, they had their houses and other properties restored to them by friendly neighbours.[19] But not all were so fortunate: as late as February 1916, a group of Armenian school-girls attending the American college in Talas were reported poisoned.[20]

A tale is still being told in Kayseri that is set in 1915 at the time of the Armenian expulsion. It captures the sense of ambivalent horror that perhaps best describes what we can know about how local Muslims felt at the expulsions. It concerns a carter with a horse-drawn carriage from Derevenk, a village close to Kayseri, who has been left behind by the army because of having only half a nose. In advance of the deportations, 'Derviş-the-Noseless' helps an Armenian family flee from the approaching state forces only to meet bandits on the road to Maraş. In gratitude for protecting them from these bandits, his passengers tell Derviş where he can find a small pot of coins hidden in the threshold of a house they have just left. On returning to Derevenk only a few days later, Derviş discovers to his horror that 'there wasn't a single house standing. None were left, only ruins. I couldn't even find where the house was, let alone the threshold.' In this tale, at least, the point of the story is Derviş's utter dismay at discovering that local people had become complicit. Salih, who recounted the tale in 2008, comments:

> Those who demolished Derevenk were our raiders, I mean the raiders of Talas and Tavlusun. The stone bricks of the old houses in Kayseri are Talas, Tavlusun and Germir's bricks. The bricks of the house demolished here, they took them and sold them. They took the window and sold it, they ripped the door out and sold it. They took all the bricks, the columns and sold them. Our men did that.[21]

What is important to Salih, in recalling the story, is the sense then, and now, of peculiar horror that some Kayserians broke faith to become treacherously complicit in order to profit from the expulsions. The age when Kayseri's 'Turks, Greeks and Armenians are the same' was clearly beginning to come unstuck in 1915, but belief in that age, its virtues and its values, strongly persists among people from Kayseri. As Salih's comments indicate, the muted sense of distance from the actions of an all-powerful state, the anxious note of complicity with unthinkable deeds carried out in one's own name, the way the story avoids the human tragedy by focusing on the destruction of property and community, and the evident anger at the way those deeds were compounded by local corruption that allowed those bricks and windows and doors to appear rebuilt, all these express the anguish of a community torn apart and still waiting to recover fully.

The expulsions still help to shape people's silent but living memory in Kayseri. As for resistance to unpopular state policies from local Muslims, what can we make of a story still reported recounting very similar conditions during the 1919–22 war with Greece? Once again the young men were all drafted and the city left to wives, children and old people. The same source, Salih, tells how the state-appointed recording clerks distributing food during war-time rationing in Kayseri are said to have used their power over rye and wheat supplies to force local women into unwanted sexual relations in return for food for their children. Salih insists: 'The man who lived through this said it, not me. He said, "I didn't hear this from someone. I'm the one who has seen this."'[22] Whatever we wish to make of such a story and its claims as a historical memory, it is worth bearing in mind that once again the bad guys here are outsiders, explicitly government employees brought in with authority to enforce state plans who use their power corruptly: a recurrent theme in Kayseri folklore as in Turkish humour generally. The other villain in these scenarios is the local opportunist who betrays the community and its values by exploiting circumstances for his personal profit. For Kayserians, he is the worst villain, the local traitor who breaks faith in pursuit of personal wealth.

In November 2011, I asked President Gül how he first learned about the expulsion of the Christians from Kayseri. His normal smile faded instantly, and after a brief pause he said, 'So many terrible, terrible things took place. We are still living with the First World War.'[23] Like others of his generation, Abdullah Gül heard tales and stories about those years from relatives who had lived through them.

> During those years, we did not have TV at home so my father's mother spent a lot of time with me and we were very close, living as a family. My grandmother told me a lot of stories. So when I was a young child my grandmother took care of me more than my mother and she loved me. Of course when we think of the days of my grandmother's childhood they were going through the First World War and she told a lot of stories about then when times were difficult. There were a lot of dramatic stories and she would sing lullabies that had dramatic feelings of sorrow from that time.[24]

In those lullabies, the spirit of loss – the loss of neighbours and community, of young men to the wars and of regional prosperity – continued to generate stories to tell as the region continued to suffer while the First became the Second World War. The Kayseri character is inextricably bound up with this powerful cultural memory of loss and 'feelings of sorrow'. Benefits to Kayseri from the republican reforms of the 1920s and 1930s were substantial but belated. Government policies of promoting industrial over agricultural development did little to mitigate the effects of a run of bad harvests during the 1920s or alleviate rural poverty.[25] During these years of scarcity, however, the commercial, entrepreneurial and independent mentality on which people from Kayseri prided themselves continued to survive even as local people continued to tell each other stories of past sorrows, transforming memories of local events into legendary history.

Based on local events that occurred during the later 1940s, Süleyman Sağlam's novel, *Embracing the Mountains* (1999),[26] captures this sense of Kayseri's proud past and the moral integrity of its business community coming under pressure from state authorities on the one hand, and local corruption on the other. Right through the 1940s, while Turkish troops protecting the republic's borders once again wrested manpower and supplies from the Kayseri region, deserters from the army turned to banditry, roaming the hills and valleys huddled about Mount Erciyes. Sağlam's novel is largely set in the vineyards clustering on these hills during the 1940s and offers a thinly veiled fictionalized version of 'a true story' of events from the era when Turkey was struggling to maintain neutrality while supplying an active army to protect its borders. It tells of villainy among the corrupt outsiders brought into Kayseri by the government, and of local heroes such as Mehmet Efendi, the charitable shoe shop owner. While struggling to make a living when no one can afford to buy shoes, Mehmet Efendi feeds his poorest neighbours while maintaining faith in President Ismet İnönü and the Kemalist reforms. 'It's the railroad company that's keeping this country afloat. And look at Kayseri! If we didn't have the state-owned airplane factory and textile mill in Kayseri, the city would be totally destitute.'[27] But the true hero above all is the freedom-loving Osman, an honourable bandit straight from folklore, living wild in the nearby mountains, beloved by all the local villagers and only ever stealing from the government for their benefit. 'Osman represented a symbol of hope for the little people. When he was in the mountains they felt they had a kind of power on their side.' And the worst villain of all is the local man gone wrong. Here this figure is named Hatem Agha, a former colleague of Osman who had 'managed to cleanse his reputation of his rather unsavoury past ... to become a person of power in the leading party. He was smart and he cultivated the kinds of behaviour that made him into a respected personage. He was trusted by the governors, the parliamentarians, the mayors, and the judges and they gave him responsibility over the hapless population.'[28] As we might have anticipated, the sly and hypocritical Hatem Agha is obsessed with gaining power to destroy the noble Osman, employing every trick known to villains who work by stealth and indirection. 'Yes,' Abdullah Gül smiled when I mentioned Sağlam's novel to him, his novel is accurate and describes the gardens where we all still lived. In Kayseri everyone has a vineyard and in the book there are stories set in them. Reading the book, I remembered all the stories of my childhood and the stories I listened to as a child. The war was very important. Of course we did not live then but we always listened to these stories from older people, of the early days of the republic when the state was weak and there were wars and bandits in the mountains.[29]

By 1950, the days of bandit-heroes had passed, but the summer gardens, suspicion of state authorities, and pride in the local business community still survive. From living memories and tales from local history, Kayseri continues to fashion its distinctive self-image as an honest, business-oriented community which pursues wealth for the common good but not personal gain. Sağlam's villain Hatem Agha gets things exactly wrong when he declares, self-importantly: 'Kayseri people are known all over Turkey for being so clever and cunning. Well, we have to be. Our wit is all we have to rely upon.'[30] He has forgotten about loyalty to the community of neighbours who are there to be relied on.

Kayseri and the republic

In 1950 when Abdullah Gül was born there, the population of Kayseri had been on the rise for some time, reaching 65,488 that year, nearly double the number of people living there in 1926. Growth declined during the war, but throughout Abdullah Gül's childhood and early youth, more and more villagers moved into the city in search of work. Most were uneducated and pious, traditional people with conservative values. For unemployed and landless villagers, the attractions of Kayseri were obvious: since 1933, it hosted an important textile factory built under the same modernization scheme as the aircraft factory where Abdullah Gül's father worked. Business was thriving. By the 1960s, population growth exceeded employment opportunities. When Abdullah Gül turned twenty-five in 1975, the population had tripled since his year of birth to 207,039, making Kayseri one of the fastest growing cities in Turkey: a trend that continues into the twenty-first century.[31]

Economically, Kayseri benefited minimally and rather belatedly from the republican modernization reforms of the 1920s and 1930s. In 1924 the state began construction of a railway line that restored Kayseri to its ancient centrality as a trade hub. The line connecting Ankara to Kayseri opened in 1927, and went onward to Sivas in 1930 and the Black Sea, reaching Samsun in 1932.

Meanwhile, in August 1925, the German aircraft company Junkers formed a consortium with Turkish businessmen and, in 1926, built an aircraft assembly plant outside Kayseri. Disagreements among the shareholders led to the plant being closed in May 1928 without a single plane ever being built there. But in 1933, the government set up the Sümer Bank for the purposes of financing industrial expansion in what were considered to be underdeveloped areas such as Kayseri. That year, the *Kayseri Tayyare Fabrikası* ('Kayseri Aircraft Factory') was reopened with a staff of over one thousand to manufacture aircraft parts for a number of US, German, Polish, British and Russian companies. Among the tasks carried out during the years that Ahmet Hamdi Gül worked there was the reverse engineering of Russian gliders – prototypes were taken apart and then machines were designed to manufacture the parts.[32]

The engine of economic growth that slowly brought Kayseri out of the doldrums of the late Ottoman and early republican years, however, was the textile mill not the aircraft factory. Also financed by the state-owned Sümer Bank, the Kayseri Textile Factory opened on 16 September 1936. A month after the factory had started production, Donald Webster, a visiting American, claimed it had already become 'the country's showcase', producing 'nearly half as much' finished cotton 'as the quantity imported into Turkey the year before the factory opened'.[33] Webster admired how the factory 'operated on a single shift' of over 2,000 workers; a number set to increase to 4,500 once 'additional living quarters had been constructed'.[34] Within a year, according to British Foreign Office figures, the Kayseri factory was producing half of the cotton produced by state-owned factories, of which there were five, and by 1940 was 'the largest in the Middle East' and still operating continuously on a single shift.[35] In keeping with other state-planned industrialization projects, the Kayseri mills were 'typical of the new industries and of the regrouping of the population which these entail'.[36] Webster greatly admired the facilities provided for workers: communal canteens supplying wholesome and inexpensive meals, sports facilities and a hospital, dormitories for the single and apartments for married families – complete with showers which proved 'a novelty to most of the laborers'. The workers were villagers, attracted by 'stories about the pleasant working and living conditions at the new factory'.[37] Many of them came up from the south, from the vast, feudally-controlled villages among the cotton fields of the Çukurova plateau, a world of exploitation immortalized in Orhan Kemal's *Bereketli Topraklar Üzerinde* ('On These Bountiful Lands') of 1954,[38] and Yaşar Kemal's *İnce Memet* ('Mehmet, My Hawk') of 1955. Migrant workers arrived on the same road from Adana along which the bales of raw cotton grown in the region came to feed the maws of Kayseri's mills. Webster noticed that 'many of them had never been away from home before and succumbed to homesickness', but he also recorded a more remarkable incident. 'Kayseri,' he says, 'had not had a history of serious malaria epidemics, but carriers infected enough mosquitoes the first summer of the factory's operation to cause a mild epidemic': some workers panicked and ran home.[39]

From the late 1930s, thousands of villagers migrated to Kayseri for work in the factories there, but culturally they barely made up for the lost Armenians and Greeks. Those who came were generally rural people unaccustomed to life outside ancestral villages. Their traditional, patriarchal values fitted well enough with the conservative character and habits of Kayseri residents, who lived close to home and family. Though some of their manners and habits often at first appeared crude to the urban and educated population of Kayseri, they were nevertheless co-religionists who spoke a common language. Their assimilation and growth were carefully orchestrated by government policy since it was their very transformation, from villager labourers into urban workers, that was at the heart of early republican reform. Indeed, the Kayseri textile mills were, as Webster said, the 'showcase' of Turkey's evidence to itself and to the world of the aggressive programme of industrialization and modernization that confirmed its status as a modern nation very much aware that the whole world was watching. As Geoffrey Lewis put it in 1955, 'the new Turks, whose constant cry was (and indeed still is), "What will Europe think of us?" did not wish to be considered a nation of peasants. "Turkey is a Western country. Western countries are industrial…"'[40] The Kayseri factory did more than produce cotton: among many local leaders, it provided opportunities for boosting the city's pride in its reputation for being a model of state planning and social engineering, a symbol of Turkey's future as it brought the nation's rural populations into the modern world. The business community of Kayseri was hungry for foreign investments and eager to forget the failed deal with the Junkers syndicate back before the war.

The American visitor, Donald Webster, was not the first Western writer to be invited to view, admire and write about the Kayseri textile factory project in 1937. Earlier that same year, even as the buildings were being put up, the machines assembled, and the future workers trained in the needful skills that would earn them a wage and modern lifestyle, Lilo Linke arrived in Kayseri after recent visits to Adana and Izmir. Since March 1935, when she arrived in Istanbul by 'mere chance', Linke had been travelling about Turkey recording, among other matters, her impressions of the government's progress towards modernization. Like Webster, she admired what she saw in Kayseri, so much so that on leaving she found herself wanting to stay on for 'a year or two' and 'to help push things forward … and so make use of my experience in the German Youth Movement'.[41] We never discover what special chance it was that brought Linke to Turkey, or why a German woman should have written a book about Turkey in English, but her observations of the Kayseri factory confirm Webster's general facts and figures, suggesting they shared an official source.

Under the enthusiastic guidance of the factory director, one Fazıl Bey, a staunch Kemalist, Linke spent several days as a guest at the project site where she witnessed for herself the management problems of persuading some two thousand villagers to behave like industrial workers. Clocking in for work at the factory gates, for example, created hours of chaotic confusion among a labour force both innumerate and illiterate, conditions that generated anger and frustration. Earlier, this had led to early morning riots that were put down with summary sackings of the rioters. ID numbers were eventually stitched onto the men's clothing, assisting them to clock in. Pilfering was also a grave concern, but despite her contempt for the workers, Linke found much that she admired in the project as a whole. She was especially fascinated by the training being given to young girls. Local women 'in Kayseri and the villages nearby belonged to the most conservative in the whole country and were shocked at the very idea of working side by side with men', Linke observes when describing Fazıl Bey's scheme of getting 'hold of girls while they were too young to be spoilt by their mothers' and bringing them up in dormitories. It appears that 'a factory of this kind needed a great number of women workers'.[42] The social revolution designed in Ankara had arrived and was transforming life in Kayseri.

The founding director of the Kayseri textile factory, Fazıl Bey himself, as well as the other managers, foremen and senior mechanics, had been trained for this modernizing mission in Russia. 'The Kayseri factory,' Linke declares, 'was the first important outcome of the Turkish–Russian industrial collaboration,'[43] doubtless echoing an official fact presented to her by the director but with her own curious enthusiasm for the Russian influences visible here. The 1914–18 war had ended age-old hostilities and bound together the new republics, 'the Soviet Union, with every man's hand against it, and Turkey, the defeated Power which refused to admit defeat'.[44] Russia not only trained the management and senior staff of the Kayseri factory, but financed and supplied the buildings and machines. All the Turks had to do was provide the raw cotton and workers. Webster would note that, after running continuously for some weeks, the Russian-made machines were inferior to English mills since they tended to break down and need constant repair, often when spare parts were unavailable.[45] They were still mostly unassembled when Linke visited, but trainees were already expected to join in an early morning routine of calisthenics, under the personal direction of Fazıl Bey, in the factory stadium which had proudly been modelled on that of Cologne. Here Fazıl Bey was already supporting the city's first football team. 'I don't want it for the sake of the sport,' Linke reports him explaining: 'They'll be forced to wear shorts and show their naked knees, and that's what matters to me. Once they dare to appear in public like that, they've broken away from tradition and are free.'[46]

In 1937, modernity and modern ideas ruled at the Kayseri textile factory. The ambitions of its director, that is, were all for rapid modernization, right down to young men exposing their knees in public. Linke was clearly a modernist herself, whose admiration for all aspects of the Kayseri factory – its health facilities, its dormitories and apartments, its educational and training schemes, its sports facilities – is only matched by her insulting portrait of the villagers who have come there to be transformed into workers, 'half animals in their dumbness and ignorance – such were the men who were slowly to be turned into a self-conscious working-class'. Linke was clearly convinced that Turkey's aims to modernize, industrialize and urbanize were an essentially admirable and indeed humanizing and progressive programme, one that she wanted to help push forward. And without hesitation she assures readers that her experiences led her to confirm that men from Kayseri are 'notorious all over the country for their cleverness and cunning in business'.[47] Yet at the same time her account reveals the human problems arising from displacement and resettlement, and the sometimes brutal logic and attitude of modernizing reformers. What was happening in Kayseri was also happening in other provincial cities in the new Turkey: Adana, Bursa, Eskişehir were all engaged in industrialization and modernization programmes, reassembling populations and urbanizing migrant villagers.

A president's father: Ahmet Hamdi Gül

In addition to opportunities for incomers, the Kayseri factories provided valuable opportunities for young and educated local people, such as Abdullah Gül's father. Employed in the aircraft factory in 1943, age seventeen, Ahmet

Hamdi Gül quickly learned the skills of the tool-and-die-maker's craft and, combining them with his keen intelligence, put them to inventive use. The factory had been taken over for military purposes during the years of war and Ahmet Hamdi found himself attached to the army, helping design and manufacture spare parts for all kinds of military equipment. He became renowned for figuring out not just how to make a one-off replica of an engineered part, but how to set up a machine that would make multiple copies to high standards. These were skills that would later prove valuable for the replication of Russian gliders. Amid this newly industrialized sector of Kayseri, one leading Turkey into the technical future, Abdullah Gül's father found himself, a pious and practising Muslim, confronting science and technology as he worked alongside highly trained aircraft designers and engineers to invent new ways of doing things. At the same time, he understood the problems arising among the workers. Russian planning models were in place at the textile project, and left-wing ideas such as workers' rights were being openly promoted and discussed in the factories.

Ahmet Hamdi Gül's aptitude for the work marked him out as a master craftsman or *üstat*, a term with traditional associations linking technical skills with a highly developed sense of moral value. Certainly Ahmet Hamdi's strong sense of justice and humanity soon led him to become active in factory organization and he became a foreman in the plant. A genial and charming young man with an infectious sense of humour matched by his deep commitment to social justice, Ahmet Hamdi would have had no difficulty leading the workers, both skilled and unskilled, who were employed at the aircraft factory. His views were respected by all the men, and his understanding of how to solve problems – that famed Kayserian skill of knowing how to resolve conflicts in a way that keeps all parties happy – kept the factory working productively while the military commanded operations there.

During these years a young man named Kemal Sadık Gökçeli (b. 1923) was assigned military service in Kayseri and was stationed at the aircraft factory. He had already spent time in prison for his left-wing political views when he met Ahmet Hamdi and the two became close friends. Ahmet Hamdi Gül had made the *hajj* to Mecca by this time. Although the young soldier was not religious, he admired the young and pious engineer, how he handled factory politics and conciliated disputes to the benefit of the workers. For his part, Ahmet Hamdi teased the soldier for his extreme left-wing views, nicknaming him *karaoğlan*, literally a 'black boy', someone who stood out from the crowd, making himself a target.[48] Later changing his name to Yaşar Kemal, the young conscript went on to achieve international fame as Turkey's foremost socialist novelist and has claimed that Ahmet Hamdi Gül was one of the first socialist influences on him. In 2007, when Abdullah Gül was inaugurated as president, Yaşar Kemal wrote a letter to the new president congratulating him on his success: he recalled working with Abdullah Gül's father and expressed his great admiration for Ahmet Hamdi as a valuable ally and comrade in the union campaigns during the years they worked together, an ally who fully understood the difficulties facing villagers who found themselves without proper voice or representation.[49]

That Ahmet Hamdi Gül, a pious Muslim, and Yaşar Kemal, a radicalized left-wing intellectual and activist, should have found common purpose in their views on labour and how to resolve problems created by the factory system is not so surprising. Although we might say that both were, in one sense, beneficiaries of the republic's aggressive promotion of industrialization and modernization, they were nevertheless critically aware of the human problems that modernization entailed. As in the nation at large, both Muslims and socialists had long had good reason to be critical if not opposed to many features of the dominant Kemalist ideology and policy. In 1926 the republican government had adopted a secular civil code that gave the state control over religious affairs, causing disaffection among traditional and pious sectors of society. Abdullah Gül recalls:

> I remember when Muslims told various stories about how it was pro-
> hibited to learn the Qur'an and how the police came and took their
> books. I listened to how my father would go out to see if the gendarmes
> were coming and he would tell others and they would rush to hide all
> their books.[50]

Even as educated Muslims were resenting control by the state over their religious lives and the choice of books they might read, socialists like Yaşar Kemal were being hounded for more openly criticizing state policies.

Despite direct Soviet assistance, Turkey's modernization programme was proudly Western, modelled on Britain and France, and it came accompanied by an uncompromising hostility to anything resembling communism. Socialists, as Ahmet Hamdi Gül and Yaşar Kemal both knew, had long been in constant danger of finding themselves being branded enemies of the state and thrown into prison. The communist poet, Nazim Hikmet, had been locked up since 1938; that same year, the novelist Orhan Kemal was imprisoned on charges that included the criminal offence of reading Hikmet's poetry aloud in public. So the Muslim craftsman and the socialist conscript discovered common cause in having legitimate grievances against the state machine. Throughout the country, traditional Muslims were confronting government modernization programmes. Ahmet Hamdi Gül and Yaşar Kemal shared a strong mutual belief in benevolence and social responsibility, and in the need to reconcile those beliefs with the innovations of wage-labour and industrial modernization. The difficulty was how to achieve that reconciliation when the government and management continued to condescend towards the workers for being illiterate peasants, unaccustomed to a life spent indoors according to clock time. Ahmet Hamdi Gül became a champion of democratic representation that took the views of the workers seriously, serving as foreman on the factory floor and later, in 1947, when trade unions were permitted, becoming an active leader of the local chapter of HARB-IŞ, a union for workers in the defence industries.[51]

Turkey's new beginnings, 1950

In a sense, the otherwise unlikely friendship and accord between Ahmet Hamdi Gül and the young Yaşar Kemal that sprang up in a Kayseri factory during the late 1940s echo a widespread and mounting discontent with the government of President Ismet Inönü, who had assumed command following Atatürk's death in 1938. The republican single-party system had produced an all-powerful governing elite who squabbled among themselves, but continued to rule in a paternalistic and authoritarian manner, telling the people what was good for them regardless of their own views and opinions. Demands for greater democratic representation had been in the air for some time, but nothing was being done. In rural areas, the small farmers who made up eighty percent of the population were still waiting to benefit from the republic. They were becoming increasingly resentful of state controls over the countryside, of armed gendarmes and tax collectors, and of restrictions on their religious life and traditional dress. At the same time, Inönü's war-time economic policies had opened a rift among supporters of the Kemalist movement who had staunchly supported the CHP.[52] Civil servants, teachers, doctors, professors, lawyers and members of the business community all suffered badly from inflationary price controls and taxation. They had become suspicious that the government no longer supported their interests. 'The position of the indigenous bourgeoisie, whose growth had been such a high priority for

Unionists and Kemalists alike, had by now become so strong that it was no longer prepared to accept this position of a privileged, but essentially dependent and politically powerless class.'[53] In 1945 the single-party system began to unravel when the CHP government of Ismet Inönü was challenged from within its own ranks. In June of that year, following heated debates over a land reform bill, Atatürk's last prime minister Celal Bayar, together with three other eminent representatives of the ruling party, proposed a motion demanding that the 1924 constitution be observed and democracy established. It was summarily rejected, but the proposals of the four – Bayar, Adnan Menderes, Refik Koraltan and Fuat Köprülü – were widely supported in the liberal and left-wing press. Inönü himself spoke on the need for an opposition party to run in the next general elections. In January 1946, Bayar and his colleagues formed the *Demokrat Parti* ('Democrat Party') on a platform of political reform and economic liberalization. Hastily conducted elections that summer left the CHP in power despite allegations of vote-rigging. But after three decades of uncontested rule, the end was in sight for the CHP.[54]

In May 1950, the 'first free elections in the history of the republic'[55] brought the Democrat Party to power and a new mayor to Kayseri, Osman Kavuncu (1918–66), a stalwart of the new party. In line with the DP slogan that promised 'unprecedented development', 1950 ushered Kayseri into a new phase of urban, industrial and commercial development.[56] A sugar factory was opened in 1953 with funding from the state-owned Sümer Bank,[57] but Kavuncu's key initiative, one that would make Kayseri a model for other industrial development projects in provincial cities throughout Turkey, was to set about establishing a crafts quarter outside the old city, purchasing land, then dividing it into lots sold on with permissions for various trades. In addition to encouraging the growth of new industries, the plan for new trade-zones also set restrictions on specific trades being carried out in the old city, such as metal working, that were operating in dangerously old buildings. The old city was itself still in poor shape, many of its houses, shops and even municipal buildings in disrepair, and the city fathers had plans for urban renewal once funding could be found. The Kayseri crafts quarter was a great success. It formally opened in 1956 and grew rapidly: by 1975 it accommodated 1,782 different enterprises, 1,159 in manufacture, 623 in trade, and was no longer outside city limits, having been engulfed on all sides by urban development. What we might call the Kayseri model for industrial development proved so successful that it was imitated nationwide. By 1972, when Kayseri opened a second industrial park, even further outside the sprawling city, 'a similar infrastructure for small businesses' could be found in most towns and cities throughout Turkey.[58]

During the 1950s, even as Kayseri was leading the way forward in municipal development schemes that brought opportunities to skilled craftsmen and small traders, enterprising Kayserians were leading the way in the private sector and founding some of the nation's wealthiest enterprises. Stimulated by investment from the USA under the Marshall Plan, which was extended to Turkey in July 1948, a number of men from Kayseri began emerging to prominence as leaders of industrial and financial companies that are still of national and international importance. Born in Akcakaya, a village outside Kayseri, Ömer Sabancı had moved to Adana in 1921 and here established himself as a labour broker who invested in cotton and oil factories. In 1948 he entered into a partnership with Nuri Has, also from Kayseri, to found Ak Bank, and during the 1950s acquired massive landholdings in the Adana region and opened further cotton and flour plants. Meanwhile Nuri Has's son, Kadir, was setting up businesses in the automotive trade, a massive growth field at the time since Marshall Plan funding was tied to the construction of new, metalled roads, a scheme aimed at replacing Turkey's antique and confused rail network with a future demand for vehicles imported from Detroit. In May 1949, the arrival of the first shipment of US tractors under the Marshall Plan was celebrated at the Dolmabahçe Palace in Istanbul. At the same time, US engineers were helping establish a Department of Highways, and Kadir Has was setting up his first successful business selling tractors and trucks to the cotton farmers of Adana. His fortune was assured with the mechanization of village farms.[59]

During the 1950s, Sabancı, Has and other entrepreneurs from Kayseri were founding international business empires. By 1972, Abdullah Gül's father had quit the aircraft factory in order to set up his own workshop, located in the new industrial park, manufacturing machine tools. Ahmet Hamdi Gül's reputation for being a fair and honest man stayed with him as he developed his own business; in 1973 he was invited to run for election in Kayseri as parliamentary candidate for the *Milli Selâmet Partisi* ('National Salvation Party', or MSP), an Islamist nationalist party formed three years previously by Professor Necmettin Erbakan, but was not elected. The company he established subsequently moved to the centre of the second industrial complex that made Kayseri once again the 'showcase' of the republic and the most productive of Turkey's industrial 'tigers'. Founded in 1972, the Asteksan factory and plant are managed today by Abdullah's younger brother Macit. Asteksan is a successful designer and mid-level manufacturer of a wide variety of fabricated metal products from bus-stop shelters to sports equipment. Ahmet Hamdi Bey – who was eighty-seven years old when I met him – still spends many days in his office at the factory, entertaining local business colleagues and the occasional biographer of his son. But he admits that the best days are those when it is time to remove to the family vineyards, tend to the grapes, and spend the evenings under the stars watching the eagles flying overhead across the face of Mount Erciyes.

Kayseri today

Kayseri today is no longer the city in which Abdullah Gül was born and grew up, but the traditions, values and character of its people live on and thrive. Going to primary school in the late 1950s, Abdullah ventured out onto muddy, cobbled streets among old, often crumbling, houses. Like other children of the time, he wore sturdy clothes and shoes that were designed to last for several years – if not generations – and were regularly big enough for him to grow into. Walking to school, there were drains that mostly did their job, and some electric street lighting, but even strolling in the heart of the old city meant passing through rundown buildings and vacant lots among neglected monuments to the city's more glorious ancient past. For decades, city funds had been limited and gone to industrialization; and there was nothing left for the full-scale inner-city renewal needed to recover from generations of neglect. Yet with great and famous architects such as Mimar Sinan and the Balyan brothers among its proud sons, Kayseri maintained a long line of skilled masons who were experts in working the local volcanic stone. A schoolfriend from those years recalls how they would sometimes pause and watch craftsmen working with stone. Growing up in Kayseri at the time, even schoolboys were aware that improvement might be in the air, and grew sensitive to the built structures of their home city. Abdullah Gül recalls the proud, old municipal buildings that had long been in need of repair:

> I remember beautiful stone buildings with magnificent huge doors and gateways that were just like those of Istanbul University. Unfortunately many of them have not been preserved. I recall one building, the former house of the governor, was much more beautiful than today – four more times beautiful! There were very old houses and narrow streets. Many government buildings of the past were very beautiful, such as the high

schools, but houses were simple and modest. For that reason I cannot have much of a longing for those times, because life was very difficult. Now the streets and houses are better and everything has improved.[60]

My own memory of first visiting Kayseri in the summer of 1996, staying in a small hotel while visiting Kültepe and other ancient sites, is that many areas of the inner city appeared to have remained unchanged for decades, and that any change was slow-coming. Mount Erciyes was with you wherever you went, and makes the city itself feel lowly. There were building sites, clearly long-term and making slow progress, with sign boards announcing the project. And there were wide boulevards that strongly evoked Paris, but with little traffic along them and remarkably few cafés. Outside the city, but still watched over by Erciyes, I recall extensive areas given over to unfinished housing projects; skeletal concrete structures that suggested no one had worked here for a long while. In the hotel I learned how people had started building when the Turkish lira had been growing increasingly worthless for investing, so those who conducted business in that currency spent it on land and building. Banks were not to be trusted, and putting your money in them in pursuit of interest would be against Islamic tradition. No one was in a hurry to finish these structures. Once the lira were all spent, building work stopped and everyone waited till the next cycle. Eventually they would finish the buildings, one floor at a time, as soon as there was money to do it.

Today, those steel and concrete frames have been completed and are inhabited by car-owning families. With the population hovering around the million mark in 2011, they have been joined by hundreds of additional apartment blocks to form extensive new neighbourhoods. Kayseri has become the nation's second largest financial centre, second only to Istanbul. Among the so-called 'Anatolian Tigers', Kayseri has also taken the lead in production for export and has its own Free Trade Zone. Cosmopolitan in many respects, it is still a markedly conservative city, one run by and for the interests of local businessmen, who are indeed hard-working, sober and more inclined to investment than to conspicuous extravagance: the recently completed Kayseri Park Shopping Centre downtown and the occasional café with Gulf-style gilt ornamentation notwithstanding. It is still hard to imagine that there are no cafés along Mustafa Kemal Paşa Boulevard, with its evident memory of Paris, where there are some shops, mostly for women looking for bridal wear and wedding gifts, but no strolling *boulevardiers*. Even the pedestrian areas between the old city walls and the covered market, where there are a few restaurants, are remarkably free of cafés and tea houses. Internal consumerism aside, Kayseri is now at the heart of a thriving Turkish economy, as if in fulfilment, finally, of the local sense of character, that inherited understanding of how to read and adapt to changes in international commerce and trade, and how to close on the best deal while keeping your clients your friends.

Supported by local-born multimillionaires who became successful elsewhere, by the 1970s Kayseri was starting to emerge from a peripheral to a central role in the growing national economy. In 1972 a volume of self-promoting proverbs and anecdotes appeared, aptly titled: 'I don't like to brag but I am from Kayseri' (*Övümmek gibi olmasın ama Kayseriliyim*).[61] At the core of the Kayseri character and the success story of the city, as just about everyone in Turkey today recognizes, is pride in business. Back in the 1970s, Europe was listening to the boasting and a new wave of Western observers came in the footsteps of Webster and Linke to assess development and to evaluate what might be about to happen. Asked his view of the key to the Kayseri character, Abdullah Gül told me:

> The people are independent and practice self-help among themselves. For instance, the first university, Erciyes University, cost the city a great deal of money but the people found the money and that is evidence. They spent so much to build it, and also the many hospitals and schools. This is also how they think about the city and about business. In the 1950s? It was still better than many places. It was very well known![62]

Early years: Kayseri and Izmir

On 29 October 1923 in Ankara, the Turkish Republic was born and Mustafa Kemal named its first president. On 29 October 1950 in Kayseri, amid anniversary celebrations, Abdullah Gül was born. The victory of Cemal Bayar, Adnan Menderes and the DP earlier that year meant that this was the first time the celebrations also marked the end of the single-party rule of the CHP. Finally, it seemed the Turkish Republic had embraced democratic reforms and proved to itself, and to the West, that it was modern and capitalist and, at the same time, in need of help to fend off the dangers of being overwhelmed by Soviet communism.

Born on this signal day in this signal year for Turkish political history, young Abdullah Gül grew up with a father renowned for his optimism, piety, good humour and skills at conciliation. From his father, Abdullah learned the importance of being a practising Muslim while understanding how religion referred to personal and private life, and how key ideas coming from the socialist left were both admirable and essential to understanding the modern, industrialized world. The heroic bandits of the 1940s who had roamed the hills around Mount Erciyes in Süleyman Sağlam's fact-based novel were being slowly and steadily replaced by industrial workers but remained local heroes, representing justice and freedom. Abdullah's earliest years were spent in a proud and ancient city that was hoping for better times, its people still suffering from decades of deprivation, yet resilient and hardworking, prepared to make the most of available circumstances. Both his parents came from families that embody these very characteristics. Adviye Hanım, his mother, was every bit as well known for her intelligence, sense of humour and generosity to others as was his father. Coming from a highly educated family of teachers and doctors in Izmir, Adviye learned at a young age to respect the scientific point of view and to think for herself, qualities that combined with her intelligence to produce a shrewd sense of wry comic irony. Abdullah Gül's parents, as one family friend put it, 'are the nicest people on earth'.

> His mother is so nice, so tolerant and embracing. She always looks on the positive side of life and that is true for the whole family. They don't sit around criticizing others but look for positive values. This is unlike many families in Anatolia who enjoy suffering, and indulge themselves in sadness and the arabesque style of melancholy. But there is no room for gloom in the Gül family. If something is bad or sad they want to move on and find something positive. All this he takes from his family background – his parents taught him to look on the bright side and not complain but to find an answer. This is unlike those who take pleasure in complaint and misery, but not the Güls. This makes him quiet, understanding and tolerant.[63]

The first-born son, Abdullah spent his earliest years among a conservative Muslim family that followed traditional habits and routines. During his infancy and early childhood, he was often cared for by his grandmother, from whom he learned those local tales of heroic suffering and sadness from the recent past.

Amid the uncles and cousins, each with their particularized status within the larger family, the birth of his younger brother Macit in 1958 made Abdullah an *ağabey* or *abi*, a 'big brother'. As in all Turkish families, even today, being an *abi* brought traditional duties and responsibilities that were waiting to be learned and fulfilled. Macit reports that Abdullah took the role of being a big brother seriously and was kind rather than bossy, sometimes joining in the younger boy's games despite the difference in age. In this conservative household, their younger sister Hatice grew up among the other girls and women. By the mid-1960s, however, grandfather Hayrullah Efendi's house had run out of rooms. Gül recalls how 'when my youngest uncle married it became too crowded so my father, being the oldest brother, decided to move out, so we moved into a modern concrete flat a few hundred meters down the street. Our new flat was on the fourth floor, and at the time this was one of the highest buildings in Kayseri. Imagine! The view we had! But now this would not be tall for Kayseri and the building is gone.'[64] Macit recalls the move and how the children found themselves cut off from former friends. When a noisy quarrel broke out between Macit and some of the local children, Abdullah 'and all the other big brothers soon joined in, but he took me aside to protect me from the other children'. Macit also recalls Abdullah helping him with school work, 'and I missed his help when he went to University and I was still in the third grade'.[65] Right from the start, young Abdullah Gül took his family responsibilities seriously.

In this, as in most respects, Abdullah Gül had a very ordinary childhood typical of the place and era. At age eight, he began formal schooling at the Gazi Paşa primary school, an old stone building situated a few hundred metres from home. 'I was back there recently, in April [2011],' he recalls, 'and the principal had prepared a surprise. When I entered my room all my former classmates were there waiting for me! I was not expecting this and didn't know some of them at first and thought they were parents of the students. It was a great surprise.'[66]

But if Abdullah's earliest years were typical for any boy growing up in a traditional Turkish family at the time, his family was nevertheless remarkable in two respects: its ability to combine piety with respect for education that emphasized openness to scientific and technical ideas, and its infectious optimism. Certainly that optimism is evident in the school photograph taken in 1962 for his graduation from the Gazi Paşa primary school; those smiling eyes surely show present and past security together with confidence in the future. As well they might: his graduation diploma shows that all of Abdullah's teachers had been impressed by his final term's performance, moving him from 'good' (*iyi*) to 'very good' (*pekiyi*) in nearly all subjects: even his worst subject, mathematics, improved from 'average' (*orta*) to '*iyi*'.[67]

Abdullah Gül's early family life was also exceptional for a young boy growing up in Kayseri in one other respect. His mother's family extended to Izmir,
and every year during school holidays Abdullah, his parents and his brother
would spend the summers by the sea staying in the city that was still one of
Turkey's cultural capitals and where daily life could hardly have been more
different from daily life in Kayseri. He recalls:

> I had a colourful childhood. Half of my family lived in Izmir so every
> summer when school closed we visited my mother's father's place in
> Izmir and spent the whole summer there, going by train, the black
> trains of those days![68]

The family would plan for weeks in advance before taking the 'black' steam
train that, in those years, took two days to reach the Aegean metropolis from
Kayseri.

For these long journeys young Abdullah was assigned some of his first
responsibilities as the oldest son of the family: supervising arrangements
before and during the journey to the coast. While the women of the household
spent days preparing food and packing clothes and other necessities for the
journey, Abdullah had the task of making sure there was enough of everything
and that everything was where he could find it. But the real challenge came
when it was time to go for the train. The train left very early in the morning
and most of the children were too excited to have slept. Among the last-minute
panics of a large family about to leave home for two months, Abdullah's most
formidable task was to ensure that everyone, with all the hampers of food and
bags of belongings and gifts, made it to the station on time. Ahmet Hamdi Bey,
who would be staying in Kayseri to work, would have gone on ahead with the
tickets to claim the seats. As Macit put it, these trips were when Abdullah 'at
once became the man of the family', in charge of conveying everyone and all
their belongings from the house to the train, then sorting out the luggage and
making sure that supplies were ready to hand. And there were a lot of supplies.
The journey took two full days. The black train took them south to Niğde,
with a stressful change of trains to be organized at Ulukişla, then on through
the holy city of Konya to Afyonkarahisar and Manisa, finally arriving on the
night of the second day at Izmir.[69] In Kayseri, I was told the story of how, one
memorable year, boarding was almost complete when Abdullah realized a
cousin had been left behind. Summoning the courage and confidence of his
young years, he successfully managed to persuade the conductor and driver to

delay the train's departure until all members of his family were safely in their seats. When I asked for confirmation, Abdullah Gül observed 'such things happened often, there were always delays'.[70] I think he was embarrassed to learn that tales of his childhood exploits had become local legend in Kayseri.

During those summers in Izmir, Abdullah Gül stayed in the house of his maternal grandfather, Ismail Satoğlu, a poet and teacher who had directed the opening of a number of primary schools in the region. The house was at Asansör, in the Jewish quarter near the Bet-Israel synagogue, and had wonderful views over Izmir harbour. Abdullah greatly admired all his grandparents, but could not help being slightly in awe of this urbane and sophisticated man who had dedicated himself to educating the Turkish people and who found his greatest pleasures in poetry and practising the ancient art of calligraphy. One year Abdullah stayed on in Izmir for a semester attending his grandfather's school.[71] While in Izmir, he also met and came to know other relatives with medical careers, intellectual interests and artistic avocations: an uncle, Ahmet Satoğlu, was professor of neurology at Ege University; a cousin, Yüksel Gemalmaz, is a doctor and well-known poet. Spending time among his family in Izmir, Abdullah Gül became accustomed to metropolitan habits and scientific discussions, and familiar with cultural values that would most likely have seemed strange and exotic to many of his school-friends who had never left Kayseri. 'Izmir,' he recalled recently, 'was a metropolis – more beautiful, more important, more diverse – it was the real end of the West at the time.'[72]

Izmir was, indeed, the most Western and, in one respect, modernized city in Turkey: the magnificent Ottoman-era villas and waterfront warehouses destroyed in the fires of 1922 had been replaced with functionalist modern buildings. But compared with Kayseri, there were more cars and taxis on the streets and there were buses shuttling about; there were more foreign businesses and businessmen; there were more electric lights in commercial areas where more shops sold more consumer goods; and on the streets and in the cafés there were respectable women wearing clothes designed in Paris, Rome and New York. The historical legacy of generations of wealthy Levantine families continued to shape cultural life: coffee-houses, restaurants, art galleries and theatres flourished as nowhere else in Turkey. Economically, if not architecturally, Izmir in the 1960s had started recovering from the devastations of 1922 and was the second biggest port in Turkey after Istanbul. Perhaps more than any other city, Izmir's recent growth had been shaped by Turkey's friendship with the USA and the Western powers. In 1952, NATO opened regional headquarters here, at about the same time that a US Air Force base was established.

What most struck the young visitor from Kayseri, though, was the sea. 'Seeing the sea when you come from Kayseri! Just imagine what that was like!'[73]

Today, many of Abdullah Gül's strongest memories of summers on the Aegean coast are of the seaside and swimming, fun at the amusement park, the cool evenings after hot days, the fruit and constant supply of fresh fish. Yet it was in Izmir that Abdullah Gül came to recognize how he belonged to a nation that reached well beyond his central Anatolian hometown with all its benefits, limitations and possibilities. To be a Turk, he realized, meant being intimately connected to an entirely distinctive regional mix of additional traditions, habits and attitudes from those which gave shape to his life at home. Bekir Yıldız, a schoolfriend from those years, recalls how 'the Izmir visits were very important to him. This was not common for everyone in Kayseri. He would return with stories of the sea but he was never snobbish or bragged about his privilege. He had an uncle there that he liked very much and would come back with stories and things his uncle had said to him.'[74] The conservative and traditional routines of life in Kayseri, and the more Western and urbane metropolitan world of Izmir, did not clash or conflict but provided more family stories and a broader perspective on Turkey and what it meant to be Turkish than was common for young men born and raised in provincial Anatolian towns. As Fehmi Koru, an Izmir-born journalist who came to know Abdullah Gül during their student years in Istanbul and London, observes: 'For someone born and raised in Kayseri he is exceptionally open-minded.'[75] That broad perspective was doubtless first taking shape from those regular childhood visits to stay with family in Izmir.

Schooldays

Back in Kayseri, Abdullah attended the Gazi Paşa primary school, located nearly across the street from home. Here he received the standard state curriculum of the time which was both secular and aimed at modernizing. In addition to standard subjects – Turkish, history, mathematics, writing, gym, music and art – it also included units on table manners, 'knowledge of life' (*Hayat Bilgisi*), and 'knowledge of the family' (*Aile Bilgisi*). His final diploma indicates that he had done well in all subjects. [76] Abdullah received his earliest religious instruction at home and during summer school meetings. 'As a family,' he recalls, 'in our individual lives we were all practising Muslims, but together with that everyone lived their individual lives free from interference. In other words religion was not a dominating factor in our lives and the ways we lived. We attended Friday prayers regularly, and tried to keep the Ramazan fast!'[77] When I asked him if he remembers his earliest thoughts about religion, and whether his distant ancestry of imams ever caused him to feel inclined to a life of piety, he replied:

> When we look at the family, my father's father was a merchant, and my mother's father was a teacher, but not a religious teacher; he opened many schools in Izmir. And even though the family is a faithful and believing one, there were no longer any professional imams or so on in the family – the Gülük days were long past! My mother's father's father was a well-known theologian, but I remember him hardly at all. I did not think of becoming religious as a child and, if I had, my parents would have sent me to an Imam Hatip School [for religious instruction]. But they didn't.[78]

Although a pious practising Muslim throughout his life, even as a child Abdullah Gül did not view religion as the determining goal in life. On receiving his diploma from Gazi Paşa primary school, he faced the next test of his manhood, one that would determine his future: further schooling or work.

And in Kayseri, the heartland of so-called Islamic Calvinism, work means commerce. 'The people in Kayseri,' Abdullah Gül explained to me,

> are very much a business-oriented people, and there was a tradition that when a boy finished primary school before sending him to secondary and high school, they used to test him, whether he had the ability for business or not. They used to put him with a friend's shop and see how he behaves: if he is active and clever or if he is shy. Then, at the end of the summer period, he would get a report. If the boy is willing, capable, it makes a difference – the report might say don't send him to school! If the boy is not very good with people, it makes a difference – so they say send him to school.
>
> I remember, I was tested! My grandfather, my father's father, his shop was very crowded those years and even on the street there were crowds. Here I had to stand, with buckets, this big, filled with ice, then bottles of soda. There were two companies making soda in Kayseri at the time, two different sources from the skirts of Erciyes. So they filled the bucket with soda and they gave me a 'sword' that you used to open the lid – putting it under and blowing the fizz about – and you shout!

'*Buz gibi gazoz!*' ['Ice cold soda!'] What a thing to be shouting! What a lot there was to shout! 'Ice cold soda! Makes all thirty-two teeth play the violin!' That's the saying! This was early marketing!

So one day my uncle came by my grandfather's shop, and when he saw how it was going, he took a bottle of soda – and he opened it and shouted, and all the people came. And he asked me to do the same. But I was unsuccessful. I never saw the report, but I assume it was not good so they sent me to school. I wanted to go to school of course, uncles and others were teachers, all went to university. So from the family I know education was important, but I was tested in that tradition. Now it doesn't happen that way, but in another way. They send children to school, often business schools, then they take over the family business. They prefer not to work in the public sector. Kayseri is very business oriented.[79]

And so it was in line with local customs developed in the vacuum left behind after the expulsion of the Armenian and Greek populations that Abdullah Gül, aged twelve, having shown promise at school but none at selling soda, began attending the Nazim Toker secondary school. Here he cemented close friendships that have survived into national and local political life: Bekir Yıldız, also born and raised in the Gülük Mahallesi, is currently mayor of Kocasinan Belediye, the largest of the five Kayseri municipalities; and Mehmet Tekelioğlu, with whom Abdullah Gül shared a desk during their secondary and high school years, is currently parliamentary chairman of the EU Commission and married to Abdullah's sister Hatice. Both these life-long friends recall how Abdullah was well known at school for being a popular conciliator, always eager to settle problems with a compromise. Nurşen Özdamar, a teacher from his high school years, also remembers this quality. During his school years, Nurşen Hanım told me, Abdullah was 'hardworking and kind, always helpful to other students, and polite in class – if other students caused distractions, he would ignore them to please the teacher.' He was not, she recalls, especially interested in religion or pious, but did have a developed moral sense.[80] Those same skills of persuasive negotiation and conciliation that had enabled him as a child to delay the departure of a train were clearly central to young Abdullah Gül's personality and sense of social responsibility. But he enjoyed games too. Bekir Yıldız recalls how he was keen on playing football, but was more enthusiastic to join in the game than skilled at it: 'we always asked him to play in goal, and he was happy there.'[81] Once again, the point is to reach an agreement and be happy with the deal, even when it means staying out of the centre-field action.

Judging from recollections of his behaviour at school by his friends and teachers, the happy, secure and optimistic twelve-year-old Abdullah Gül who appears in the photograph for his primary school diploma was clearly still all those things: a smart and well-adjusted young man in the making. Yet by 1962, Abdullah was already personally aware of the political troubles that were shaking the nation.

The 1960 coup

On 27 May 1960 a military coup overthrew the DP government and set about ruling through the National Unity Committee (NUC).[82] Later that year, on 29 September, the NUC closed the DP and put its leaders on trial before setting about imposing a new Constitution that, amid a number of liberalizing reforms, also strengthened military powers over political life.[83] During the months before the show trials at Yassıada began, President Celal Bayar, Prime Minister Adnan Menderes and other DP ministers were imprisoned in Kayseri. 'There was in Kayseri,' Abdullah Gül recalls, 'a very strong prison and members including the president were brought there and I recall our neighbours making baklava and taking it to the prisoners.'[84] However much consideration or even thought the young Abdullah may or may not have given to national politics during his first ten years, the sudden incarceration of the president and his senior ministers in the local prison brought the harsher world of power unforgettably before him. Martial law had been declared, and the streets right outside his home, streets along which he had walked to and from school, were now under night-time curfew and patrolled by armed guards during the day. In family gatherings, memories were recalled and tales retold of former times when the people of Kayseri had found themselves unwillingly caught up in the affairs of an authoritarian state. In Kayseri and Izmir, the Gül and Satoğlu families were, like educated families everywhere in Turkey, anxiously gripped by the regular news broadcasts that were now being transmitted on the newly arrived radio.

> And then I remember the 1960s coup and we were living very centrally in the city. We were not allowed to go out from the house – we just peeped outside and I remember seeing gendarmes at the entrance to the street. My grandparents and neighbours were very sorry because

they used to love Prime Minister Menderes very much, and they were
very sad at what was happening.

When I was in secondary school I remember listening to my grandparents telling stories of those times after the 1960s coup when there
were the hearings at Yassıada. Everyone got together to hear the radio –
which was difficult to tune – and I heard the comments of the family
and they were very sorry and I am sure that what I heard contributed
to my earliest understanding of political matters and sensitivities
toward them.[85]

Born the year that Adnan Menderes had come to power, Gül had spent his
earliest years in the midst of a family and community that had supported and
benefited from a decade of his government. How could these terrible things
be happening to the leaders they supported and continued to admire?

Like the reasonable majority of devout and educated Muslims, the Gül
family had welcomed the DP's concessions to religion even as they recognized
and appreciated how much they had gained as citizens of the republic. A
wealthy landowner from Aydin in the west, Menderes was a popular speaker
who had endeared himself to Muslims by reintroducing Arabic as the language for the call to prayer instead of the awkward 'modern Turkish' version
imposed by the CHP. At the same time, Menderes and the Democrats had
pursued policies of rapid internal growth, pursuing economic reforms that
introduced a new era of entrepreneurial opportunities for businessmen,
shifting government investment from industrial to agricultural production.
Fortunes were being made in the private sector from subcontracting to state
enterprises, in transportation and in the cotton-based industries of Adana
and Kayseri. With US aid, the length of metalled roads increased from 1,600
km to 7,000 km over the decade, ending the development of rail links and
replacing public with private transport networks, but providing agricultural
villagers with better access to markets. In the same decade, the number of
motor vehicles tripled, from 53,000 to 137,000, leading to a flourishing of small
repair shops and service stations.[86] Thanks to US aid packages, the number
of tractors rose from 1,750 in 1948 to more than 30,000 in 1956, and Turkey
became one of the world's leading exporters of wheat.[87] On coming to power,
the Democrats were keen to make their Cold War alliances clear. On 25 July
1950, mere weeks after assuming office, Menderes dispatched Turkish troops
to join the UN forces in Korea. In February 1952, Turkey entered NATO
and officially joined the 'West' in the Cold War.[88] The early, golden years of

DP rule had encouraged optimism and brought prosperity to many with an economy that grew 'at a rate of between 11 and 13 percent'.[89] By the middle of the decade, however, inflation was starting to produce dissent in many quarters of the political spectrum.

Until 1958 at least, the Democrats under Menderes remained generally popular, especially in rural areas and among conservative families like the Güls who were prospering. In limited ways, the modernization programme first announced by Atatürk decades ago had finally begun benefiting families, like the Güls, living in rural and provincial areas.[90] Radios were becoming increasingly widespread, bringing news of national and international events even as they happened, and housing standards were improving.[91] In 1962, Abdullah Gül's immediate family moved into a new, modern four-storey building; at the time it was the tallest building in the area and had modern facilities that worked most of the time.

But not everyone was happy with Menderes and the Democrats. There were those of extreme religious beliefs who were unappeased by the nominal easing of religious restrictions just as there were extreme secularists who feared that the DP had gone too far in encouraging religion to re-enter the political sphere. Nor were all the new government's other policies popular, many of them directly aimed at intimidating the opposition in pursuit of financial gains for the governing party. In thirty years of power, the CHP had become enormously wealthy while the new governing party needed funds. In 1951 the Democrats closed and seized the assets of the *Halk Evleri* ('People's Houses') and *Halk Odalari* ('People's Meeting Rooms') – cultural institutions run by the CHP – thereby reducing educational provision in rural areas to put something into the party coffers. Two years later, they seized all the material assets of the CHP for the state treasury.[92] Members of the CHP who continued to regard themselves as Turkey's natural leaders now found themselves in opposition, under constant threat of having all their party assets seized. In 1950, the Democrats had released Nazim Hikmet from prison, but remained fiercely anti-communist: Hikmet chose self-imposed exile in Moscow. In keeping with their Cold War alliances, the DP banned all left-wing parties, sending their leaders to prison or into exile, and set about controlling the press and using the state-controlled radio for its own purposes. After a second electoral victory in 1954, Menderes, who 'had always found it very hard to accept criticism ... now became positively allergic to it'.[93] This authoritarian tendency became ever more apparent as Menderes set about purging universities, the civil service and judiciary of any form of opposition.

In 1955, Menderes's support for anti-Greek demonstrations in Istanbul and Izmir backfired. In recent years, the Turkish press had been following events in Cyprus with more than usual interest, signalling alarm at increasing evidence that the Athens government was backing Greek-Cypriot demands for control of the island. Inspired by the passionate rhetoric of Archbishop Makarios, Greek-Cypriot demands for *enosis* – union of the entire island with mainland Greece – had pressured the Greek government to take the case for union to the UN. In December 1954, the UN General Assembly declared that 'it does not appear appropriate to adopt a resolution on the question of Cyprus'.[94] Makarios was furious. Within three weeks, on 11 January, he gave the go-ahead for the use of violence in support of Greek-Cypriot claims. From April, with the blessing of their patriarch, the Nationalist Organization of Cypriot Fighters (EOKA) set about attacking British military and government offices, but Turkish Cypriots also came under attack right from the start since they constituted the majority of the island's police force. In August, at a conference on the Cyprus question, Menderes firmly declared that 'this country will absolutely not accept any change in the status of Cyprus either today or tomorrow that will be against the interests of the [Turkish] state'.[95] His firm stance gave tacit legitimation to those in Turkey who were infuriated by the increasing violence of the EOKA campaign and anxiously seeking to do something. In early September, demonstrations were organized in Istanbul and Izmir to support Turkey's claims to Cyprus. When these quickly led to widespread violence against Greek businesses, the police were under instruction not to intervene. More than five thousand Greek shops and houses were ransacked before the government declared martial law, and the Turkish press set about attacking Menderes and his government for damaging Turkey's reputation abroad.[96]

Tarnished but undeterred, Adnan Menderes and the DP were returned in the elections of 1957 with a diminished majority. In his election speeches, President Bayar promised to put Turkey on the road to becoming a 'little America' within thirty years, but it was a country he had never visited and his optimism was equally unfounded.[97] Soon after re-election, Prime Minister Menderes made his first move against the military, arresting nine army officers for plotting against the government. By August 1958 the Democrats had so lost control of the economy that they were forced to accept an IMF plan of devaluing the lira by an astonishing 321% and increasing prices for which the state treasury received US$359 million in loans.[98] Meanwhile, Ismet İnönü and the CHP opposition were not idly standing by but engaged in a vigorous anti-government propaganda campaign. Both parties exploited public feelings in the press and on the radio, bringing political debates ever more into provincial and rural households. Public feelings ran high as the 1950s came to an end. Farmers who had received IMF aid brought in a bumper harvest in 1959. In January that year the nation heard on the state-owned radio how Menderes had escaped from a deadly air crash because he was chosen by God to lead his people. Party loyalties led to hostility, even violence. While campaigning, Inönü found himself subject to attacks in DP strongholds. In February a CHP rally he was addressing in Konya was broken up by police: 'early in April 1960 troops were used to stop him holding a meeting in Kayseri. When he refused to turn back, the troops were withdrawn.'[99] In 1960, political life was turning nasty. In April Menderes closed the universities, sparking student riots in Istanbul and Ankara. On 27 May, the army seized power.

For young Abdullah Gül, experiencing the 1960 coup was a personal turning point. It was his family's responses to the military takeover of May, and the trials leading to the execution of Adnan Menderes, Finance Minister Hasan Polatkan and Foreign Minister Fatin Rüştü Zorlu in September 1961, that first inspired him to imagine taking an active role in the nation's political life.

> I remember that granddad – my mother's father – and everyone in Izmir – their frustration! They were so angry at what was happening. And while they were talking they said '*babayiğit*' – he is a 'brave heart' with good ethics who defends them in a brave way. They were saying that there is no such 'brave heart' that would go and tell them the truth and make them face reality. I remember hearing this as a child and when everyone went away I went to grandfather and told him that I can be that 'brave heart' and go to them and tell them what they needed to hear! He was very angry because he was very sensitive being a teacher. My granddad was a careful artistic teacher dealing with calligraphy and writing poetry – he published a book – and he wrote me verse letters from Izmir, so after listening to the family asking for a '*babayiğit*' I came out and said I would do it and he got very angry – to protect me![100]

Perhaps under other circumstances, Abdullah's childhood ambition to think of himself as a *babayiğit* might have seemed amusing since, aged eleven, he was hardly the right physical size or shape and a *babayiğit* is usually a big man. Among numerous colloquial terms in Turkish defining different kinds of masculinity, a *babayiğit* is a man of the people who is both fearless and honourable, but he is most often very strong physically, large and unbeatable. Abdullah had the right spirit and moral impulse, but hardly the right body. The executions of Adnan Menderes and his senior ministers shocked the nation, inspiring a young boy from Kayseri to become a hero and please his family. Although he would never forget his grandfather's kindly anger and warning about entering politics, the urge to tell the authorities 'what they needed to hear' never went away.

Kayseri Lycée, 1965–69

It is hardly surprising that Abdullah Gül's earliest memory of encountering and becoming personally engaged with the world of harsh political events should involve an emerging sense of duty amid the disturbances brought by the 1960s coup and its aftermaths. His emerging views and opinions at the time were clearly shaped by his family: practising Muslims who were conservative and traditionalist yet open to the ideals of social justice and a fair society, to scientific and technological developments; people who were optimistic and forward looking, uninfected by the melancholic nostalgia and alienation felt by many conservative people that had been brought about by decades of living under a secularizing and modernizing state. The Güls had survived the lean decades and were prospering. His father's technical professionalism and notable energies on behalf of organized labour in the factories would also have provided a broader sense of what it meant to be a responsible and pious Muslim than was being declared by the anti-Westernization rhetoric of more extreme Islamists.

Abdullah Gül's intellectual engagements continued to develop widely during his high school years against a backdrop of the exciting but increasingly disturbing world events that were being described 'in radio broadcasts as Turkey underwent democratization, liberalization, radicalization, and militarization.'[101] During his first year at high school alone, a Soviet cosmonaut became the first man to walk in space; India and Pakistan went to war; the USA, Great Britain and the Soviet Union all demonstrated their nuclear weapons in tests throughout the year; and amid widespread anti-war demonstrations, President Lyndon Johnson increased US military intervention in South East Asia. Closer to home, the interim government of Suat Hayri Ürgüplü that formed in February was swiftly replaced by Süleyman Demirel's *Adalet Partisi* ('Justice Party', or AP) government in October elections.

In September 1965, even as Pakistan was invading Indian Kashmir, Abdullah Gül began attending Kayseri Lycée. Founded in 1893 to train future bureaucrats, the school has a long, prestigious and indeed heroic past. During the war with Greece, the school buildings were evacuated to house the Grand National Assembly when it moved to Kayseri to avoid the approaching Greek armies. Meanwhile, all the senior students aged sixteen and seventeen were recruited into the armed forces. Most of them lost their lives or were severely wounded during the decisive battle of Sakarya which lasted from 23 August to 13 September 1921, but turned back the invading Greeks. On 14 October 1924, Mustafa Kemal and his wife Latife Hanım visited the school and praised its intellectual rigour. While a student, Abdullah would have heard how the great leader had written in the school visitor's book: 'We saw here passionate and prosperous teachers and students of the Republic.'[102] A monument memorializing Atatürk's visit stands in the school courtyard today. By the time Abdullah enrolled, Kayseri Lycée had proved a successful gateway to places at universities in Ankara and Istanbul, having graduated numerous prominent statesmen, businessmen, artists, scientists and writers.[103] At registration, he wore glasses and adopted a serious expression for confronting the school camera:

> There used to be a famous ophthalmologist in Kayseri and he told my father I needed glasses and if I wore them as a child I wouldn't need them later. So I wore them and the other kids had fun teasing me because no one else had them.[104]

The teasing soon disappeared once the glasses had done their job – he still has good eyesight and only occasionally uses reading glasses – and Abdullah quickly established a reputation for being hardworking, honest and helpful to other students and teachers alike. 'Students gossip and tell stories about each other behind their backs, but he was never like that,' recalls his teacher Nurşen Hanım.[105] The young man pictured in his school records on his arrival in September 1965 was clearly far too thoughtful and reflective to be easily taken in by idle school gossip and backbiting. There were more important and challenging things to be thinking and talking about. The smiling twelve-year-old had become a thoughtful young man of fifteen.

During the first few weeks after the start of term, Abdullah Gül attended the political rallies being held in Kayseri for what would prove to be the most important general elections since the military coup of five years earlier. After a series of unstable coalition governments under Ismet Inönü, change was in the air. A young and dynamic leader, Süleyman Demirel had taken charge of the Justice Party (AP), which had emerged as the heir to the Democrats and major challenge to the CHP. Unlike the Democrats with their origins amid what had become a metropolitan Kemalist elite, however, Demirel's AP 'was a party in which, and through which, self-made men from the countryside and from the smaller (but fast-growing) provincial towns became a dominant force'.[106] Demirel himself was conservative, pro-capitalism and outspoken, declaring in June that policies being proposed by the CHP were 'the road to communism'.[107] For Abdullah Gül and his teenage friends, these were exciting times. 'For the first time, such topics as socialism, capitalism, land reform, foreign policy and economic development were debated at length', and in public.[108]

> When I was in secondary school, the first elections were being held and the Justice Party was there and in the city centre the parties all came and made public speeches. I remember going with some friends including Mehmet Tekelioğlu. We went and listened to the speeches. These were my first encounters with politics and sometimes we joined the rallies.[109]

The elections of October 1965 proved a landslide victory for Süleyman Demirel and the Justice Party. The chairman of the Kayseri organization of the AP at the time was Abdullah's uncle, Abdullah Satoğlu, so there was no doubt a sense of special excitement at being on the winning side in the Gül household.

When Demirel came to power in 1965, the republic had been trans-formed by a new constitution that was 'markedly different from the 1924 Constitution',[110] which was a revolutionary document designed to protect the newly established, secular and republican state. Constitutional changes following the coup of 1960 created what some have termed a democratic 'Second Republic' that replaced the authoritarian state that Atatürk and Inönü had set up. Aimed at ending the monopolization of power within the National Assembly, the new constitution established a second legislative chamber, the Senate, and introduced a system of proportional representation that prevented any single party achieving dominance. The Grand National Assembly now consisted of two chambers: a Senate of 150 members elected by majority vote, and a National Assembly of 450 members, elected by proportional representation. The president was appointed for seven years by the two chambers, and in turn appointed the prime minister who appointed the Cabinet. Although the military leaders of the 1960s coup had always insisted they sought to defend rather than gain power for themselves, the new agreement created the National Security Council (*Milli Güvenlik Kurulu*) which gave the military direct political power for the first time. But numerous social and political freedoms were also nominally extended for the first time: new parties were free to organize; restrictions on universities and political publications were lifted. Demirel took over a reformed state with a growth economy and an expanding population of young people attending university: enrolments at universities would double between 1950 and 1960.[111] The coup had proved good for business; living standards and incomes were generally on the rise, especially in agricultural and provincial areas where they had been low to start with.[112] A self-made businessman himself, Demirel was a popular speaker who spoke the language of the people, a skill Inönü had never achieved.

During his Lycée years, Abdullah Gül joined his family's admiration for the government and its leader, but he was also reminded of his grandfather's stern advice about the dangers of the political life. He watched while Süleyman Demirel, espousing traditional Islamic values, struck forcefully against the rising tide of left-wing movements while riding the wave of a growth economy. Between 1963 and 1969, when Demirel was forced from office by the military, 'real incomes went up almost continually, by an average of 20 per cent'.[113] But growth without adequate development proved his undoing, and young Abdullah noticed how the political system turned against Demirel, just as his grandfather had said happened to all politicians. After being returned to power in 1969, amid violent clashes between left- and right-wing groups, Demirel tried to recover the economy and invigorate industrialization by new tax reforms. He had already alienated liberals and intellectuals, but now lost much of the support of his party base among the Anatolian tradesmen and landowners. Briefly forced to resign in February 1970 by the right wing of his own Cabinet, Demirel left office following an ultimatum from the military on 12 March 1971.

Necip Fazıl Kısakürek and *Büyük Doğu*

Abdullah Gül's high-school years at Kayseri Lycée were times of growing political debate and confrontation throughout Turkey and the world. By the time he signed on for his first term, Abdullah and friends Bekir Yıldız and Mehmet Tekelioğlu were already engaged in an independent programme of intellectual self-development. During their final year at secondary school, amid the political excitement of the times, the three friends had discovered a common distrust of the way they were being taught and had formed their own reading group in line with the 'Great Ideas Clubs' – *Fikir Külübleri* – that had emerged as national forums for debating social and political issues.[114] At high school, they agreed that most of the teachers were fine – often young and enthusiastic – but the version of Turkish history and culture they were being taught did not quite fit with what they had all learned from stories told at home and what they could tell from their own observations. Music classes that made them memorize the lives and titles of works of foreign composers whose music no one listened to were especially unpopular. What of Turkish music and culture? And what of Turkish history? Abdullah Gül remembers how 'intellectual life was very much active in Kayseri. In high school we were struggling as we questioned our teachers, and we questioned what they told us of history. This was a main area of debate, the official history and the real history, so that was one of the controversial things in Turkey at the time.'[115]

When they arrived at Kayseri Lycée, the three young friends joined the school's reading club of twenty or so students from other years. Together, they explored writers and works they considered important that were not on the school reading lists.

Here Abdullah met Şükrü Karatepe who was already in the second class; they became lifelong friends. 'The way forward was not school, or family, but this reading club,' he recalled in 2011, 'those years were a different mood, with different thoughts and ideologies.'[116] In the nation at large, and among friends, debates continued to rage over the question of Turkey's secularism and modernity, over what it meant for Turkey to desire modernity by allying itself with the West, and over what any of these issues meant for the everyday lives of Turks as individuals. In addition to national and international history, they read the classical European novelists that were becoming available in translation: Camus, Dostoyevsky, Tolstoy. Here they discovered images of a society different from their own, a secularized world inhabited by characters struggling to preserve themselves and their beliefs as individuals in the face of a crumbling civilization. Bekir Yıldız recalls that Abdullah Gül was keen on the French novelists who showed how problems within the family led to feelings of personal isolation and alienation, but was also intrigued by international relations. 'We read classics of east and west, meeting weekends in a small room to read and discuss them. Abdullah Gül became very interested in relations between the French, the English and Russia. This group led us all to understand a larger world and ways of thinking that was beyond the perspective of Kayseri. This was the *Büyük Doğu* moment.'[117]

The '*Büyük Doğu* moment' would define and shape Abdullah Gül's intellectual development for the rest of his teenage years and beyond. Meaning 'Great East', *Büyük Doğu* was the title of a journal that, since 1943, had also become a widespread nationalist Islamic movement led by the founding editor, Necip Fazıl Kısakürek (1904–83). Ever since the Kemalist state had set about secularizing the republic, the Muslim majority of the citizens had resented having their traditional, and often localized, spiritual life and daily rituals being taken over by the state. They had seen their imams transformed into civil servants, and found themselves being banned from wearing traditional clothing, notably headgear, that was taken to have religious symbolism. From 1932, it had also meant having to hear the call to prayer in modern Turkish. The secular state went so far as to abolish the Caliphate – the most important institution in Sunni Islam that had long brought Turkey prestige and international importance. And the state banned the Sufi orders and other local religious assemblies that, for generations, had provided a traditional and conservative people with rituals and routines that gave shape to their lives and distinction to their communities. While many Islamic religious orders dissolved, others went underground and new leaders appeared with new and modern ideas about relations between Islam and the modern state.

The most influential of the first generation of new modern Islamists to respond to republican reform in terms of Islamic revival was Said Nursi (1876–1960), who came to be called *Bediüzzaman*, 'the wonder of the age'. A Kurd from Bitlis who had dedicated himself to the religious life as a child, Nursi developed advanced and indeed innovative ideas about how Muslims should respond to Europe, modernization and the secular state.[118] His teaching was based on explaining the message of the Qur'an to large audiences, encouraging the pious to read and meditate. He sought a modern version of Islam, teaching Muslims to seek the unity of God while also embracing science and modern technologies for advancing the cause of Islam and the well-being, prosperity and self-respect of Muslims. His biographer, Şerif Mardin, explains:

Said Nursi's contribution was a reaffirmation of the norms set by the Qur'an in which a way was found to re-introduce the traditional Muslim idiom of conduct and of personal relations into an emerging society of industry and mass communications.[119]

During the 1930s, Nursi was among the first to make successful use of increasing literacy and cheap print to distribute his ideas widely to small towns and villages, producing a series of Qur'anic commentaries that, collected together, comprise the *Risale-i Nur* ('The Epistle of Light'). After 1950, when the multiparty government marked the 'defeat of Turkish Jacobin secularism', Nursi's ideas spread into a powerful nationwide movement of followers called *Nurcu*.[120] Nursi's message was internationalist, concerned with Islamic values and the future union of Muslims everywhere, and this did not sit well with secular nationalists in Turkey. Frequently arrested for rejecting secularism and nationalism, Nursi lived to see his thoughts inspire an internationally influential movement that one leading expert has called 'the most powerful and effective socio-political community in contemporary Turkey'.[121] Of several religious movements to originate in Turkey inspired by Said Nursi, the most important and influential is the 'community of Fethullah Gülen'. Like Nursi, Gülen (b. 1938) emphasizes reading the Qur'an in the light of contemporary circumstances, but his movement – called *Hizmet*, or 'Service' – is more directly engaged in social activism, mostly through publishing educational materials and establishing schools. Since the 1980s, the Gülen movement has developed a wide international following, and continues to arouse controversy in Turkey and elsewhere: more on Gülen and Hizmet in Chapter 6.

Said Nursi was among those released from prison by Menderes and the Democrat government of 1950, but the movement he inspired did not take hold of the Gül family in Kayseri. Ahmet Hamdi Bey would certainly have been familiar with his pamphlets, and shared Nursi's commitment to pious behaviour and the conviction that Muslims could and should embrace modern science to improve their lives. But whatever conversations young Abdullah Gül listened to that were taking place among his elders at gatherings of the Kayseri and Izmir families, there seems to have been little enthusiasm for the Nur movement. Doubtless Nursi's almost exclusive focus on endlessly interpreting passages from the Qur'an would have seemed unattractive to the widely read teachers, poets, merchants, technicians and doctors of the Gül and Satoğlu families. With a father keen on reading Western fiction, Abdullah's family influences invariably steered him towards a wider view of the world than that of the *Risale-i Nur*, to one that embraced Western culture. For his own part, given his general disinterest in religion as a child, Abdullah would have found the Nur movement limited and intellectually stifling: *Büyük Doğu*, however, offered a wider view of the world. As he reflected during an interview in 2005: 'The most important intellectual who had a major impact on my worldview was Necip Fazıl Kısakürek. He was not only an intellectual but also an activist and fighter against all forms of oppression.'[122] Here was a model for a young man who, aged eleven, had imagined himself a *babayiğit*.

Necip Fazıl also taught a modern version of Islam but it differed from Nursi's constant emphasis on interpreting the Qur'an. Fazıl consistently emphasized how culture was as crucial a means of personal and moral development as was doctrinal understanding, and that this principle also held true for political life. As a result, he argued, cultural progress was the key to Turkey's future as a Muslim nation that could be proud of its history. Unlike Nursi, 'by stressing Turkish nationalism and the Ottoman legacy, Kısakürek played an important role in the nationalization of Islam',[123] rather than the relegation of the nation to a universal Islam. Where the Nur movement, with its deep roots in Sufi mysticism, taught spiritual understanding and the primacy of Islam and *shariat* over political life, Fazıl taught a vision of Turkey within the history of Islamic civilization that kept national culture to the fore. What was needed, he argued, was a rebirth of Turkish culture that looked not only to Islamic civilization but also to the modernist achievements and failures of Western Europe. 'He envisaged his "Great East",' observes historian Carter Vaughn Findley,

> as a utopia, in which the material achievements of the West would be grafted onto the spiritual roots of the East. His 'ideological weave' amounts to an authoritarian, Islamic-nationalist pastiche that would have turned Turkey into a paradise somewhat like Franco's Spain ... [but] does not live up to Islamic norms of intercommunal relations.[124]

Gül admits that he has become somewhat embarrassed by some of Fazıl's ideas, but continues to admire the vision and sense of Turkey's cultural importance that Fazıl projected.

Throughout the late 1950s and 1960s, Necip Fazıl was among a group of Islamic writers, such as Nurettin Topçu (1909–75) and Sezai Karakoç (b. 1932), who emerged in the wake of the Nur movement to stimulate and to lead Islamic discussions about how to respond to the changes and challenges of the modern world. It was their writings and ideas, rather than those of the *Risale-i Nur*, which shaped discussions at family meetings of the Satoğlus and Güls when Abdullah was growing up. In 1957, Uncle Abdullah Satoğlu was inspired by Necip Fazıl to found a 'Great Ideas Club' in Kayseri,[125] where the intellectual climate, as elsewhere throughout the country, was indeed marked by 'different thoughts and ideologies'. Islam, nationalism, secularism, modernization, science, socialism, capitalism and communism: all were being hotly debated in the periodicals and 'Great Ideas Clubs'. The big question among Muslim writers and intellectuals concerned what it might mean to be Turkish, a Muslim, and a citizen of a secular republic all at the same time. This, the questioning of identity, has often been called a symptom of the 'postmodern' condition, though in Turkey as elsewhere, it also properly belongs to the condition of modernity, with all its cultural explorations of alienation amid technological progress. For three aspiring young intellectuals entering high school in 1965, entry to these debates came via the person and ideas of 'a new kind of literary figure and new phenomenon in Turkish "print capitalism"', Necip Fazıl.[126]

For Abdullah Gül and his friends, *Büyük Doğu* was more than simply a journal of ideas. Fazıl's ideal of a 'Great East' or 'Great Orient' was a world vision and a grand one that held enormous appeal for many in Turkey at the time who were pondering their faith and sense of being Turkish. Amid the new roads and the burgeoning presence of trucks and cars and automotive repair shops, and the arrival of Coca-Cola, not to mention the global political disputes being described on the radio news bulletins; amid all this, what was happening to life in Turkey? Was it really becoming 'little America'? Could that really be a good thing? In this context, the very name of Fazıl's movement, 'Great East', brought into focus a confident insistence that being a Muslim was not to be backward, as Kemalist modernizers loudly insisted, but rather that Islam was a progressive force promising a great and prosperous future for Muslims, for Turks, and for Turkey. Reading the Qur'an and works by religious thinkers was important, but for Necip Fazıl putting ideas, values and beliefs into practice was paramount. Here was a teaching that was both appealing and made a great deal of sense at explaining how top-down reforms, right back into Ottoman times, had not always been beneficial. Under the authoritarian control of the Kemalist state, new problems had been created by following Western and secular ideals, models and practices too closely without regard for Islamic values or for local and historical differences. Dispirited and disenfranchised, the Turkish people had become frustrated and depressed: cultural rejuvenation was the solution.

This view, that current problems could be solved by Turkey turning to its

own history and geography and realizing that Islam represented a civilization that was both modern and inspirational, had first started to circulate
during the war years in *Hareket Dergisi* (1939–74), edited by Nurettin Topçu.
Topçu envisaged the formation of a Turkish–Islamic national identity based
on personal faith giving shape to social morality and practices. Necip Fazıl
developed and explored these ideas in the pages of *Büyük Doğu*, in his books
and lectures, and shaped them into an inspirational personal programme for
all readers who shared a vision for the nation's future in Islamic terms. Political
scientist Hakan Yavuz outlines the 'three pillars' of *Büyük Doğu* ideology:

(1) Turkish–Muslim society had lost its 'ties' with the past by losing its
'language,' morality and historical memory as a result of Westernization
policies. (2) The Kemalist reforms deliberately sought to 'destroy'
the inner spiritual power of the Turkish nation. (3) This project of
de-Islamization could be reversed with the rise of a new 'ruling elite'
(*yönetici sınıf*) who shared a Turkish–Islamic cognitive map (*zihniyet*)
of revival.[127]

Fazıl's version of anti-secularist nationalism pitted Turkish Muslim culture
against the contemporary secular West, arguing that Turkey should direct
its future in line with its own distinctive geography, culture and history that
combine Ottoman, Western and Eastern elements. Yet like Topçu and other
Muslim thinkers of this generation, Fazıl had drawn many of his ideas and
values from Western philosophy and the very culture he was criticizing.
During the 1930s and 1940s, he had first established his reputation as a leading
Turkish poet in the high-modernist style, expressing the angst and alienation
that was fashionable among European poets of the time.

When Abdullah Gül first met him in the late 1960s, Necip Fazıl was very
much a distinguished grey-haired poet and author, a charismatic personality
with a national following and a compelling message. After taking his degree in
philosophy from Istanbul University, Fazıl had travelled to Paris where he read
Baudelaire and developed a taste for gambling and alcohol. At school, Fazıl
had been a classmate of the great Turkish communist poet Nazim Hikmet.
'Both were already writing poetry and they were jealous of each other – so
when Hikmet went left, Fazıl went right and eventually became religious and
liked by conservative nationalists.'[128] In Paris, Fazıl found himself deploring
modernity and the evident decay it had brought to the grand ideals and claims
of Western civilization:

Paris, which with its civilization symbolized the West, exhibited on its front page designs of miraculous refinement which, however, turned out to be etched on a background of plastic, the latter, in fact, attracting to one's eye what it disguised, namely, ruin and darkness; a civilization that was condemned to hit its head against one wall after another and play hide and seek from one crisis to another.[129]

On his return to Turkey, Fazıl, like T. S. Eliot – another poet-critic of modernity and its signs of decay – worked in banks while making his name as a poet of modernist angst. Şerif Mardin discusses how his earliest poem from 1921, 'The Tombstone' (*Mezartaşı*), is suffused with high-modernist pessimism, addressing death by adapting a Sufi tradition of meditation on inwardness that he sets in opposition to the outwardness of modernization. In doing so, he also attacks the tendency among republican intellectuals and writers to be exclusively outward-looking, whether to the West, to the Soviet Union, or even in the search for Turkish origins in central Asia. Fazıl's early poems typically offer stable images of the past through evocations of familiar locations and of traditional objects in normal settings, thereby conjuring an ideal order that was in danger of being disturbed by modernization. Similarly, according to Mardin, Fazıl deployed metaphors from nature, of seeds and growth, to suggest an organic spiritual element too often ignored yet which remains central to the Turkish people and their land.[130]

In 1934, after meeting a Nakşibendi Shaykh, Abd al-Hakim Arvasi, Fazıl's angst-ridden modernist-bohemianism took an Islamic turn and he 'opted for an increasingly spiritualist orientation, which with time became that of a true believer'.[131] Like many a convert, Fazıl turned fiercely against non-believers and publicly opposed the enforced secularism of the state, often finding himself imprisoned for his views. In formulating and teaching his 'Great East' ideal, Fazıl used modern language, genres and media aimed at the younger generation who would, he hoped, grow to form an ideal Islamic community in Turkey that would provide a model for the Islamic world at large. In pursuit of these goals, in addition to editing his journal, Fazıl organized and lectured at *Büyük Doğu* 'thinkers' clubs', becoming 'a beacon for the conservative, Islamic-inclined Turkish youth of the time'.[132]

When Necip Fazıl arranged to come to Kayseri and formally establish a *Büyük Doğu* club, Abdullah Gül and his schoolfriends were on the organizing committee that had invited him. Gül's intellectual development took shape from those earliest years of his direct and personal involvement with Necip Fazıl and *Büyük Doğu*:

> When I was in high school we organized a club that used to meet and read and discuss the works of Necip Fazıl and my intellectual life started in those days. As you know, even though Necip Fazıl is a poet, in his literature he expressed strong political views. Before I joined the university my baseline was strongly influenced by those days and I think my current understanding was laid during those meetings and discussions in high school.
>
> So there was Necip Fazıl! In Kayseri one day! And this was my first understanding of things. Fazıl's thought was different from others; a great intellectual. He was thinking; he was very much open to the outside. I started at that point, which was very much different from other conservative and religious centres of the time. There was struggle in Turkey and intellectual life in Kayseri was very lively and active; not in terms of religious activities but there were these clubs. These clubs held different opinions, read different books, held different seminars. So in all those years I formed myself within this atmosphere. Of course my family was very important; my uncles, my grandfathers, and the 1960 coup d'état made a big impact on the mind of many families. So in all those years I listened to them; first definitely within the house, then in the clubs where there was intellectual debate in those years.
>
> Necip Fazıl had an Islamic view but the way he interpreted history and many ideas was very open-minded. In those high school days anyone seeing my books would see everything from left to right and world classics – not a monolithic approach but a wide interpretation of everything. If you look at these so-called Islamic or religiously identified intellectuals, they also originated during those years. Many movements were national, traditional, Islamic. But when I was fourteen and fifteen, I was also reading classics – of the East and the West.[133]

Despite their difference in age, Abdullah Gül and Necip Fazıl remained close acquaintances for many years to come, the young student often turning to his 'master' or *hoca* for advice and ideas. In his last year at Kayseri Lycée, Abdullah and his friends Mehmet Tekelioğlu and Ahmet Taşçı organized a *Büyük Doğu* conference in Kayseri, inviting Necip Fazıl as a key speaker and presenting him with a letter, dated 3 July, declaring their gratitude and support in a rather florid style and vocabulary designed to evoke Fazıl's poetic idiom at its most recondite. The Turkish original, I am assured, resists translation, so I include it here in the original with a rough translation supplied by Yusuf Müftüoğlu of the presidential office:

İslam davasının zerre tavizsiz müdafii Üstadımız'a İslam davasının agora meydanlarında sağırların kulağını patlatacak gür seslilikte aksiyoneri Büyük Doğu Gençliği'nin ruh gıdası mecmuanızı tekrar çıkarışınızdan dolayı size minnettarlıklarımızı arzeder, hangi şartlar altında olursa olsun hal neyi icap ettirirse ettirsin yüzde yüz emrinizde olduğumuzu bildirir hürmetlerimizi sunarız. Yarın elbet bizim elbet bizimdir. Gün doğmuş gün batmış ebet bizimdir.[134]

To our very dear Mentor, the adamant defender of the Islamic cause: We express our gratitude to you for republishing your magazine, the food for the souls of Büyük Doğu Youth, the activists of the Islamic cause whose loud voice at the agora arenas disturbs even the deaf, and declare hereupon, along with our respects, that we are one hundred percent at your service, under whatever circumstances and whatever the situations require. Tomorrow is ours, definitely ours. The Sun may rise and set; eternity is ours.

While now admitting that he finds some of Fazıl's later ideas embarrassing and misguided – in his later years Fazıl became an advocate of racial purity – Gül recalls the power of his poetic language to describe and capture feelings in ways that inspired him as a young man to understand how morbid feelings of resentment and frustration at injustice need to be turned to social if not political action. Şerif Mardin has suggested that the appeal of Necip Fazıl's message derived from offering a kind of three-step approach to being a modern Muslim. 'His success among young Muslims was due to his ability to set together the three elements that underpinned the Muslim canon: affection, honor/heroic deeds, and repentance and redemption. A dynamic element which Necip Fazıl introduced into this Islamic setting was his continued sinning and repentance after he met the Shaykh.'[135]

Yet for Abdullah Gül and his high-school friends from the Kayseri reading club, their activities and interests were far from concerns over sin, repentance and redemption. The first two steps were enough for them: affection and heroic deeds. Melancholy and existential despair are not part of the Gül family make-up either. The nuances of Fazıl's language appealed to them for resonating with familiar Muslim values and ideas, putting them into modern contexts and social arenas. Rather than agonizing over spiritual redemption, however, the three friends were more concerned with cultural and social activities and with intellectual and political debates. During their last two years at high school, Mehmet Tekelioğlu recollects that their major interests and energies went to organizing social and cultural events alongside the reading group, and that Abdullah was more concerned with history and politics than spiritual introspection. Şükrü Karatepe recalls moments of active exuberance:

> We were always interested in politics, and attended meetings in the big square. Sometimes we demonstrated against speakers! I remember the *Işçi Partisi* ['Labour Party'] came to Kayseri and the group protested them. With Abdullah Gül among us, we went to the meeting and protested – we were not opposed to socialism, we were never against socialism as such! But at that time the guy speaking was saying strange things![136]

Theirs was a serious, but by no means agonized and introspective adolescence. Throughout his high-school years, Abdullah Gül began observing current events from the perspective of what he was reading about Turkish history from the Tanzimat reforms of the nineteenth century to the present. As he did so, he became increasingly aware of how the establishment of the early republic had created a political system – and a secular middle-class bureaucracy to ensure its running – that was not serving the interests of many sectors of the country, and how many of the reforms of that time were oppressive. From this critical reading of history – which in schools was highly partisan and largely ignored the Ottoman past – Abdullah Gül developed early on a sense of the need for an accurate understanding of the past to recognize the origins of current problems.

Abdullah Gül grew up among the happiness and security of an affectionate and caring family, one that had already inspired him with intimations of earning personal honour through undertaking heroic deeds on behalf of those his family supported. And perhaps because, from his earliest years, he was already experienced at acting publicly on behalf of his family, he never embraced or took his identity from Necip Fazıl's third step of spiritual gloom and angst, of 'repentance and redemption'. Instead, Abdullah Gül has drawn characteristics from his family's open-minded optimism and his birth-city's virtues of social responsibility, dedication to hard work, conciliatory disposition and skills, while keeping his personal religious beliefs private. His was in many ways an extraordinary early life, one spent in Kayseri and Izmir, among pious Muslims who talked of science, socialism and progress, who read secular novels and wrote poetry. From here, the *Büyük Doğu* movement supplied him with ways to explore how Islam and the Ottoman past were central to understanding how Turkey was connected to the rest of the world, and how modernization and culture were the keys to the future.

To the summit of Mount Erciyes

In their final year at Kayseri Lycée, one of the social events that the reading club organized was a trip to Mount Erciyes. Bekir Yıldız remembers that Abdullah Gül 'was always good at resolving conflicts or disputes in the planning and organization,' and the day started well with everyone arriving on time to take the minibus and plenty of provisions for the picnic. 'That evening,' Yıldız recalls:

> Abdullah Gül and two friends returned from a walk and they were hoping to climb to the top but they had no equipment. They had met with two English boys who did have equipment, so we all set off together and made the summit. Although it was light at the top, we couldn't see over the other side and it was unrecognizable. By the time we climbed back down to the picnic site at 2000 metres it was dark and midnight. The minibus had already left, though some of the other boys had stayed on so we all shared the tents of those two English boys. The next day we all had to walk 15 kilometres home and were crippled for the next week![137]

Inspired by the sublime experience of their climb to the summit of Erciyes, excited by their meeting with English students who proved as hospitable as Turks, they all aspired to great and new horizons beyond Kayseri. During those days when their feet were slowly recovering, the group continued to meet after school and, according to Bekir Yıldız, 'we all fantasized about moving to Istanbul, the centre of culture and arts and civility, and how we all wanted to go to university there'. In 1969, succeeding in their ambition, Abdullah Gül, Bekir Yıldız and Mehmet Tekelioğlu all moved to Istanbul to attend university.

2

Istanbul, England and Saudi Arabia 1969 to 1991

O n several occasions, Abdullah Gül has repeated that his political ideas and vision for Turkey developed during his student years at Istanbul University. If ever there was an exceptional time to be a student with an interest in world affairs, it was surely the late 1960s. During his high school years, he had listened to radio broadcasts describing how the entire world seemed to be politicizing and taking up arms, especially in areas of the Muslim world: at university he tried to make sense of it all. There had been coups, attempted coups, and even revolutions: Algeria (1965), Iraq (1965 and 1968), Syria, Ghana and Indonesia (all 1966), and Greece in 1967. In May 1967, India appointed Zakir Hussain (1897–1969) its first Muslim president; in July 1968, Saddam Hussain came to power in Iraq. A great blow to Arab pride – and so of concern to Muslims everywhere – the Israeli victory in the Six Day War during the summer of 1967 encouraged the formation of the Organization of the Islamic Conference (OIC) in September 1969. Turkey was among the founding members.[1] Earlier that month, Muammar Qaddafi led a successful revolution in Libya, delaying by a day to avoid conflict with a concert by Oum Kaltoum. The year 1968 opened with the Prague Spring followed closely by the Tet Offensive in Vietnam; the assassination of Martin Luther King in April proved especially alarming to Muslims throughout Turkey. Was the Soviet threat coming closer, even as the US military machine was proving vulnerable? What could it all mean?

As more information about the world was becoming available to Turkish audiences, there was a lot more that needed explaining. There were events taking place that made little or no sense. These were also years of unexplained happenings, cover-ups, and early misinformation campaigns. In January 1968, inexplicable disasters began to strike military hardware. A United States Air Force B-52 bomber, carrying four nuclear warheads, crashed into the coast of Greenland, leaking widespread radioactive contamination.[2] That same month, no fewer than two submarines, one belonging to Israel and one to France, both sank for no obvious reason and with loss of life.[3] When a US submarine mysteriously disappeared on 22 May, the disaster was kept secret until 1998.[4] But other events were making international headlines. On 22 March, Danny Cohn-Bendit and seven others occupied the University of Nanterres, setting off a chain of protests that, by May, would almost topple the French government. Even as reports of protesting workers and rioting students became regular features of the radio news broadcasts in Turkey, atrocities were taking place at Mai-Lai that would remain unreported and unknown for nearly two years. In Turkey, the USA was in bad repute with left, right and nationalists of all persuasions. Since 1964, when President Lyndon Johnson had insulted national pride by peremptorily instructing Turkey to back off over claims on Cyprus,[5] anger at everything that was being reported of American activities overseas had intensified widespread suspicions of the US and the West. In this era of Cold War politics the USSR remained the ultimate threat to Turkey, but anti-US sentiment became increasingly hostile in Turkey as throughout the world. Even as the left and moderate press agreed to deplore American insensitivity to Turkey, widespread anti-American demonstrations broke out, starting in 1964 with state-sponsored rallies objecting to US favouritism towards Greece in Cyprus, and becoming more militant by 1968 under left-wing student leaders. Anti-US demonstrations, accompanied by increasing violence, would continue until the military takeover of March 1971.[6] These were exciting and stimulating times to be a student in Istanbul and it seemed impossible not to become involved in global events.

Istanbul University, 1969–76

When Abdullah Gül left Kayseri to study economics at Istanbul University, Turkish students had already begun exercising their power to influence national politics. Back in April 1960, after all, it had been anti-government demonstrations staged by students, including cadets at the Army War College in Ankara, that 'proved to be the spark which provoked' the military coup, leaving one dead.[7] By 1969, violent student protests in the US, Germany, and France were recent news. Abdullah Gül's parents were very proud that he had achieved a place at a major metropolitan university and confident that he was not a troublemaker, but had good reason to be worried nevertheless. His brother Macit recalls: 'Although Dad was a technician, he was very happy to see Abdullah go since it meant that the family was continuing to advance.'[8] In these days before the telephone, everyone in Kayseri looked forward to reassurance from his weekly letters home, which would be read aloud several times.[9]

By 1969 when Abdullah Gül enrolled in Istanbul University, student protests had become a familiar feature of the Turkish political scene and university campuses were dominated by a variety of left-wing and radical groups. Widespread rioting and bloodshed soon followed. Once again, as in 1960, the initial push came from students who were enraged at support for the USA. For the first time, a serious and substantial left-wing challenge to republican business-as-usual had emerged; it was highly critical of Turkey's foreign policy. The student movement and the left which had entered parliament in the 1965 elections had broken with convention by challenging the state over Turkey's foreign policy and Cold War alliances. Fired up by the near success of French students at toppling De Gaulle's government back in May, left-wing students protesting the arrival of the US fleet into Istanbul in July 1968 were the first to clash violently with police: Vedat Demircioğlu, a law student at Istanbul University, died after being thrown out of a window during a police raid.[10] Left-wing violence provoked reaction.

For Turkish students of the nationalist right, the fight against the ever-present spectre of communism provided obvious and ample reason for organizing against the left-wing groups which had taken over university campuses.[11] By December 1968, both alarmed and provoked by violent demonstrations by left-wing students in Germany, the USA and France, young right-wing nationalists who called themselves *Ülkücüler*, 'Idealists', but were commonly known as *Bozkurtlar*, 'Grey Wolves', began organizing campaigns to intimidate 'leftist students, teachers, publicists, booksellers and, finally, politicians'. Followers of the ultra-nationalist Colonel Alparslan Türkeş, one of the most radical of the officers behind the 1960 coup, militant extremists among the *Ülkücüler* began organizing training camps for *komando* groups in 1966; graduates of these camps would take upon themselves the task of keeping the streets and campuses free from left-wing demonstrations and violence.[12] By October 1968, Türkeş could boast:

This year, sixty tents have been set up in Istanbul for commando and judo training, fifty in Ankara, and thirty each in Izmir and Adana … Over one thousand youngsters have been trained at camps in various parts of the country. In coming years, these activities will spread throughout the land, and tens of thousands of youths will be readied for the day feared by communists and freemason-capitalist collaborators.[13]

For those on the extreme nationalist right-wing, this conflation of communism with anti-communist Freemasonry and capitalism evidently made sense: after all, Süleyman Demirel had been accused of alleged Masonic credentials. However unlikely such a conspiracy might now seem, Türkeş was a charismatic and inspiring leader who managed to convince his youthful supporters that religiously inspired Freemasonry was somehow part of a communist plot that not only justified but more importantly demanded violent nationalism. By early 1969 they were almost ready to act. On 14 January, left-wing students in Ankara set fire to the US ambassador's car outside the campus of the Middle East Technical University (METU). Among them was Deniz Gezmiş, a student leader who had been active in Istanbul since 1968, who now represented a militant group, the 'People's Liberation Army of Turkey' (*Türkiye Halk Kurtuluş Ordusu*).[14] Perhaps not so ironically, METU is one of Turkey's elite universities; it was modelled on the Massachusetts Institute of Technology and set up by US funding. Until the end of the 1990s, METU was the only university in the country allowed to teach in a foreign language, namely English. But it was demonstrations against the US fleet in Istanbul a month later on 16 February that led to Turkey's 'Bloody Sunday', when anti-US demonstrators in Beyazit Square were attacked by *komando* militants while the police watched without intervening. There were two more deaths.[15]

During the course of the 1960s, increasingly rapid social changes had been causing disaffection, culture-shock, and feelings of isolation among large segments of the Turkish population, especially young people.[16] On the nationalist right, extremists among the *Ülkücüler* organized themselves along military lines even as the left student movement in Turkey was doing what left organizations regularly did, splitting along theoretical lines.[17] Grounded in debates within Marxist theory, there were those who argued that since Turkey was still largely feudal, the revolution needed intellectual leaders to lead the ignorant masses. Others argued that Marx's theory of the Asiatic Mode of Production needed to be critically examined and adapted to Turkish history before it would be possible to elaborate a proper campaign. While students on the left, armed with a theoretical critique of the Turkish state that did not quite fit, continued to argue and splinter into new groups over how to turn theory into practice, nationalist students and other militant extremists united over their single-minded belief in the nation and the righteousness of armed defence. By early 1970, extremist groups had broken away from the mainstream left to take to guerrilla warfare against the state while extremists among the Grey Wolves continued public attacks on left-wing demonstrators; sometimes, it seemed, with the connivance of the police. Demonstrations, street-fighting and violent attacks by left- and right-wing militants continued until the army cleared the streets in March 1971.

Student activism: MTTB

In the late summer of 1969, when Abdullah Gül and his friends stepped down off the bus from Kayseri, student life in Istanbul was unavoidably political and often violent, but not all of the time. Although attending different courses at different universities, Abdullah Gül, Bekir Yıldız and Mehmet Tekelioğlu lived with other students from Kayseri with whom they shared a similarly conservative background in what was familiarly known as the 'Kayseri Dorm', the *Kayseri Öğrenci Yurdu*. With their intellectual formation in Necip Fazıl's ideas they found a natural home for themselves in the *Milli Türk Talebe Birliği* (MTTB), the 'National Turkish Student Association', an organization of disparate conservatives and members of the nationalist right where Turkish history, culture and values were on an agenda that also included opposition to violence. First established in 1916 as a youth movement engaged in exploring pan-Turkic ideas and cultural connections, MTTB soon fell apart from internal disputes in 1920. It had been reborn in the 1930s, publishing a newspaper, *Birlik* ('Union'), which proclaimed an ultra-nationalist agenda causing the organization to be closed in 1936. Re-established once again in 1945, by 1968 MTTB had evolved into 'a cultural and arts group with right-wing but non-violent views on nationalism'.[18] As Bekir Yıldız put it, 'We were practising Muslims but not Islamists.'[19] Members staunchly supported efforts at eradicating communism, and responded to the rise of the left-wing student movements that were dominating university politics by campaigning under their own slogan, *Milli Ruh*, or 'National Spirit'. Between the theoretical Marxism and tendency to violence of the student left, and the ultra-nationalist extremism and violence of the Grey Wolves on the extra-mural right, MTTB provided a more agreeable entry into student life for the conservative young intellectuals from Kayseri. In his letters home, Abdullah Gül was able to reassure his parents and family that he was living among like-minded friends and keeping safely away from trouble.

In Istanbul, Abdullah Gül and his friends soon became active members of MTTB. Gül started arranging cultural and social events that brought new friends and connections with students in dormitories and at universities elsewhere in the city. In keeping with cultural interests developed during his high-school years organizing *Büyük Doğu* events, Gül advocated keeping politics out of ideas. He energetically put his experience and management skills to the task of organizing screenings of avant-garde French films in order to compete in the cultural stakes with screenings of recent films at the *Sinematek*, run by left-wing intellectuals.[20] Gül also served on the jury of poetry-reading contests, arranged visits to the theatre and weekend trips to beaches along the Black Sea coast. MTTB provided a national network that kept him in close touch with Şükrü Karatepe, who was studying law at the University of Ankara. The national network also brought Gül back in contact with Fehmi Koru, a distant cousin from Izmir. Born the same year, they had shared classes when Abdullah spent a semester in Izmir. Fehmi Koru was now attending university in Izmir and representing MTTB on the national council. They became even closer friends after Koru graduated from Izmir and moved to Istanbul for further study. They met regularly at board meetings, attended rallies held in each other's cities and shared views. In 1976, along with Şükrü Karatepe who had completed his law degree, they would all study together in London.[21]

Through his activities on the council of MTTB, Abdullah Gül also made new contacts and developed friendships that have followed him into his political career, although during the days they were students together, the idea of entering politics would have seemed most unlikely for any of them. Nonetheless, even without imagining a political future, during his student years Gül was showing an instinctive aptitude for networking. Notable new friends from that period who would become founding members of the AK Party and serve in Cabinet posts after 2002 include current Deputy Prime Minister Beşir Atalay and Sami Güçlü. From Keskin in Kırıkkale, Atalay was a leading figure within MTTB in the law school at Ankara University when Gül arrived in Istanbul. They became close friends with common intellectual interests and kept in touch while Atalay pursued an academic legal career that, in the early 1990s, would take him into state planning in the days of Turgut Özal's presidency: Atalay entered parliament in 2002 and has been a member of the Cabinet with different appointments ever since. In 1970, Sami Güçlü, later MP for Konya and Cabinet minister in the first two AKP governments, arrived from Konya to study in Istanbul where he met Abdullah Gül through MTTB events. Gül was already a leading figure and a regular speaker, well-known for having 'a broad world view'. 'Even his political opponents liked him for being approachable and human,' Güçlü told me:

> His friendly approach in debate was admired even then, and these are skills that continued into his later political career. Members of MTTB were mostly students from villages and small towns, none of them metropolitans from Istanbul or Izmir or Ankara. But unlike them, the president was clearly different, more cultured and worldly in his outlook.[22]

Even as he became more and more actively involved in organizing for MTTB, Gül at this time had no thoughts of entering national political life. Student activism was one thing, but a career in politics another. Among his MTTB colleagues, Gül followed Necip Fazıl's teachings, devoting his intellectual energies and activities to understanding the nation through learning about its history and its culture. How did contemporary events and struggles taking place in Istanbul and throughout the nation fit in with the national past, both in its Ottoman and its republican cultural eras, and how did Turkey today fit into a broader understanding of the world and the future of civilization?

From Necip Fazıl, Abdullah Gül had learned and continued to believe that culture not politics was the best way forward. During his student years 'he became personally involved with writers and artists in Istanbul, unlike other members of MTTB', and arranged readings by poets and writers, and visits to galleries displaying works by contemporary and classical Turkish artists.[23] In addition to organizing a photography club, Gül helped write and edit a weekly MTTB newspaper, 'Milli Gençlik Dergisi' ('Journal of National Youth').[24] He also took charge of the book club, expanding the list from famil-iar works by Necip Fazıl, Nurettin Topçu and Sezai Karakoç – writers whose books still make up the bulk of the MTTB recommended reading list to this day[25] – by including formative works by left-wing writers and poets such as Idris Küçükömer (1925–87) and Attila Ilhan (1925–2005). Translations had started to appear of influential books by foreign Islamic thinkers such as Seyyid Kutub (1906–66), a founding member of the Muslim Brotherhood and one of its first martyrs,[26] and Muhammad Hamidullah (1908–2002), a prolific writer on Islamic jurisprudence from Hyderabad.[27] Abdullah Gül was keen on debating how their ideas for reframing the relation between religion and politics might shed light on what was happening in Turkey. He also introduced George Orwell, Alexander Solzhenitsyn and other modern novelists to the list of Western writers on the reading list. Urged by Abdullah Gül, MTTB organized meetings with living writers, some on the left, who became personal friends; an enthusiastic photographer in these years, Gül was also especially keen on inviting film directors who were in Istanbul to speak to them.[28]

Friends from that era agree that, among the Muslim nationalists who made up the MTTB group, Abdullah Gül was well-known for being energetic, determined and intellectually engaged, 'a cultured person'. For him, Necip Fazıl remained a key personal inspiration. Since their first meeting in Kayseri, the two had kept in touch, trusting and respecting each other across the generational divide between them. In Istanbul, Gül organized annual lectures at which the eminent public poet and intellectual would try out his new speeches on them, and then revise his talk before taking it on tour at meetings throughout the country.[29] At the same time, friends also agree that Gül's interests were already becoming wider than those shared by most members of MTTB, especially his open engagement with what some of the left intellectuals were thinking. Having learned respect for the ideals of social justice from his father, Gül also seems to have inherited Ahmet Hamdi Bey's ability to win respect for his enthusiasm and organizational skills. In March 1971, he was elected to represent MTTB at Istanbul University.[30]

For the next few years, his new office brought Abdullah Gül the responsibility of organizing a national student festival to celebrate the nation's great victory at Gallipoli. Held close by the battlefields inside a militarized zone at Çanakkale with special permission from the military authorities, these festivals were attended by hundreds of university students who had come from across the country. At these, Gül delivered his earliest public speeches, claiming to speak in the name of Turkish students. In 1973, following attacks on the Turkish consulate-general in Los Angeles by militant members of the Armenian diaspora, Gül helped organize protests outside the French and Austrian embassies on behalf of MTTB, later representing the organization at meetings with the consulates to discuss the situation.[31] Amid the incipient crisis brewing over Cyprus, on 18 March 1974 at the Çanakkale Student Festival, he made his first directly political speech, recalling the words of an MTTB resolution from 1954 that had declared: 'We proclaim yet again to the whole world that Cyprus is Turkish and we call the entire Turkish Nation to the defence of our cause.'[32] Later that summer, he addressed a huge demonstration of over five thousand that had assembled in Beyazit Square following the arrival of Turkish troops and the partitioning of Cyprus.[33] Although they were still constantly concerned for his safety, Adviye and Ahmet Hamdi Gül were pleased that their son had become an important figure in MTTB and was publicly upholding values they shared.

During his student years in Istanbul, Abdullah Gül was slowly starting to become that 'brave heart', the *babayiğit*, of his childhood fantasy, standing up and speaking what he believed needed to be said. Yet he recalled his grandfather's warning about the dangers of political life, even as he found himself becoming subject to its threats and dangers. Becoming a leader of MTTB brought Abdullah Gül public visibility. With it came valuable experience at compromise and conciliation that confirmed his belief that persuasion was better than violence or force. While his religious beliefs and conservative views made him an enemy to most on the left, his outspoken attacks on the use of violence even on behalf of the nation made him a traitor to the extreme right. Along with the other leading members of MTTB, Abdullah Gül grew accustomed to seeing his picture posted on campus walls with demands, often amounting to threats, from left organizations that he be removed from the university. Despite always adopting a moderate position and voice, Gül became accustomed, like all student activists, to being heckled while speaking at open meetings. On one occasion at a student rally, an enraged extremist pointed a gun at his head and told him to be quiet: friends recall with admiration how he quietly and quickly talked his way 'into a peaceful resolution.'[34]

The 1971 military intervention

When it happened on 12 March 1971, the military takeover by memorandum put a temporary end to much of the political violence. Earlier that month Deniz Gezmiş and his People's Liberation Army of Turkey had kidnapped four US soldiers, holding them captive on the Middle East Technical University campus. 'Army units launched an all-out attack on the student dormitories, killing three … Gezmiş released the US soldiers to prevent further bloodshed'[35] even as the generals were making their move. Having learned that Prime Minister Demirel's AP Cabinet 'no longer enjoyed the full support of his own party', the generals presented President Cevdet Sunay with a memorandum demanding reform and threatening to take power if the current government did not resign: Demirel had no choice but to quit.[36] In May 1972, Gezmiş and two other left-wing student leaders were executed for using violence to destroy the constitutional order.

The imposition of martial law that followed disrupted student life and gave Abdullah Gül and his friends cause to reflect back to the military coup of 1960. Now, after a decade of unprecedented growth and freedom, the universities were being closed and students were forced to go home. Riding the bus back to Kayseri, Abdullah Gül and Mehmet Tekelioğlu discussed how to understand what was going on and what their position as intellectuals and their role as activists should be. 'At the time,' Tekelioğlu recalls,

> public opinion was often anti-student; given the variety of positions that student groups were adopting, it was widely thought that students clearly knew nothing about the real world and were ivory tower idealists regardless of their ideas. We were concerned not to be like this, and in our discussions came to recognize how the events of 1971 and 1960 were both long-term effects of various errors made during the first republican era. Later, the 1980 coup only confirmed us in this view. Our efforts since 2007 to revise the constitution have very much been a result, an attempt to address those problems that are still in place.[37]

Recalling childhood recollections of 1960, the MTTB group could now recognize the recurrent problem of the constitution; its tendency to protect the state at the expense of the people. The 1961 reforms had addressed some political imbalances introduced by the constitution of 1924 – which was designed to solidify a revolution rather than to establish a democracy – but in attempting to liberalize society at the same time as the economy, they had also created new problems by introducing a Keynesian mixed economy with a strong state planning component. Once more, the state was in charge. On the other hand, allowing greater freedom of expression, assembly and publication, the reforms opened up the political sphere to increased public scrutiny and debate; but also to violence.

The reformed constitution of 1961 contained a number of social targets for which any new government would be accountable: these included achieving 'a standard of living benefiting human dignity', while promising free trade unions, social security and medical care. But it also contained a clause that made pursuing these social goals conditional, stipulating that 'the State shall carry out its duties to attain the social and economic goals provided in this section only in so far as economic development and its financial resources permit'.[38] With such a loophole, social programmes were often neglected even as new freedoms allowed popular criticism and protest. 'Perhaps as important as the new institutions,' Feroz Ahmad suggests, 'were the explicit guarantees of freedom of thought, expression, association and publication, as well as other civil liberties, contained in the new document,' including the right to strike.[39]

During the course of the decade, those very freedoms enfranchised and politicized not only the growing number of university students but also the increasing number of unionized workers. In rural and provincial areas, living standards did improve and the economy did grow, but loudly promised social reforms, or at least the funding for them, lagged well behind. While keeping his eye on the approval and support of the West, Süleyman Demirel promoted import substitution – radios, telephones, central heating equipment, bathroom fittings and such like no longer needed to be imported from foreign manufacturers. At the same time, he encouraged joint operations between Turkish companies and multinationals such as Fiat and Renault. Coca-Cola moved in, and would soon close down the small independent companies producing local *gazoz*, such as those bottling the waters from Erciyes that Gül had failed to sell as a schoolboy. In 1971, looking back over a decade since the reforms, Gül and his friends saw how political elites were continuing to govern in the authoritarian and paternalistic style of Atatürk and İnönü Paşa, using their power to tell the people what was good for them, and following the constitution only when it suited their interests.

What seemed clear to the young nationalists was not that modernization of the economy was a problem in itself, but that Turkey was imitating foreign models and losing its cultural identity in its rush to become like America.[40] By mid-decade many thought Süleyman Demirel had come to embody all that was objectionable in Western capitalism and Turkey's vulnerability to US influences, cultural and political: on this, the highly articulate left could agree with the nationalists and influential Kemalists who were ensconced in the state apparatus and among the urban elite. And they were joined by the religious right, who – ever keen to promote a conspiracy – loudly proclaimed Demirel to be a Freemason who was undermining and destroying Turkey's culture and morality.[41] Back in that crucial month of May 1968, Professor Necmettin Erbakan first came to public attention, declaring that Demirel had turned Turkey into 'an open market for Europe and America.'[42] In January 1970, he formed the National Order Party (*Milli Nizam Partisi*), the first party committed in Turkey to political Islam. The new party was claiming to represent the lower-middle classes who were suffering from the rise of corporations and monopolies throughout Anatolia. Even as industrial production of automobiles and consumer goods for the home market grew – overtaking agriculture in 1973 as the largest sector of the Turkish economy – the 1961 constitution had opened the way by guaranteeing workers' rights. Many unions went on strike in the 1970s, flexing their newly formed industrial muscles. Under attack from all sides, Demirel failed to satisfy the demands of big business alongside those of a newly enfranchised labour force. Unlike 1960, it was not student demonstrations that sparked the semi-formal military takeover. Rather it was the workers' strikes and mass-mobilizations of 15 and 16 June 1970, together with the subsequent escalation of violence by Guevarist student groups, which triggered a faction within the army to force Demirel's resignation and assume power on 12 March 1971, instead of the left military coup they had hoped to unleash.[43]

Abdullah Gül and his friends understood all too well that this intervention, like the previous one of their childhood memories, was in key respects a reaction against an authoritarian state that, armed with a constitution and power to interpret it, dictated all the rules and enforced them from above. As oppositional voices became louder, it seemed, political leaders became increasingly authoritarian. For all his skills at addressing ordinary Muslims throughout the country, Demirel, when it came to enacting policies, had continued to ignore their cultural aspirations. What Abdullah Gül and friends were unlikely to have understood at the time was a signal difference between the two events that would have telling consequences later: the 1960 coup had been led by a coalition of radical officers representing different generations and backgrounds united by a common vision of restoring constitutional democracy and little else, while the intervention by memorandum of 1971 was planned and executed by the military high command. The army itself had changed. When it seized power for the second time it was less concerned – at first – with enforcing constitutional democracy than with suppressing the violence of extremist militant groups, whether students, workers, communists or nationalists. Looking back to 1960 in 1971, what was most apparent to the MTTB intellectuals were the recurrent problems produced by simply revising the constitution inherited from the first republic. But as would become apparent in 1980, it was even more complicated than that since by 1971 the army had already become a semi-autonomous force within national political life.[44]

The officers who led the coup in 1960 had a substantial list of grievances behind them, and there were considerable differences of opinion except on the need for reform. Since the 1940s, most especially after Turkey's entry into NATO in 1953, a gap had increasingly opened between an old guard of officers who had been educated before the war and resented NATO influence, and a new and increasingly important group of younger officers who had been trained in sciences, foreign languages, modern methods and technologies. Government military spending had been increasing rapidly as it invested in new NATO-friendly equipment and hardware, but salaries for younger officers remained pegged at pre-war rates. For them, faced with inflationary prices and no raises in pay, living standards kept going down. Following the coup of 1960 the military quickly secured its own interests by entering business on its own behalf. With the new constitution of July 1961 in place, the army incorporated itself by creating the 'Army Mutual Assistance Association' (*Ordu Yardımlaşma Kurumu*, or OYAK), a pension fund which soon expanded into a major financial company with holdings in insurance, automobile production, food canning, cement, hotels and tourism.[45] Following the new agreement, in March 1962 the National Security Council (*Milli Güvenlik Kurumu*, or NSC) was created, giving the military a direct say in government policy and certain powers to intervene. Retired admirals and generals were appointed ambassadors and directors of banks, giving the army direct influence in foreign affairs and the national economy. 'By 1962,' Feroz Ahmad comments, 'the army had become an autonomous institution recognized by Turkey's ruling circles as the guardian and partner of the new order it had just helped to create.'[46] The next year, the National Intelligence Organization (*Milli Istihbarat Teşkilatı*, or MIT) and Office of Military Intelligence were established.

So by March 1971, the officers within the high command who organized and led the coup were not only fully confident of their own authority but in charge of a vast amount of manpower and equipment. They also had access to information about almost everyone in the country, including members of the various militant groups that were robbing banks, kidnapping US servicemen, and bombing the houses of left-wing university professors. Among the professors not being targeted was Necmettin Erbakan, but he too represented a serious thorn in the side of the military since his Islamist *Milli Nizam Partisi* ('National Order Party', or MNP), founded in January 1970, was openly denouncing Kemalism and secularism, thereby 'infuriating the armed forces'. As the New Year opened, the previous summer's strikes inspired industrial workers throughout the country to follow suit: during the first three months of 1971, there were more strike days than in any previous year in the republic's history.[47] On 12 March, ever vigilant against the threat of communism, whatever form it might appear to be taking, and just as keen to assert itself against Islamic anti-Kemalism, the military high command took action and handed Demirel a memorandum demanding his resignation. The army had set themselves up to be guardians of the secular, democratic republican state.

For Abdullah Gül and his friends in the MTTB group, concern over changes in the military was less urgent than the need for a rethinking of how Turkey's history had unfolded in their own lifetimes. Unlike the extremists among the Grey Wolves, they publicly condemned all violence and rejected military force as the way forward. Although they were by no means Kemalists, they took very seriously Atatürk's declaration in his famous Nutuk speech of 1927 that young people must take the lead in shaping the future of the new republic: this had been among the founding principles of MTTB.[48] And they believed that the future should be shaped through cultural and social development and not be imposed by force backed up with the threat of violence. When the Turkish State Theatre performed a play celebrating the life of Sultan Murad IV, formerly viewed as 'one of the most tyrannical of Ottoman sultans', the MTTB group could recognize a piece of crude propaganda, aimed at legitimating authoritarian state rule and the violent repression of dissent.[49] For them, the political chaos of recent years was not to be explained by simple allusions to Turkey's Ottoman past, but as the result of how the constitution had been framed to create and legitimate an authoritarian state. 'Those years,' Mehmet Tekelioğlu recalls, 'were a time of generating lots of new ideas about how to address long-term problems with the Turkish constitution and political life.'[50] Among those voicing new political ideas with an explicitly Islamist agenda was Professor Necmettin Erbakan.

Early political activities

While Necip Fazıl's synthesis of Islam and civilization continued to shape Abdullah Gül's intellectual and cultural development, Erbakan's project began to define the shape of some of his early political views and experiences. Offering an alternative to Alparslan Türkeş's ultra-nationalist *Milliyetçi Hareket Partisi* ('Nationalist Action Party', or MHP), Erbakan's *Milli Nizam Partisi* ('National Order Party', or MNP) had been swiftly closed by the military authorities in 1971, but resurfaced in 1973 as the reformed *Milli Selâmet Partisi*

('National Salvation Party', or MSP). Their slogan, 'Great Turkey – Again!' aimed to evoke the Ottoman past as a time 'when the state was Muslim as well as powerful'. Erbakan's populist message 'laid far more stress on conservative Muslim values than the other parties', and declared the need for moral as well as social and economic reform. Staunchly anti-Western, Erbakan deplored the way Demirel's government had focused on economic programmes to develop what he termed 'soda-pop and assembly industries' (*gazoz-montaj sanayii*) at the expense of improving living conditions for most of the people. Erbakan also opposed seeking membership of the European Common Market, declaring it to be a conspiracy of Catholics and Zionists hoping 'to melt Muslim Turkey away within a Christian Europe'. Instead, he proposed that Turkey should establish a 'common market' with other Muslim nations.[51]

In 1973, the organizers of Erbakan's new party in Kayseri sought out Ahmet Hamdi Gül, with his impeccable local reputation for personal integrity and high moral standards. Better still, he had never been a party activist or even contemplated running for political office, so he had no political skeletons in his closet. They managed to persuade him to put his name on their ticket for the general elections scheduled for October that year. Although his father was not elected, family ties to Erbakan's MSP were established that would later offer Abdullah Gül his first direct experience of party organization.

Erbakan and his party did well enough in the 1973 elections to join several short-lived coalition governments, first with the CHP, which had been led by Bülent Ecevit since the previous year, and with the next coalition, led by Süleyman Demirel, that came to power in March 1975.[52] It was in the preparations for the 1975 elections that Abdullah Gül first learned about party campaigning and the elation of electoral success. The MSP candidate for Kayseri that year was Recai Kutan, a career politician who later helped Necmettin Erbakan form the *Fazilet Partisi* ('Virtue Party', or FP) in December 1997 and, when that party was closed in June 2001, formed the *Saadet Partisi* ('Felicity Party', or SP). In the run-up to the March elections, Abdullah Gül was a member of Kutan's campaign team together with Bekir Yıldız, Şükrü Karatepe and Irfan Gündüz, all of whom entered politics and became MPs or mayors.[53] Şükrü Karatepe recalls how, during this campaign, Abdullah Gül gave an impromptu speech during a rally in the public square in Yeşilhisar, a substantial town outside Kayseri.

Demirel was there and had just spoken before a huge crowd. Then there was supposed to be a speaker for the National Salvation Party from Istanbul, but he was a professor who feared he would lose his job if Demirel heard him and so he backed off from speaking. So Abdullah Gül took the opportunity to take the microphone and made his first square speech. In those days we had these phrases, 'We Say This! Give your vote to Kutan!' and it was all very funny. We were young and enthusiastic, getting up and speaking among all these people![54]

Kutan was not elected that year. However thrilling being part of what would prove a losing team must have been, Abdullah Gül had no plans at the time to become a politician.

Academic ambitions

Even as they debated the nation's future, few of the MTTB group in Istanbul were contemplating political careers for themselves after graduation. Abdullah Gül and friends from that time all insist that none of them ever thought that he, or any of them, would enter politics as a career. Being an active student organizer was one thing, even if it entailed developing a flair for persuasively addressing large audiences, but pursuing a political career was something else. Politics was very much a closed shop and a rather nasty business that belonged to other kinds of people.[55] For this generation of conservative students with provincial backgrounds, most often the first in their families to attend university, entering politics after graduation was as unthinkable as a career in any other sector of the state bureaucracy. The public sphere at the time was elite and secular, making it unappealing to conservative and devout students. And none of them were keen on futures in the private sector.

Mehmet Tekelioğlu explains: 'The private sphere at the time was largely Koç and Sabancı enterprises, and these did not seem to be directed at benefiting Turkey and Turks so they did not seem suitable directions. So it was that many members of this group decided that the best way to go was to pursue academic appointments.'[56] Here too there were obstacles such as finding financial support. At the time, academic jobs still usually went 'to the sons and daughters of the old Ottoman families and metropolitan elites, and only a few professors were willing to support our ambitions,' recalls Bekir Yıldız. At Istanbul University, however, some of them were fortunate to study with two influential Islamic opinion-makers, Professors Sabahattin Zaim (1926–2007) and Nevzat Yalçıntaş (b. 1933).

During the late 1960s, Yalçıntaş had been a member of 'a right-wing group of scholars and intellectuals' that in 1970 formed the *Aydınlar Ocağı*, or the 'Intellectuals' Hearth', which promoted discussions of nationalism and the careers of young scholars from conservative and provincial backgrounds.[57] Its first chairman was Ibrahim Kafesoğlu (1914–84); members included future President Turgut Özal and his brother Korkut.[58] In the wake of the 1980 coup, Yalçıntaş and Kafesoğlu would play leading roles in developing the Turkish-Islamic Synthesis (*Türk Islam Sentezi*), a project aimed at extirpating the Turkish left while diffusing tensions between the Sunni majority, Shi'ite Alevis and Kurdish nationalists.[59] A more directly political ambition was to rebuild bridges between Türkeş's National Action Party and Erbakan's National Salvation Party. From the 1940s onwards, there had always been some fractures between the two traditions of conservative nationalism about whether Turkey's future should follow from its Turkic or its Islamic past.

As the name suggests, the Intellectuals' Hearth sought to bring thinkers from the two traditions together, united against the left and beginning to rise through the bureaucratic ranks in ministries but divided between the two parties as a result of the Nationalist Front Coalitions of 1975–79. In looking to the future, Yalçıntaş actively encouraged the careers of conservative students, such as the group at MTTB with academic ambitions. 'These were teachers who changed their lives,' observed Bekir Yıldız, 'representing the group's desire for freedom, they provided direction and helped encourage those who wanted to pursue academic futures.' And the members of MTTB at the time included many who did successfully pursue academic careers. Sami Güçlü showed me a group photograph of friends from the Istanbul University years who had all pursued academic careers after graduation: Abdullah Gül, himself, Mehmet Tekelioğlu, Ibrahim Mete Doğruer, Kemal Gündoğdu, Numan Yazıcı, Harun Taşkin.[60]

After graduating from the Department of Economics in 1974, Abdullah Gül stayed on at Istanbul University to conduct research under the supervision of Professor Yalçıntaş. During those years he cemented friendships that have followed him through academia and into politics. Having spent their first two years living in the Kayseri Dorm, Abdullah Gül, Mehmet Tekelioğlu, and Rifat Bescili had together moved into a basement flat in Fındıkzade, a neighbourhood inside the walls of the old city. 'We called our home the Bodrum Palace,' Gül explained, 'because it was in the basement!'[61] *Bodrum* means underground vault or dungeon.

> One of my old housemates, Rifat Bescili, recently went to see if the building is still there, and he knocked at the door of our old flat. A lady answered and he said 'Did you know that the President used to live here?' and the woman got angry and said 'are you kidding me!' So he went away. [laughs] It has always been a very respectable area. Later we moved outside the old walls to Bakırköy and our flat there was on the third floor.[62]

Here Abdullah Gül continued his reputation for cooking Kayseri-style *kuru fasuliye*, an inexpensive but tasty dish of white beans that had been his child-hood favourite, and feeding the cash-strapped household of students and any of their friends who had come over to talk; which was most evenings.[63] In the aftermath of the 1971 military coup, he became especially interested in debating the ideas of several influential and controversial writers of the time, keeping alive his high-school habit of mixing up the books on his shelf between those of left and right, and doing the same with the MTTB reading list. From the right, the group continued to read and discuss recent essays by Necip Fazıl, Sezai Karakoç and Nurettin Topçu who were promoting a future for Turkey that only a restoration of the nation's Islamic past could produce. Gül had also become an admirer of Cemil Meriç (1916–87), a right-wing liter-ary critic and essayist, who wrote about French literature and Indian culture, becoming an attractive inspiration to students of Gül's generation who were on the intellectual and nationalist right, but more open to the world than the religious right of the times.[64]

Nevertheless, in 1975 the publication of Erbakan's Islamic treatise *Milli Görüş* ('National Vision') caused a great deal of excited discussion and debate, as it would do for years to come.[65] Here, Erbakan railed against the low status of Islam in modern Turkey, calling for a 'just order' that would restore Islam to the centre of Turkish society, and directing Turks working in Europe to hold firm to their identity as Muslim Turks. As one veteran of those times recalls:

> the religious right, until the 1980s, was very much like an arid land; intellectually there was nothing going on. The influential thinkers on the right were not interested in democracy or human rights, but they were popular with many uneducated people at the time because the left was not producing arguments that ordinary people could easily understand. The left eventually proved marginal in their own way too,

of course, since they never produced any intellectuals or artists with enduring influence.[66]

But Abdullah Gül recognized that there were new and exciting ideas about democracy and the Turkish past coming from the left and he put some of them on the MTTB reading lists for discussion. He was much taken with the arguments of Idris Küçükömer who, in 'Düzenin Yabancılaşması' ('The Alienation of Order'), had argued that notions of a political left and right no longer made any sense in Turkey where the Kemalists of the CHP, who claimed to be left, were really of the right. They had proved themselves to be authoritarian and disrespectful of the demands from civil society, autocratic not democratic, and primarily concerned with protecting the privileges of the political elite. Idris Küçükömer played on the Turkish meaning of 'civil society' which also connoted opposition to military-inspired and enforced modernization. Meanwhile conservative leaders such as Adnan Menderes had become popular heroes, even to some on the left, for responding to the needs of ordinary citizens.[67] What did this say about the Turkish people? And what might it mean for democratic political life in Turkey?

By introducing MTTB to such writers, Abdullah Gül 'put himself at the centre of the debates over left and right taking place at the time'.[68] He also became fascinated with the writings and ideas of the influential left-wing novelist Kemal Tahir (1910–73), whose reputation and political influence reach beyond his fiction. In 1938, while working as a journalist, Tahir had been arrested for sedition along with Nazim Hikmet and spent the next twelve years in prison. Here he met ordinary people from all over Anatolia and, listening to their stories, began writing. After his release in 1950, unlike Hikmet, he stayed in Turkey and made a living from writing film scripts and popular fiction under pseudonyms in order to be able to write historical novels dealing with serious events and issues. Remaining a great sceptic who challenged everything from a left perspective, Tahir, like Küçükömer, was raising evident problems that Muslims clearly needed to address but for which traditional Islamic teachings offered no obvious solutions. Reading and discussing these writers' works, Abdullah Gül came to grapple with some of the key debates among Marxists of the time. Tahir, like others, maintained that while Marx's theory of the Asiatic Mode of Production was evidently inaccurate, his need to invent it showed how Asian societies are not structured according to Western models. It followed that, since there was no bourgeoisie or proletariat, socialism needed to be different in Turkey. In the same way,

Tahir set out to show, the novel in Turkey needed to develop its own generic features rather than simply following those of the West. Gül also worked with Turkish film-makers, encouraging them to create new forms and styles that would embody the specificity of Turkish history and identity.[69] These were not arguments approved of by those communists in Turkey who followed sectarian allegiances to Moscow, Beijing or Guevarism, but they made a great deal of sense to Abdullah Gül and to many young Turkish nationalists. From left-wing disputes over how to understand and act upon Turkey's exceptional historical development emerged 'one of the debates over which left and right youth came together' in those years.[70]

Even as he was beginning his doctoral research on economic relations between Turkey and Muslim countries, inspired by debates being generated by Erbakan's plans for an Islamic 'common market', Abdullah Gül kept his intellectual and cultural interests to the fore of his personal development and student activities. His years leading MTTB equipped him with valuable experience at brokering compromise and conciliation, providing him with a reputation for being a 'kindly leader' with a 'broader view than most student leaders, so he won the respect of other groups and even some on the left came to our meetings because they wanted to know what he had to say'.[71]

> In those days we were idealistic, not thinking of becoming rich but trying to find ways to solve social problems and were driven by concerns over ways to improve conditions and guarantee the nation's future. Most intellectuals of the time were not nationalist or Islamists, unlike Gül, and indeed most nationalist Islamist student groups of the time were not driven by intellectual concerns.[72]

During the early 1970s, Abdullah Gül 'followed all the influential writers. He was not a great intellectual with original ideas of his own, but he was open to big ideas and still likes to follow ideas and evaluate different approaches to come up with a solution'.[73]

'Scholars of Özal'

During those undergraduate years, personal qualities apparent from his high-school activities had come to the fore and were taking more muscular shape: the intellectual curiosity and drive; the organizational ability to make things happen; the engagement with 'big ideas' whether coming from the left or the right, East or West; the desire and ability to see through and conciliate what seem to be established and entrenched positions; the energetic activities on behalf of cultural nationalism; the commitment to make a change for the bettering of the nation. Combined with his years of service to MTTB and his reputation for being a practising Muslim in his personal life, these were all recognized qualities that, with the support of Professor Yalçıntaş, won him a two-year scholarship from the *Türkiye Milli Kültür Vakfı* ('Turkish National Culture Foundation') to study English in England. Established in 1969 by a group of businessmen, the Foundation was directed by Turgut Özal, at the time an economist working in the private sector.[74] These generous scholarships were designed to provide future academics with advanced training in the English language to prepare them for undertaking doctoral research of an international calibre. In 1976, when Abdullah Gül set off for England, Fehmi Koru and Şükrü Karatepe were also awarded similar scholarships.

Having completed his law degree, Şükrü Karatepe had been interning as a barrister in Kayseri and hating every minute of it:

> One day while I was working as a lawyer in Kayseri I was sitting in the park feeling angry. Abdullah Gül and his uncle Professor Ahmet Satoğlu came walking along. They were very calm and peaceful and asked me why I was feeling angry. I said that I felt as if Erciyes, the mountain, is getting higher every day and the plateau is falling down into the ground. I said that I feared one day Kayseri would disappear! And his uncle said I have an answer! You must go to England. Abdullah is going and you should go too. This idea made me very happy, so I applied and went three months after Abdullah Gül. We spent five months together at the Pittman School near the Post Office Tower in London. Turgut Özal was president of the National Culture Foundation that gave us these scholarships. So we are scholars of Özal! And this made us very happy.[75]

In more than one way, the figure of Turgut Özal would continue to haunt the future careers of Abdullah Gül and friends.

England, 1976–78

After a year in London, among friends from home and new friends from the community of Turkish students and expatriates, Abdullah Gül realized he was spending too much time speaking and thinking in Turkish and not practising and living in the language he had come to learn. For his second year he moved westward into the countryside and attended English courses at the University of Exeter, where Turkish students were fewer on the ground and nearly all the students spoke middle-class English all the time. This shuttle between London, the bustling metropolis, and Exeter, the bucolic cathedral city, brought the young Turkish nationalist face-to-face with life as it was really being lived in the secular, capitalist West. It changed the way he thought about many things.

London, 1976–77

Abdullah Gül arrived in London even as the hottest and driest summer on record was beginning to break up but was still a constant topic of conversation among those who had lived through it. During June and July, temperatures had reached astonishing peaks that the English, still thinking in degrees Fahrenheit, spoke of as the low to mid 90s (32–5 Celsius). By July, the ensuing drought was the worst known 'since records were first kept in 1727'.[76] During September, it remained unusually hot even though temperatures had dropped slightly in London and there was suddenly a great deal of rain.[77] In the heart of the city, in the rather cramped and airless classrooms of the Pittman School of English on Goodge Street, Abdullah Gül's language instructors introduced the students to phrases such as 'cats and dogs', and other useful idioms for understanding the English preoccupation with animals and the weather.

During his time in London, Abdullah Gül lodged at 38 Mapesbury Road. From here it was a short walk to Kilburn Park underground station on the Bakerloo Line – the Jubilee Line had not yet been built – for getting to and from the Pittman School. Then, as still today, this substantial double-fronted Victorian house was leased by FOSIS, the Federation of Student Islamic Societies. Since its establishment in 1963, FOSIS has provided an umbrella organization for Muslim student groups coming from different parts of the Muslim world, and it was through this organization that Abdullah Gül made many friends.[78] While Gül lived here, the house 'had such a beautiful garden', but it suffered from old and out-of-date plumbing.[79] There was no central heating. Hot water came from a gas geyser that made a terrific noise and filled the bathroom – shared by the tenants – with steam. And like the gas heaters in the rooms, it worked only because you fed coins into a meter with an endless capacity; since the supply of coins was always about to run out, so too the gas supply was always likely to cut off. 'Growing up in Kayseri,' Abdullah Gül reflects, 'we would be proud when the temperature was lower than in Sivas or Erzurum, so I knew about cold cities. In Kayseri we used to wake up with ice on the window in the morning as if there were flowers! But in London humidity made us feel so much colder. I never felt so cold as in London.'[80] Today, the FOSIS house has central heating, but the garden has been paved over for a car port.

Abdullah Gül's landlady at the time was an Englishwoman who had married a Turkish Cypriot. With her husband, she lived on the ground floor of the house where she had grown up, and Gül recalls how she 'could not have been kinder' to her rather earnest Muslim tenants. During the early 1970s both Turkish and Greek-speaking Cypriots had been arriving in London, and there were substantial communities taking shape in Hackney, Harringay and elsewhere. These were all respectable people, keen to fit in and get along with others. Out in Kilburn, the neighbours on Mapesbury Road went out of their way to be kind to the Muslim students who had arrived among them. On the evening of 24 November 1976, there was an unexpected knock on the front door of number 38. It was an elderly lady who lived across the street. She had just seen the evening news on the BBC reporting on the earthquake that had struck Van and Muradiye in the east of Turkey. She wanted her Turkish neighbour to know so he could phone home. Abdullah Gül had already gone to bed, but his landlady 'woke me up telling me to use her phone to call our parents now!' As it happened, the Gül household had one of the new private telephones that had started to feature in Turkish provincial homes, and although the price of international calls was exorbitant, his landlady insisted on paying. 'This was a very generous gesture when phones were still rare. Otherwise I went out to use a booth with even more of those coins!' Honoured by her generosity, Abdullah Gül was able to report that evening how the disaster had taken place far from his home and family, though she shared their sadness as further news came in that nearly four thousand lost their lives. 'Later, I learned that she is Jewish. But I never thought it made a difference. I had the chance to experience the world in London. There are so many different people and cultures, races, religions, and it's only in London you can find so many different differences.'[81]

A practising Muslim, Abdullah Gül bore the brand of his native city and felt that religious faith was a matter of personal piety and more important than religious difference. While studying in London, he realized that the nearest place of worship to the Pittman School was the church around the corner on Tottenham Court Road. A V-2 bomb in 1945 had destroyed the original Tabernacle that had been built there in 1756 for Revd George

Whitefield. The new structure, opened in 1957, had recently become home to the American Church in London, who are still in residence there. Keen to practice his religion, Abdullah Gül dutifully sought out the local vicar for permission to pray here.

> He was so polite and said we could pray in this side room. He was so polite but I felt I was disturbing them. There were all these people who would come, and I felt I was a burden on them. But he would open the room for me and even disturb meetings that were taking place there so that I could pray, so I knew I was being a nuisance and after a while I found somewhere else.[82]

For Fehmi Koru, this incident was 'an eye-opener', thinking when Abdullah Gül first approached the vicar that 'if a Christian came into a mosque and asked the imam to pray, this would be very awkward'.[83] But Abdullah Gül seems to have been blithely confident that, since such differences should not matter they didn't, and he was rewarded with the vicar's generous agreement. Years later, he still expresses bemusement at 'those pious Turks and Islamic fundamentalists' who found the story shocking when it was reported in the Turkish press.[84] In London, Abdullah Gül discovered that democracy had established religious freedoms unthinkable at home. London, as Fehmi Koru put it succinctly, 'broadened our imagination'.[85] In the nature of historical ironies, the Pittman School of English moved from their Goodge Street premises before closing, and the building is now a mosque run by the Muslim World League.

For Abdullah Gül, a further signal feature of life in London that broadened his understanding as well as his imaginative grasp of the wider world was meeting Muslims from other nations.

> For Friday prayers we used to go to Regent's Park Mosque. This was different because it was my first time praying outside Turkey and meeting with many different Muslims. I used to think Islam belonged to the Turks! We once had the caliph! That is what they taught us, and they taught us to be sober! But Muslims are also very colourful! People from Pakistan, Senegal, from Africa all praying! In London I met black people from all over the world for the first time. The imam was okay. Friday prayers were full of course, and the Muslim Turks were praying in a very disciplined way with very formal manners. When I saw people carrying their shoes inside the mosque, I was surprised. That's

one of the things that Turks pay special attention to, but I realized it was different for other Muslims and the way they behave inside the mosque. I was shocked at first, but soon learned that Muslims can be very relaxed – there were even some people sleeping inside the mosque. So while in London I learned there is a great horizon of people and a great difference among the Muslims of the world, and I learned all this in London.

In Jeddah, of course, we used to travel to Mecca and Medina so we saw the people there. But this was not a shock like London. In prayer there were other styles and this made me wonder if my ways were right. The imam in London was not strange, but he was speaking in English so it was useful to listen. Life at the mosque was also social, people coming to meet each other. And the black Muslims impressed me enormously – they were arriving in Jaguars and Rolls Royce cars and so were clearly very successful.[86]

The imam at Regent's Park Mosque at this time was Dr Sayyid Mutawalli ad-Darsh (1930–97),[87] an Egyptian who had trained at Cairo's most important centre of Islamic learning, Al-Azhar, where he began his career as a lecturer in theology. During the mid-1960s, he learned English in Dundee before spending the next years teaching in Lagos, Nigeria. In December 1971 he moved to London and became imam at Regent's Park Mosque. When Abdullah Gül heard him speaking, ad-Darsh was addressing local questions from an Islamic point of view: how might Muslims live righteously in a Christian culture? At the time ad-Darsh was an active member of numerous international Islamic councils and a member of the board at FOSIS, and had already published pamphlets on *Islamic Health Rules, Islamic Family Law,* and *The Prohibition of Intoxicants,*[88] all of them based on his Friday speeches. A vigorous campaigner for the recognition of Muslim practices in Western countries, ad-Darsh promoted Islamic values within modern contexts. He would have said nothing that Abdullah Gül might have found either remarkable or objectionable: the Qur'an should be recited in Arabic, but Islam could be taught in any language; Muslim women living in the West should dress modestly but need not cover. For educated young Muslims brought up in the Republic of Turkey, there was nothing startling here; the real surprise was finding out just how differently Muslims from other parts of the world practised their faith.

If Friday meant Regent's Park, Sundays meant Speakers' Corner at Hyde Park where Abdullah Gül discovered the wonders of democratic free speech.

'We went nearly every week.'[89] Here they were astonished at the openness with which people with extreme ideas could address public audiences. Abdullah Gül recalls nationalist speakers from Pakistan, Senegal and Sri Lanka openly attacking the British government.[90] Hearing such speeches coming from the mouths of foreigners was shocking. At that time in Turkey, such free-speaking would lead to arrest, imprisonment, probably torture and, for foreigners, deportation. But here, major controversial topics were being discussed from all available political angles: there was the new Pol Pot regime in a place now called Kampuchia; the continuing Irish problem and its attendant violence; the shift in South East Asia as North and South become the Socialist Republic of Vietnam; changes of government in the US and UK; Mao's death in December. There were also major crises in the UK: strikes continued throughout 1977 even as inflation hit summer highs of seventeen percent; demonstrations in London and Birmingham by the racist National Front provoked violent riots; and the Yorkshire Ripper remained at large inspiring terror in readers of the popular media. One Sunday, Gül first learned about what was going on in South Africa from a student group protesting apartheid. He was shocked by what he heard about racial segregation in that country, and was especially astonished by posters showing benches in a South African park, one marked 'Whites Only', the other 'Blacks Only'. He tells me that he kept one of these posters and has deposited it in the presidential library inscribed with the date, as a memento of how legitimate student protests have successfully challenged iniquitous governments.[91]

When Abdullah Gül and Fehmi Koru arrived in London during that sweltering summer of 1976, Palestine had been a very hot topic for some months and there were several sides needing to be attacked and defended. Since January, anti-American Muslim intellectuals had had a field day following the US veto of a UN resolution calling for a Palestinian state. Syria's intervention against the PLO in Lebanon that May, followed by the Entebbe raids in July, only provoked even more hostility among speakers and the crowds in London with views on Israel and Palestine. At Speakers' Corner, amid the speeches and debates on all these emotive political crises, there were lessons to be learned about the rhetoric of public performance.

There was a Palestinian speaker who was regularly there, waving a Palestinian flag and selecting a member of the audience to speak to directly, addressing his comments to that person directly. The Palestinian was saying interesting things and he was clever at using arguments. If someone came to heckle him he always overcame that kind of opposition and was very funny. He used to treat issues in surprising and different ways. Instead of putting everything in one way and forcing the opposition into a corner, he would take them into his confidence by speaking to them personally – 'I am not a monster! I have no bad feelings to you! If you accept the state of Israel, why not agree that we should have a state too?'[92]

Accustomed to the paternalistic and demagogic style of political oratory practised in Turkey, Abdullah Gül became fascinated with the variety of different approaches to public speaking on display in Hyde Park. Alongside the familiar rabble-rousing practised by fierce Irish Unionists and angry Maoists, he witnessed the persuasive force of other approaches among the Buddhists peacefully protesting against China and the Christian groups protesting nuclear weapons. On those Sunday visits to Hyde Park, Abdullah Gül learned about the modes and tricks of good oratory, but he also came to understand and respect the democratic right of free speech, and to reflect on how the lack of democratic freedoms in Turkey was a major cause of problems that were holding the nation back. How could an uninformed people govern themselves when political leaders used their ignorance to tell them what to believe, and then proceeded to control their behaviour and limit their freedoms to talk, read and listen?

From Necip Fazıl and others, Abdullah Gül had learned to admire while distrusting the West, to see through its vaunted claims to civilization and modernity and to recognize its decadence and its will to power. That first year in London caused him to start revising his opinions. England was in a bad condition with strikes and massive inflation, yet the standard of living wherever he looked was generally much better than in Turkey: capitalism did, it seem, provide education, health care and welfare provisions beyond anything comparable at home. There were, of course, surprising and even shocking features to life in London. There were more people from more different countries than he could have anticipated. There was the increasingly ominous racism of the National Front, though the violent clashes that their marches provoked were nothing like the attacks of the Grey Wolves. In London, young people behaved in public with an intimacy that would have been unthinkable in Turkey, even in metropolitan Istanbul. They touched, kissed, drank and even took illegal drugs in public places. Fehmi Koru recalls attending a Santana concert at Alexandra Palace where some boys were smoking opium. 'This was a real shock. When they learned we were Turkish they thought we knew about opium, but we had never seen it before. And I didn't realize that people who smoke opium liked to hear Santana. He was my favourite.'[93] In London, Abdullah Gül and his friends went to the cinema, theatre, concerts and exhibitions, and mixed with those they met. The Pittman School ran a weekly film club, and here they saw European films that would not appear in Turkey for some years. Antonioni's *Blow Up* was a great hit, but Abdullah Gül continued to prefer French art-house directors, Godard and Resnais. London provided religious, political and cultural experiences that were challenging and mind broadening.

When you move to live in a foreign country, you cannot avoid becoming newly aware of where you come from: being Turkish in Turkey is different from being Turkish in England. Abdullah Gül and his friends often discussed this experience, this new way of thinking about being Turkish, and compared themselves with the Young Turks who had engineered the end of the Ottoman state.

> In our discussions at the time, we thought about the young Turks of Abdulhamid's time who were not happy and went to live abroad in Europe. When discussing what will happen in Turkey, we asked would there be a better government? We always identified with the Young Turks in Europe seeing better governments and better societies and we wondered how this experience affected them? We always compared ourselves with them in the 1970s, and Abdullah Gül was much affected by what he saw in England.[94]

In Turkey during those years, Bülent Ecevit and Süleyman Demirel were swapping back and forth between unstable coalitions of ever shorter duration. Ecevit's secular-left CHP government of 21 June 1977 lasted less than a month before Demirel and the conservative AP took over again. With historical hindsight, we can see that the conditions leading up to the military coup of 1980 were in place and becoming more potent. But at the time, watching Turkish politics from London, what was becoming ever more clear to Abdullah Gül was the need for Turkey to become more Westernized, more democratic and socially open like London and Europe. Here, you were free to practise your religion; living standards were higher for everyone; the streets were not patrolled by armed forces in uniforms or otherwise; and even the riots seldom proved deadly. Europe was not the decayed civilization bemoaned by Necip Fazıl and the angst-ridden high modernists, but a model of how democratic freedoms and Western capitalism were, despite economic crises and labour strikes, actually providing benefits desperately needed by most people in Turkey. These experiences helped shape the articles that he helped Fehmi Koru write for publication back home in *Yeni Devir* ('New Revolution'), at the time a key focus for debates among Muslim intellectuals in Turkey. '*Yeni Devir* was published to put the Islamic side of the argument,' Abdullah Gül explained, 'but that was not always our idea! Fehmi was more prominent in writing these essays and he went on to become a journalist. I was more, you might say, of a ghost writer!'[95]

London also provided Abdullah Gül with an immersion in confronting how Turkish nationalism was not just about Muslim identity, Turkey and the Turks, but also about neighbours and foreign relations.

This was my first experience abroad and I realized that there were other people in the world with different views. There was a Greek guy in my class at a time of bad relations over Cyprus and we talked about it and he became my best friend, he said so too. We realized that we shared many common forms of social unrest – the colonels in Greece and the many coups in Turkey. We shared stories of hard times from our childhood and discovered so many of our traditions were the same. So what was the difference that was separating Turkey from Greece?[96]

FOSIS provided the ideal setting for finding new ways of thinking about problems in Turkey in an international context. Among those he met at FOSIS to talk about the political challenges facing Muslims in other countries were several young scholars who would return home to become leading figures, such as Mustafa Osman Ismail (b.1955), who was Sudan's foreign minister from 1998 to 2005, and became that country's longest-serving politician. Gül also recalls discussions on the need for reform in Muslim countries with Anwar bin Ibrahim (b. 1947), finance minister (1991–98) and deputy prime minister (1993–98) of Malaysia, where he has been leader of the opposition since 2008.[97] An experienced student activist who now thinks of himself as having been a 'revolutionist' at that time, Abdullah Gül soon found himself organizing a forum for discussing and debating questions confronting Turkish students in an international frame. Conditions in Turkey were pretty grim and this group became the rather sonorously named *Müslüman Öğrenciler*

Birliği'nde Türk Öğrencileri Yardımlaşma Derneği ('Mutual Association of Turkish Students of the Islamic Students' Association'). [98] However bad conditions in England were, they were worse in Turkey. Fehmi Koru recalls how in Turkey 'there were people waiting in queues, to buy margarine! Demirel said "we need 70 cents" things were so bad. It was much worse than England. In those years before 1980, we lost more than five thousand young people to terrorism.'[99]

Becoming more and more involved with organizing discussions on how best to serve Turkey and prepare for the nation's future, Abdullah Gül once again started bringing people home to talk while he cooked great pots of *kuru fasuliye*. Among Turkish students living in London, Abdullah Gül quickly became proverbial for the energy he put into both cooking and talking; 'we said that he always carried a cooking pan with two plates, two forks and two spoons in his bag wherever he went!'[100] Sometimes he would show up at the house at 94 Drayton Park Road near Arsenal stadium where Fehmi Koru, Şükrü Karatepe and other Turkish friends were living. Koru remembers: 'I was a very serious student and would be upstairs in my room reading and he would show up chatting downstairs about how to serve Turkey and what to do for the future! He was preparing himself for political command even in those days – he was so busy he forgot to learn English!'[101] Abdullah Gül agrees that cooking Turkish food and talking endlessly to Turkish students about Turkey in Turkish was not helping him to learn English.

> I found myself cooking for all the guests! I thought: I can no longer tolerate this so I must leave this place! I was a revolutionist and found myself stuck in the kitchen, cooking simple foods in London. And that is why I moved to Exeter. In the daytime we stayed in a house belonging to FOSIS, it was a beautiful area, this house, on the brown line after Kilburn – the station was Kilburn on the Bakerloo line. But many people were always coming from Turkey, students, to see me and I had to spend time with them and we talked about home – about saving the country from the valley of the wolves – and about the government and not talking or learning English. A friend at Exeter invited me to go there.[102]

And so it came about that Abdullah Gül packed up his books and his student activism, and moved to provincial Exeter to concentrate on his language studies.

Exeter, 1977–78

For Londoners, even today, Exeter is a remote place; not perhaps as far-off as people from Istanbul view Kayseri as being, or people from Kayseri view Van, but distant nevertheless. In 1977 that was promising to change with the official opening of the M5 motorway in May, but it still takes a good three hours to travel to London, and much longer by car during the holiday weekends. Like other English provincial cathedral cities in the 1970s, Exeter attracted a certain kind of middle-class English visitor and even the odd foreign tourist but was otherwise strongly regional in its resident population and wary of strangers. There were pubs with quaint 'Olde Worlde' signs where locals went to drink, and there were Indian and Chinese restaurants as well as fish-and-chip shops, but the kebab stands, handy guide-books to city sites, and the student night clubs by the quay had yet to arrive. Like Kayseri, Exeter boasts a substantial architectural history with Roman and earlier remains, and a much admired cathedral that was under construction even as the Selçuk Honat Hatun mosque complex was being completed. Promoted from a college to full independence as a university in 1955, the University of Exeter was becoming increasingly important nationally for attracting well-qualified undergraduates with private school backgrounds. At that time it was sometimes jokingly said that when it became a full-scale university, Exeter hired bright young lecturers from Oxford and Cambridge who promptly joined the golf club. Be that as it may, given its proximity to the magnificent Dartmoor National Park, Exeter promoted itself as a splendid place to practise rural sports such as horseback riding, and it attracted students who brought their own horses and, as was still fashionable as well as legal in those days, came to hunt. The university no longer openly advertises itself as a good place to bring your own horse, but the memory of the queen's granddaughter Zara Phillips, who did just, that lingers on. The Turkish show-jumping champion Dilara Pars studied here in preference to a well-known university in Istanbul.

When asked his strongest and first memory of Exeter, Abdullah Gül replied with glee:

Exeter: what I remember is the Turk's Head pub sign. It was hanging and there was an Ottoman *kaptan-başı* on the main street! It was on the way from the centre to my house so I used to walk by it every day. Sometimes when I saw it I used to go over and wonder what people thought. Did they think I looked like that?

The Turk's Head is no longer a pub. It became an Italian restaurant in 2005, but the 700-year-old building with the wood-carving of a fierce and turbaned 'Turk' peering from above the entrance remains a landmark attraction on Exeter's High Street just as the enigma of how the old pub got its name remains unsolved.[103] Although puzzling to a young Turkish nationalist, any ancient hostility seemed long forgotten in the way local people behaved, and Abdullah Gül was very happy during his year at Exeter. 'Exeter University is very beautiful … I wished I had been able to stay there. That is something I always wanted to do!' In his classes he became friendly with other Muslim students, 'mostly from different Arab countries and some Turks, and we organized some events. There was a *mescit* [prayer-room] on campus at the time.'[104]

While missing the intellectual excitements of London, Abdullah Gül soon came to understand and enjoy the amenities and enchantment of the English countryside. He sometimes travelled back to London to catch up with news and friends, but also went for long walks on Dartmoor at weekends. During the week, he took to strolling for hours along the river, sometimes with books to stop with and study. The green beauty of the Devon countryside contrasts sharply with the stark sublimity of Kayseri, and it became clearer and clearer how people belong to their land, their weather and their geography every bit as much as they belong to their history.

> My house in Exeter was two storeys. It was the ground floor with another Turkish student. When you go out from the centre to the river, you cross the bridge then one or two hundred meters, we were on the right side. Next to where I lived was a farm with horses. Every Sunday they used to go there, small girls, to see the horses. From time to time I was offered to go with them and went riding in England. So another thing I learned there was how the English people like horses. Every Saturday there were horse events on TV – show jumping for instance.[105]

Between them, the rousting and heckling of Speakers' Corner and the weekly ritual of small girls indulging their passion for ponies brought Abdullah Gül to understand how life in England differed greatly between the city and the country, and just how different both of them were from the way 'the West' had been described by left and right at home in Turkey. There was clearly more thinking to be done about the West, about Europe at least, about democracy and capitalism, and about the intimate links, geographical as well as historical, that bind a land and its people together. There were obvious object lessons to be learned about free speech and education and welfare provision. After two years in England, what Abdullah Gül came to understand more vividly than ever before was how a people truly belong to their own past and their own land, and that Turkey would only develop through democratic reforms that would improve living standards for everyone living there, not simply the metropolitan and business elites. The constitutional system in place since the coup of 1960 and the 1971 amendments was simply not working to advance these ideals.

Before returning to Turkey in 1978, Abdullah Gül went back to London to go shopping for presents to take home. He was booked onto the same flight to Istanbul as Fehmi Koru, and the two of them spent so much time talking that they left one of the most important gifts to the last moment. What would they take back for Necip Fazıl? With only hours left to get to the airport, they stopped on Regent Street. Here, their panic only increased once they realized how expensive everything was.

> We couldn't afford to buy something too expensive but needed to find something of sufficient quality. But there were too many expensive shops. We bought a lighter, paid a lot of money for it, and a tie pin. When we arrived in Istanbul, we went to his villa at Erenköy and while waiting outside he came to us and we chatted. We offered our humble gifts. He shouted 'Neslihan! Come and look at what my loved ones brought to me!' When his wife arrived and saw the lighter, which was very delicate, she declared 'It's mine!' And so he ended up with just the tie pin.[106]

At home in Kayseri, Abdullah Gül's London shopping was also appreciated. Macit, normally prone to sobriety of expression, brightened into a broad grin as he recalled his brother's arrival home:

> When Abdullah returned from England he brought me blue jeans and a green jacket with a red lining! This was the first time such clothes were seen in Kayseri! Levis were nowhere in Kayseri! I was so happy to get these presents. I was seventeen and had the coolest clothes in town![107]

It is perhaps no more than a curiously ironic coincidence that Abdullah Gül might have brought the first Levi jeans to Kayseri in 1978 since 'virtually every major brand of jeans on earth today uses Turkish denim' produced in Kayseri. In 1953, Orta Anadolu was one of the new textile companies established in the industrial park close by Ahmet Hamdi Bey's workshop. In the early 1980s, Levi Strauss took them on as partners, retooling operations for producing denim. Five other denim plants soon followed, and Kayseri now produces denim worth over $2 million a year, while Orta Anadolu alone makes one percent of world denim.[108]

Return to Turkey, 1978–83

Back in Turkey, Abdullah Gül brought England with him, not just stylish clothing but in the ways he now viewed Turkey and its problems. He had seen how freedom of speech and open debate challenged and defused extremist views even as, and because, it allowed them public expression. He had seen how strikes and anti-fascist rioting could lead to street fighting in England, but in Turkey on his return there were daily armed attacks and political assassinations with promises of more to come. Left-wing guerrilla cells carrying out targeted assassinations of politicians and judges seemed to be operating without any clear objectives other than provoking fear and instability. The pro-Marxist Turkish Workers Party (*Türkiye Işçi Partisi*, or TIP) made matters worse by claiming alliance with left-leaning Alevis and Kurds who became mistakenly identified as communists and thereby frightening 'the Turkish military establishment, which still saw Turkey as a bulwark of the anticommunist West in the Cold War'.[109] Once again, left-wing violence was provoking reactions.

Under the command of Abdullah Çatlı – a name we will encounter again – extremists among the Grey Wolves had formed links with the international anti-communist organization Gladio, and imagined they were protecting not only Turkey but the entire civilized world by shooting left-wing students and carrying out massacres of Alevis (Turkish Shi'ites). And they seemed to be protected by the state. 'There were indeed signs,' comments Mehmet Ali Birand,

> that the 'Grey Wolves' ... were given preferential treatment by security forces already stretched to their limits by mounting street terror. However, in the relations between the militants of the right and the security forces the key word was 'nationalism'. When the young right-wing militants or would-be terrorists were confronted by the

law- enforcement agencies, they claimed affinity simply by stating that they were 'anti-communist nationalists' in favour of 'law and order'.[110]

On 4 July 1980, an extremist 'group of right-wing Sunni Turks attacked Alevi neighbourhoods in the town of Çorum, killing 26 people and destroying 36 homes and 12 stores'.[111] This was not Abdullah Gül's vision of nationalism, law, order, or of how to promote the future of Turkey and the well-being of the Turkish people. The violence that was returning to political life in the closing years of the 1970s was both terrible and intolerable. Amnesty International estimated that there were nearly ten assassinations a day, totalling more than five thousand by decade's end.[112] By July 1979, that average had risen to twenty a day.[113] In October, shortly after Abdullah Gül arrived back, Alparslan Türkeş's Nationalist Action Party called upon the government to impose martial law. On 9 October, as if in self-fulfilling prophecy, seven students supposed to be members of the pro-Kurdish Workers' Party (PKK) were murdered in Ankara, sending the press into a frenzy of conspiratorial reports about unsolved assassinations of journalists and academics, condemning how the perpetrators were seldom caught or brought to trial. Then matters deteriorated even further. On 19 December in Kahramanmaraş, 'the worst in a series of pogroms of Alevis' that had been 'organized by the Grey Wolves left more than 100 people dead'.[114] Gül himself reflects:

> The ideological violence of the late 1970s was a by-product of the Cold War rivalries all across the world. But in Turkey it was rather fiercer than any other European country since Turkey was a flank country of NATO alliance opposing communism. Violent attacks were mutual indeed and in some cases they were carried out in order to trigger sectarian strife in Turkey. In recent years there were several studies trying to shed light on this dark period of Turkey's political history. They were suggesting that 'the deep state' was behind many of these attacks hiring provocateurs from both sides. So attributing the overall violence primarily to the Ülkücüler as many early scholars did was inaccurate. There were thousands of rightist activists (including Minister Gun Sazak from MHP) who were killed by the Marxist Leninist and Maoist organizations at the time.[115]

After a decade of unworkable coalitions, by 1980 it had become clear that the political system was in tatters, provoking violence from extremists of all

persuasions.[116] Despite martial law, the number of deaths from political violence and terrorism continued to increase: there were 1,250 deaths between
January and August alone.[117] Unable to control the violence, the coalitions
had also failed to control the economy. Ineffective regulations had encouraged runaway hyper-inflation. Foreign exchange was at an all-time low, no
longer fed by the remittances of overseas workers as it had been since 1973.[118]

To Abdullah Gül, this murdering of fellow Muslim Turks was not nationalism but something deeply wicked and terrible. While the intellectual left had
yet to resolve contradictions in Turkey's exceptional historical development
and the 'lunatic left' had begun registering its protest 'by dotting crowded
public places in Ankara and Istanbul with booby-trapped banners and placards',[119] there were still extremists among the nationalist right who continued
along the path of violence in the name of saving the nation from those they
considered subversive. But it is no longer clear that all the attacks attributed
to the Grey Wolves were what they appeared to be. At the time it seemed
as if the militant tendency among the Grey Wolves had spread everywhere,
coming dangerously close to Kayseri. On 18 June 1980 in nearby Nevşehir,
Bülent Ecevit and other parliamentary delegates were fired upon while
attending the funeral of a local Republican People's Party delegate who had
recently been assassinated.[120] At the time, the incident was widely reported
to have been instigated by the Grey Wolves, but a Nevşehir resident, who
briefly trained in the local *komando* camp at the time, insists that the attack
was orchestrated by agents working for the government to warn Demirel at
the same time as spreading violence that could be blamed on Türkes, Çatlı
and the Grey Wolves.[121] For Abdullah Gül, already a well-known and easily
recognized figure on the nationalist student right, the best thing to do was
to concentrate on pursuing his academic career. These were clearly times to
follow grandfather's advice, keep a low profile, and stay away from politics.

Under the supervision of Professor Nevzat Yalçıntaş, Abdullah Gül set about
writing his research on Turkey's economic relations with other Muslim
countries. In 1978, he became an instructor in the Department of Industrial
Engineering that had just been formed by Professor Sabahattin Zaim at the
newly established Sakarya University. Less than ten years old, the university
was a brand-new complex situated several hours from Istanbul on the road to
Ankara. Here he taught economics to engineers, and met up again with Sami
Güçlü who was also starting out on an academic career teaching at Sakarya.
Along the road from the university campus, the nearest town of any size is

Adapazarı, which was then a medium-sized market town with two business-class hotels and little else.[122] Sami Güçlü recalls how 'at the time Sakarya was a provincial backwater with no cultural or intellectual life beyond a single tea shop'. The area was still scarcely populated and too remote to have any cultural facilities or venues, but not entirely a wasteland where nothing could be grown. The students were first-generation undergraduates coming from homes in villages and small towns where the only book in the house would be a Qur'an; reading was not a usual activity for them, but they were keen and eager to learn. Before he could organize a reading club, Abdullah Gül first had to persuade the university authorities to open a book store, something that had been ignored in the rush of planning and development.

> The bookstore – which employed ten students – was the first in town and soon became a centre for cultural meetings. Most students became involved in some way with the activities of the bookshop regardless of political persuasion, so lots of meetings at which left and right met and discussed matters of common concern as much as differences. The shop encouraged students to read beyond the syllabus of their courses.
>
> As a teacher, Abdullah Gül was universally liked: he gave out copies of Necip Fazıl's books. He is also very keen on Turkish folk music, and I remember that a special favourite in those years was the song 'Şen olasin Ürgüp Dumanin Tütmez'. Literally this says 'Be happy Ürgüp because your smoke cannot be inhaled', but means 'Be proud Ürgüp because your people can breathe clean air.' This song reminded Abdullah Gül of a good friend who had died young.[123]

Available on YouTube being performed by numerous different artists, this melancholic air and lyric from Nevşehir, popularly known as *Cemalım*, laments the untimely death of a young man, balancing the memory of loss with an insistence on hope for the future that is often missing from the *arabesk* style of songs that were also popular at the time. Here, as it were, was a possible allegory for Turkey at the time: a sad and mysterious tale of premature tragic loss that needed to be recalled and lamented, but in a spirit of hope for the future. For the young university lecturer, culture and education were still the best means for realizing that hope.

Marriage and coup, 1980

Meanwhile in Kayseri, with her first-born son now back home in Turkey and in possession of an income, Adviye Hanim turned her thoughts to how he must now be in need of a wife. For mothers of her generation and traditional background, it would have been unthinkable not to take this matter firmly in hand. Among her acquaintances she knew one Ahmet Özyurt whose daughter Hayrünnisa was studying at the Çemberlitaş High School for Girls in Istanbul. Originally from Kayseri himself, Ahmet Özyurt ran a retail business in Tahtakale in the Eminönü area of Istanbul but regularly returned to Kayseri, staying in a house that his father, Halil Ibrahim Özyurt, had built there.[124] The Gül and Özyurt families were friendly, and there were connections via the Satoğlu clan. Meetings of all the interested parties were duly organized and agreements eventually reached on all sides. Abdullah and Hayrünnisa were happy enough to be engaged, but they insisted on waiting until after her next birthday. 'One of the things that has attracted attention,' Hayrünnisa told me, 'has been my marriage at a young age. Marriage at an early age is always considered an important topic in Turkey. People think it is because of tradition or perhaps due to family pressure ... My marriage was not like that. I can only say it was fate or destiny.'[125]

So it was that a year later, on 21 August 1980, Abdullah Gül and Hayrünnisa Özyurt were married. Looking back, Hayrünnisa recalls some of her initial doubts:

> I must have felt the difficult years ahead of us even then because I told Abdullah Bey, perhaps even during the first time I met him, that I did not feel positive about politics. He told me he would not go into politics. I made that point because his interest in politics was obvious even in those years: because the years when we were growing up were the most difficult years in Turkey. I was a child in the seventies and at that time there were times when it was difficult to go out on the streets. Those were the years when there were heavy clashes between the left and the right and it was difficult even to go to school then. There were clashes between left and right wing students at universities. Abdullah Bey was actively part of the events when he was in the university. I could not have a positive view of politics because of this general environment. In fact, I was proven right with regard to my concerns because the coup took place the day after we came to our house after our marriage in 1980.[126]

But her major concern, and one that became a condition of her agreement to the engagement and marriage, was that she should be free to finish high school from home. On this there was full agreement, though circumstances would prove adverse. A further matter over which neither of them had any direct control was the wedding ceremony itself, which was very much arranged among the wider families. For her part, Hayrünnisa had grown up in Istanbul where she had developed certain modern ideas, so the traditional wedding festivities were full of surprises. When I said that I had heard somewhere that the wedding celebrations had lasted for two weeks, she laughed and said:

> No, it was four to five days. It did not last forty days and forty nights, but four to five days ... It was a beautiful wedding. Kayseri was preferred for the wedding because of our ties with Kayseri on both sides. It was perhaps not so easy for me because I had only been to Kayseri for short periods of time ... Our wedding was similar to other weddings held in those days. Then, everybody preferred traditional weddings. Wedding meals would be cooked at home. Cooks would come to the house and prepare the food. There would be a henna night. I don't know if there are still weddings in Kayseri that last four to five days like this, but most weddings today are held out of the house in wedding halls or hotels. In those years however, organizing a wedding somewhere other than your house would be considered inappropriate. In fact, I may have contradicted tradition in some ways because I was born and raised in Istanbul and I can say that I was not brought up very traditionally. I don't mean this in a negative sense, but just to say that I was not used to some things. We were married on the 21st of August. We stayed with Abdullah Bey's family for a while after the wedding. We were in our house in Istanbul one day before the coup.[127]

The plan was to move into a rented flat in the Asian suburb of Erenköy from which Abdullah Gül would easily commute by train between Sakarya and Istanbul University. Hayrünnisa's own family were also about to move there from Beyazit, where the streets had become unsafe, to help while she completed her high school examinations. That, at least, was the plan.

Once family farewells in Kayseri were over, it was late on the evening of Thursday 11 September when the newly-wed couple arrived home in Erenköy. That night, their first in their new home together, the third political intervention by the military in as many decades took place. When I asked him about arriving back with his new wife just in time for the 1980 coup, Abdullah Gül offered a clear account of what were obviously memorable events about which he has often reflected:

> When I got married, we had the ceremony in Kayseri and then stayed on some days, then returned to our house in Istanbul. And that was the first day of the coup. But we didn't have TV and didn't know anything about it. So the first morning back I went to Sahrayi Cedid mosque for Friday prayers and realized things were different – it was only half-full and people were silent and there was a strange atmosphere. So I asked someone what was going on. And he told me that the coup had taken place and I felt afraid because those were interesting days and I couldn't figure what this coup was. The left and the right and Marxists were all being involved, so I had no idea what was going on. That was the first day.[128]

That evening, he nervously pondered his own position and once again recalled his grandfather's warning about how speaking out in public could be too dangerous. He had kept a deliberately low political profile since returning to Turkey, and had always avoided any involvement in violence, but who knew who the leaders of this coup might be, or what they might have in mind, or how they would behave? Ever in tune with an inherited optimism, Abdullah Gül recalled being able to look on the bright side of things.

> I was just thinking that the house we rented was brand new and how nice it was and I was teaching at the university, I was well known, active and my ideas were well known. So I felt safe because no one would know my new address and we would be fine and have a nice month of honeymoon. But at five o'clock in the morning a young officer came to the door and said that I was among the first being summoned under the '*Bayrak* ['Flag'] Operation' to be apprehended. He was a young lieutenant. According to Turkish traditions we don't keep people standing at the door so I asked him to come in and wait while I prepared to go with him. And because of Turkish hospitality I asked my wife to offer him coffee while I prepared, so we offered him coffee. Afterwards I wondered why I did such a thing and remembered I was inspired by my mother's mother.[129]

Amid laughter that almost brought him to tears, Abdullah Gül recalled how his grandmother had once offered coffee to a burglar:

> When we were away visiting, a burglar stole things including a beautiful watch of my father's and he took things and ran off – it was a pocket watch, a half-hunter with a chain. We all returned home, and months went by until the police phoned my father and asked about his watch, since they had caught the man and to confirm things – the police brought the man to describe how he had broken in, and my grandmother offered coffee to the police and to the burglar, and the police were astonished, and I realized that I was inspired by my grandmother.[130]

Asked for her memories of these first days of married life, Hayrünnisa recalled them clearly:

> There was a coup and my first question of course was to ask what a coup was? Why was it happening? I tried to understand the curfew and the coup. On that day, I did not for a moment think that my husband would be detained. The next day … the coup was declared on the 12th of September and he was taken on the next day in the early hours of the morning on the 13th of September. It was about five to six o'clock in the morning. I really had a hard time understanding it. Why, what for, what was his crime? I was newly married, how was I to explain this to people? What would the neighbours think? One thing I cannot forget about that morning is how Abdullah Bey asked me to prepare coffee for the soldiers who came to take him. I prepared their coffee. I don't know whether I could do the same today.[131]

Under conditions of extreme anxiety, such as being arrested at five o'clock in the morning on the second night of being at home with his new wife, Abdullah Gül found sufficient reserve of exemplary family manners to help manage the unfolding calamity to his best advantage, persuading the soldiers to let him stop to make a telephone call.

> When I left the flat I realized there were soldiers everywhere and I was surprised and wondered what to do since I had a new wife at home and we didn't have a phone. So I asked if I could make a call and I had an

auntie on the next street and we went there and phoned Kayseri and
I told them your daughter-in-law will be alone, they were taking me
away. They took me to Metris prison, so we crossed over to the other
side and I was shocked when I arrived. I was the only person there,
not just the first! So I really didn't know what kind of coup this was! I
was the only one arrested! Later, many people poured in and the place
was heaped up, sometimes three to a bed.[132]

Back in Erenköy, the young bride was also finding the limits of her patience
and fortitude tested. A close friend explained:

You must understand that Hayrünnisa is a very strong woman. She married when very young and one might expect she would be oppressed
and compliant, but she is not. She was only sixteen when she married,
but her family respected individuality although they were also very
traditional in other ways. Her father wanted her to be educated and so
she was raised in a good school. Although a woman, they wanted her to
be educated like a son and perhaps have a career. She was brought up
to feel important in her family, so when she married she had matured
early and was not daunted or compliant. In 1980, after her marriage,
Abdullah Gül was arrested and taken away so she found herself in an
awkward position. She was away from her parents and so was alone
welcoming neighbours and other visitors who came to congratulate
them, and not let on that Abdullah Gül had been taken away. Imagine;
she was sixteen, had just left home, and had to pretend as if nothing had
happened. If the neighbours knew, she would be excluded. So people
would come by to congratulate her. She would make them coffee and
chat – then go off to the bedroom and cry a little – then return and
carry on the conversation.[133]

These were hardly auspicious circumstances in which to be beginning married life. For both, the arrest and separation were bad enough, but left alone
at home in Erenköy without knowing what was going on made matters even
worse. Amid it all, Hayrünnisa's father was taken seriously ill.

We had no information. I cannot remember exactly for how long,
but we did not hear from him for a while. I had a chance to see him
briefly when he was taken from Istanbul to Adapazarı. It was short, but

I could at least see that he was fine. Then he was taken to Adapazarı. At that time, my father was hospitalized for a heart condition. There was a curfew, those were difficult times. When I think about it now, I ask myself how I managed to overcome all that. He was in Metris for about ten days and then sent to Adapazarı. One month in total… He was released one month later.[134]

When I asked about his treatment while in Metris Military Prison, and whether he was put in cells with hostile prisoners, Abdullah Gül replied:

I was subjected to intensive interrogations for one and a half months but they couldn't find any reason to keep me, so they released me. My brother Macit was also jailed, but they kept him for six months and he had very difficult times there. My ideas were well known, the rightists and nationalists were all brought in together. So no hostile prisoners – no mixing of left and right, they grouped political factions together, but in other places they sometimes mixed in criminals and political enemies. But when I was in Metris we were grouped without criminals.[135]

Information remained scarce. For a long time, no one inside the prison could know or understand what was really going on. Those six weeks were not intellectually stimulating times.

Later we slowly learned from newcomers what the coup was and who was doing it and what they were ordering. It was a regular army coup within the frame of the command chain, and this was a relief since there were many extremists who might have taken over. But sitting in prison I thought that having a proper command chain through the army was better. And that is why we were able to return to democracy faster than if it had been an extremist coup. These were the early days of the coup and there was chaos, so in prison we didn't have much to discuss since we still didn't know what was happening. My concern was that I couldn't communicate with my wife and tell her I was fine and well and weeks went by without anyone hearing from me. The officers knew I taught at the university and one of them who was friendly towards me agreed to phone my wife and that was how I was able to let her know that I was well.[136]

Being among the very first to be arrested might be said to have had some advantages. The prison officers and interrogators were less routinely hostile. Torture had yet to become routine. The cells were cleaner and, initially at least, less crowded.

During the weeks that Abdullah Gül was detained, there were over 11,500 further arrests under the new military government led by generals who were following a carefully conceived strategic plan.[137] 'The main aim of Operation Flag was to deliver a final, body-blow to terror',[138] and it did not take the authorities long to recognize that Abdullah Gül's activities on behalf of MTTB and his links with professors Erbakan and Yalçıntaş had nothing to do with the massacres committed by the Grey Wolves. One of the very first to be arrested and interrogated, Gül was also one of the first to be discharged without suspicion before the overcrowding in prisons and courts created procedural delays and backlogs. 'By September 1982, two years after the coup, 80,000 were still in prison, 30,000 of them awaiting trial.'[139] Abdullah Gül later came to understand what was going on all too well: after all, Macit 'had very difficult times' in gaol, being suspect for supporting a high school organization after graduation.

The coup of 1980, code-named 'Operation Flag', had been in the planning for some time. Alarmed by unprecedented levels of daily political violence, and furious at the way the political leaders were squabbling among themselves, General Kenan Evren and other members of the military high command had already announced their discontent in a letter addressed to President Fahri Korutürk in December 1979. Meanwhile, they had continued with plans for 'Operation Flag' which would place the country under control of the National Security Council. The broad political aim was to undo what they considered to be damage resulting from the 1961 constitutional reforms, which they regarded as dangerously liberal, while also clearing out the entire existing political classes by closing all existing parties and arresting party leaders. Professional associations and trade unions were suspended, strikes declared illegal, newspapers closed. His ear evidently open to rumour, Alparslan Türkeş had already gone into hiding when his arrest was announced, but he gave himself up two days into the coup. Demirel and Ecevit were initially put under protective custody and deliberately held in the same military facility, but were soon released. Türkeş and Erbakan, however, were brought to trial, charged with seeking to undermine the constitution: both were eventually found not guilty. But the arrests and trials continued unabated. By 1982, the courts had passed no fewer than 3,600 death sentences, of which twenty were actually carried out.[140]

Sakarya University and early married life, 1980–83

Abdullah Gül continued to stay away from politics after his release from Metris Prison, completing his doctorate while teaching and organizing cultural and intellectual events for the students at Sakarya. He wanted to spend any spare time at home with his new wife and withdrew from taking on any roles that might make him publicly conspicuous. But he continued to engage in discussions and new ideas about the nation's future with friends. In the aftermath of the coup, Professor Nevzat Yalçıntaş and the 'Intellectuals' Hearth' held regular meetings at which they were developing a scheme later known as the Turkish-Islamic Synthesis. This system argued that Turkish history revealed a special relationship between pre-Islamic Turkish peoples and Islamic civilization. Indigenous Turkish culture and Islam, it was further held, 'shared a deep sense of justice, monotheism and a belief in the immortal soul, and a strong emphasis on family life and morality'. Here was a nationalism that appealed even to many of the staunchly secular military commanders, including General Kenan Evren – now president – for its vision of an Islam that was friendly to the state and celebrated patriotism as a religious duty. As the junta purged the media and universities – three hundred professors were dismissed by the end of 1982 – former editors, university rectors and board members of the ministry of education were replaced by leaders and nominees of the 'Intellectuals' Hearth'. Courses in religion and ethics became part of the school curriculum for the first time in the history of the republic.[141] Religion might have made it into the school books, but some things had not changed in the educational system. Being married, Hayrünnisa was obliged to complete her high-school education at home – which she did with top marks. But when she showed up at school to take her final exam, she was barred on the grounds of wearing a headscarf.

Abdullah Gül was busy at the time with his new academic job, marriage and completing his doctorate so 'very rarely' attended meetings of the 'Intellectuals' Hearth'.[142] Even as compelling as he found his professor's ideas about Turkish history and Islam providing keys to framing a new nationalism, Gül remained uncertain, especially about the popularity of these ideas among militants. The very icon of *Mehmetçik*, the patriotic Turkish soldier who heroically defends Islam, that appealed to Evren and the junta, also drew heavily on language and ideas that had been popular among followers of Alparslan Türkeş. 'I got to know soldiers during the 1980 coup of course!' and understood only too well how some were nicer people than others.[143] There was nothing wrong with soldiers or the army as such, but the world of armed violence remained as strongly repugnant as ever. Although the military life had never been appealing, Gül soon found himself in uniform and sometimes even enjoying himself. Recalling his military service, Abdullah Gül told me:

> I went into the army late in 1981 and served four months. In those years there were lots of young men at the age [for military service] and for that reason a new rule said university graduates only need serve four months. Again, I was one of the first. I was newly married and living in Istanbul so it was relatively easy. I was stationed at Tuzla barracks. In Turkish culture, army service is special and not doing it would be an absence. You cannot be a whole man unless you serve! Things are changing now, but those ideas were very powerful then. The months were very strict military training. We were kept in barracks and not allowed out. It was near Izmit away from Istanbul but I was lucky to be there. I was thirty years old and the others were all university graduates and I have some fond memories. Four months is a short time![144]

Once out of uniform and back at work and living at home in the rented flat in Erenköy, construction noises from across the street began disturbing the mornings.

> We are newly married in Erenköy and one morning Hayrünnisa woke me up. We faced an old wooden mansion that had been torn down, and we could see that it was being turned into new flats and she suggested we buy one of the new flats. And I was amazed because we had so little money, it was out of the question then, not even possible to think about it and I didn't want to give her hope so I said so – and she felt a bit heartbroken – and she said I am not asking it from you I am asking it from Allah![145]

A university instructor's salary was a stable income, but barely enough to make ends meet without regular help from Ahmet Hamdi Bey when the rent came due. During the summer of 1982 a number of new brokerage houses and even banks defaulted, having offered unrealistic interest rates, wrecking the currency rates even further.[146] The national economy was in a mess and costs kept rising. The young couple shared hopes for a more prosperous future but differed on their expectations about how soon it could be achieved.

> We were barely making ends meet and father was helping. One day we were crossing the bridge in her father's car and we saw a bright green Honda Accord and Hayrünnisa asked why don't we buy that car? I couldn't believe my ears since we had no money. Yes: life teaching at the university was comfortable but didn't pay very well.[147]

By 1983, Hayrünnisa was pregnant with their first son and career prospects for a young lecturer could not have been worse. Working at the Sakarya campus had become gloomy and sometimes fearful. Abdullah Gül applied for a job in the new Islamic Development Bank in Jeddah, Saudi Arabia.

> They were difficult years. It was still the coup and when I went back to the university the atmosphere was uncomfortable. The coup had spoiled the university environment and was blocking my possibilities of progress. With a new wife and lost hopes for advancing my academic career, I saw the announcement in *The Economist* and my supervisor, my old professor Nevzat Yalçıntaş, suggested I apply for the Jeddah job which I did. It was a fresh breath for me career-wise, and financially, for me to go there.[148]

With his professor's approval, Abdullah Gül submitted his doctoral dissertation on economic links between Turkey and other Muslim countries, and set off to explore his topic further at first hand among the international community of Muslim bankers assembled in Jeddah. The move not only solved the problem of a blocked career. It would soon prove to be another valuable period of life lived as a 'Young Turk', stimulating reflection on Turkey's continuing crises from an expatriate's point of view, only this time, being abroad also meant being well paid.

> So all these things happened in a few months. In Jeddah everyone has a car since there is no public transport. So with my salary and the loans from the bank that I worked for, we bought a car, a bright green Honda Accord. I first went alone to Jeddah since she was pregnant with our first son and still says she is sorry that I wasn't there for the firstborn. But after he was born, I was able to find time away and came home to take them back to Jeddah, and when I arrived to take them back, we bought an apartment in the building in Erenköy with a loan from the bank. So we got what she wanted by Allah! When she saw

this generosity!! She reminds me and still sometimes says 'I am not asking for something from you!'[149]

For the second time in his life, Abdullah Gül had become an expatriate.

Jeddah, 1983–91

Friends were at first taken aback by the suddenness of the move, but quickly understood it was for the best. Şükrü Karatepe recalls:

> Yes, it was a surprise, but after the coup Abdullah Gül was not happy working in the university after his arrest and constantly being watched by the army. One of the political targets of the coup were young and educated people, so they were constantly interfering in teaching appointments and promotions. Turkey closed off while the world was changing. The army didn't see outside changes, but many in Turkey did and they engaged with the rest of the world once the army were no longer in control. Abdullah Gül went to Jeddah because he didn't want to live under the closed Turkish state, but we knew that one day he would return to Turkey and enter political life.[150]

For Hayrünnisa the move also made a certain amount of sense. As she reflected, 'no one likes to leave one's family and country', but early married life under the coup had been frustrating in more than one way. Her ambitions of completing her high-school diploma working from home in Erenköy were painfully thwarted because 'there were many things that were forbidden in Turkey in those years', such as the curfew and being 'banned from going to school. I encountered this for the first time in an exam; I was dismissed from an exam because of my headscarf.' New regulations also meant that, being married, she was not eligible to be enrolled. She continued to study nevertheless, fondly remembering evenings spent reading while Abdullah was working on his doctorate: 'We have a contest in our family with regard to reading books. Abdullah Bey always says that I read faster.' Day to day life, however, was dull, difficult and heavily restricted. 'The times were not free in Turkey then to go out to dinner,' she observed. The prospect of moving from the rented flat in Erenköy with its old-fashioned plumbing and solid-fuel heating to a new, modern house while her husband earned a much higher salary had obvious appeal. Only the timing of the move was unfortunate.

I was pregnant with Ahmet. We had lost three children before that. I had to rest throughout the nine months of my pregnancy and I gave birth while Abdullah Bey was in Jeddah. So, I went to Jeddah much later. One of my saddest moments was perhaps around the time when Ahmet was born. These should have been the days when I should feel happiest, but I was sad because Abdullah Bey was not with me. Abdullah Bey was able to see Ahmet for the first time when he was three and a half months old. Although he wanted this child very much, I remember him seeing Ahmet as a stranger. Such alienation may take place because he was not there at the beginning. It happens. He was probably expecting to see a small baby when I arrived but, though Ahmet was still a baby, he was quite large, a big baby.[151]

When she arrived in Jeddah, 'Everything was ready because Abdullah Bey had already made many preparations knowing that we would be going there to join him. So, I went to a house that was already settled.'[152]

The year that Abdullah and Hayrünnisa Gül arrived in Jeddah was a momentous year in Turkish politics. In 1983, the first elections to be held since the coup brought new parties and new leaders onto the ballots. The National Security Council had finally resolved to permit three parties to form: a 'nationalist democratic' party representing the generals' interests, a 'populist' party representing the Kemalists and the rump of Ecevit's Republican People's Party, and Turgut Özal's *Anavatan Partisi* ('Motherland Party', hereafter ANAP) which, despite obstacles, represented everything else that the generals permitted. Election results revealed a broad consensus among conservative Muslims, nationalists, economic liberals and social democrats that brought Turgut Özal to power.[153]

An engineer from Malatya with a broad popular appeal, Turgut Özal was able to capture votes from the new industrialists, the farmers and small businessmen, as well as the nationalist and religious right: in many ways, this was the constituency who would later support Abdullah Gül and the future AKP. With family ties to the Nakşibendi dervish order, Özal was a self-made businessman whose family had moved to Kayseri where, like Abdullah Gül, he is among the most honoured graduates of the Kayseri Lycée. An engineer interested in economics, Özal was very much influenced by the Turkish-Islamic Synthesis in planning the ANAP programme, but secularists' suspicions towards him were partly allayed by his powerful commitment to neoliberal economic policies. He had been appointed by Süleyman Demirel to head the State Planning Office, but left to work in the World Bank following the army intervention of 1971. During his years as a senior consultant in the Washington headquarters of the World Bank, Özal personally witnessed the emergence of free-market economics, later known as the 'Washington Consensus' of neoliberalism. In the final months before the coup, while serving as secretary for economic affairs, Özal had drafted Turkey's policy plan designed to release credits from the IMF and had been trusted by the generals to advise them on economic matters. He was a great admirer of Reagan and Thatcher.

Once in the prime minister's office, Özal came to dominate the political stage in Turkey for the next decade, introducing neoliberal economic policies and seeking a higher profile for Turkey in regional and international affairs. It has often been observed that, in its economic policies and westward-facing foreign policy, the AKP has been following initiatives first opened during Özal's time in power. He was an admired but controversial figure who 'replaced the inward-oriented, import-substitution policy pioneered in the 1930s with an export-led growth strategy, so adjusting to the global trend toward privatization'.[154] Amid mounting charges of corruption, he won re-election in 1987 but not the local elections of March 1989. Such was his popular power and prestige, however, that in October that year he became president when Evren retired. 'The point about Özal,' as one scholar comments:

> is that he switched sides and loyalties from being Demirel's economics supremo enforcing the IMF and World Bank adjustment programme of 24 January 1980, to offering his services to the military government. But he was on his way to outmanoeuvring the military, landing the premiership in 1983, despite their displeasure. Özal's legacy is that his model of building a coalition among the four major currents in Turkish politics – namely the Islamists, the nationalists, the centre-right conservatives and some elements of the centre-left – would provide a model for the AKP twenty years later. Özal opened the gate from which Erdoğan and Gül would pass, leaving Erbakan behind.[155]

During the 1980s under Özal, Turkey changed a great deal even as what political scientist Hakan Yavuz calls 'opportunity spaces' opened up in economic and political life.[156] But there were major obstacles. In 1984, the PKK took up armed resistance in the cause of an independent Kurdistan, and the atrocities on both sides began in earnest. In 1987, Özal's government applied for Turkish membership of the European Community, only to be postponed two years later. Since taking office, through liberal reforms Özal had encouraged industrial development for export markets leading to brief periods of economic growth, but provided no solutions to inflation or the inefficiencies of Turkish financial institutions. For many, the growing economy seemed to be a good thing as banks extended credit for the televisions and washing machines and refrigerators that had become household necessities for increasing numbers of Turks.

In July 1988, Prime Minister Özal publicly declared that Turkey had achieved a new era of progress and modernization as he opened a second bridge across the Bosporus. In October Istanbul's first shopping mall, the Galleria in Ataköy, welcomed its first shoppers. By 1989 private television companies were, though illegal, broadcasting in Turkey, while the spread of easy credit was becoming an inflationary drain on the national economy.

Özal remained bullishly optimistic about Turkey becoming a more important regional power. In 1990, hoping to increase Turkey's prestige in the Middle East, Özal supported US plans for the First Gulf War despite the way UN sanctions on Iraq had long been damaging the economy. Early in 1991, the war itself produced further economic problems, exacerbated by increased PKK attacks on Turkish forces on one hand, and the massive number of Kurdish refugees from northern Iraq seeking sanctuary in Turkey to escape Saddam Hussein's chemical weapons. Financial aid from the US worth $850 million did little to recompense the cost of relief operations, or lost revenues. Yet Özal had planted Turkey firmly in the US political imagination as an invaluable ally with ambitions: as one US commentator put it at the time, Özal's policies 'add up to ... the most expansive Turkish thrust since the Ottoman Empire's collapse at the end of World War 1'.[157]

In many ways, Özal's ambitions for bringing Turkey greater prosperity and international prestige would not be achieved until the new century, during the first term of the AKP. Abdullah Gül was, and remains, a great fan of Özal, sharing his belief that economic and political reform was essential for bringing Turkey greater prosperity and international prestige, and that such modernizing reforms were entirely compatible with Muslim belief. First as prime minister and then as foreign minister in the first AKP government of 2002, Gül pursued financial, economic and foreign policy reforms initiated by Özal.

Meanwhile in Jeddah, Abdullah Gül kept in touch with events in Turkey and elsewhere in the world by listening to the BBC Turkish Service.[158] Life here was at first a shock, 'because of the heat'.

When I first went to Jeddah I never thought I would stay so long. Early on a friend met me at the airport and I was surprised to learn that he had been there for as long as four years. I couldn't imagine. But I ended up staying eight years because conditions were very good and I enjoyed my stay there.[159]

Gül became fascinated by his job as a researcher for the Islamic Development Bank. It brought him into daily contact with bankers from all over the Islamic world while providing access to files on every country. 'We were given topics to write briefs on, and there was a lot of travel on missions to various places – Pakistan, Iran and Indonesia during its most difficult times. I visited these places at this stage of learning about the world.' With wars in Lebanon and between Iran and Iraq, the Kingdom of Saudi Arabia at the time was an interesting place to observe and learn about the Middle East. There was a great deal of fascinating and valuable inside information to be gathered about the Arab and Islamic world beyond Turkey.

Meanwhile life in Jeddah offered many real and substantial pleasures, especially those of challenging and well-rewarded work and a comfortable family life.

My best family life was there because we did all things together. Kübra was born there. We all went to buy bread, or collect water. We had to of course; if Hayrünnisa needed to shop or go to the dentist, I had to go too. Apart from work hours we were always together with each other. Back then, I liked that. Now back in Turkey all that has changed and we are too much apart. Jeddah has another feature since all the region is full of holy places and we were able to visit them frequently and this was very positive for us.[160]

Yet another plus was that there was a substantial community of Turkish people living and working in Jeddah at the time.

The Turkish community was two groups. There were a big number of construction companies with hundreds of thousands of Turkish workers. There was also a group of professors with PhDs and experts at the bank, so we never felt isolated. It was boom times of financial resources so we lived well, and it was friendly, and as a family we lived very comfortably.[161]

For Hayrünnisa too, life in Jeddah was a great improvement over conditions back home, and proved ideal for bringing up her growing family. Living in the land of the Prophet Muhammad and the holy sites of Islam added a special satisfaction. When their daughter was born in April 1985, Hayrünnisa's mother's mother suggested that she be named Kübra, not a traditional family name, but one derived from a poetic term suggesting 'sublime' and 'lofty' that is used to describe the first wife of the Prophet.

> Kübra was born in Jeddah. They are seventeen months apart. They are like twins. Ahmet was eleven months old and I was pregnant with Kübra when we went on Haj for the first time. Looking back now, I think Jeddah was an ideal place to raise children. There was no problem with catching a cold, they were in good health. There were good schools for education. In those days, Jeddah was much more developed than Turkey. Although not as beautiful as Istanbul, Jeddah was a new and comfortable place. For example, diapers did not exist in Turkey, but you had them in Jeddah. Same for baby food as diapers … Things were much better there than in Turkey. I remember taking diapers with me from Jeddah when we came here for the summer. Working hours were adjusted according to the heat so Abdullah Bey was at work by 7.30 a.m. and back home by 3.30 p.m. He may have also told you that people would take a nap after coming home, but the children and I would be bored at home and would want to be out by 5–6 p.m. immediately after having dinner. One of the things Abdullah Bey regrets about those years, as he still says, is 'how he could not sleep as much as he wanted in Jeddah'. However, from the point of view of spending time together as a family with the children, the time in Jeddah was very good. The same was true for education; we would speak Turkish at home and they would learn Arabic, English and French at the same time outside.[162]

It was in Jeddah that, despite local laws, Hayrünnisa learned to drive a car. After Friday prayers, the two of them would drive the green Honda out to a development area with roads but no built structures and Hayrünnisa would take the controls, practising so intently that 'as soon as we came back to Turkey she passed her test and got her licence first time'.[163] Hayrünnisa cheerfully admits that she didn't know of the ban on women driving in Saudi Arabia until after arriving.

As a person, I cannot stand it when things are forbidden. I had not heard that it was forbidden to drive in Jeddah. I remember very well how we went to the grocery store one day and Abdullah Bey went to the market and I was waiting for him with Ahmet in my arms when the car in front of us wanted to move out and I put Ahmet in the back seat and tried to pull the car out of the way slowly. All of a sudden, I remember fifteen to twenty people gathering around me. I did not understand what was going on, I was wondering why these people were staring at me. Abdullah Bey came immediately and told me that women are forbidden to drive and that that was why they were looking at me. This was my first encounter with bans in Saudi Arabia. This was the ban in Saudi Arabia, then there were bans in Turkey.[164]

For the most part, Hayrünnisa kept busy looking after the children and their education. Jeddah was ideal, she explained:

The children were learning to ride horses and to swim as well as three languages. I remember very well that the cook was Turkish because Turkish food was popular and, for that reason, they had brought a cook from Turkey. The school was owned by Princess Iffet, wife of the late King Faisal. Kübra started going to school at the age of three. I was very much involved. I used to go to their school very often. In fact, I attended Arabic classes in Ahmet's school for a while. I would go to school after dropping him off at his school. I was famous in Jeddah for my knowledge about the schools there. Foreigners, Turks coming there would ask me because it was well known that 'Abdullah Bey's wife will find out or know the best teacher, the best school'.[165]

Family evenings at home were regularly scenes of studying, with Hayrünnisa and the children working away at Arabic calligraphy and Abdullah preparing reports for the bank or writing academic papers.

During the Jeddah years, Abdullah Gül 'came to be known as a shy banking expert who spent his time reading; his wife was more outward socially'.[166] They returned to Turkey most years, but in 1985, his parents and brother came to visit them. Macit vividly remembers their 'lovely house in the city, not a compound', and the friendly Tunisian neighbours. He speaks of cheering himself by remembering the car journey between Medina and Jeddah. 'I had just finished university and started working with my father as a mechanical engineer, but I had no driving licence so *ağabey* did all the driving. I was so proud of him, and the countryside was unlike anything I had imagined.'[167]

At the time of his family's visit, Abdullah Gül was organizing plans to salvage the meat that he had seen wasted in Saudi Arabia as a result of the millions of pilgrims making ritual sacrifices. Astonished that so important an Islamic practice should waste so much valuable food, Gül looked for a working solution. 'With so many millions of sheep killed at the same time, I saw the meat going rotten with three or four million animals being slaughtered.' His plan was to set up a refrigerated transport chain from the slaughter sites, cleaned up to provide wholesome meat, to the port of Jeddah where ships would deliver the meat to starving Muslims in Africa and Afghanistan.

> So Turks became involved with bringing in the vets and the butchers, and they came to Jeddah for ten days. We would leave the bank and work with them – and the bank supported it! 'Let us take time from work to help distribute all that meat by establishing a cold chain', they all agreed. It started during my time there and I worked on it every year and it gave me great experience in working internationally.[168]

Even as he was gaining international experience, organizing practical solutions to obvious problems, the 'shy banking expert' was also reading and mastering the debates over Islamic banking and attempts to develop 'opportunities for those wanting to bank without interest', as he succinctly expressed the problem.[169] At the Islamic Development Bank and elsewhere, that problem was being addressed in terms of replacing the notion of earning variable interest on investment capital with the notion of making a profit from resale of a purchased commodity. A 'sharia-compliant' bank, for example, might extend a loan for a customer to buy a car and simply mark-up the price it then charges the customer for repayment by a certain date. In order to square the twin circles of development and investment while avoiding interest, such banks need to operate through financial instruments that entail ownership of products or things that can be sold on at an agreed, fixed profit.[170] The building boom throughout the oil-rich Gulf states and Middle East generally is one highly visible result.

His work in Jeddah was giving him insight into and experience of life inside the wider Islamic world, its limits and restrictions among which openings could sometimes be found. He gained personal experience of the difficulties and problems living within a theocratic state and could not help but contrast life in the Kingdom with life in the UK even as he gained insight into other Islamic states.[171] As one colleague put it:

> Jeddah was very international. There were Indian bankers and intellectuals from Indonesia and Malaysia that he talked with. There were many Indian Muslim intellectuals and they taught him about Iqbal.[172] Here Gül also saw all the problems and deficiencies of Saudi Arabia and the whole: the corruption, illiteracy, inefficiency, violence, civil disruption, the irrational use of resources, the extravagance. But he also saw the potential – the resources, the human power, the young – and he recognized a strong heritage that could be revived, but he was very clear about the problems.[173]

Apart from anything else, this 'comparative perspective on life in East and West' showed him the crucial need for more and better education in the Islamic world and in Turkey.[174] Although it had not been part of any plan, Gül's years in Jeddah proved to be both incentive and invaluable preparation for the next phase of his career.

A visit home to Turkey, 1991

In 1991, general elections were once again looming in Turkey as Hayrünnisa and Abdullah Gül were planning their annual visit home to see family in Kayseri and Istanbul. It was time for Ahmet Münir's *sünnet*, the circumcision ceremony that would mark his entry into manhood. The visit was supposed to be a shorter stay than usual. Despite his many years' experience of organizing and arranging long-distance trips, Gül was finding the pleasures of international air travel wearing thin with children and all their belongings to take care of. Aged eight and six, Ahmet Münir and Kübra had already proved to be good travellers, but the amount of personal luggage required for lengthy visits to Turkey could prove onerous. He recalls:

> This year I asked if we could go with little baggage and spend just two weeks before coming back. This was the year for my first son to have his circumcision. So we went to Kayseri for this important ceremony – *sünnets* and weddings are important for boys – girls only get the wedding! They are very important for the family. In modern life they go

to hospital but it is still a special day and the whole family prepares. So we went to Kayseri to my father's house. It was a time when there was an unstable coalition with general elections every few years. These were the lost years of Turkey![175]

Arriving home in Kayseri, Abdullah Gül was invited to run as candidate for Necmettin Erbakan's *Refah Partisi* ('Welfare Party', or RP) in the forthcoming elections: he accepted and won. What had started as a short visit home for Ahmet Münir's *sünnet* changed the course of Abdullah Gül's life and the future of Turkish politics. He would spend the rest of the 1990s serving his party and government, a delegate member of the Grand National Assembly representing his native city, experiencing the machinery of European democracy at first hand while representing Turkey's interests internationally in Strasbourg, and becoming an influential voice in foreign policy.

3

The Refah Years, Ankara
1991 to 1997

I n his work at the Islamic Development Bank, Abdullah Gül had been
addressing questions of interpreting the Muslim's place in the world from
very pragmatic directions and in very practical terms shaped by what was
actually going on in Islamic countries with autocratic regimes. Developing an
informed international perspective from his dealings with colleagues from
Malaysia, Pakistan and the Gulf countries, he became only too aware of the
injustices arising from zealous applications of traditional practices wrongly
or manipulatively attributed to Islam by authoritarian regimes when they
conflicted with democracy, prosperity and human rights.[1] As political scientist Hakan Yavuz observed, 'at the Bank, he became deeply aware of the
problems in the Muslim world, and was always uneasy about the prevailing
socio-political conditions.'[2] In London, but more forcefully in Jeddah, he had
learned to see how being a practising Muslim was not the same as being an
Islamist of the kind that sought to turn the clocks backwards by repressing
civil rights and advocating isolationism. Watching the Arab states fumble
with their oil wealth, he became more convinced than ever that states ruled
by authoritarian regimes using Islamic pretexts were not serving the best
interests of their people, which were better served under democratically
elected governments.

Invited – or perhaps more accurately, persuaded – by old friends to run
for election to represent Kayseri in 1991, Abdullah Gül shifted gears from
banking to politics. It was a career move that shocked some family members
but, as things turned out, greatly aided the party he joined. Signing up to
Erbakan's Islamist Refah Party was not obviously a wise move. The military

were no longer directly in control of the government, but governments were changing too often to be anything other than compliant with the wishes of the generals. And since the generals cast themselves as the protectors of Atatürk's secular legacy, joining an Islamic party likely to be closed down at any minute had obvious drawbacks. But it would be six years before that happened, and in the meantime Gül would prove adept at winning votes for himself and his party while gaining himself a reputation at home and abroad for honesty, his firm belief in democratic due process, and a commitment to improving living conditions for everyone in Turkey, especially those who had suffered from religious discrimination.

This was just the start of the 1990s, the 'lost decade' during which thousands lost their jobs amid repeated economic crises, and thousands more lost their lives through war in the south east. No fewer than eight coalition governments – interrupted by two brief periods of single-party rule – would fail to manage an already inflationary economy. Being weak and temporary, coalition governments repeatedly allowed the military unlimited financial resources on the pretext of waging war against the *Parti Karkerani Kurdistan*, the 'Kurdistan Workers' Party', better known as the PKK. Now an elected politician, Abdullah Gül began shuttling between Kayseri, Ankara and Strasbourg, remaining outwardly loyal to his party and its leader even as he began finding himself increasingly sceptical of Erbakan's methods and policies.

Turkey since the 1980 coup

While the Güls had been living in Jeddah, there had been four general elections in Turkey. Following the 1980 coup, new political leaders had emerged and new parties had come into being, often only to dissolve or morph, even as experienced but banned leaders remained active behind the scenes. Since the 1983 elections, the first to be held since the coup, Turgut Özal's Motherland Party (ANAP) had headed a series of governments that had set about loosening the restrictions initially imposed on political life by the National Security Council. In the run-up to municipal elections in 1984, the Grand National Assembly had agreed to allow back some of the parties that had been banned the year before – including Erbakan's Refah Party. As a result, ANAP held its majority with 41.5% of the vote, while the new *Sosyal Demokrasi Partisi* ('Social Democracy Party', or SODEP) led by the late Ismet Inönü's son, Professor Erdal Inönü, took second place with 23.5%. Süleyman Demirel, still banned from political life, was covertly heading the *Doğru Yol Partisi* ('True

Path Party', or DYP) which took 13.5%. That year Erbakan's resurrected Refah Party attracted a mere 4.5%.[3]

Adjusting to the newly formed parties had led to a rather odd set-up since 'a number of parties that demonstrably had a sizeable portion of the electorate behind them were not represented on a national level at all'.[4] Based on regional and national thresholds, the electoral system favoured large parties since any party failing to achieve a regional threshold saw the votes they had received taken away and distributed among the parties that did achieve this threshold. Tinkering with the system, Özal precipitated a constitutional referendum to allow former party leaders to return and adjusted the thresholds before calling for early elections in 1987. At these ANAP's majority dropped to 36.3% but kept its majority in the National Assembly since only Erdal Inönü's new party, the *Sosyaldemokrat Halkçı Parti* ('Social Democratic Populist Party', or SHP) and Demirel's DYP achieved the threshold, with 24.8% and 19.2% respectively.[5] Erbakan's RP improved on its previous count, taking 7.2%.

Two years later, in 1989, Turgut Özal survived a would-be assassin's bullet but not the growing evidence that the corruption charges that had been made against him were not simply political slander. In that year's municipal elections, Inönü's SHP came out on top with 28.3% and Demirel's DYP came second with 25.6%. With Özal's reputation disgraced, ANAP fell to third with only 21.9%, but it was enough to enable them to shift Özal into the safety of the president's office before leaving power. Once again, Erbakan's Refah increased its total, taking 9.8%.

A big decision

For Abdullah Gül, this was hardly an auspicious moment to abandon a career in international banking in order to join a minority party that, despite marginal improvements in gaining votes, seemed destined to lose. Among his close friends, Beşir Atalay was hotly opposed to his decision to return from Jeddah and advised against it, insisting that the RP 'was not a good place'. Atalay was working in state planning at the time, had become familiar with the workings of the government and had become an admirer of Özal and a critic of many of Erbakan's goals.[6] Why would a young man, one with a growing family, quit a highly paid job in international finance to enter such a political arena on behalf of a party that could not win enough votes to have any influence on what was going on? The decision was not easily made and was certainly not popular with several close members of the family. In so many obvious ways it made little sense to abandon a career and way of life that were intellectually challenging and socially stimulating, provided excellent international schools for the children, and guaranteed financial security for the family. Why would 'a shy banking expert who spent his time reading' give it all up for an entirely uncertain future in politics?

One answer is that lifetime habit of reading and the ways it was making him revise and develop his ideas about Turkey and its place in the future world. While living in Jeddah, Abdullah Gül had kept up with his reading even while learning to understand, better than ever, the problems of the decade. The BBC provided reasonably reliable world news, while books and periodicals from home kept him up to date with intellectual and political life back home in Turkey. Erbakan's RP may not have been doing well in the elections, but the 1980s had seen the emergence of an interesting new group of Muslim intellectuals writing about Turkey and producing new and challenging ways of talking about Islam and Turkish identity. Many of these were writers of his own generation and a shared provincial and edu-cational background: Ali Bulaç (born 1951 in Mardin), writer, publisher and founding editor of the national daily *Zaman*; Rasim Özdenören (born 1940 in Maraş), novelist and columnist for *Yeni Şafak*; Ismet Özel (born 1944 in Kayseri), inspirational poet and author; Ilhan Kutluer (born 1957 in Biga), professor of theology and author of books on faith and science; Ersin Nazif Gürdoğan (born 1945 in Eskişehir), engineer and columnist for *Yeni Şafak*; and Abdurrahman Dilipak (born 1949 in Adana), Islamist journalist and founding editor of *Yeni Devir*. According to cultural historian Sena Karasipahi, these 'Muslim Intellectuals' set about reclaiming and rede-fining 'Islamic values' through an 'intense and severe criticism and overall negation of Western civilization', often claiming that 'democracy, secularism, and modernism are not compatible with Islam'.[7]

Reading such arguments, Gül tended to disagree as he reflected on what he was learning about faith-based political systems from his work at the bank, and developing his own increasingly clear views on these questions from meetings and discussions with powerful figures and intellectuals from Islamic countries. His comfortable life in the Kingdom had not lessened either his intellectual interests, his sense of national belonging, or his memories of living in England where conditions were not as described by political Islamists. He was far from prepared to abandon modernity or Western civilization, and failed to be convinced that there were any necessary contradictions between his personal faith in Islam and his belief in the advantages of democratic government. He approved of how these writers maintained a sense of Muslim identity while continuing to engage their ideas with religious beliefs, values and ideals that he most often shared. But he also remained convinced that hostility to modernity and the West was misguided; religious faith as such is personal, while religiously inspired political ideals were usually neither practical nor realistic. Life in England and Saudi Arabia had taught him the difference between belief and facts on the ground. The democratic West promoted religious freedoms for all, while states founded on political Islamic agendas that curtail democratic rights and freedoms were failing to serve the best interests of their people in terms of development and wealth-distribution.

Friends back in Kayseri recognized how Abdullah Gül had been gaining experience and an international abiding that was shared by very few others. They came to regard him as someone who might, once again like one of the Young Turks of old, return from exile with useful knowledge gained overseas and bring it to the aid of Turkey. Some, like Sami Güçlü, still remained personally loyal to the *Büyük Doğu* ideal of avoiding political life, but even he happily joined with Mehmet Tekelioğlu, Bekir Yıldız, Irfan Gündüz, Şükrü Karatepe, Azmi Ateş, Bahaeddin Cebeci and other friends who all agreed that Abdullah Gül would be a perfect candidate to put some youthful energy into Erbakan's party in Kayseri. In company with some old friends and representatives of new business interests, including RP chairman Şaban Bayrak, Mehmet Tekelioğlu approached Abdullah Gül during his visit to Kayseri and asked him to run as Refah candidate. Erbakan was still attracting supporters, and the party needed some new faces and new ideas from a younger generation. Their persuasive energies at offering an opportunity for new political possibilities was doubtless a second reason that Abdullah Gül left his job to return to Turkey and represent his hometown.

A third reason for agreeing to run as candidate for Erbakan's RP in 1991, perhaps more abiding than the others, is a predisposition of character inherited from his family and its values as well as the culture of the very hometown he was hoping to represent. Alongside his wide and continuing intellectual interests, Abdullah Gül had a strong practical bent, a technician's frame of mind. Like his father he is good at, and enjoys, the challenge of solving problems. When there are organizational difficulties, like his father he understands the need to help all sides come to an agreement. Seeing waste resulting from the *kurban bayramı* in Saudi Arabia, he brought everyone together to redeem the meat, using modern methods to help Muslims just as Islam intended. When there were practical answers to existing problems, Gül was becoming skilled at spotting and bringing systems and agents together to realize them. Entering his forties, he had become adept at encouraging and organizing groups and campaigns on behalf of his beliefs. While friends in Jeddah thought of him as a quiet banker who read a lot, friends in Kayseri and Istanbul knew he had considerable experience at persuasive public speaking and campaign organizing. Although his early intellectual development owed much to the *Büyük Doğu* commitment to ideas rather than politics, the impulse to become a *babayiğit* and stand up for what he believed in had never really gone away. Perhaps now was the time to defend 'good ethics ... in a brave way', to return to Turkey with the needful experience, skills and knowledge that finally made it possible to 'go and tell them the truth and make them face reality'.

Having agreed to stand for election, the shy banker swiftly 'emerged as a vibrant personality who was, and is, motivated by his beliefs rather than personal ambition'.[8] Those beliefs and values had been shaped in Kayseri where public service and loyalties to the local community were deemed both virtues and duties. The neoliberalism of Özal's reforms during the 1980s had created an economy once again no longer able to keep up with its own growth, producing the worst inflation for years.[9] The economic chaos of the late 1980s was proving to be Özal's greatest failure. Gül had been gaining direct insight into the instabilities of the Turkish economy since 1985, when the Islamic Development Bank oversaw the foundation of Turkey's first Islamic bank, the Faisal Finance Bank, which assumed a mere 0.8% of the nation's commercial banking deposits through an alliance with MÜSIAD.[10] By then Gül had come to understand international finance and recognized how growth without adequate financial institutions was at the heart of many problems that were facing Turkey. According to economic historians Ziya Öniş and Fikret Şenses, 'the critical turning point in Turkish neo-liberalism was the decision in August 1989 to open up the capital account completely', since from then on, 'the Turkish economy was fully exposed to the forces of financial globalization'.[11] From discussions with analysts at the Islamic Development Bank at the time, Gül was all too aware that 'the Turkish economy was ill-equipped to deal with the forces of financial globalization', because chronic instability of the macro-economy, and inadequate regulation of the financial sector, had already produced what Öniş and Şenses describe as 'an economic structure characterized by pervasive rent-seeking and corruption'.[12] It was time to return home from Jeddah in hopes of being able to make a difference.

Kayseri and the 1991 elections

The decision to run for office in Kayseri was not easily made. Brother Macit recalls there were, unusually, long silences at home. Some family members were simply refusing to talk about the possibility of Abdullah quitting the well-paid position in Jeddah. For his own part, Macit had always wanted his *ağabey* to come home, but never thought he would do so in order to run for parliament. Ahmet Hamdi Bey also welcomed the thought of having the family closer to home once again; he also understood the perils, but was confident that his firstborn son was able to make up his own mind. Hayrünnisa was pregnant and not best pleased by the prospect of abandoning the advantages of excellent health care and family life available in Jeddah. Others kept their thoughts to themselves.[13] Abdullah Gül remembers his surprise and uncertainty over the invitation.

> When the general election was called, all my Kayseri friends – as well as friends from Istanbul – asked me to be a candidate. I was very surprised. At the time I was over the moon with my job, it was very comfortable. And I was following the country. I was reading the papers and in touch with my old friends, so there was pressure on me that I should become involved. My wife didn't want this. She didn't want to come back because she was happy in Jeddah. Life was comfortable there.[14]

Accepting the invitation would probably be a waste of time since the odds were well against Refah winning enough votes to count. At the time, the two thresholds were twenty-five percent within the province and ten percent within the country. With expectations of eight percent in Kayseri and nationwide, Erbakan's RP was unlikely to be sending any deputies to Ankara. Fully aware of the risks, but finding himself rather taken with the idea of pleasing his friends by running for office, Gül found another way of thinking about the odds of winning.

> I tried to convince my wife that I would not be elected in any case! But at least we will spend some time with friends, relax, and then go back to Jeddah. She held out and saw I was upset, but I said okay we would return. We went to Istanbul to take the plane to Jeddah and she saw that I was not happy and then she changed her mind and I got

permission. So the next day I went to Kayseri and became the first on the list of candidates.[15]

The slate of candidates being put forward for election by a political party would normally list the chairman's name at the top. But in 1991 the Refah chairman in Kayseri, Şaban Bayrak – who was now Macit's father-in-law – tactically broke with tradition. He boldly put Abdullah Gül's name at the top of the list and his own name in fifth place, creating a great deal of local gossip that swiftly made the young candidate a household name. 'So there was a fresh move within the party,' Gül recalls. 'The new generation saw me as representing them and we went and organized the first modern campaign in Turkey.'[16]

With friends from his university years, Abdullah Gül launched that 'first modern campaign' in Turkey by examining recent opinion polls, and by canvassing to find out what people wanted, then offering to help them when it was possible to do so, but promising no more than that.

> First my friends helped me understand recent polls from the regions and helped me understand what people wanted. This told me what I needed to say to appeal to the people. And so I learned and said all of these things. The real change in the party is that my voice was very much different; my statements convinced Kayseri people that they could trust me and believe what I told them. My academic background impressed them.[17]

Voters in Kayseri that year greatly admired the new young candidate for his honesty, noticing that he was already making well-informed arguments even if they sometimes proved critical of his party leader. 'He impressed voters with this evidence of his honesty since it was expected new candidates would be devoted to their party leader. But Abdullah Gül was openly critical, and this showed you could trust what he said.'[18] Ever hostile to the EU, Erbakan had long proposed a common market of Muslim countries, and had gone so far as to imagine them sharing a common currency. But from what he had seen and learned in England and Jeddah, Gül understood the folly of such a plan, and said so openly. Right from the start of his political career, he showed himself loyal to the party he was representing, but with open differences from the vision of its leader, Erbakan.

The party saw that the Muslim countries should come together. They were talking about this. TV in local areas started picking up on this. So when they asked me do we want a single money system and so on, my explanation was different. I told them that is not possible. What Erbakan is proposing is being exaggerated. Why not think of a Commonwealth like the British one? Muslim countries have independence and their own direction so why not solidarity? Look at Canada, Indonesia, Cameroon, Bangladesh – they come together and have special solidarity among themselves using their common history for their own benefit. So why not among the countries that were once the Ottoman states and were all together for many years? There are many countries and states that should not be enemies but in lively cooperation. This was convincing to them. But if you say *Milli Görüş* or talk of Islamic armies, people don't believe in it or want it. That is what the Kayseri people believed when they voted for me.[19]

Abdullah Gül's 'modern campaign' was such a success that Kayseri sent all seven of its Refah candidates to parliament that year, having taken an astonishing thirty-two percent of the provincial vote.[20] In the conservative industrial heartland, this new voter-friendly approach to politics, one that put people's interests to the fore while offering them no promises in outmoded language, had paid off well. The campaign tactics that had proved successful in Kayseri would be imitated and developed throughout the decade, bringing Refah to the centre of political power. At his first attempt, and in a very short time, Abdullah Gül had shown himself to be a popular, innovative and successful politician.

Politics and family life

Although Abdullah Gül's sudden change of career and return to Turkey were eventually welcomed by his family, it entailed a good degree of disruption to plans and moving about for a full year. Hayrünnisa admits: 'When the election results were announced everyone was cheering and happy, but I was crying.' She had arrived in Kayseri for Ahmet Münir's *sünnet* seven months pregnant with Mehmet Emre, her third, and was especially anxious at the sudden change in plans. 'When I was pregnant with Mehmet, I had a severe case of food poisoning and had to be hospitalized. You might say that almost all of Saudi Arabia knew of Mehmet. Because it was a food poisoning case, even

the Ministry of Health was involved and Mehmet was closely monitored to
ensure that he would be born healthy. There were concerns about the baby's
health because I was on medication.'[21] With Abdullah busy packing up his
office in Jeddah and moving his work to Ankara, everyone agreed with the
doctors that the best plan was for Hayrünnisa to stay in Istanbul among her
family and to deliver her next child there. Ahmet and Kübra temporarily went
to schools in Istanbul, while a private tutor came in to help them improve their
written Turkish. A month after Mehmet was born in November, Hayrünnisa
returned to Jeddah for ten days to pack up.

> We said our farewells to friends and went for a last *Umrah*. We could
> not take the children there, of course, but Mehmet was with us because
> he was a baby. We sold our furniture, things and car, so it was very busy.
> We were at Erenköy until September 1992. The children started school
> in Ankara in September, so we moved there. We stayed at Erenköy at
> most for a year. As you know, I was born in Istanbul and I love Istanbul.
> When in Jeddah, we used to discuss with friends 'whether it is better to
> live in Ankara or Istanbul'. I would always say Istanbul. I never thought
> or imagined that I would come to Ankara and live there for twenty years
> or that I would live in Ankara as long as I have and have a political life.[22]

Abdullah Gül recalls the astonishment of his colleagues in Jeddah when they
heard he was leaving: he was the first employee ever to resign from the Islamic
Development Bank since it had been founded in 1974. And he admits that
the transition back to Turkey was difficult at first, especially for the family.

> Hayrünnisa and the children were living in Istanbul so she could be
> close to her family with the new baby. I was moving between Ankara
> and Kayseri all the time, and travelling to Europe and other places. For
> the family this was not so good as life in Jeddah. In Jeddah my wife was
> on her own with the children eight hours every day, and for sixteen
> hours we were all together. And now sometimes I was away from the
> family for weeks at a time.[23]

With a clear sense and acceptance of a shaping destiny beyond her imagined
plans, Hayrünnisa was soon so happy to be home among her family with
a healthy new baby, and so busy helping Ahmet and Kübra with their new
schools, that nostalgic memories of life in Jeddah soon shifted to frustration

that Turkey was still so far behind in so many things. In their time away she had observed how some parts of Turkey had become richer and richer, proving the country's wealth and capacity. But in so many ways the people were still poor and the country lagging behind in education and health care. Together with the children she stayed on in Erenköy until the following September before moving to Ankara for the children to start schools there.

When I asked her if the big moments in her life – leaving school to marry someone involved in politics, moving to Jeddah, moving back from Jeddah – were all changes that she was initially reluctant to make, Hayrünnisa laughed and said that the 'big moments in her life' were her children, and that she was not 'reluctant' to do any of these things.

> We were in politics for many years. Counting from 1991, this is twenty-one years, going through various stages … We do not have control over this life, of course. One cannot determine things in life. Perhaps it is destiny or Allah's will. I think Allah prepares you for life in stages.[24]

For Hayrünnisa, the move home to Turkey was further evidence that her life took directions that were not so much beyond her control as beyond her imagined expectations. Some wishes had come true, but in peculiar ways, and that very fact suggested it was best to go along and learn as you went.

Although family life in Ankara would never return to the Jeddah pattern of being together for hours every day, Sundays were set aside for them all to be together. 'It is very easy to live in Ankara,' Hayrünnisa admitted:

> Compared to Istanbul, it is so much easier to live in Ankara as a city and in terms of lifestyle, but Istanbul poisons you so much that you still like to live in Istanbul although it is much more difficult to do so. I stayed away from politics maybe because from the outside, it looked artificial to me. It looked as if you had to seem different than yourself. I am a more realistic person. I like to say what I think. I could not hide my feelings very much. In politics, you may have to hide your feelings. My personality is such that I do not like to be in the forefront very much. I always defended what I thought to be right and if something felt wrong to me, then I always spoke the truth without being harsh.[25]

Alongside a sense that the big picture sometimes looks like destiny, Hayrünnisa is a 'strong woman' who has no doubts about what she thinks needs to be done and, like her husband, strongly feels the need to speak out. Having grown up to be suspicious of the political classes, marrying a young, dynamic and successful politician was clearly not going to prove easy. Her husband's remarkable success meant that everyone in Erbakan's party expected her to become visibly active in their organization, but this was not a role for which she had ever felt herself suited or for which she had prepared. Becoming a politician's wife would prove yet another step in a life she had never imagined for herself.

> At the first party meeting I attended, I realized that that was not my world and I did not remain silent and expressed my views. When I came home and told my husband, he said that I had done the right thing. Looking back, I see that what I defended back then is very relevant to what is happening in the world today. In other words, I could see the future back then. This was because I had lived abroad, in that world. The meeting was about the Middle East. I told them at that meeting that the lifestyle of the people in some of the countries in the Middle East, although they were Muslim countries, did not make the Muslims living in those countries happy. I said this because someone was making a speech, someone who was a foreigner was making a speech which did not reflect the realities of that world and I did not choose to remain silent, just listen and go home. I remember going to the wife of the late Erbakan and the wives of other leaders of the party and saying that what was stated in the speech was wrong, that it would harm our party and I did not agree with those views at all and that the realities of the world and the Middle East were not as expressed.[26]

Hayrünnisa's first foray into the arena of party politics never made the press, but the immediate response among party members so impressed her that it would be her last for a while.

> My opinion attracted a lot of attention, perhaps more than normal due to the fact that I was very young. From then on, we made a pact with my husband. I would take care of the house and the family. He would pursue his political career. I would not expect much from him in order for him to be successful. In fact, I had no time or opportunity to expect anything from him. I would be dealing with the education of the children and other things, but not joining party activities. Looking back

now, I see that I did the right thing because I have seen from friends and neighbours how they suffered for neglecting their children.[27]

While taking care of the children, Hayrünnisa herself returned to her studies, and her pursuit of education would soon bring her to media attention. Ardent in her belief in education, and especially education for women, by 1998 Hayrünnisa had become confident enough to take the next, previously unimagined step, and seek the spotlight that she had earlier endeavoured to avoid. In Jeddah, she had started taking lessons in English and had continued in Ankara. Having finally achieved her ambition of completing high school, university was next. Once again, a challenge had arisen, but this time she felt ready to face it directly.

In 1997, after the military had closed down Necmettin Erbakan and Tansu Çiller's government, the new secularist coalition of Mesut Yılmaz, Bülent Ecevit and Deniz Baykal set about enforcing regulations to counter the influence of Islam in education. In addition to restricting graduates of religious schools from attending universities, they also enforced a ban on women attending university wearing headscarves, a regulation that had previously been ignored. The headscarf ban 'struck a blow against conservative women who wanted to get ahead', as Nicole and Hugh Pope put it:

> More than 60 per cent of Turkish women cover their heads, and secularists never saw much of a threat in the traditional *başörtü*, the headscarf tied under the chin, worn mainly by rural women or immigrants in the big cities. But a new generation of young urban conservatives was no longer content with a traditional lifestyle. Unlike their mothers, the young women wanted access to higher education and to the public space. Instead of the *başörtü*, they wore the *türban*, tightly wound around their heads and covering their necks, incurring the wrath of Turkish secularists, who rejected their attire as the uniform of political Islam.[28]

Hayrünnisa was clearly among those being targeted, but was a few years older than most and in a position to protest the ban. On Tuesday 8 September 1992, together with her husband, their attorney and some journalists, Hayrünnisa set out to register in the Arabic Language and Literature Department at Ankara University but was 'unable to register because her photograph, required for registration, showed her wearing a headscarf'. Abdullah Gül took the opportunity to observe how 'the sad point is that if we were living in London or Paris today, my wife would not be faced with such an obstacle'.[29] Hayrünnisa refused journalists' questions, but soon followed through with a formal complaint to the European Court of Human Rights. She eventually dropped the case in March 2004, explaining to the press at the time:

> I launched a case because I wanted my 'education right' back. However, after this case, my husband first became the prime minister and then the foreign minister. As a result, this case became a political event … I decided myself to withdraw this case and gave instructions to my lawyer to give up the claim. When my husband became the foreign minister, I became both the plaintiff and the defendant of the case.[30]

Not all were convinced. Journalist Ilnur Çevik commented that 'her current move really boils down to a good public relations effort in Europe but no more'.[31]

Outside Turkey, secular wrath over a matter so seemingly trivial as what someone wears on her head may seem strange. Yet it is perhaps worth recalling how, in 1925, Atatürk himself had initiated legislation banning men from wearing the fez: within a year, 'twenty or so' death sentences had been pronounced for 'violation of the new hat law'.[32] Perhaps some of the antagonism towards the *türban* can be attributed to repressed memory and guilt over those deaths.

Starting a life in politics, 1991–95

The 1990s, Turkey's 'lost decade' of repeated economic crises, political corruption, and the escalation of the war with the Kurds, also witnessed the steady emergence of Refah as a party to be taken seriously. That was largely thanks to the efforts of Abdullah Gül and the younger generation within the party. Having observed how Turgut Özal had taken charge of the political scene after the 1980 coup by forming broad alliances, Gül and colleagues watched and planned as the old secular parties crumbled before the economic and political crises of the decade. They were ready to take over in 2002 with a new party and a programme of reforms that captured a broad base of electoral support. Meanwhile, by adopting Gül's approach to election campaigning during the 1990s, Refah went from strength to strength, delighting some and alarming many others.

There were plenty of cameras when Abdullah Gül arrived in Ankara, a young hero of the winning party. When he took his seat in the *Meclis*, the Grand National Assembly, he was one of the youngest members representing Refah. Although his signal campaigning success in Kayseri had not been equalled elsewhere, it drew him to the attention of the older generation of politicians from all parties. He was soon appointed deputy party leader with the job of speaking on behalf of Refah during parliamentary sessions. For Necmettin Erbakan and his old guard, here was a talent to promote: the party had increased its national vote and was all set to begin building on that success.

In the elections of 20 October 1991, Refah took seventeen percent of the national vote, only a few points behind Erdal İnönü's SHP in third place with twenty percent. Süleyman Demirel's DYP came out top with twenty-seven percent, while the Motherland Party (ANAP), now led by Mesut Yilmaz, came second with twenty-four percent. Through alliance with the ultra-nationalist supporters of Alparslan Türkeş, who had reformed in 1983 as the *Milliyetçi Çalışma Partisi* ('Nationalist Working Party' or MÇP), Refah sent no fewer than sixty-two delegates to parliament that year.[33] With Turgut Özal in the presidential office – still boasting of his alliance with George Bush in the First Gulf War – Demirel formed a coalition government with İnönü amid a wretched economy and with increasing 'terrorist' and military violence in the south east.

Political violence had also come back in new forms. Since 1989 a new terrorist threat had emerged from the Marxist-Leninist left in the form of *Dev Sol* ('Revolutionary Left'), a guerrilla organization that was assassinating judges, generals, admirals, policemen and retired officers. Since the return to civilian government in 1983, PKK attacks on government and military bases in the south east had escalated, leading to retaliation by the military who were aided by a number of licit, and covert, organizations. In 1985, Özal had inaugurated the paramilitary 'village guard' system (*Köy Koruculari*), arming local groups to fight the PKK. These had soon become 'semi-tribal bands settling scores with their enemies and expelling villagers who refused their protection.'[34] Although purporting to save the nation from 'terrorist' threats that were real enough, the army was not very popular and proving to be a drain on the economy. No longer visibly involved in electoral politics, the generals and officers were now defending the secular state from behind the scenes, providing tacit support to clandestine organizations such as the 'Gendarmerie Intelligence and Counter-Terrorism Centre' (*Jandarma Istihbarat ve Terörle Mücadele Grup Komutanlığı* or JITEM). With intelligence networks operating everywhere, the generals were keeping a watchful eye on the shifting among and between parties that followed the 1991 elections. No threat to them was Deniz Baykal's split with Erdal İnönü to revive the CHP since it promised, as the true heir of Atatürk's party, to defend the secular state. The presence of Necmettin Erbakan and his Islamist Refah Party in government was, however, a situation that needed to be monitored carefully.

The emergence of Refah in 1991 shocked many at the time, and it continues to worry many Turks today, marking, as it does, the penetration of Atatürk's secular republic by an openly Islamic party. Refah's early success certainly represents the increasing power of conservative Muslims who viewed the West with suspicion and had benefited least and suffered the most from the inflation of the Özal years. But inflation would continue through the 1990s, reaching a massive 150% at the end of 1994,[35] and the decade would prove to be one of rapidly changing unstable coalition governments. While dithering with the economy and largely impotent against violence, the 1991 government struggled to put through a series of reforms, some of them inherited from Özal's time, that included permitting the Kurdish language in certain circumstances, as well as allowing academic freedoms and freedom of the press. But the first coalition could not survive Özal's death in April 1993, which sent Demirel into the presidency and brought Tansu Çiller onto the scene as the camera-ready, surprise new leader of the True Path Party (DYP). With Mesut Yilmaz now leading Özal's Motherland Party (ANAP), and the recently revived CHP under Deniz Baykal, there were new faces at the helm of the political parties as the country prepared for the next municipal elections. These were held in March 1994 and the results confirmed secularist fears that Islam was on the rise. Erbakan and the RP campaigned with the slogan of promising a 'Just Order' (*adil düzen*) that would oppose communism and protect small business from the self-interest of state-supported monopoly capitalism.[36] Refah took 19.1% of the national vote. The best that Prime Minister Tansu Çiller could do to keep DYP in first place was a mere 21.4%, barely in the lead over Mesut Yilmaz and ANAP with 21%. The 'true winner' that year was clearly Erbakan.[37] Having dropped the earlier alliance, Erbakan was clearly better off without the ultra-nationalist Alparslan Türkeş and his supporters, who had relaunched themselves in 1993 as the *Milliyetçi Hareket Partisi* ('Nationalist Action Party', or MHP).

In 1994, Refah changed the face of Turkish electoral politics by winning such a large portion of the vote in municipal elections that it provided indisputable evidence of widespread support for a party promoting Islamic ideals.

Erbakan openly began demanding constitutional reform to remove article 24, which guaranteed the secular political system. Islamic nationalism had entered the political discourse. The urban secularists and press went wild. Winning control over six major cities, Refah had shown the strong alliance that could be produced among small businesses and the growing numbers of urban poor living just outside the major urban centres. Refah's success was partly the result of the voter-friendly approach pioneered in Kayseri, but was also the product of broad-scale grassroots organizing, especially among women who visited remote areas to inform people of their electoral rights. Refah women's groups were especially active among the conservative and sometimes illiterate poor who had moved into the massive clusters of often hastily erected buildings known as *gecekondu* that had spread around Istanbul, Ankara, Izmir and other major cities.[38] For its ideas and public face, Refah had attracted younger candidates nationally, and it was a group within this new generation of party delegates, Abdullah Gül and Recep Tayyip Erdoğan among them, whose ideas and approach brought the party even more shocking victories in the general elections of December 1995: that year Refah came top with 21.4%.[39] During the 1995 campaign, the party adopted a number of themes in elaboration of the 'Just Order' suggesting the early influence of the new generation, including 'social justice, domestic peace, regional equality, religious freedom, ethnic impartiality, respect for labour, interest-free economy and an end to corruption'.[40]

Refah's electoral victory in December 1995 confirmed the strength of their popular mandate, marking 'a true watershed in Turkish history'.[41] A party whose leader was calling for the end to the secular foundations of the Turkish Republic had taken the largest number of votes in the secular republic established by Atatürk himself. President Demirel had little option but to invite Erbakan to form a Cabinet, and his failure to do so was not entirely predictable. With 19.7% and 19.2% respectively, Yilmaz and Çiller were, however, unlikely allies and their coalition lasted barely four months before Yilmaz agreed to Refah demands for Çiller to be investigated on charges of alleged corruption. Indignantly resigning from the coalition, Çiller amazed everyone by then throwing her lot in with Erbakan and together this unlikely couple formed a coalition government on 28 June 1996. 'This alliance,' Abdullah Gül explained,

> was a very pragmatic solution to a particular moment – the most pragmatic solution! The political arena was full of intrigues at the time.

We called it 'The Byzantine Games'. This was a development of recent political culture, the times when there was no majority party. There were many parties working even more pragmatically to exclude Refah! So this was the most pragmatic solution for us.[42]

Tansu Çiller, for her part, also pleaded a pragmatic defence, explaining that while she was in favour of the secular state and 'not terribly fond of Refah, she believed that taking Refah into the mainstream of Turkish politics was the only way to maintain social peace and preserve democracy'.[43]

I remember watching Çiller and Erbakan's first joint television interview with friends in Istanbul. 'Amazing. It's as if Maggie Thatcher and Ronald Reagan have come together again. Not amazing, grotesque!' a boisterously left-wing friend observed. And I recall thinking that 'amazing' really was the more accurate term to describe seeing Turkey's first Islamic prime minister sharing the platform in alliance with a woman who so clearly admired Margaret Thatcher, a woman highly unlikely ever to have accepted second place to an Islamist. However amazing the Erbakan–Çiller alliance still seems, it nevertheless made Erbakan a powerful spokesperson for Islam in Turkey. 'At the time,' Abdullah Gül recalled, 'fanatic defenders of laicism felt threatened, but not those who were sincere defenders of contemporary secularism.'[44] The rise of Refah in the early 1990s was being watched ever more closely.

MP for Kayseri

Right from the election campaign that led to victory in 1991, Abdullah Gül was active in bringing about the party's years of political success. In Ankara, in addition to duties as deputy party leader, he was immediately appointed to a five-year term on the Planning and Budget Committee of the Ministry for Economic Affairs. He was also elected to represent Turkey on the Parliamentary Assembly of the Council of Europe (PACE), where his international background and ability to communicate fluently in English swiftly made him an energetic and respected player. His new jobs were suited to his ambitions and abilities. Gül set out to introduce a new world-view into Turkish politics. Turning aside from the myopic nationalist introversion that still held sway among many of the older generation in his party, he sought out better relations with the West and the Muslim world both, rather than only pandering to Western capital. From the start of his political career and throughout in his dealings with Erbakan, he insisted on a different approach to thinking about Turkey's relations with its neighbours and its role in the world, an approach in line with Özal's outward-looking neoliberalism that, far from turning its back on the West as Erbakan wanted to do, sought closer alliances.

> I came into politics out of the blue so went through a very rapid adaptation period. I was also involved in party issues and making the party position clear because they made me a lead deputy of the party to speak on behalf of the party in the *Meclis*. At the time, Refah was perceived as an Islamic movement that had nothing to do with contemporary values and democracy, so I was advocating what we really stood for. I said that we were religious people but we were at peace with democracy and contemporary values. I was among the prominent figures trying to transform the party to take the centre stage of politics. I had brought the modern election method into the party, so the party understood how they needed young people with dynamic ideas. We were not against Erbakan, but there was a generation difference and a different understanding of how to go – he was more classical and his understanding was more conservative than ours. For us, we were open to the outside world, and as people with faith we had a different intellectual perspective.[45]

These were differences that, in due course, would lead to the split from Erbakan and the founding of the AKP.

Once elected to office for Kayseri, Abdullah Gül immediately began taking most seriously his responsibilities to those who had elected him. Along with the other victorious Refah delegates from Kayseri, he quickly broke off ties with Alparslan Türkeş's party in Kayseri, a move that anticipated Erbakan's policy for the national party; it had been a tactical alliance and after the elections the MPs from Türkeş's cadres returned to their party. He kept in regular touch with the Kayseri community and visited most weekends.

Mustafa Boydak, today's director of the *Kayseri Sanayi Odası* (KAYSO), the Kayseri Chamber of Industry, came to know Abdullah Gül during the 1991 election campaigns. He recalls how, after election, Gül returned every week to meet with local community and business leaders to find out and help with their problems and needs. 'And whenever people came to Ankara from Kayseri he would help them in any way he could. He would even give them their bus fare if they were very poor and help find them jobs or whatever they needed. Sometimes there were disputes about land, and they brought him these, and he always sent them away happy with what he said.'[46] Boydak also recalls how Gül brought that same infectious optimism to his dealings with business leaders, inspiring them with confidence in troubled times.

> Kayseri at the time was experiencing only middle growth, thanks to Sabancı in part. It was already a top ten city for commerce and trade. But by 1991 growth did not happen rapidly. The coalitions were in power and rapid growth was not possible. Refah was not too powerful so there was little sudden progress after 1991, but people in Kayseri were happy with Gül. He was young. He was local. Every week he returned to Kayseri to talk and see what was needed; what were the problems. He was an honest speaker who didn't tell lies or make promises. His PR was very good and he built confidence.[47]

In Kayseri, growth had flattened off. Özal's economic reforms had benefited big holding companies like the Koç and Sabancı groups. Several Kayseri-based companies were also flourishing thanks to the construction boom taking place in the Gulf and other Arab countries. But by 1991, the local economy was stagnating even as the nation entered a recession and the banking system was in chaos. Access to new consumer goods, and credit to buy them, had changed the habits and expectations of many even as high inflation had weakened real earnings and brought poverty to the unemployed, especially those living on the edges of Istanbul and Ankara.

The 1980 coup had initially been good for business confidence in Kayseri as elsewhere. Once he came to office in 1983, Özal had ended traditions of state control over the economy and had agreed on a deal with the IMF that entailed shifting to decentralization, promoting privatization, encouraging export-driven industrial growth, and freeing the market from state controls.[48] As in other provincial industrial zones, the number and output of Kayseri's factories had grown rapidly during the later 1980s. Even while established industries like textiles were retooling and increasing production of denim for jeans, and carpets to meet vast new export demands, new factories with no obvious advantages for being there – such as locally convenient natural resources to exploit – were opening up and rapidly expanding to meet new domestic markets. Wood had to be imported from the Black Sea, but workshops and factories making furniture for the growing number of apartment dwellers were flourishing.

When Abdullah Gül entered parliament, production figures for Kayseri's furniture and textile factories may have been healthy enough, but all was not well locally or nationwide. Even as the economy continued to grow with hyper-inflation once more out of control, the gap between very rich and poor was widening rapidly. Serious urban poverty was becoming widespread even as new millionaires with their yachts graced the pages of the new celebrity magazines. Since the end of the 1980s, a massive tourist boom along the coasts was making construction companies, hotel owners and some local entrepreneurs wealthy. Foreign investors were now free to build in Turkey and huge, but often empty, luxury hotels started to appear in coastal areas. By 1995, about seven million foreign tourists were visiting Turkish resorts annually, contributing to uneven local development and erratic local wealth-distribution even as a booming black market in laundering foreign currency through empty hotel rooms emerged.

True to their reputation for being 'very business oriented', Kayseri businessmen in the early 1990s began seeking foreign currency in exchange for their goods, but remained sceptical about foreign investment practices and ownership of infrastructure. Orta Anadolu's dealings with Levi Strauss in the early 1980s had shown that it was possible to attract investment development loans from foreign investors without selling off the company to foreign interests, legitimate or otherwise. But many businessmen in Kayseri were still very uncomfortable with, if not piously opposed to, dealing with investors who calculated interest on loans.[49] And as if to confirm their views, the number of bankruptcies and closures of Turkish financial institutions had been on the rise since 1989.[50] In 1991, Turkey entered the first of four recessions that were to mark the decade.[51]

During his earliest visits to Kayseri that year, Abdullah Gül set about helping the business community to turn towards foreign markets without becoming involved in forms of foreign investment clearly linked to interest-bearing arrangements or black markets. His years of work with the Islamic Development Bank provided him with just the experience and knowledge needed to advise Kayseri businessmen how to engage with global markets without compromising their beliefs. Mustafa Boydak is certain that 'it was because of Abdullah Gül's advice and inspiration that Kayseri businesses turned from domestic production to international ambitions'. Gül encouraged them to follow Özal's neoliberal approach to foreign trade and investment, while keeping an eye on self-sustainable banking practices that would prevent capital leaving the region and country. The Kayseri business community was agreed on the moral need to avoid the corruption that could easily follow from rapid development financed through foreign investment. Gül, their MP, was eager to share his international perspective and understanding of so-called 'sharia-compliant' or 'participation' banking, which largely operates trade financing through mark-up funding – whereby the bank purchases goods and resells them at a simple, fixed mark-up – or forms of profit-and-loss sharing contracts, rather than debt-based financial instruments.[52] Ever self-reliant, Kayseri businessmen listened closely and set out to control their own financial systems as the key to stable growth.

During his first months in office, Abdullah Gül met with members of the Boydak family, whose businesses were suffering from the recession. The story of brothers Mustafa and Sami Boydak, and their six sons, is worth telling briefly since it illustrates the entrepreneurial spirit and achievement of the Kayseri business community, as well as their struggles, values and attitudes. In the 1950s, the two brothers moved from their hometown of Hacılar on the outskirts of Kayseri to the new industrial park, set up shop and for the next twenty-five years produced hand-made furniture to order. In 1976, after visiting trade fairs in Europe, the Boydak brothers returned to Kayseri with some new machines and started making furniture by mass-production techniques. During the 1980s, amid the rapid increase in the number of people moving into apartment buildings, their signature sofa-bed, the *çek-yat*, became a national bestseller. By 1991, the Boydak factory was making 1,500 sofa-beds every day.[53]

Meanwhile the next generation of Boydaks had been entering business. Sami's son, Mustafa Boydak – the current director of KAYSO with whom I spoke – was working at the time in middle management at HES Cable in Hacılar. Unlike the family-based Boydak furniture factory, Turkey's first electric cable company had been founded by a consortium of local business-men forming a joint company. HES Cable 'enjoyed meteoric success in the 1980s on the back of major public investments in Turkey's infrastructure'. In 1985, however, HES took out credits to expand production, thereby 'skirting the traditional Islamic prohibition on debt-based financing'.[54] Not all of the founding partners were comfortable with this decision and arrangement, and in 1991 the company joined with the Boydaks to form one of Turkey's earliest participation banks, Anadolu Finans.[55] Islamic banking was new in Turkey. These were pioneers and their pious undertaking was both brave and risky. The new bank could hardly be expected to have solved the problems of that year's recession. Mustafa Boydak recalls how:

> the Boydak family bank was initially called *Anadolu Finans* and was an early participation bank. In the 1991 crisis they were forced to sell off sixty percent of their shares [in the family business], but in 1999 were able to buy the company back from former partners. This is how we learned to work together.[56]

Although inflation, recurrent recessions and banking problems would continue, the Boydak group continued to grow through the 1990s, generating subsidiary companies and eventually absorbing others, including HES Cable, into Boydak Holding. Growth followed from continued innovation. In 1993, the furniture company 'revolutionized its marketing' by establishing 'its flagship brand, Istikbal ("Future"), with a catalogue and fixed prices applied across the country'. In 2000, 'Boydak created a second more up-market brand, Bellona, to compete directly with imported furniture. Bellona soon became the country's second-biggest furniture seller after Istikbal.'[57] By 2004, Boydak Holding had grown into 'a conglomerate comprising 22 companies and an export network spanning 70 countries', with more than 12,000 employees and a turnover of US$1.2bn.[58] It has continued to grow since, and offers as good an example as we are likely to find of how the Kayseri business community, often referred to as 'Islamic Calvinists', have led the way in Turkey's economic boom in the new century.

According to Mustafa Boydak, Abdullah Gül provided 'psychological encouragement' at moments of crisis, a characteristic that has made him an inspirational leader. In 2001 the Turkish currency lost half its value, and the government set out to regulate the banking sectors.[59] 'Business life was terrible,' Boydak explained, but:

> Abdullah Gül came to Kayseri with a group of MPs to express their concern. With my brother I met with them and explained how bad things were. Normally we paid employees their salaries on the tenth of the month but by the fifteenth we had no money and couldn't afford to do so. Gül asked how this came about and we explained that factory production was down by over fifty percent. At this point, my brother

started to cry and Gül was very clearly affected by this, declaring strongly 'This day will pass! You are a fine family and will prosper!' This kind of psychological encouragement is a key to Gül's power and importance as a leader who offers sympathetic understanding rather than commands.[60]

As the economic crisis worsened, the participation banks struggled to stay alive. Of the five such banks at the time, Anadolu Finans suspended activities while the others were being hard pressed by their depositors making constant withdrawals. A parliamentary committee made up of Abdullah Gül and several other MPs was appointed to investigate the participation banks.[61] Mustafa Boydak recalls:

> Our bank was not being managed properly and the government refused to approve selling it off. With my brother I went to Ankara to see the MPs involved. One of them, despite being a Kayseri MP, was haughty and announced that, 'Our job is bad enough and you are making it worse!' We then went to Abdullah Gül but were very depressed and nervous following our reception by this other MP. I was so worried and nervous I smoked the first cigarette of my life! Gül listened to us and helped us talk through and understand the problems we were facing. Even so, we needed approval from the Treasury Authorities and were expecting that we would have to go into receivership. The visit to Abdullah Gül was for information about how best to do this, but he insisted that the bank would survive if we adopted suitable management strategies. He told us 'Relax! The bank will be fine if you change your management.' We did, and ten years later it is a major success. So Gül is a major booster and psychological support in times of anxiety and trouble.[62]

Having survived the 2001 financial crisis, in 2005 Anadolu Finans combined forces with another participation bank, Family Finans, owned by the Ülker Group, 'the worldwide giant in biscuit, chocolate and various food products', to form *Türkiye Finans*.[63]

Providing 'psychological support', Abdullah Gül helped inspire the Boydaks and other Kayseri businessmen at the very time that Kayseri was emerging as the leader of the 'Anatolian Tigers'. These are provincial cities that, by the mid-1990s, had been singled out for managing impressive growth rates despite the weak national economy.[64] By 2004, the economic power of Kayseri and other cities such as Bursa, Denizli, Gaziantep, Kahramanmaraş, Kocaeli, Konya and Malatya, had given Turkey 'the fastest economic growth rate of all OECD economies'.[65] Kayseri's slow but steady march to economic success during the early 1990s can be attributed to the entrepreneurial and communitarian spirit of the business community, one based on belief that the virtues of hard work and community responsibility take precedence over accumulation of wealth for its own sake. Although no businessman himself, as his failure to sell soda had long ago taught him, Gül understood the underlying financial problems and was otherwise entirely in sympathy with their conservative values and social imperatives. When I asked him about working with the Kayseri business community during the 1990s he said:

> During discussions between Turkey and the EU, some researchers from the EU came to Kayseri and conducted research there and they came up with a study about 'Islamic Calvinists'. I liked that. Business people in Kayseri are conservative people with religious families. They are big on tradition but at the same time open to the outside. They look out to the world; that is the main characteristic of the city. At the same time, the people are independent and practice self-help among themselves. For instance, although Erciyes University is a state university and the state is supposed to finance it, Kayseri people are very philanthropic and they spent almost as much as the state on buildings and the faculty. This is how they think about the city and about business.[66]

When the European Stability Initiative report in question was published in 2005, Abdullah Gül was soon quoted in the European press for declaring himself 'a proud Islamic Calvinist'.[67] The report itself, the latest in a line of Western rediscoveries of how important a model for the country could be found in Kayseri, was highly enthusiastic about the way the city's growth and business community showed once and for all that Turkey was a viable partner for Europe. The twenty-first-century European observers measured their assessments against those made by van Velsen back in 1976 and were highly impressed to discover how the local Muslim community had embraced commerce and industry to prove themselves national and international leaders well beyond the expectations of three decades ago. As every educated Turk knows from the Ottoman past, Islam has never been a barrier to commerce and international trade. What Europe was learning was how successful conservative Turkish Muslims were becoming at industrial production and global finance systems.

Ankara and Strasbourg, 1991–94

During his first years in parliament, as much as he was able to help boost the spirits of Kayseri's businessmen, Abdullah Gül found himself learning more about national difficulties, but largely unable to do very much about major problems. He was in the government, but not in power. In Ankara, he was appointed to the Planning and Budget Committee where, from what he had learned during his years in the Islamic Development Bank, he could see that Turkey's difficulties were tangled with global trends about which there was little that he could do. Reading the reports, listening and discussing, his work on the committee taught him how much of an intractable mess the Turkish economy and banking system was in. It also confirmed his belief that many of the underlying problems resulted from decades of political mismanagement and corruption made possible through inequities in the electoral system as well as loopholes and political inequities built into the constitution produced by the 1980s coup.

With no clear economic policy, the Demirel–İnönü coalition Cabinet proved incapable of solving the rising gap between rich and poor. The year 1991 had begun with general strikes and the financial drain of the First Gulf War.[68] Coalition Cabinet ministers looked after the financial interests of their party supporters while leaving the military to its own devices; parliamentary delegates could do no more. Driving the economy further downhill, the military budget to pay for 'security' operations against the PKK continued to grow, only proving the ineffectiveness of the policies of the government and military high command as the violence continued. Heavy-handed and often clandestine operations by the military against Kurdish 'insurgents' regularly backfired. 'The army fought the PKK, but also burned villages and tortured their residents before forcing them to flee.'[69] The government seemed worse than powerless as the media broadcast scenes of excessive military violence.

Back in the summer of 1991, just as Abdullah Gül and his family were arriving in Turkey for their son's *sünnet*, the army assassinated the Kurdish leader Vedat Aydın in Diyarbakır, where his funeral turned into a riot during which government soldiers fired into the crowd, killing dozens.[70] A year later in August, army forces razed the entire Kurdish town of Şırnak in retaliation for a PKK attack. Meanwhile, the leftist guerrillas of *Dev Sol* continued targeting right-wing judges and Islamic anger started to boil over. The assassination of investigative journalist Uğur Mumcu on 24 January 1993 confirmed the suspicions of many that, in addition to the elected government, a secretive 'deep state' of generals, judges and politicians – some of them retired – was at work behind the scenes, protecting the best interests of the secular republic, and that they were in command of covert tactical forces. It had been widely rumoured that the assassinations of eminent Kurdish activists – including the writer Musa Anter in September 1992, and the union leader Zübeyir Akkoç in January 1993 – had been carried out by armed commando cells working in concert with this 'deep state'. It was certainly public knowledge that Mumcu had been investigating just such claims when he was killed by a car bomb. Once again, violence was breeding violence. In July 1993, thirty-five people were killed in Sivas when an angry rightist mob set fire to a hotel where Aziz Nesin – an Alevi and a socialist writer who had translated sections of Salman Rushdie's *Satanic Verses* into Turkish – was scheduled to speak. The hotel quickly became a symbol for Alevis of the discrimination they have suffered, while exemplifying how political and religious violence remained in fashion throughout the 1990s, Turkey's 'lost decade'.

The Council of Europe

Powerless in the face of Turkey's domestic turmoil, Abdullah Gül found his earliest years in government also bringing him face to face with Europe at a time when European politicians were trying to make sense of the dissolution of the USSR and the former Yugoslavia. Since 1989, Turkey's bid for entry into the European Community had been on hold, but Gül was firm in his belief that the debates in Europe offered models of democracy that Turkey needed to understand and emulate. Here in European democracy, rather than *Milli Görüş* nationalism and Erbakan's vision of an economic union of Muslim countries, was a successful federation of different countries with different cultures, religions and resources, who were actively combining mutual interests despite the recent past of a terrible war. In Europe, democratic reform and the rule of law were bringing prosperity and freedom from violence. Gül understood all too well how Europe did not always live up to its own standards, especially with regard to Muslims. Yet the European model offered better ways to learn how to advance the interests of the Turkish people than could be found in any of the existing Islamic states.

On 3 February 1992, Abdullah Gül was delighted to be formally appointed a representative of Turkey on the Parliamentary Assembly of the Council of Europe (PACE). This was a post he would hold until September 2001, during which time he 'was the window of his party to the outside world'.[71]

> When I was elected for Kayseri, the parliament appointed me a delegate to PACE, we were twelve from Turkey I think. However, I was alone representing Refah, and the youngest of the Turkish delegation; many of them were very prominent politicians. And this was the first time that Refah was represented in Europe. I was very active because in those years there was the war in the Balkans. I used to talk a lot on these issues to the Assembly and made many friends, some are still friends and remember me. I learned many things there and it helped with my political development, understanding how democracy can work. I agreed with the policies of the Council and believe in their principles of human rights, the sovereignty of law, transparency of government, political pluralism – I have always supported these ideals.[72]

Since its foundation in 1949, the mission of the Council of Europe has been to bring the countries of Europe into agreement on standards for human rights, rule of law, democracy and cultural cooperation. Established on a treaty agreed between member nations, the Council is perhaps best known today for operating the European Court of Human Rights that enforces the European Convention on Human Rights. The Council is formed of two houses, the Committee of Ministers – composed of governmental deputies – and the Parliamentary Assembly. With only investigative and advisory powers, the Assembly represents member states through delegates drawn from democratically elected members of their national parliaments – who must include members of oppositional parties. With his excellent command of English and his international experience in Jeddah, the new MP for Kayseri was his party's obvious choice to join the team of representatives from Turkey.

Taking his place as a member of PACE for the first time in Strasbourg on 4 February 1992, Abdullah Gül at once made his name known to other members of both houses, the Parliamentary Assembly and the Committee of Ministers. During an opening joint session at which the Committee of Ministers offered oral answers to questions put by national representatives,

Gül tabled a question directly aimed at the central ideals of the Council itself. With its declared promotion of democracy, why, he asked, had the Council remained silent about the military coup in the former European colony of Algeria? The reply was not recorded, but Gül's question is and shows how swiftly he began sharpening his rhetoric.

1. Recalling that the Algerian people realised their first free and multi-party general elections to choose their democratic representatives;
2. Recalling also that both this democratic process and the free will of the Algerian people have been blocked by a violent military intervention;
3. Bearing in mind that the Council of Europe is an organisation mainly concerned with human rights and democracy, and with the violation of the right to self-determination of people even outside Europe,
4. To ask the Chairman of the Committee of Ministers,
   a. Why has the Council of Europe kept silent in this matter, a silence that was an implicit approval of the military coup;
   b. Whether the Council of Europe supports free elections and democracy, or should we keep quiet when military coups and juntas suit us;
   c. What action does the Council of Europe plan to take to start the democratic process in Algeria.[73]

At his first appearance before PACE, Gül announced himself to be an independent and critical observer of the way that Europe was not quite managing to achieve its own ideals in respect of promoting democracy in former European colonies. This was a position he would reiterate tirelessly in Strasbourg. At the same time, Gül also found a natural place for himself as a member of two committees, Rules of Procedures, and Culture and Education. On the latter, he was able to exercise his long-held commitment to promoting culture, and on the former he was able to learn how an intergovernmental organization such as the Council was constituted and operated within its own rules.

Abdullah Gül's regular if sometimes mundane tasks as a member of the Committee of Rules of Procedures included confirming the records of representatives, and their substitutes, making sure not simply that they were who they claimed to be, elected members of parliament, but that each national delegation included representatives of an opposition party. A founding member of the Council, Turkey sent twelve representatives, the same number as Spain and Ukraine, but fewer than the eighteen each sent by France, Italy and the UK. Given its imperial Islamic history, followed more recently by a military coup not entirely unlike that of Turkey in 1980, Gül became especially interested in learning about Spain, with its Islamic past, and how more recently it had recovered from the Franco regime to take its place as a European democracy. Meanwhile, the standing job of the Committee of Rules of Procedure offered him more than formal gate-keeping duties, since its general function is to update and maintain the integrity of the Council's statutes. This was a task very much in line with Gül's long-standing interest in questions of constitutionality, offering the chance not only to study those statutes in detail, but to observe and comment on their efficiency as well as their shortcomings. In March 1993, he was among the team that prepared reports on reforming the Council and revising its statutes.[74] Their recommendations were adopted two months later.[75] Abdullah Gül had become part of the continuing historical process of European self-definition.

In many ways, Gül could not have joined PACE at a more intellectually exciting and politically challenging moment. The end of the Cold War had generated new nation states formed from the break-up of Yugoslavia and the Soviet Union. Many of them were eagerly applying to be accepted into the European Community. In the early 1990s, Turkey emerged as a powerhouse of stability amid post-Cold War turbulence.[76] The big debates at Strasbourg concerned who was and who was not European; what was and what was not a democratic European state. In September 1992, a lengthy report was presented to the Assembly by the Committee on Political Affairs exploring 'The Future of European Construction' as a question of how Europe might expand beyond its traditional 'Western' borders.[77] In the following months Gül worked with groups to sharpen that focus with specific resolutions regarding Europe's Muslim populations. Discussions in Strasbourg provided insight not only into how the Council of Europe managed its constitutional affairs, but also how Europe was engaged in the complex and challenging struggle to define itself faced with a flood of applications for membership. Through research and consultations with working parties, Gül's work at PACE brought him direct involvement in shaping the European debate over democracy and the constitution of Europe itself.

On 7 May 1992, Abdullah Gül presented his first formal motion to the Assembly and, once again, it challenged the Council to live up to its own self-defining standards, particularly with regard to protecting the lives of Bosnian Muslims. The Socialist Federal Republic of Yugoslavia had formally ceased to exist as of 27 April; the next day Serbia and Bosnia dropped 'Socialist' to form the Federal Republic of Yugoslavia. Under Serbian command, there were thousands of soldiers from the former national army still active in Bosnia-Herzegovina. On behalf of fifteen signatories, Abdullah Gül's first motion before the Assembly proposed that 'the special guest status of Yugoslavia should be withdrawn' because of 'the unceasing violence and bloodshed in Bosnia-Herzegovina by the Yugoslavian National Army and the irregular forces which it supports, despite declarations of 15 April 1992 and 1 May 1992 as well as the United Nations Security Council Resolution 749 (1992)'.[78] Although 'Yugoslavia' no longer existed, no one would have failed to recognize that Serbia was the target, so Gül's proposal to withdraw 'special guest status' was not simply a procedural matter of concern to a member of the Committee of Rules of Procedures, a clerical issue of keeping the records straight. It was also a call for action over the continuing slaughter of Bosnian Muslims.

In response to Gül's efforts, the Committee of Ministers were able to sidestep the question of eligible membership by reaffirming their policy of seeking to establish 'official contacts' with Croatia and Slovenia, while hoping to open contacts with Bosnia-Herzegovina 'if developments permitted'.[79] Nothing was said about Serbia for the time being, but only a few weeks later, on 30 June, the Parliamentary Assembly passed a resolution granting the parliaments of Slovenia, 'together with that of Croatia ... special guest status within the Assembly', while also recognizing the sovereign independence of Bosnia-Herzegovina. The June resolution even went so far as to condemn 'the authorities of Serbia' for 'the denial of fundamental human rights and freedoms to ethnic Albanians in Kosovo, and to Hungarian, Muslim and other minorities on the territory of Serbia', while also endorsing the United Nations sanctions on 'the Federal Republic of Yugoslavia (Serbia and Montenegro)'.[80] But Bosnia and its Muslim populations continued to slip from official notice. Beyond condemning attacks on relief convoys 'by the authorities of Serbia', the Assembly 'reaffirm[ed] that the crisis in Bosnia-Herzegovina ... constitutes a serious threat to peace and security in Europe'.[81] The next day, however, PACE did accept a recommendation to establish 'an international court to judge war crimes' to be 'convened under the auspices of the United Nations', but in the most general terms, referring only to crimes committed during 'recent conflicts'.[82] Abdullah Gül was learning how democratic due process was a matter of patience and keeping up the pressure.

Undaunted, Gül pressed the point that recent embargoes against Serbia were insufficient; direct support for the Muslims of Bosnia also needed to be on the agenda. On 1 February 1993 when the next session of PACE opened in Strasbourg, he sent a question to the Committee of Ministers for oral answer:

> To chairman of the committee
>   Mr GÜL,
>   Noting that, from the very beginning of the Yugoslavia crisis, he has displayed firm support for Croatia and Slovenia, but that he has not given the same support for Bosnian Muslims,
>   To ask the Chairman of the Committee of Ministers, how he can explain this paradoxical position.[83]

Whatever the discussion on that occasion might have been, the formal response appeared two days later when the Assembly passed a concise and fully informed resolution condemning 'the massive and flagrant violations of human rights in the territory of the former Yugoslavia, committed mainly by the Serbian militia in Bosnia-Herzegovina'. In response to concerns for the Bosnian Muslims, the February resolution opened with specific details, declaring:

> profound consternation ... at the perpetuation of crimes against humanity such as the murder of innocent victims, concentration camps, torture, the systematic rape of women belonging to minority groups, and in particular to the Muslim population, as a deliberate means of destroying these minorities, 'ethnic cleansing' and the deportation of entire populations.[84]

Without naming guilty parties, the resolution nevertheless adopted language sufficiently precise to guarantee that the Council of Europe had acknowledged its constitutional mission to 'provide legal enforcement mechanisms' to bring these specific 'crimes against humanity' to trial.[85] In September that year, further resolutions were passed addressing the refugee crisis and the special situation of women and children in the former Yugoslavia.[86] In the same month, PACE responded to a United Nations Security Council resolution concerning 'setting up an international tribunal' for prosecuting crimes 'committed in the territory of the former Yugoslavia since 1 January 1991'.[87] Abdullah Gül had not been alone in his efforts, but among his first major achievements as a member of PACE was being part of the team that advised on establishing the International Criminal Tribunal for Yugoslavia, set up by United Nations Security Council Resolution 827 in May 1993, and scheduled to complete trials by 2014.[88]

In 1993, while thousands of Bosnian refugees were still arriving in Turkey, Abdullah Gül continued to encourage European efforts on their behalf.[89] He also joined multinational efforts to defend the human rights of co-religionists in other areas. He was among a group that proposed a motion condemning the deportation of Palestinians from Israel.[90] Advocating on behalf of Muslims enabled him to keep faith with his own beliefs and principles while also being responsible to Erbakan and his party with its Muslim supporters. But he was also a representative of Turkey and that was often proving difficult. When Gül first joined PACE, Turkey was under close scrutiny by the Council regarding its human rights record and its war against the Kurds. A resolution adopted on 30 June 1992 on the 'Situation of human rights in Turkey' had been highly critical, and an embarrassment for the Turkish representatives.[91] Gül disapproved of government-supported military activities against ordinary people in the name of fighting the PKK, and disagreed with every position that branded all Kurds terrorists, but was not yet ready to break ranks with his party or colleagues in Strasbourg. In April and again in October, he joined the other delegates from Ankara when they walked out of the Assembly during readings of motions on the situation of the Kurds in Turkey. The second motion was especially scathing of 'the massive violation of human rights by Turkish security forces against the Kurdish minority', recording that: 'A violent assault, launched by the Turkish army and paramilitary forces on 21 and 22 March 1992 upon the Kurdish populations in and around the towns of Cizre, Şırnak and Nusaybin in south-east Turkey, is still in progress.'[92] Further embarrassment followed in October when a written question was put to the Assembly asking whether the June resolution on human rights 'should lead to ex officio action by the Committee of Ministers' that would censure the Turkish delegates.[93] The Committee took no action on this proposal, but representing Turkey was not always pleasant or easy when it meant seeming to approve of violence.

Abdullah Gül has never supported armed violence of any kind. He was deeply critical of Turkey's military actions against the Kurds and soon broke ranks with his Turkish colleagues in Strasbourg. In November, he conspicuously refused to sign their motion concerning the 'Fight against the PKK's terrorism in Europe'.[94] Ever an ardent supporter of the fight against the PKK itself, Gül has been equally loud in voicing his criticism of malpractices of the security forces in this struggle, while insisting that the solution could only be achieved through democratic reforms. On other issues, he generally supported the national front, signing on to efforts to end pollution in the Black Sea and to condemn Armenian incursions into Azerbaijan.[95] While working on help- ing Europe redefine itself, Gül was being forced to think hard about Turkey in terms of European standards and the possibilities for change. Supporting his nation's military violence against the Kurdish people was as unthinkable as promoting clean fisheries was crucial.

Abdullah Gül's work with the Committee on Culture and Education also allowed him to pursue intellectually challenging questions of concern to Muslims in Europe concerning their status and the challenges they faced. Between January and July 1993, he helped prepare team reports and draft rec- ommendations that were adopted in September on the 'Fight against racism, xenophobia and intolerance'.[96] Gül became directly involved with debates concerning the place and role of culture, matters that had long interested him. He assisted the Assembly with research and drafting reports aimed at promoting cultural cooperation and ethical journalism.[97] He learned how Europe regulated international sports events, and about attempts to improve the condition of young people and gypsies throughout the 'new Europe'.[98] As one close colleague put it, 'PACE was his real school!'

> After the years in Saudi Arabia, he starts coming to Strasbourg and follows the European debates. He followed the nature of their agenda and the terms of debate in Europe and found this very interesting. He made close friendships with many European politicians on all sides. It was a big learning experience. When he became prime minister in 2002, he had plenty of experience: eight years in Saudi and ten in Europe.[99]

The continuing rise of the Refah Party

For Abdullah Gül and other members of Refah, 1994 was another year of signal victory. Their grass-roots style of campaigning had given them control over all the major municipalities in the March elections, most notably bring- ing Recep Tayyip Erdoğan into power as Mayor of Istanbul while Gül's old friends Şükrü Karatepe and Bekir Yıldız became provincial and municipal mayors in Kayseri. Nationwide, there was no longer any doubt that a growing majority of conservative Muslims was coming to dominate electoral politics. The secular and military establishment trembled at the prospect of increasing religious power and what it might lead to, holding informal meetings behind closed doors to discuss the future: a hostile press encouraged fears that Turkey was becoming an Islamic state, a theocracy like Iran, where women would all have to cover in public and drinking *rakı* would become a crime.

Events leading up to the elections had once again brought Turkey's standards of democracy under censure and diplomatic embarrassment to Gül and the other Turkish delegates. In January 1993, the Constitutional Court in Ankara had closed down the pro-Kurdish *Halkın Emek Partisi* ('People's Labour Party', or HEP) for suspected links with the PKK. By May, its leading members, including Leyla Zana, had rapidly regrouped to form the *Demokrasi Partisi* ('Democracy Party', or DEP). On 2 and 3 March 1994, less than three weeks before the municipal elections, six DEP deputies were arrested on charges of advocating Kurdish separatism. In mid-April, a mere two weeks after enjoying Refah's victories in the Turkish local elections, Gül was back in Strasbourg battling proposals to withdraw diplomatic immunity from the Turkish delegates, an action that would oblige them to withdraw from Assembly meetings. Gül and his colleagues swiftly responded and their status remained intact. When, however, the Constitutional Court in Ankara closed down the DEP that June, and brought charges against six members that would result in death penalties, the Council of Europe started to build a case censuring Turkey for its violation of democratic and human rights.[100] In 2002, the European Court of Human Rights finally brought judgement, declaring the closing of the DEP to have been contrary to the European Convention on Human Rights.[101]

On such issues Abdullah Gül found himself in a quandary. He was well accustomed from his student years to facing opposition and hostility; but what if the accusations he was facing as a representative of Turkey were correct? Turkey really did suffer from an unworkable electoral system that made a mockery of democracy. How was it possible to represent national interests when there was so much about Turkish politics that was not only distasteful but contrary to his deepest beliefs in democracy and conciliation before violence? In Strasbourg, he distanced himself from the official position of the Turkish state when it came to supporting military action and refusing to negotiate with Kurdish representatives, at the same time deploring the actions of the PKK as much as those of the Serbian militias.

In Ankara, the practice of using the Constitutional Court to close down parties and silence minority groups was but one of many features of Turkish political life that he disliked and hoped to change. And he knew it was the kind of change that only constitutional reform could achieve. Less immediately tractable to constitutional change, the Kurdish issue could not be properly addressed until the fighting stopped: but challenging the apparently autonomous authority of the Turkish army at this stage would be both futile and personally dangerous. And not all problems were home grown. He watched as the Erbakan–Çiller coalition government's 'new stability' programme of economic reforms failed even to address the systemic failure of Turkish banks to cope with 'the vagaries of financial globalization'.[102] International confidence in the Turkish banking sector crashed in 1994 from 'investment grade' to 'risky', leading to a massive thirty-eight percent devaluation of the currency and helping to produce an inflationary record of fourteen percent. This was the second of the four recessions to hit Turkey during the 'lost decade'.[103]

During his first years in government, busy as he was, Abdullah Gül often reflected on his own position within the party he was representing, and how – like Turkey and even Europe – it was in need of reform. In Jeddah and Strasbourg, he had grown used to working with colleagues who were internationally-trained experts in their fields, unlike many of the old-guard leaders of political parties in Turkey who talked only to each other. As much as he admired Erbakan for his visionary ideals and populist appeal, Gül had never been fully convinced by his *Milli Görüş* version of nationalism with its hostility to Europe and the West; it was too narrow and too unversed in the ways of the world. Nor was he favourable towards the party's advocacy of a system of 'multiple legal-orders' that would allow communities to self-govern according to their own beliefs. From Strasbourg he knew that the debates on coexistence and multiculturalism had moved on from half-baked attempts to revive the Ottoman '*millet*' system – by which self-regulating communities of religious minorities were tolerated – in the name of 'civil society'.[104] The way forward for Turkey was not to be found in old Ottoman and Islamic law books. Recollecting those early years he told me:

> We were trying to professionalize the party from the start. But we soon realized this was not possible because the leaders were old and controlled everything. And people knew that the method at the time was not right, but from respect to the leaders they were not talking about it, keeping their ideas to themselves.[105]

Erbakan and other senior members of the party were, as Turkish politicians still tend to be, demagogues who like to stab the air with their index fingers while telling people what they should believe, whom they should distrust, and what they should want. After participating in European democracy at work, and becoming increasingly aware of its possibilities, Gül was more convinced than ever before that the RP was being run on unworkable lines, making unreasonable promises, pursuing inconsequential policies, and – like the republic itself – in need of reform.

Even during his high school and university years, Abdullah Gül had always been independent minded, seeking leadership roles within clubs and organizations that he supported and then using them to press his own agenda. At MTTB in Istanbul during the highly charged political atmosphere of the early 1970s, he steered the organization away from confrontation and violence to approach political questions by way of history and culture, promoting poetry, photography, art and the Western novel. In London, he had found FOSIS a useful framework within which to set up a discussion group of Turkish students. But that independent mindedness did not mean that Abdullah Gül was hostile to teamwork; on the contrary, he understood and valued the importance of learning from and hearing the advice of experts and colleagues. In 1991, he had agreed to run for office more because of the convincing arguments of his old friends that he could make a difference than his belief in many elements of Erbakan's party programme.

> What I saw in England and Jeddah was very important and had a great impact on me when I entered politics. People within the party were traditional, local, nationalist, Islamic. It was only me in Refah who was open to the outer world because of my experiences. I still preserve the same identity from my background, but I became open to the outer world. I attracted attention by taking a rational approach to problems. From the eyes of opponents I was considered to be Islamic, but my rational approach was showing the difference and drawing attention.[106]

During those first years in government, Gül continued to consult with his old friends from Kayseri and MTTB about party reform, while at the same time he began looking outside the party for Turkish intellectuals who would help him find informed ways of addressing the real problems in rational ways.

Refah victories and the Reformist Group

With local elections scheduled for March 1994, Abdullah Gül started planning months in advance. Thinking ahead to the elections, he recognized that a key priority for Refah, and his own vision of its future, was to bring like-minded people into the party to run for office and that Kayseri was an obvious place to establish an unassailable foothold on the political grid. Late in 1993 he set off to Bursa where his old friend Şükrü Karatepe, now an assistant professor of law at Izmir's Ege University, was speaking at an academic conference on questions of state and religion. Karatepe recalls being surprised to look out from the conference platform and see his good friend Abdullah Gül sitting in the front row and smiling.

> After the discussion he said he had come to see me to talk. Well, he said, why don't you become a mayor? No! I said. I was collecting my academic papers for promotion to professor. He said that I could become professor any time! Come to Kayseri and stand for the mayor! Then he called me once a week and asked if I was ready to collect my things and move to Kayseri! And eventually I did. It was my wife made me do it! [laughs] The mayor at the time was from Melikgazi and he called my wife and said '*Yenge*! If he won't come, we will lose the election and it will be your fault!' Bekir Yıldız also called and said to me one day that he would hit me if I didn't stand! He is a sportsman and would do it too! He called me *nazlı*, and said I was behaving like a shy girl![107]

Amid the friendly good humour, the friends from Kayseri and MTTB were pushing each other to take the ideas they had discussed for so long and to put them into political practice. Bekir Yıldız was running as Refah candidate for the mayoralty of Kocasinan Municipality, the most important urban sector of Kayseri. Mehmet Özhaseki, who had grown up a family friend of the Güls, was standing for the mayor's office in the nearby Melikgazi Municipality. According to Şükrü Karatepe, by helping to direct the Refah campaign along lines that had worked so well three years previously, 'Abdullah Gül changed all manner of political life in Kayseri' in 1994.

> We set out to find what was going on. I spent four months studying local government in Turkey asking 'what in Kayseri can we do to reform things?' We produced analytical reports and published three of them. We visited everywhere and talked to people and found what they thought: this was Mehmet Özhaseki, Bekir Yıldız and myself – and we found out how people were living. From these talks we prepared our political programme, and we then used all three television channels

for promoting our plans over several months. Abdullah Gül was often working with us on the public relations.

So by the time of the election, all the other parties were adopting our ideas. The head of the Anavatan Party, Şevket Bahçeoğlu who was also a candidate for mayor of Melikgazi came to me and told us that we had raised the standards of political life in Kayseri.[108]

Refah swept the board that year in Kayseri and all three were elected, continuing in office to become founding members of the reform wing within Refah that would eventually become the AKP. Bekir Yıldız has been re-elected mayor of Kocasinan ever since, while Mehmet Özhaseki won Melikgazi that year, moving when elected to replace Şükrü Karatepe as mayor of Kayseri in 2004 and is still in that office.

All three proudly claim that their victory in 1994 finally put Kayseri on the fast track to becoming what it is today, the most powerful of the Anatolian Tigers. With Abdullah Gül advising from Ankara, Şükrü Karatepe put his academic research on hold and immediately set about growing the provincial budget and developing the city itself, aggressively seeking funds from Kayseri businessmen such as Kadir Has. Working together, the Refah mayors set about what Mehmet Özhaseki calls 'key development projects'. Without prompting, he took a breath and proudly listed ten of them on his fingers:

The Yamula Dam and hydro-electric plant; exploitation of natural gas; setting up a world-class public metro system; new sports facilities including the Kadir Has stadium; improved civic infrastructure; the Erciyes sky-resort project, costing 270 million Euros; four new universities and two more being planned; a new highway to Ankara with a speed-train service coming; the Guinness Book of World Records for opening 139 factories in a single day; setting up four new industrial parks and the Free-Trade Zone.[109]

'All this development was planned from 1994,' Özhaseki concluded with a grin. But shorter-term goals were directed at the general elections to be held in 1995. How could the party ensure national victory on a comparable scale?

Abdullah Gül had also been thinking of longer-term strategies beyond securing Kayseri for his friends and for Refah. In Ankara he was casting his search for colleagues beyond party ranks, and was interested to hear friends and colleagues mention academic and other experts who were like-minded, conservative Muslims but who shared his international experience and perspective. In 1992 Murat Mercan had arrived back in Turkey with a PhD in Information Sciences from Florida University to take up an academic post at Bilkent University in Ankara. Turkish universities, rectors and hiring committees especially, were and still are always keen to hire Turkish candidates with the international prestige of an overseas doctoral degree. Adding to his allure, Murat Mercan's doctoral work had been so impressive that it had already gained him his first academic job in the USA, at Cleveland State University. For the higher administration at Bilkent, hiring such a candidate to return to Ankara, where they were lavishly creating Turkey's model private university, provided an ideal opportunity to boost their academic credibility for international standards of research. Having planned to return home to Turkey one day, Mercan accepted the offer, leaving behind the post-industrial urban Midwest of Ohio for the high-modernism of the Bilkent campus. He was clearly eager to report his arrival at Bilkent when I talked with him in 2011 and struggled to restrain an urge to laugh.

> Can you imagine, here I was, a professor at a wealthy, Turkish, private university dedicated to science and secularism. I wore a shirt and tweed jacket, slacks and shoes from the States, and everyone looked at me. I was the only one there with a beard right down to here![110]

Pausing briefly from puffing away on his *shisha*, Mercan gestured silently with the mouthpiece, genially emphasizing how the times of wearing a chest-length beard had passed long ago. After drawing and exhaling another plume of aromatic smoke, he continued:

> In 1992 when I moved to Bilkent I had an interest in political life. I was one of very few conservative professors there. One day in 1993 a friend said that Abdullah Gül wanted to meet: he was MP for Refah from Kayseri. Early the next year we met for lunch at the *Meclis* and chatted. We shared common concerns and ideas and our friendship developed. Abdullah Gül was looking to revamp the party. In those days he wanted to improve the party by bringing in people with Western experience who were also conservative in values: he aimed to change the image of the party with new faces and new ideas. He wanted to improve Refah by introducing outward-looking members, both outward to the West, and outward to people in Turkey.[111]

So as early as 1993, Gül was already setting up a network to plan party reform, encouraging friends and colleagues to run for office, and seeking the advice of academic experts who were conservative but shared his international perspective. With Murat Mercan in Ankara, Abdullah Gül formed a political ideas group to discuss and plan national and party reform: among those involved in these informal discussions were old friends and colleagues from the party and from academia, including Sami Güçlü and Mehmet Tekelioğlu. But over the next few years, others would be included from the younger generation of Refah mayors and delegates who were interested in modernizing the party. The group would eventually formalize to confront the political crisis of 1997 by calling itself the Political Research Centre, and from here would be founded the AKP.

Recep Tayyip Erdoğan

Looking back to the 1990s, no one with whom I spoke could remember the earliest significant meeting between Abdullah Gül and Recep Tayyip Erdoğan. This is not, perhaps, simply willed forgetfulness since the two seem to have been within each other's radar for a long time. Born in 1954, Erdoğan was of a slightly younger generation of student in 1970s Istanbul, but the two crossed paths at MTTB meetings and became friends. From the working-class neighbourhood of Kasımpaşa in Istanbul, the younger man was a business student paying his way by playing semi-professional football. Erdoğan was a man of action, full of energy and inspired by resentment at injustice, ready to move quickly on impulse. For Erdoğan, belief in the Islamic ideals of *Milli Görüş* led him to join the Beyoğlu youth branch of Erbakan's party, which provided a forum to launch assaults on the great enemies of Turkey. In 1974 he wrote, directed and performed an allegorical play, *Mas-kom-ya*, attacking freemasons (**mas**on), communists (**kom**ünist) and Jews (**Ya**hudi) as enemies of Turkey and ideologists of evil.[112] It would not have amused Abdullah Gül.

Although Gül and Erdoğan had different political ambitions during their student years, by the time of the 1991 elections they recognized common goals: Gül persuaded Erdoğan to run as a Refah candidate for Istanbul that year, assisting with his campaign.[113] Both were elected, but Erdoğan was prohibited from taking his seat on a technicality.[114] Nevertheless, the political connection had become personal and the charismatic Erdoğan became directly involved with the reformist group in Ankara after again capturing the Istanbul vote to be elected and successfully appointed mayor in 1994. Refah victories in the general elections of 1995 only brought the two young politicians into closer dialogue, even as they brought Erbakan into the office of the prime minister.

For Abdullah Gül, the elections of 1995 marked a turning point in Turkish history, one that promised future challenges and victories. On the eve of the elections in late November, he boldly declared to Jonathan Rugman, a journalist for the *Guardian*: 'This is the end of the Republican period.'[115] Gül also endorsed Erbakan's call for a change to the constitution regarding secularism; endorsing a change from secularism in the form of state control over religion (laicism) to secularism in the form of religious freedom: these were ideas he had been developing while working on democratizing religious freedom at PACE, and they were rather different from Erbakan's ideas.[116] Gül's bold statements made at the time would come back to haunt him when the opposition press in 2007 set about accusing him of advocating political Islam, of which more in due course. In 1995, soon after the results were announced, Şükrü Karatepe recalls they were discussing how Turkey was changing in the 1990s, already the 'lost decade', and reports Gül saying: 'We have the Belediye, we have a base in central government, now we need to look at the nation's economics!'[117]

For many in Refah, the party's success in the general elections of December 1995 seemed to fulfil hopes generated by the municipal victories of March 1994. With his characteristic optimism and a growing confidence that he understood how to make things happen, Abdullah Gül was already looking beyond recent victories to the task of addressing the big questions of Turkey's continuing economic crises and the need for political reform.

> When we entered the coalition government, it was not easy. The whole decade was unfortunate for Turkey. There were unstable coalitions running the country – it seemed like a new government almost every year – and this was damaging the country. Refah and the other parties were mostly old guard who were paying no attention to what people were suffering. Refah emerged as populist. The mayors were very successful, working hard for their people, and maintaining high transparency, which was much appreciated. And there was a young generation in the party. We were becoming visible within the political arena at the time – the newcomers. Although Refah was not new, there was a new generation.[118]

Gül was only too aware that victory dreams can prove unreliable, and kept up planning Turkey's future and political reform with a widening circle of friends and colleagues that included Erdoğan, Bülent Arınç, Abdüllatif Şener, Yaşar Yakış and other founding members of AKP.

Minister of state, 1996–97

In the Erbakan–Çiller coalition government formed in June 1996, Abdullah Gül was made party vice president and government spokesman, entering the Cabinet as minister of state with the principal task of advising Erbakan on foreign affairs. He was also appointed to serve on the board of TRT, the state-owned broadcasting company, and was presented portfolios for relations with Muslim countries in the Balkans and the new Turkic republics formed from the break-up of the Soviet Union.[119] The Turkish press were quick to observe that the member for Kayseri was being called 'the shadow foreign minister of the RP-DYP coalition government'.[120] Despite known differences of opinion over religion and Europe, Gül was still Erbakan's obvious choice for these appointments because of his languages and increasing expertise and international reputation in foreign affairs. To assist with the increased workload, Gül brought in expert colleagues from academia. Murat Mercan took leave from duties at Bilkent to travel with him as his personal chief advisor, monitoring international events and coordinating the Political Research Centre in Ankara while they were on the road. He also solicited the help of his old friend Sami Güçlü, now a professor at Sakarya, who was temporarily seconded from academic duties to serve as a chief advisor to Erbakan's office (*Başbakanlık Başmüşaviri*).

Together, Abdullah Gül and Sami Güçlü confronted the formidable task of negotiating with Turkmenistan and its autocratic and Turcophilic president, Saparmurat Niyazov, who had renamed himself Türkmenbaşı, 'head of the Turkmen', in imitation of Mustafa Kemal renaming himself Atatürk, 'father of the Turks'. With enormous oil wealth to play with, Türkmenbaşı was no supporter of wealth-sharing, democracy, or any opposition to his ideas. But he followed Atatürk in pursuing modernity and decreed that there would be alphabet reform: in this case from Cyrillic which had been imposed by the Soviet authorities to a Latin script. Gül was responsible for encouraging the several Turkish banks and construction businesses that were operating in Turkmenistan, and came to recognize a pattern of economic recklessness and financial mismanagement with which he was all too familiar from dealings with oil-rich states with autocratic, albeit Muslim, leaders. During a state visit to Ankara in November, Türkmenbaşı thanked Turkey for previous help, observing that there were over twenty Turkish enterprises operating projects in his country and that he welcomed more. Gül responded by agreeing that increasing trade was a common goal since the previous year's figure of $170 million 'did not reflect the real potential and that it should be at least $1 billion'. That said, Gül continued by diplomatically pointing out that there were simple problems standing in the way, such as 'problems involving the payment' of Turkish companies, which needed to be 'solved at once'.[121] With a shared and long-term belief in using culture to address political problems derived from their understanding of Necip Fazıl, Abdullah Gül and Sami Güçlü devised a plan: they would promote education in Turkmenistan. On a visit to Turkmenistan the following March, Gül announced that 'cultural affairs were as important as economic relations', and that the Turkish government would assist alphabet reform by printing course books with the new letters.[122]

In recalling this project, Sami Güçlü suggested to me that it typifies how Abdullah Gül had developed and refined a political manner and style of doing business that has proved so successful since, one that simply involves bringing opposite sides together to focus on a common problem and then working together to solve it to the benefit of all sides.

> There was a general sense of anxiety at the time; this was all happening as the military was plotting against us. Meanwhile we were working hard on Turkic affairs and Turkmenistan was Romanizing its alphabet. The two of us worked to assist this project by providing them with books printed in Roman script. We had the right printing presses, but this was a very expensive and complex project, but it is typical of Abdullah Gül's approach: when he can help he will go out of his way to do so. The project to supply three million course books was very costly, and Abdullah Gül sought assistance wherever it could be found. He approached the general director of İş Bank, who at the time was Ünal Korukçu. This was a risky and strange thing to do since İş Bank was long established as a Republican People's Party bank; it is the bank of Atatürk and the Kemalists. But Abdullah Gül was able to bring them on board once they heard what the project was, and they agreed to help. Now listen as I tell you the consequence!
>
> As the economy continued to go awry, Erbakan developed plans to modify the banking sector and called a meeting of leading bankers

to try to resolve problems with Turkish banking. Ünal Bey from Iş Bank was at this meeting. Abdullah Gül tapped him on the shoulder and quietly told him to let him know if there were any problems with the various plans being proposed by Erbakan, and to explain what these might be. As it happens, Ünal Bey was not expecting to bother reporting problems at the meeting since he considered there would be no point in doing so. But Ünal was so taken by this offer of Gül's that he did report what he thought were problems with the proposal. Gül thought about them and later reported to Erbakan who agreed to work with Gül and Ünal to resolve them. So: Gül is clearly adept at understanding the psychology of those in power, regardless of their political views, and uses that understanding to bring about resolutions to problems that might otherwise remain intractable. For Iş Bank, this proved to be a key moment in resolving the banking crisis of the time since it enabled the bankers and government to open up the discussion of their respective needs and interests.[123]

By the time the ceremony took place in Ankara at which the Turkmen ambassador was presented with the three-millionth book in October 1997, the Erbakan–Çiller government had fallen, but the new state minister for Turkic community affairs – Ahat Andican – 'praised former State Minister Abdullah Gül and Prof. Sami Güçlü for their personal efforts in the initiative'.[124] At least one Turkish journalist at the time remained sceptical that books would be enough to challenge the autocracy of President Türkmenbaşı, but joined others in praising the project.[125] A year later, when Ünal Korukçu retired from his ten-year directorship of Iş Bank, he observed how the bank had recently been named as 'the second most reliable financial institution in Turkey after the Turkish Armed Forces', showing an impressive 143% increase in profits between 1997 and 1998.[126]

An emerging foreign policy expert

Alongside his new ministerial duties in the Erbakan–Çiller coalition government, in Strasbourg Abdullah Gül continued to defend Turkey's position on Cyprus, questioned minority rights in Greece, helped draft a charter on freedom of religion, and pressured for gender equality in education. In Ankara, meanwhile, Turkey's foreign policy had fallen into 'utter chaos'.[127] This was partly the result of unstable coalition governments appointing revolving-door foreign ministers. But to make matters worse, Tansu Çiller's erratic and some-times uninformed interventions had brought the Foreign Ministry itself – once a bastion of traditional values and worthy of respect – into disrepute among the Turkish political classes and beyond. Elsewhere, regional crises were boiling over. The killing in the former Yugoslavia was increasing; NATO was bombing Serbian forces in Bosnia-Herzegovina. UN inspectors in Iraq were still failing to solve the disarmament problem. When Saddam Hussain sent his army to capture Erbil in the summer of 1996, the US retaliated with attacks by cruise missiles in 'Operation Desert Strike'. Russia was at war in Chechnya. Israel was at war in Lebanon. The weakness of the Foreign Ministry to offer the govern-ment clear positions during these crucial months provided Abdullah Gül with opportunities to develop a voice in, and command over, foreign affairs that were beyond his formal position. As Philip Robins observes, Gül is an early example of those 'state ministers who have exercised considerable influence in foreign affairs even when not holding the portfolio' of the Foreign Ministry itself.[128] Ironically, if you will, this was among the structural anomalies in the system of policy making and governance that Gül was most eager to reform: the post of minister of state no longer exists.

Abdullah Gül quickly began taking a lead in shaping Turkish foreign policy, whenever possible steering Erbakan's views into more reasonable and practi-cal directions, rephrasing or recasting some of his leader's more immoderate positions into tactical language that left other options still open on the table. In August he sparked controversy by boldly telling reporters that the party was not against indirect talks with the PKK. Erbakan's position had remained the same as ever: there were no Kurds, only terrorists. But Gül in turn remained true to his conviction that conciliation was always the best result, and that dialogue was the means to achieve it, not violence. One of Erbakan's first moves after becoming prime minister had been to make a state visit to Iran, alarming secularists throughout Turkey and worrying the US State Department. When he returned, Gül publicly defended Erbakan's visit, arguing that it was not about Islam but about Turkey's sense of responsibility to establish good work-ing relations with all of its neighbouring countries, including Iran. Following this defence of Erbakan's visit to Iran, Gül implicitly criticized his leader's well-known position by using the same argument to defend dealing with the PKK. 'There is no one in the government or the state that is thinking about bargaining with the PKK,' he pointed out, but continued: 'If our deputies, journalists, businessmen are exerting certain efforts in this regard, we are not against these.' His aim – and he was speaking on behalf of the entire party – was to make sure there would be no more 'mothers of martyrs ... shedding tears'. Erbakan immediately responded by repeating how the party of which he was leader 'would never sit at the table with terrorism'.[129] The young minister of state may not have persuaded the prime minister to change his tune, but by publicly challenging his leader on this issue, he was opening up new ways of thinking about Turkish foreign relations and policy while making clear his own position on the need to stop the violence in the south east. In this he shows himself to be the kind of democrat who believes it is better to talk to your enemies than it is to kill them; they may, after all, become your friends one day.

When I asked him if working with Erbakan was sometimes tiring, President Gül laughed and replied:

> Erbakan was a clever man and master of a style of rhetoric that became a habit. It became a certain method. My main difference from him in politics at the time was about his rhetoric; it sounds well but is dangerous and not useful. People trusted me because I didn't use it.[130]

And he selected issues on which he was prepared to show his loyalty to the party leader. Erbakan was an outspoken anti-Zionist and hostile opponent of the European Community. On 3 November 1994, still an opposition backbencher, Gül spoke on behalf of his party chair when he challenged Tansu Çiller's visit to Israel to discuss strategic and security partnerships 'at a time when virtually all of the Occupied Territories was still under Israeli control'. Gül also opposed plans to sell water to Israel, and objected to suggestions that 'Turkey should be helping Israel find business opportunities in the Turkic republics'.[131] Where Erbakan was anti-Zionist and regularly anti-Semitic in his comments, Gül targeted Israel's policies, not its right to exist or the religious beliefs of its people.

Later that month, November 1994, Abdullah Gül issued a controversial public statement on Refah's position regarding Europe that showed he was developing the rhetorical craft of leaving important disputes open to future developments while shifting responsibility for difficulties back to the other side: 'Our opposition to the European Union is based on the idea that we are from a different culture, we have a different identity and a different economic structure than European countries.'[132] This was not the same as Erbakan's hostility and blunt refusal even to entertain the idea of Turkish membership of Europe. Gül clarified the position in stronger language the following March:

In Turkey's relation with the EU, everything is one-sided. Whenever European interests are concerned, Turkey yields and makes all kinds of concessions. In short, this policy of surrender is the outcome of a rigid policy of becoming a member of the EU regardless of the cost to Turkish national interests. As long as the government continues with this mode of thinking, Turkey will never be allowed to enter into the house of the European rich but will rather be asked to stay in the dog house [*bahçedeki kulübe*] in the garden. Turkey's entry into the EU is an imaginary tale. Turkey will never be allowed to join the EU and Turkey cannot become a member because the EU is a union of Christians.[133]

Unlike Erbakan's opposition to Turkey's application, Gül's emphatic position – informed by what he learned at Strasbourg – was that the question of Turkey joining Europe could not yet be asked, much less debated, so long as the EU remained a religious and cultural closed shop. Rather than backing his leader's categorical refusal to talk to Europe, he challenged European leaders to address their own barely hidden religious agenda.

On some general matters there was little disagreement between the prime minister and his foreign advisor, but Erbakan did not always follow Gül's informed recommendations. There were other forces at work shaping the way Erbakan behaved. Tansu Çiller's trip to Israel had involved military contracts and the generals were becoming impatient. Since April, the army had been conducting 'Operation Hawk', attacking PKK bases in the south east, and they were keen to learn about new targeting techniques and to acquire up-to-date hardware. In July 1996, Gül spoke out opposing the attacks and 'insisted that there would be no new military accord with Israel', but he was ignored. On 28 August, Erbakan found himself reluctantly giving in to pressure from the army and he signed the deal.[134] Perhaps to reassert himself after being humiliated by the generals, Erbakan immediately and energetically pushed ahead with his long-held plans for an economic union of Islamic nations by setting off on a tour of Muslim countries in Africa. And it was perhaps the apparent encouragement his proposals received earlier that year in Indonesia and Malaysia that led Erbakan to ignore Gül's strenuous and personally informed warning to leave Libya out of his African tour.

The problem was not just Erbakan but Ecevit and everyone of that age. They had this 'third-world countries' approach and wanted to associate themselves with administrations of countries like Libya and Iraq on the basis that they had an anti-imperial stance to Europe and the West. I disagreed with this categorically – these were the first instances where we openly disagreed. I disagreed with their categorical argument that any state taking an anti-imperial stance was an ally. But they couldn't hear.[135]

Oblivious to good counsel, Erbakan went ahead with plans to visit Libya. But he managed to set himself such an ambitious schedule that he was not even able to arrive in Tripoli in time for Qaddafi's festival celebrating twenty-seven years of his revolution. Abdullah Gül went instead.

On 1 September, together with Namık Kemal Zeybek, a minister of state representing Çiller's party, Gül landed in Tripoli. They had been sent 'to negotiate for payment owed to Turkish contractors for work done in Libya amounting to $320 million'.[136] Qaddafi publicly and personally snubbed them on their arrival for not being Prime Minister Erbakan. He later humiliated the Turkish delegation even further by making them stand before the international press in the hot sun while he harangued Turkey at great length for its treatment of the Kurds.[137] Gül understood all too well the diplomatic nightmare that would await Erbakan if he were to visit Tripoli; even Tansu Çiller advised him strongly against going, but he went anyway. As Gül had warned, on 5 September, Erbakan and a large group of Turkish journalists were treated to a second performance of Qaddafi's lengthy and fulsome attack on Turkey's Kurdish policy. The international press were there, and Turkish journalists went wild. The New York Times picked the story up on Saturday 7 September, reporting that 'Mr. Erbakan appeared shocked by Colonel Qaddafi's comments' and quoting his response: 'We don't have a Kurdish problem. We have a terrorism problem.'[138] This is just the kind of comment for which Erbakan was famous and which had always worried Gül: pithy, easy to grasp, forceful, cast in a populist idiom, easy to understand if you didn't think about it too much and dangerously misleading. In addition to recognizing Erbakan's failure even to understand the key link in Turkey between national and ethnic identity, Gül also recognized how such kinds of denial did not make the problem go away, and in this case was so dangerously beside the point that it would only make the problem worse. For the moment, as reluctant as ever to speak in support of Turkey's untenable Kurdish policy, he took the old-fashioned diplomatic approach of dodging the question and loyally fibbing rather than betraying his leader. According to the New York Times: 'State Minister Abdullah Gül of Turkey said, "We would never have imagined when we came here that Qaddafi would say things like this.'''[139]

October that year was a month of important meetings and conferences. Amid international criticism of Erbakan's Libyan adventures, Abdullah Gül's name began appearing regularly in the national and international press. This provided a sure signal of his increasing importance in foreign affairs, but his work for Erbakan was usually ignored. It was, however, reported that he advised Erbakan not to visit the Sudan, and was listened to this time.[140] However, it attracted no attention that Abdullah Gül and Murat Mercan had been struggling all year on plans to transform Erbakan's vision of a league of Islamic nations into a practical and realizable project. Knowing that a full- scale economic union along European lines would never work, Gül reckoned that Erbakan's scheme did offer some attractive small-scale economic possibilities for promoting Turkish exports while also extending Turkey's diplomatic grasp.[141] Consulting with Erbakan as he set off on his promotional tours of Asia and Africa, Gül and Mercan drew up draft discussion papers and proposals in preparation for a constitution to be presented at a conference held in Istanbul in October on 'Cooperation and Development'. Here 'the idea of cooperation among major Muslim developing countries was mooted by Dr. Necmettin Erbakan' in what came to be 'the first step towards the establishment of D-8'. Also known as 'Developing-8', D-8 officially began to operate following further discussions, drafting of terms, and a summit meeting held a year later – on 15 June 1997 – in Istanbul at which heads of state from Bangladesh, Egypt, Indonesia, Iran, Malaysia, Nigeria, Pakistan and Turkey ratified the Istanbul Declaration on 'development cooperation'.[142] The D-8 continues to promote economic cooperation among member states from its headquarters in Istanbul.

But in October 1996, Erbakan was attempting to recover from the disaster of his visit to Libya while preparing for local by-elections. At the Refah Congress held in Ankara on 13 October he presented a programme of compromise with the secular establishment, claiming that his party was a proponent of secular government and the true inheritor of Atatürk's legacy. He was hailed for moving his party 'from radical Islamic to moderate centre'.[143] Many in the party were disappointed, but the loyal columnists writing for pro-Islamic newspapers such as *Yeni Şafak* celebrated 'Refah's new image as the Islamic version of Kemalism'.[144] Enough voters were clearly persuaded for Refah to take thirty percent of the vote in the November local by-elections.[145] This was yet another signal victory for Erbakan and Refah. But it was about to turn sour. Prime Minister Erbakan was soon to find himself under the spotlight, being held accountable for events beyond his control – and perhaps even prior knowledge – that marked the beginning of the end of Refah's rise to power.

On Sunday, 3 November, even as the votes were being counted, a car crash in the small town of Susurluk killed three people. The subsequent investigation revealed just how complicit the political classes had become in the corruption and bloodshed that had marked the 'lost decade' of the 1990s, bringing down the Erbakan–Çiller government and forcing the closure of the Refah Party. Erbakan's 'Islamic version of Kemalism' was stillborn.

4

From Refah to AKP
1997 to 2001

E ver since Uğur Mumcu's assassination in 1993, sections of the Turkish press, and many Turkish people generally, had become increasingly alarmed that something nasty was going on behind the scenes. For those who already thought this way, the 'deep state' that Mumcu had been investigating had once again revealed itself, blatantly seeking to cover up the underhand games it was playing in national affairs. Most Turks knew there were ample historical precedents providing reason to believe such ideas, and many suspected that much of the recent violence was the result of some form of covert state authority. The torture and executions that followed the 1980 coup were of recent memory, but many were also familiar with longer ago, when the Ottoman court had employed extra-judicial operatives – these were often official appointments such as the palace gardener whose job included strangling important troublemakers with a silk rope. The Young Turks of the Committee of Union and Progress who brought the republic into being carried on the tradition with the covert use of *fedaiin,* those young army officers who 'volunteered' to carry out assassinations and other messy operations in protection of the new republic: we might recall the figure of Yakub Cemil, once sent to assassinate Mustafa Kemal, who would later violently expel the Armenians from Kayseri and other provinces.

What Mumcu's death signalled was a growing public interest in finding out what relation, if any, such groups and activities had with the state, elected or 'deep'. For the secular and liberal press, still horrified by Refah's rise to power and what that might portend for the future, military rule and counterterrorism operations in the Kurdish provinces were disturbing enough. But when reports came in that police in Istanbul attacked and killed young Alevis from the Gazi neighbourhood in March 1995, and in December that police in the western city of Manisa had arrested and tortured sixteen young people, many believed that the state was out of control: or, more alarmingly, that there were elements of the state, including the police and military high command, operating beyond the control and knowledge of the elected government. Such suspicions and fears were confirmed in early November 1996.

Susurluk and the 'postmodern coup', 1996–97

On Sunday 3 November 1996, even as the local by-election votes were being counted, there was a car accident outside Susurluk, a small town south of Istanbul and the Sea of Marmara on the road between the ferry port of Bandırma and the small city of Balıkesir. Four people were in the Mercedes that crashed into a truck and rolled over into a ditch. Three of them were killed. Once the four were recognized, the unavoidable question of what they were doing together in the same car proved simply irresistible. The press and politicians went wild. Within a month of the accident, early answers had led to trails of evidence linking the police and army security forces, a former member of the ultra-nationalist *ülkücüler*, members of the National Intelligence Agency, and international criminal organizations that were actively trafficking heroin and laundering money through Turkey. Connecting all of these were leading politicians, including Tansu Çiller. On 28 February, at a regular meeting of the National Security Council, the General Staff presented Erbakan with a list of demands that the Cabinet was to enact. Initially reluctant, Erbakan eventually agreed to their demands. In June, he resigned his office as prime minister after his demands for a comprehensive inquiry into the affair were curtailed by the 28 February process.

The driver of the Mercedes that crashed in Susurluk, Hüseyin Kocadağ, was a career policeman who had risen to become deputy chairman of security for Istanbul. He had also achieved the status of a minor celebrity in the gossip pages of the Istanbul press for being a fancy dresser, a manager of Fenerbahçe Sports Club, and for alleged links to the criminal underworld. His reputation eventually earned him sideways promotion to a less volatile position as director of the Istanbul Police Education Centre. In 1995 he had been involved in the police attack on Alevis in Gazi. When his body was removed from the car, it was clear he had been drinking and that he 'had died in a horrible manner'.[1] What was less clear was what he was doing driving the others. The bodies of those taken from the back seat were those of Abdullah Çatlı and a model who may or may not have been his girlfriend at the time, Gonca Uz. She was travelling with fake identity in the name of Melahat Özbey. On his body, Abdullah Çatlı was found to be carrying an authentic Turkish passport, but it too was in a false name. The second-in-command of the *ülkücüler* since the late 1970s, Çatlı was wanted in Turkey following a death sentence for killing seven student members of the Türkiye Işçi Partisi. Along with a convicted murderer notoriously working for MIT, one Mahmut Yıldırım, code-name 'Yeşil' (Green), he was also alleged to have organized the assassinations of hundreds of Kurdish businessmen on the suspicion they were supporting the PKK. He was also being hunted internationally by Interpol, having escaped from a Swiss prison where he had been incarcerated for heroin smuggling. There were rumours he had facilitated the attempted killing of Pope John Paul II. Early reports on the Susurluk accident suspected that his relationship with Gonca Uz was business related, whatever else it might have been, since 'it is known she was formerly the lover of Kürşat Yılmaz, one of the famous names in the underground world' in which Hüseyin Kocadağ was also rumoured to be involved.[2]

That a rather dodgy former police and security chief with a reputation for violence should be in the same car as a wanted murderer and heroin dealer with a known history of organizing violent attacks and a model with known underworld connections, all this was alarming and shocking but perhaps not entirely surprising. What turned a bizarre accident into a national crisis that would topple Erbakan's government and initiate investigations that are continuing into the second decade of the next century, is that the fourth person in the Mercedes, and the only survivor, was Sedat Bucak, a member of parliament for Tansu Çiller's DYP representing Şanlıurfa. Sedat Bucak was well known to be a Kurdish warlord from Siverek in Urfa province who had profited from state counterterrorism policies – the notorious 'village guards' system. 'With an army of 90,000 people belonging to his clan and the latest weapons' supplied by the state, Bucak 'had declared war on the Kurdistan Workers Party (PKK) and cleared Siverek, Hilvan and Ceylanpınar from the organization.'[3] In the 1980s, Hüseyin Kocadağ served as chief of police in Siverek.[4] That a junior member of Tansu Çiller's party should also have been in the car 'introduced a new dimension to state/mafia relations'.[5] Although granted parliamentary immunity at the time, in 2004 Bucak would be convicted of criminal involvement and sentenced to a year in prison.[6]

Within days of the accident, Doğu Perinçek, former leader of an outlawed Maoist party who had become an outspoken anti-Kurdish nationalist, pointed the finger at Tansu Çiller, claiming that 'those in the car were the branches of Çiller's organization within the state'.[7] As if to confirm the beliefs of those anticipating a conspiracy, Çiller immediately defended Çatlı saying: 'Those who fire bullets or suffer wounds for this state will be remembered with utmost respect by us. They are honourable men for us.'[8] Former prime minister Bülent Ecevit entered the arena and confirmed suspicions even further, announcing in parliament that 'Turkey is facing the greatest crisis of its 73 years as a Republic.'[9] Ecevit recalled how, on coming to power in 1974, he had first learned that a gang of state-supported operatives had been secretly organized to combat terrorism. Following the 1980 coup, their activities had increased, but President Özal had objected to making their existence official: as a result, according to Ecevit, 'these forces calling themselves "*ülkücü*" (idealists) turned to gambling and drug trafficking in the name of protecting the state': cash for the cause.[10] Following Özal's unexpected death in 1993, the National Security Council met and made the organization of death-squads official.

The *New York Times* reporter Stephen Kinzer shrewdly observed at the time that, while 'many Turks seem to accept the idea that their Government might behave this way at moments of crisis', matters were different now that there was mounting evidence 'that at some time in the last five years, the criminal gangs began to work as enforcers for private interests tied to members of the political elite'.[11] Prime Minister Erbakan could do little other than to promise a full investigation, knowing that in doing so he was risking the collapse of his coalition government. If there were members of parliament using their authority to collaborate with criminals and death-squads, what else might be going on behind the scenes?

The events of 28 February 1997, sometimes referred to as a 'postmodern coup', made it four times since 1950 that an elected government of the republic had been derailed by the military. In some ways, the unravelling of information following Susurluk set the scene for a political crisis that had been in the making since the Refah Party's rise to power. The generals and political elite, eager to protect the secular republic by any and all means, had been carefully monitoring what they considered to be the rising threat of political Islam. As soon as Erbakan formed a coalition government, Abdullah Gül recalls, there had been audible rumblings of discontent:

> From the very beginning, the political establishment and the media made war against [Erbakan's] government. It had some faults but none

of them justifies the actions against the government. They were thinking that Islamists were running the country even though it was a coalition. There was talk of Iran at the time and fears of moving that way, but we can never become Iran as you can tell from Ottoman times. But the negative PR was so intense against the government at the time – that is how it was done – there was force used, but no weapons, not an armed coup but forceful threats and it caused too much damage to Turkey.[12]

Amid the fears and confusions arising from investigations into the accident at Susurluk, the generals finally moved when their fears of political Islam were provoked too far by a municipal event in Sincan, a small town outside Ankara.

On 30 January 1997, the Refah mayor of Sincan – one Bekir Yıldız, an opportunist Islamist and not Gül's high-school friend from Kayseri – had organized a 'Jerusalem Night' with speeches enthusiastically calling for the liberation of the holy city from Israel. Such rallies with their strong language were not unusual in Refah strongholds where Erbakan's fiercely anti-Zionist rhetoric captured votes. But among the invited guests was the Iranian ambassador, and the army were not amused. Two days later, their tanks rumbled through the streets of Sincan.[13] On 28 February, at an extraordinary meeting of the Cabinet, the National Security Council presented Erbakan and Çiller with a detailed memorandum of measures to suppress 'religious reaction' (irtica) that the government was herewith to enforce: an ultimatum that Erbakan was forced to sign.

Detailed evidence about who did what leading up to and during the events of 28 February 1997 was still being revealed during trial hearings that began in April 2012. But the major implications soon became clear enough: in the name of protecting the secular status of the republic from encroaching threats, the army had overthrown the government without taking up arms or even leaving the barracks in a virtual and hence 'postmodern' coup. The constitutional reforms of 1982 had established the militarized National Security Council as a 'permanent organ of the state' with executive authority to regulate government affairs, powers that rendered a physical coup needless. At a nine-hour meeting, Erbakan and Çiller were informed that irtica, extreme 'religious reaction', had become the greatest threat to the state.

Since many feared that the secular republic was clearly in danger of being about to be taken over by political Islam, the National Security Council proposed measures that the Cabinet would have to take: these included tightening control over Islamic brotherhoods, closing religious Imam Hatip Schools (which had originally been established after the 1980 coup as a bulwark against communism!), marginalizing the conservative businessmen of central Anatolia (the so-called 'green' capital of the Islamic Calvinists), and shutting down Qur'an courses and all media outlets perceived to be anti-secular.[14] The National Security Council memo also outlined plans to appoint the 'Western Working Group' (*Batı Çalışma Grubu*), a body of unnamed 'intelligence experts' to be funded and given the task of seeking out and investigating 'threats from radical Islamists throughout the country and abroad': this group was reported to be still active in 2000.[15] Days went by and the generals grew impatient at Erbakan's delay in ratifying their executive demands while he launched a last-ditch attempt to rally support for a 'democracy' campaign among leaders of the other parties. As sociologist Haldun Gülalp comments: 'Testifying to the lack of democratic culture in the Turkish political mainstream, none of the other parties were interested in searching for a common platform of democratization with Refah.'[16] Not only the party, but democracy itself, was paying the price of Erbakan's reputation and extreme positions.

During those tense weeks following 28 February, Abdullah Gül was only able to play a minor role, that of advisor offering guidance – which would not be followed – to an increasingly distracted prime minister. At a formal meeting in Ankara with the President of Kyrgyzstan, Gül was offended when a uniformed soldier interrupted the discussion and asked the prime minister to accompany him outside the room. When Erbakan eventually complied and it became clear what was happening, Gül went into the corridor and once again protested with Erbakan that compliance was not a good idea.[17] As if worn out by his own delaying tactics, however, Erbakan reluctantly signed off on the army's demands, effectively abandoning the electoral power of his parliamentary majority, and giving in to the power of the generals with their goal of ending the possibility of Turkey becoming an Islamist state in any significant sense.

Party reform, 1997–2001

Abdullah Gül was shocked to watch as Susurluk unravelled amid mounting evidence of corruption and conspiracy among seasoned politicians, international criminal gangs, and special security forces only to result in an attack on the one party within the government that not only had the largest number of democratically elected delegates, but also had the least to do with the unfolding scandals and conspiracies. Refah was clearly being scapegoated for Erbakan's rhetoric and the Islamic tendency he shared with many of his powerful supporters; that much was clear to all. Never one to be quick to assign the blame, Gül had nevertheless always been highly sceptical of many of Erbakan's alliances and declarations, not just the language in which they were expressed to gain votes, but also his use of Islam to promote ultra-nationalism and hostility to European democracy: this stance was clearly wrong. Gül became even more convinced of his early belief that religion, as such, should be left out of political decisions just as much as religious life should be free from state control. There was no disagreement with Erbakan over their common dislike of the way that Article 27 of the constitution enshrined laicism, but that did not necessarily mean there was agreement about what needed to be done about it. And now Erbakan's rhetoric had lost the day.

Abdullah Gül's experiences in England and his work at PACE had convinced him that only continuous democratic debate and reform guaranteed people of different religious faiths the freedom to worship in their own way without interference from the state. While this was not Erbakan's vision of an Islamic Turkish state, Gül avoided publicly contradicting his party leader on religious matters and what constitutional revision on the secularism question should involve. Gül was determined to leave Islam, and most certainly political debates among Islamic jurists, out of his political language: denouncing state-enforced secularism in favour of religious pluralism was a different matter. Just as he believed that the state should not prescribe the way people practised their religions, so he held that religion should not be used to solve political questions. Gül had become firmly opposed to state-organized control over religious practice, and was no special friend of Israel or Iran, the two theocracies which had recently inflamed the Sincan incident. He also recognized all too well the dangers of rabble-rousing in the name of religious difference and of singling out foreign states and labelling them enemies – conciliation or patient silence were far better tactics. He had strongly opposed Çiller's arms deal with Israel, but kept quiet when Erbakan signed off on it under pressure from the military. At the same time, his years representing Kayseri, working closely with and witnessing the successes of his own generation of Refah colleagues and the city's business community, had strengthened his belief in the values he had learned growing up there. The Islamic Calvinism of Kayseri was a pragmatic ethics involving community service, not the *Milli Görüş* nationalism of Erbakan and his core supporters; nor was it the spectral Islamic takeover feared by the military and secular establishment.

Abdullah Gül had seen how the social and economic achievements taking place in Kayseri were entirely compatible with basic Islamic principles and this was a feature that had attracted Refah supporters generally: putting moral order into the national economy by opposing monopoly capitalism, promoting small business interests, while at the same time opening the economy to international trade. This had been among Turgut Özal's lessons in Turkish politics; making neoliberal policies work for the largest groups of voters. By continuing to uphold these policies, the RP had captured the conservative vote throughout Turkey, uniting followers of the religious orders with provincial small business people, and expanding their following beyond the provinces to the ever-increasing urban populations of working class and unemployed voters from conservative and religious backgrounds. The vast majority of these voters were not people who wanted to be at war, with Israel or the Kurdish people, any more than they wanted to live in an Islamic state like Iran: the voters that had brought Refah to power were indeed largely politically conservative Muslims, but not all were attached to Erbakan's vision of Islamic nationalism and perpetual war in the name of religion.

Shortly after Erbakan formed his coalition with Çiller, scholar Haldun Gülalp shrewdly observed that Refah's success had been a 'radical' rather than 'conservative' event since the party 'does not rely exclusively on support from religious orders, and its ideologues are mostly graduates of secular universities fully conversant in Marxist and post-modernist theories'.[18] Traditionally, political parties in Turkey behaved like the loyal children of paternal leaders, but Refah had started breaking the pattern. Within the party, Abdullah Gül, Recep Tayyip Erdoğan, and the new generation of RP mayors throughout Turkey who differed from Erbakan and his followers had brought with them different electoral groups. They were still conservative Muslims but with a broader, often international outlook, and a stronger commitment to improving the standards of living among their constituents through economic reform. If Erbakan's links with the Nakşibendi orders informed his own views, won him votes from those who followed his lead, and made the generals suspicious, successful Refah policies were being forged from a broader understanding of Muslim and national identity than that envisaged earlier by Erbakan's *Milli Görüş*. By 1996, Refah campaign propaganda focused on themes of 'social justice, domestic peace, regional equality, religious freedom, ethnic impartiality, respect for labour, interest-free economy and ending corruption'.[19] Islamic belief remained central to Refah's success, but for Gül and the new generation of 'ideologues' within the party it was never a political goal. As one close colleague put it:

Gül hated being called Islamic! He said that it has values as an ethic, but we are human beings and parties are made of people. So if we call ourselves Islamic and we make a mistake, this will be attributed to religion! And this is common. When there are corruption cases, people blame Islam! So he never liked being called Islamic, and his aim was to bring reform along European lines, and to bring religious freedom such as he saw in England.[20]

Political Islam has never been on Gül's agenda, but in 1997 the generals thought otherwise about the party he represented and its leader. When there is corruption, some people blame Islam.

Refah's final days

In May, the Constitutional Court began proceedings against Erbakan and senior members of Refah were indicted.[21] In defiance of evidence emerging from the Susurluk investigation, the chief prosecutor called for the RP to be closed because 'it had become the focal point of criminal [i.e. anti-secular] activity'.[22] That same month 161 commissioned and non-commissioned officers were purged from the army on suspicion of Islamist sympathies.[23] By early June, the generals were issuing statements based on reports from the Western Working Group in which they warned that Refah was connected to a widespread Islamist movement, was receiving financial and military support from Iran, Libya and Saudi Arabia, and that RP delegates were connected to Islamist business interests in Germany.[24] However unfounded such charges were – and it was recognized at the time that there was a great deal of bluffing involved – they were serious enough. Given Refah's electoral mandate, this was clearly a full-scale assault being made on parliamentary democracy by a hostile military and judiciary. Even the *New York Times* was quick to pick up on the story and deplored how the actions of Turkey's 'restive generals ... amount to a backdoor coup against parliamentary democracy'.[25] On 18 June, Erbakan gave up under pressure and resigned, immediately adopting 'democracy' as his new slogan. Mesut Yılmaz became prime minister and speedily set about implementing the new laws advocated by the military.

By December, in anticipation of Refah being closed down, Erbakan and his lawyer, Ismail Alptekin, founded a new party, the *Fazilet Partisi* ('Virtue Party' or FP), proclaiming the restoration of 'democracy' their key objective. In January 1998, the Constitutional Court finally closed Refah and banned

Erbakan from political office for five years. Most RP delegates joined Fazilet, and the new party attracted members from the conservative Motherland Party (ANAP), including Cemil Çiçek, Abdülkadir Aksu, Ali Coşkun, and Abdullah Gül's professor Nevzat Yalçıntaş. With Erbakan directing policy from behind the scenes, the first Fazilet Party congress was scheduled to be held on 14 May – to commemorate the date when, in 1950, democracy had arrived in Turkey with the election of Adnan Menderes.[26] Recai Kutan would be nominated party leader.[27]

With the collapse of Erbakan's government in the summer of 1997, Abdullah Gül returned to being MP for Kayseri, but fewer duties meant more time for addressing urgent and longer-term problems within the party. Sami Güçlü recalls:

> Abdullah Gül was always critical of Refah policies and operating strategies, and even before 1997 understood that reform could not take place within the existing structures that led from Refah to Fazilet. Those within the party of like mind recognized that young leaders were needed if the party were to succeed in improving its ratings from twenty percent, so a group within the party following Gül set up a reform programme.[28]

With Gül no longer a government minister able to employ a full-time assistant, his colleague Murat Mercan returned to Bilkent University and busied himself consolidating the Political Research Centre, an informal think-tank of mostly foreign-educated intellectuals and academics that had been meeting since 1993, and handling public relations. Staying in daily phone contact with Gül in the *Meclis*, Mercan began working closely with Melih Gökçek, Refah mayor of Ankara since 1994, and maintained regular communications with the Istanbul working group led by Erdoğan. Mercan recalls:

> We set out to handle the crisis together, managing to maintain a mix of relations with the Western media, Western-educated intellectuals, as well as leaders in business and finance. We established a foundation, the Political Research Centre, and this was the origins of the AK party. Abdullah Gül was chairman; I was coordinator of the Political Research Centre as we worked on new ideas for the party. We kept

close links with Tayyip Erdoğan and established these two branches, Istanbul and Ankara, and these became the new party.[29]

Early meetings of the Political Research Centre included Refah delegates Bülent Arınç, a legal expert from Manisa, and Abdüllatif Şener, a financial expert from Sivas, while Gül's old friend from the MTTB years, Beşir Atalay became a key figure in the team with his informed criticism of Erbakan's management of Refah from an insider's understanding of government bureaucracy.[30]

Throughout the summer of 1997, Abdullah Gül was singled out by the Turkish press for being among the leaders of a reformist group within Refah. Within weeks of Erbakan's resignation while the case to close Refah was still at an early stage, Gül was named for representing a 'younger generation' who 'reportedly hold the older generation responsible' for the party's loss of power, and who also 'reportedly believe that the RP's closure could lead to a healthier start for Islamic politicians'.[31] But this was not Gül's stated position at the time any more than being an 'Islamic politician', or being openly disloyal to Erbakan and the party, were ever part of his public political agenda.

In the months before Refah was shut down, Abdullah Gül energetically campaigned to prevent the party being closed by drawing international attention to events in Turkey, where the case being made against a party with a substantial majority was clearly a violation of democracy. He travelled to Chicago and Washington, DC during August, lecturing on 'Islam and Democracy' and lobbied for support against Refah's closing.[32] At home, he openly challenged the undemocratic actions of the army, accusing them of making 'the worst mistake they have ever made', and instructing the generals to quit politics. During a television interview Gül declared that the case being brought by the prosecutor to close Refah had been written by the military and was 'not based on any lawful grounds'.[33] On 17 September, accompanied by journalists, Gül visited the tomb of Adnan Menderes where he tendentiously announced that the former prime minister who had been tried and executed by a military court 'became a martyr to prove the supremacy of the popular will'. Such resonant and allusive visits to key monuments of the nation's history are crucial to the rhetoric and performance of politics in Turkey. The visit provided Gül with occasion to lay down a challenge to the judiciary: 'The Refah Party will not be closed. It would not be in line with the democratic tradition to ban Turkey's biggest party, biggest political movement. Prosecutors may request anything. It is the judge's decision which matters.'[34] In November,

Gül attended a not-entirely 'secret' meeting of Turkish and US officials held in England to debate attempts to close Refah alongside the possible use of the US air base at Incirlik 'in case of any attack on Saddam'.[35] By December, even as Erbakan was giving up hope and establishing Fazilet, Gül continued to seek to draw international attention to the injustice of what was happening to Turkish democracy, and exposing the need to set limits to military power.

On Wednesday 10 December, while the EU was deciding on whether to proceed with Turkey's application for admission, Abdullah Gül called a press conference at the parliament and repeated that 'the Refah Party had been forced to quit the government by undemocratic methods', further noting that former members of the National Security Council had recently been appointed to positions on company boards. Once again, he raised the question of law and democratic due process, appealing to the judiciary to be mindful of European standards of transparency since 'the EU was not only an economic community, but ... had standards on the issues of democracy, human rights and freedom'.[36] In December, Lee Hockstader of the *Washington Post* took notice, reporting from Kayseri on how a 'campaign, led by the army, Turkey's most powerful institution and the guardian of its secular state' to close down the RP had recently led to Gül's old friend and political colleague, Kayseri mayor Sükrü Karatepe, receiving a prison sentence.[37] A year previously, following ceremonies celebrating Atatürk's death, Karatepe had declared that there was no true democracy in Turkey because of state mandated secularism. 'The dominant circles,' he had announced, 'threaten us to live like them – if we do not they are ready to accuse us ... Do not think that I am secular just because you see me in this colourful official suit.'[38] In October 1997, these remarks had earned him a one-year sentence for 'inciting feelings of hatred and enmity in people by focusing on religious differences',[39] which Hockstader offered as obvious evidence of 'a campaign in Turkey to silence and marginalize Islam-based parties, institutions and media'. Hockstader concluded: 'It is widely expected that the Constitutional Court will rule against the Refah Party and ban six of its top officials from political activity for five years.'[40] Gül took the opportunity of responding to the piece in the Turkish press with a rhetorical flourish, announcing: 'If we are banned it will be a crime but it will be a happy crime. It will help us to come back even stronger. We'd be a victim, and the attitude of the Turkish people is always on the side of the victim.'[41]

Right up to the end Abdullah Gül continued to make public statements insisting that Refah would not be closed. Doing so enabled him to start setting new terms that he hoped would shape the debate about, and future of, democracy in Turkey. His aim was to establish an agenda for needful reforms with an eye to how Turkish democracy lagged behind European standards and undoubtedly deserved its poor reputation. In Strasbourg, he had learned how far behind Turkey really was in terms of democratic process and rule of law, and he was keen to bring the need for reform into political discourse in Turkey. It was a difficult juggling act. On one hand, he was seeking to hold on to the wide base of support for Refah that he had been instrumental in developing, while on the other he needed to steer the party away from political Islam.

In late December, during an interview over the formation of the Fazilet Party, Abdullah Gül was once again cast as an unofficial spokesman for a number of 'young RP deputies who have been criticizing members of the party's executive council who have been in the party for 30 years'.[42] At issue from the start was the name of Erbakan's new party since in Turkish 'Fazilet', meaning 'Virtue', can be taken to have Islamic connotations such as obeying the rules of the Qur'an. Gül and other members of the Political Research Centre drafted a general statement on behalf of the 'young deputies' who opposed the new name and what it signified: 'It is again an Islamic name', the group announced, declaring further that they thought Fazilet 'is not suitable for a party name. There should have been a worldly name for the new party, not an Islamic one. A new movement cannot be finalized with this name.' Voicing one of Gül's major concerns of previous years, the unattributed statement insisted that Islamic rhetoric was not suited to uniting the party with its electoral base, and that future success depended on a different name around which party delegates could rally support: 'If a suitable name is found, perhaps we can be successful. However, our deputies must appear strong, otherwise we might lose our grassroots. Our grassroots must not think that we were unable to endure this critical transition period.'[43] Speaking personally, Gül was adamant that, 'We don't believe that the Welfare Party will be closed', thus preserving the public appearance of hope for democratic rule of law in Turkey and a future for the RP. But he knew these were forlorn hopes.

Clearly aware that Refah's days were numbered, Abdullah Gül publicly framed the crisis in terms of improving democratic standards and establishing rule of law; the military and secular elites would hear the challenge. He declared that the Constitutional Court could not find against a party that had behaved 'within the framework of the Political Parties Law and the Constitutional Law',[44] less in hopes of influencing the decision than establishing that Turkey should be capable of democratic behaviour, despite its recent past. Closing the party, he pointed out, would be an entirely 'political' decision since the accusations were all directed at party delegates rather than party policy or behaviour. 'Although it is a political trial, we believe that the law will prevail and that constitutional law will behave within the framework of its articles and international law.' Opposing politics to the law in this way, he recalled recent events in Turkish political history of which European observers were only too well aware:

> We know that Turkey is not experiencing a normal period nowadays. On the other hand, if we look at our country's past, we have witnessed a prime minister's execution and the imprisonment of many party members, and later on, the same party members have become prime ministers or presidents. Thus anything can happen in Turkey. From that point of view, if a political decision is made, I will not be surprised.[45]

Speaking on behalf of the younger generation of Refah delegates who were unhappy with the directions Erbakan's new party was taking, Gül insisted that 'there will be no disintegration' of the party but, if it is closed, 'we [will] continue to act within the framework of the democracy that is foreseen in Turkey ... We don't impose any ideas on people. We represent people's thoughts.'[46] Gül will return to this political formula throughout his career: in 1997 the version that he was keenest to promote was Turkey's need for further and continued democratic reform, whatever happened to the party. In Strasbourg he had learned how democracy took time and patience; it was a process in need of perpetual revision and reform in response to circumstances and 'people's thoughts'. This was a case he would be making again in the course of the months ahead and remains an abiding principle in his political thinking, the need to respect public opinion even when it conflicts with his own analysis of a problem.

The Reformist Group, 1998

Meanwhile, to no one's surprise, on 16 January 1998, the Constitutional Court closed Refah and pursued indictments against senior members. James Rubin, a US State Department spokesman, instantly declared that the decision 'damages confidence in Turkey's democratic, multiparty system'. Speaking to Stephen Kinzer of the *New York Times* that day, Abdullah Gül agreed that the ban was 'a shadow on Turkish democracy' but confidently added, 'we will have another political party'.[47] On 24 April, his close friend Sükrü Karatepe entered Yahyalı prison to begin serving four months of his one-year prison sentence.[48] Three

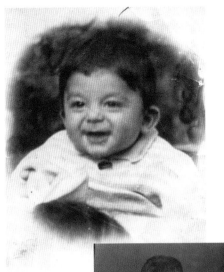

Above left: Abdullah Gül aged 1.

Left: Abdullah Gül aged 3.

Above right: Abdullah Gül graduates from Gazi Paşa Primary School, 1962.

Below: Ahmet Hamdi Bey at work.

Kayseri Lycée, late 1960s. Abdullah Gül is standing, second on the right.

Abdullah Gül addresses a MTTB student rally at Çanakkale, 1972.

Necip Fazil Kisakürek with members of the Istanbul MTTB group, 1974. From the left: Mehmet Tekelioğlu, [?], Yaşar Karayel, Necip Fazıl, Abdullah Gül, [?], Professor Saffet Solak.

London, 1976. Ali Ihsan, Fehmi Koru (in front), Abdullah Gül, Mehmet Tekelioğlu.

Hyde Park, London, 1977. Fehmi Koru, Abdullah Gül, Şükrü Karatepe.

Abdullah Gül during his military service, Tuzla Barracks, 1981.

A family day out on the Jeddah Corniche; mid-1980s.

At home with Kübra and Ahmet Münir in Jeddah, 1989.

Abdullah Gül with Dr Asaf Ahmet, Islamic Development Bank, Jeddah, 1989.

A family visit to the Dolmabahçe Palace, Istanbul, early 1990s.

Abdullah Gül addresses the Parliamentary Assembly of the Council of Europe, Strasbourg, 1993.

Abdullah Gül with Necmettin Erbakan and Şevket Kazan, Ankara, 1995.

Abdullah Gül, Turkey's Minister of Foreign Affairs, Dr Benita Ferrero-Waldner, Minister of Foreign Affairs for Austria, and Jack Straw, Secretary of State for Foreign Affairs, UK, attending an informal NATO–European Union working lunch, 3 April 2003.

Abdullah Gül with Condoleezza Rice at a NATO Council meeting, 8 December 2005.

President and Madame Gül welcome Queen Elizabeth and
Prince Philip to Turkey, Istanbul, 14 May 2008.

President Gül and Queen Elizabeth II
at Westminster, November 2010.

President Gül visits Kayseri; Mount
Erciyes in the background, 26 June 2011.

President and Madame Gül with Prime Minister
and Madame Erdoğan, Istanbul, 29 May 2013.

days earlier, Recep Tayyip Erdoğan was sentenced to prison under Article 312 for inciting religious hatred. He would eventually serve four of the ten months of his sentence between April and July 1999. Key among his crimes was making a speech in which he quoted a poetic fragment: 'The mosques are our barracks, the minarets our bayonets, the domes our helmets, and the believers our soldiers.'[49] Doubtless aware that the poem had been composed by Ziya Gökalp, the celebrated and conspicuously secular nationalist ideologue, the court ignored the poetic irony and interpreted Erdoğan's use of the line as a means of advocating armed struggle in the cause of political Islam.

Since his first disputed election for the Refah Party in 1991, Recep Tayyip Erdoğan had attracted both wide support and notoriety in his native Istanbul and beyond. During his time as mayor of Istanbul, he had sorted out major water, pollution and traffic problems, while also taking a firm line on municipal corruption and investing heavily in the city's infrastructure. Among many people in Istanbul as well as political colleagues, there was evident concern that he was being punished unjustly and undemocratically.

Beşir Atalay recalls how, shortly after news of Erdoğan's prison sentence was announced, Gül pondered whether he should run for the vacancy in the mayor's office in Istanbul. '"No!", I told him,' Atalay reports saying, '"You are not fit for that job, you need to be in Ankara representing the state as a whole!" I managed to stop that idea. Istanbul was not suited to his talents.'[50]

Over the next few months the reformist group held regular meetings in Ankara to discuss the immediate political future and the need for a new approach, not simply to policy, but to public relations. 'The new replacement government was so corrupt,' Gül recalls, 'and the problems were all ideological as happens in developing countries with weak democratic structures – the agenda of the government, whatever it might be!'[51] Capturing the political high ground by promoting democracy was clearly a priority goal, both in the party and the nation at large.

At gatherings of the Political Research Centre in Ankara, concerns about Erbakan's newly formed Fazilet Party and problems with its organization and programme were discussed with some dismay. Fazilet was being established within a structure ruled by an old guard of conservative Islamic nationalists, a joining of forces between ideologues representing both *Milli Görüş* and the Turkish-Islamic Synthesis. The party's founders were largely Erbakan's cronies, many of them members of an Islamic association of lawyers.[52] Fazilet was not aiming in directions that the reformist group had been thinking about, and would clearly never attract the growing numbers of voters that Refah had managed to build up with its broader, more modern approach and policies that had been working so well. 'During the Fazilet period,' Murat Mercan recalls, 'there were many who told Abdullah Gül to leave and form a new party. But he said: "A fundamental principle is that it is impossible to succeed if you simply change parties." So, despite many temptations to leave, he stayed with Erbakan and Fazilet', displaying the same loyalty he had shown to Refah. Yet as early as January 1998, even as Erbakan was organizing his new party from behind the scenes, the pro-Islamic newspaper *Yeni Şafak* reported: 'Refah Party's four young guns, Tayyip Erdoğan, Abdullah Gül, Melih Gökçek and Bülent Arınç, are making secret preparations for the "Erbakan-less period." A series of meetings have been held in Ankara and Istanbul.'[53]

Whether Abdullah Gül and the other 'young guns' had been named by a deliberate press-leak from the Political Research Centre or not, throughout 1998 and 1999, the national media eagerly pursued rumours of divisions within the ranks of the Fazilet Party, paying special attention to how Gül, Erdoğan, Arınç and Şener were leading the reformist group. According to the press at the time, and to subsequent scholarship, what was at issue was nothing less than the nature and future of political Islam in Turkey based on the not unreasonable presumption that Fazilet represented its newest phase and was doomed to fail. For Abdullah Gül, Islam as such had no place in what he termed 'the framework of the democracy that is foreseen in Turkey'. The rights of Muslims and others to practise their religious beliefs freely was an issue that could only be solved by removing religious affairs from the control of the state – as still enshrined in the 1924 Constitution – as part of a general and systematic overhauling of political life starting with reforms that would introduce greater transparency of government and the rule of law. Democratic reform would remove the suspicions of the secularists while preserving the rights of those, like himself, who wished to observe their religious faith.

In an interview with Scott Peterson of the *Christian Science Monitor* of January 1998, Gül made his own position clear enough while appearing to be speaking on behalf of the party. Peterson reports:

What his party wants is not enforced Islamic dress on women, enforced Islamic education, or imposed Islamic law, Gül contends, but a meeting – and mutual respect – of the joint Western and Islamic traditions in Turkey. Though some Refah hard-liners have called for turning Turkey's decades-long secular tradition on its head, Gül speaks of the 'Islamic headscarf and the miniskirt walking hand in hand'.[54]

Gül's aim, here as elsewhere in his speeches at this time, was to promote democratic freedoms that included better wealth distribution and improvements in education and women's rights, while removing questions of religious faith from politics.

During the early weeks of 1998, Abdullah Gül supported Erbakan and the successful establishment of the emerging Fazilet Party. But the activities and aims of the Political Research Centre in Ankara were becoming widely known and perceived as a growing split within the party: the tactic was to urge Erbakan and his cadres to see the need for party reorganization and to adapt. By mid-February, along with Erdoğan and Arınç, Gül was widely being tipped as a leading contender for possible leadership of a new party. This 'younger generation' of deputies, which also included Şener, was reported to 'have already produced ideas for the structure of the new political organization and its principles as well'. This group was reported to argue that rhetoric and policy both needed to change, abandoning a vision of militant Islam for 'a full civil party discourse' that would protect 'democracy and human rights ... not only for pro-Islamic people but for everybody from various strata of society'.[55] In tune with discussions among members of the Political Research Centre, even Erdoğan had slowly softened his rhetoric over the years, earning him a reputation for being a moderate in contrast with Erbakan.

By 1998, the shift in Recep Tayyip Erdoğan's public rhetoric and reputation was becoming clear to all observers. Following Refah's 1995 election victories, he had notoriously declared that 'the 21st century will be an era in which systems that are based on Islam will come to power in the world'.[56] But by January 1998, Erdoğan was reportedly 'known to be more moderate and modern minded than Necmettin Erbakan and his staff', and was 'being considered as a candidate for the leadership of the Refah movement when the era of its legendary leader, Necmettin Erbakan, comes to an end'.[57] Even to the liberal press, Erdoğan's recent poetic allusion to bayonets and minarets had merely 'harmed his image' rather than confirmed his allegiance to political Islam. With his prison sentence making him an obvious martyr to the cause, he gained increasing personal support among Muslims who felt they had been victimized by the secular state.

In the lead up to the first founders' meeting of the Fazilet Party in May, Abdüllatif Şener emerged as the chosen spokesman representing the reformist group aiming to achieve 'a full civil party discourse'. Known to be a close associate of Tayyip Erdoğan, Şener dodged the question of whether Erdoğan would be running against Erbakan, deferring to 'the democratic wishes of the party'.[58] At the time, Erdoğan was awaiting sentence on charges of *irtica* – political reaction – that would bar him from political office, but his widespread popularity and charisma made him the obvious choice to test the waters of party reform. Here the tactic was to keep Erdoğan's name in play alongside Şener's, maintaining a united public front among the reformist group, while also advertising that it enjoyed a choice of strong leaders.

In the weeks before the founders' meeting held on 14 May, Abdullah Gül kept his name out of the running for leadership but made his own position clear once again, insisting that democratic reform based on European principles together with a non-violent approach to national problems were at the heart of his vision for the party and for Turkey's future. Whoever was to take over fronting the party after Erbakan, Gül would be in charge of the reform programme. Since January he had been attending meetings of PACE in Strasbourg, where – amid debates over Kosovo – the imminent execution of Karla Faye Tucker in Texas had sparked a widespread debate on capital punishment. On 5 February, two days after Tucker was killed by lethal injection, PACE called on the US and European nations to abolish capital punishment.[59] With the arguments against capital punishment firmly in mind, in mid-May – days before the FP held its first council meeting – Gül made headline news by declaring his support for a draft bill proposing to end capital punishment in Turkey that was being tabled by delegates from the opposition CHP. The draft proposed to reverse the capital sentences passed against Deniz Gezmiş and the left-wing student leaders executed back in 1972, and called for a future ban on capital punishment. Gül spoke out in support of the opposition party's bill, using the occasion to draw attention to the deplorable current state of democracy in Turkey and demonstrating to colleagues in Europe that he, at least, believed in the same values as they advanced. Here he found himself in what at the time seemed a paradoxical position: that of being Turkey's delegate in Strasbourg, a practising Muslim representing a party reputed to be Islamist, yet condemning capital punishment by defending the memory of an executed left-wing student:

We were members of the opposition student movements during the period of the March 12 coup in the 1970s. They saw us as enemies. When I was serving as president of the student organisation [MTTB], I lost one year at the university because of this group of activists, including Gezmiş and his friends. Now, after 30 years, I sign this draft bill for democracy, not because I admire them. In the past, it was Adnan Menderes, Deniz Gezmiş; today it is Sükrü Karatepe and Greater Istanbul Mayor Recep Tayyip Erdoğan. We don't know what will happen to other people tomorrow. This situation shows the state of our democratic standards.[60]

Alone among his party colleagues, Gül was acutely aware of just how closely Europe was watching what was happening in Turkey, and he was regularly embarrassed by what they saw and heard at meetings in Ankara. Asserting to a home audience that capital punishment had no place in a democracy enabled him to urge the party to adopt a position that was not only his strong personal belief but also one that would direct the nation towards recognizable European standards in human rights.

Meanwhile by holding to his own 'fundamental principle ... that it is impossible to succeed if you simply change parties', Gül managed to remain loyal to Erbakan and the new party that, while banned from politics himself, the former Refah leader was directing from not very far behind the scenes. Yet at the same time, Gül remained indirectly critical of the route along which Erbakan was leading the party. Between the founders' meeting in May 1998 and the general elections of 18 April 1999 – at which Fazilet lost the previous majority enjoyed by Refah and dropped to third place – Gül said nothing to disparage Fazilet or its leadership. He preferred to use his position within the party as a platform from which to continue mounting a public criticism of standards of democracy and human rights in Turkey. Relations with Erbakan had cooled off considerably from the time when they had worked closely together on foreign affairs, but rather than publicly criticize his leader, Gül preferred to promote his own agenda.

Despite his loyalty, Abdullah Gül would twice appear to be snubbed by Erbakan. At the founders' meeting in May 1998, he and Bülent Arınç were conspicuously not appointed to the party executive; they were 'vanished', as one columnist put it.[61] For party leader, Erbakan installed Recai Kutan – a founding member of the RP whose successful election campaign representing Kayseri in 1975 had been Gül's first experience of political canvassing. For deputy chairman, Erbakan appointed another political colleague from that campaign, Irfan Gündüz, now a professor of divinity at Marmara University. Professor Gündüz was not the only academic brought in at the expense of a seasoned politician to add intellectual respectability to the party: Erbakan had even invited three women to join the party council, including Western-educated Professor Oya Akgönenç of Bilkent University, and the controversial journalist

Nazlı Ilıcak.[62] Of the former Motherland Party conservatives who had joined Fazilet, Abdülkadir Aksu and Gül's professor Nevzat Yalçıntaş, both accepted party posts. Cemil Çiçek and Ali Coşkun, however, turned theirs down, refusing to become 'stuntmen' performing for a party in which they would have no say.[63] They agreed with Gül and the young reformers that Erbakan had created a party with only two objectives: appearing different from Refah and ensuring personal loyalty to himself, even if that meant appointing women to the party council. Kutan struggled to throw off his image as Erbakan's puppet, wisely widening the party by eventually bringing Çiçek, Coşkun and Gül back into the party administration and listening to their ideas.[64]

At a press conference in November, Abdullah Gül and Bülent Arınç spoke on behalf of the reformers when they described plans to widen the party's reach and appeal. Gül explained at the time:

> We are putting forth the intellectual line and principles of the party. With a deliberate process of discussions, we are setting a new style. We are trying to get rid of narrow perspectives and a narrow party structure and to create a more liberal, more democratic party structure ... But this must not be done in a pragmatic or opportunistic manner. In the left too there are many very honest and capable names ... We are thinking of inviting many names from the left.[65]

But such plans were a little too much, too soon. By the time of campaigning for the April 1999 election, Erbakan used his lobby within the party to turn down Gül's nomination for the position of mayor of Istanbul – which Erdoğan had been required to resign in September after the high court of appeals upheld his prison sentence – in favour of Ali Mürfit Gürtuna, a person widely known to have been 'imposed on the party from outside by Necmettin Erbakan'.[66] For his part, Gül's ambitions were to set forth his agenda for a reformation of national politics; he had no desire to be mayor of Istanbul.

The EU agenda

Following the Fazilet Party founders' meeting at which he was left off the party executive, Abdullah Gül spent the summer of 1998 working closely with Murat Mercan while in Ankara drafting proposals for the constitution of a new party that would correct all Erbakan's errors. They kept in daily telephone contact with Arınç, Erdoğan and Şener. In public, Gül directed his energies to future possibilities for Turkey in Europe by speaking out on the very issues on which he had parted company with Erbakan: capital punishment, human rights and democratic reform of political institutions, ending government support for pre-emptive military actions against the Kurds, improving relations with Europe and the West, and removing Islamic rhetoric from political discourse. With an ever-patient eye to the long term, Gül was looking to open up Turkey's place in the world, and to bring it fully into the European Union by reforms that would conform to the highest of democratic standards. In Strasbourg as in Turkey, he remained formally loyal to the repute of his party and nation while all too often agreeing with many of their harshest critics. The years at PACE had increased his respect for and understanding of freedom of speech as a democratic practice at work.

> I learned many things there. Joining the debates helped with my politi-
> cal development and my understanding of how democracy can work
> to solve problems such as those we were facing in Turkey. I agreed
> with the policies of the Council and came to believe strongly in the
> ways we were talking about human rights, the sovereignty of law, the
> importance of pluralism – I have always supported these ideals. When
> I visited PACE as prime minister in 2002, I made a speech and said
> that this was my School of Democracy.[67]

It was here, in the 'School of Democracy', that Gül learned something that Erbakan and other Turkish politicians of his generation could not grasp; that Turkey needed to stop making excuses for its obvious mistakes, and instead needed to admit to problems and then seek to solve them, when necessary, by careful reform of its political institutions. It was around this time that, when there were discussions at the Political Research Centre in Ankara about the new party vision, Gül proposed that it should be called the 'Reform' Party, using the familiar English term to make their aims abundantly clear at the risk of offending only a few old-fashioned nationalists.[68]

At the time in Strasbourg, Abdullah Gül and colleagues were confronting a full-scale attack that they had been anticipating for some time. Since 1989, Turkey's application to join the European Community as a full member had been postponed, though a customs union was agreed in January 1996. In December 1997, however, amid the political chaos resulting from the Susurluk incident, a European Council meeting in Luxembourg repudiated Turkey's status as a candidate for full membership. European parliamentarians hostile to Turkey were busy building on that success by preparing an investigation into human rights abuses in the south east. On 3 June, Ruth-Gaby Vermot-Mangold, representing the Swiss Socialist Group at PACE, presented a report on the 'Humanitarian situation of the Kurdish refugees and displaced persons in South-East Turkey' that raised 'serious human rights concerns'.[69] In recalling the situation, President Gül told me:

> When I was in Strasbourg as a member, Turkey was not in good shape democratically and we were always under attack. There were always urgent debates about Turkey and they all used to criticize us heavily; sometimes they went beyond reason in their criticism. But they had many points and I knew that many of these were right because we were not democratic. But we were under attack and there were no friends of Turkey at that time, only the Turkish delegates who used to say 'no' to all the resolutions against Turkey when everyone else was for them. So we were always fighting, but there were so many times that I was joining the others. I was quiet when they were attacking us, but saying to myself 'you are right' because sometimes they exaggerated but sometimes they had good points. So in the vote sometimes I used to abstain – the killing had to stop you see – and my friends were all worried, they did not approve of the killing but felt they had to vote against the resolution because it was against Turkey. There were many resolutions against Turkey concerning unsolved murders, and these said that the murderers should be caught. My colleagues as a reflex always voted 'no', but I was selective about the items and I voted 'yes' for things I believed reflected the truth of what was going on.
>
> So my vote was never a categorical rejection of every resolution against Turkey but a qualified approach. Right now I still know many of those people and they noticed I was not always voting automatically so they came to respect my views.[70]

Gül's refusal to reject categorically each and every proposal critical of Turkey had already gained him respect among European parliamentarians at PACE. When the Vermot-Mangold report was first presented, Gül and his Turkish compatriots were able to delay implementation of the unrevised document, pointing out, among other things, that 'the report was completed without its rapporteur leaving her desk to go to the Southeast'.[71] The delaying tactic enabled Gül to lobby for support among sympathetic European colleagues.

When the revised recommendation was adopted three weeks later, rather than openly condemning Turkey, it 'invite[d] Turkey to take steps to dialogue' with the insurgent Kurds.[72] For Gül, the problem still remained to be solved since 'the killing had to stop', but the revised language was a momentary success that provided useful arguments for him to take back to Turkey.

A week after the initial proposal was delayed, Abdullah Gül gave an extensive interview in Istanbul to Ilnur Çevik, editor of the English-language *Turkish Daily News* in which he turned the debates in Europe to advance his own political goals of increasing democracy and respect for human rights in Turkey. One of his major themes throughout the interview was the need to increase support for Turkey among European nations by acting in ways that proved Turkey was both willing and capable of achieving European standards. There was, he warned, a real danger that Turkey might lose such support as it had in Europe by missing the opportunity to demonstrate its commitment to cleaning up its human rights record: above all, that meant stopping the violence against the Kurds. The initial European report, Gül recounted, had only been sent back for revision thanks to 'goodwill efforts by some friendly European parliamentarians', but he quickly added that he refused to 'deny continuing human rights abuses in Turkey' that needed to be ended.[73] In Europe, he explained, 'the Socialist group there is very prejudiced' against Turkey as well as being 'the strongest group of the Assembly'. The recent delay for revisions to their report had only been possible because he was able 'for the first time' to bring together 'Liberals, Conservatives and Christian Democrats' to object to the report as initially tabled. 'The proposal is now rejected,' he pointed out, 'but the way it was rejected is very interesting.'

> There were some European deputies who supported us. Achievement was reached by counterproposals submitted by us along with the supportive votes given by those Europeans. I have records of the speeches made at the Assembly. The reactions against Turkey were very strong. Questions were asked on whether there is democracy in Turkey, or who is governing Turkey. Is the military directing Turkey? Are civilians directing Turkey? Is there a parliament in Turkey? How much power does the prime minister or president maintain? These questions were asked by the parliamentarians who provided their support for Turkey. There are many questions about Turkey pertaining to human rights infringements; the time has come for Turkey to accomplish what is expected from her.

By relaying in this way the not-unreasonable confusion and indeed ignorance about how Turkey was currently being governed that remained current even among Turkey's supporters in Europe, Gül deftly indicated the need for political reform and not merely a better public relations campaign. Eager not to lose support in Europe, he was even more eager to stimulate recognition within Turkey that abuses of human rights must end. Without directly condemning government approval of military operations against the Kurds, he described and deplored the conditions under which the populations of entire villages were being displaced and then simply abandoned. For this he scolded the government and its complicity with the military, insisting that the forced depopulation of Kurdish villages must cease and that those thousands already displaced must be properly cared for:

> You must take these people and settle them in a suitable location, or provide them financial support and assistance for their resettlement ... Such incidents should not take place in Turkey. Turkey must achieve the mission of attaining civilian and democratic governments. All human rights infringements must come to an end in Turkey.[74]

What this interview makes evident is the way that Gül was addressing immediate problems while carefully illustrating a political agenda for reform in Turkey that he could present persuasively in both Ankara and Strasbourg. Following what he has termed his 'realistic and pragmatic approach',[75] rather than offering a general solution to the conflict, Gül outlined actions that the government should and could take to put 'an end' to abuses of human rights. This was not only a matter of increasing support from Europe, but an urgent call for the government to acknowledge its responsibilities to democracy and human rights in Turkey.

Abdullah Gül ended the interview by pointing to further infringements of human rights taking place in the universities. He observed how European colleagues could not believe how 'young men with long hair and earrings and young girls with headscarves [were] being dismissed from universities'. On 8 September, he accompanied Hayrünnisa and their lawyer to stage a protest when Ankara University refused her permission to register. September was a month for protests. When Erdoğan's sentence was confirmed by the appeals court, Gül organized a petition among European delegates in Strasbourg condemning the decision, one which 'gives the distinct impression that the judiciary is used for political purposes in Turkey'.[76] Of the fifty-two signatories to the petition, the name of only one other Turkish delegate appears, that of Ismail Ilhan Sungur, representing Fazilet from Trabzon. Rallying support for Erdoğan among Turkish colleagues in Strasbourg was evidently tougher than holding on to the support of European colleagues for Turkey.

On 15 September, the PACE group monitoring human rights in Turkey presented a 'draft information report' based on three fact-finding missions.[77] In his 'comments' on the draft report, which he presented to the European Assembly on behalf of the FP in January 1999, Gül elaborated largely and in detail on many of the positions he had taken in his interview with Ilnur Çevik the previous summer. Comments on the report from other Turkish delegates suggest something of their distance from European conceptions of democracy and human rights, perhaps helping to explain the reluctance of their party leaders to join the protest over Erdoğan. The CHP and MHP delegates objected to the report on the grounds that the writers clearly mis-understood secularism in Turkey: a necessary but insufficient argument. The ANAP delegates quibbled, objecting to the term 'Kurdish minority' since, they pointed out, the only 'minorities' in Turkey were those named in the Treaty of Lausanne. Meanwhile the DYP delegates lengthily returned to a debate about Atatürk's vision of the nation, employing such bewildering conclusions as 'The nationalism of Atatürk does not mean rationalism.' In contrast, Gül summarized his own position by noting that, 'despite prejudiced and incomplete information':

> We agree especially with the approach regarding human rights, free-doms and democratic standards presented in the report. Turkey should be together with the contemporary democratic countries and should improve her standards of democracy, human rights and freedoms just because her citizens deserve it.

Rather than attacking the report and defending Turkey, Gül set out from the position that 'Turkish democracy ... has some deficiencies and shortcomings', several of which he mentions. He noted how democracy is limited because 'the bureaucracy, especially the military, police forces, public prosecution, senior civil servants' are all 'untouchable ... with regard to their powers and influence'. The current government had not, as it claimed in December 1997, pursued improving human rights but 'just the opposite'. He agreed that the 'village guard' system 'should be abolished'; that the judicial system, especially the power of the military State Security Courts (*Devlet Güvenlik*

Mahkemeleri), needed overhauling; that the National Security Council and military had too much power in civilian affairs; that even though Lausanne does not define a 'Kurdish minority', the 'democratic rights of all citizens should be enlarged'; and he emphatically agreed with the report that the Turkish constitution needed reform: 'We share the view [that] the improvement of individual freedoms in our constitution in line with the European Convention on Human Rights is the desire of our people and all the political parties.' In words directed towards Ankara as much as the assembly in Strasbourg, Gül concluded:

> We believe that in order not to be subject to such accusations that our people do not deserve, we should undertake the necessary arrangements as soon as possible by our own will.[78]

Erbakan, if he knew what Gül was saying, would not have recognized a position that he would care to endorse, yet in Strasbourg, Gül's strong and credible stance kept a cross-alliance group of European supporters listening to what he had to say. The subsequent decision of the European Council in Helsinki on 10 December 1999 to restore Turkey as a candidate for full membership was clearly conditioned by sympathy for the suffering caused by the earthquake in August. Much of the political support for Turkey among European politicians, however, had already been set in place by Gül's lobbying efforts, which were all the more persuasive for his 'qualified approach' to criticism. And in Ankara too, his call to 'undertake the necessary arrangements' for constitutional reform were being listened to.

1999

Looking back, Abdullah Gül's old friend Fehmi Koru recognized how 1999 was something of an *annus mirabilis*.

> What a year that was! When I looked back at the events shaping the year 1999 I feel amazed. It almost started with the capture and trial of Abdullah Öcalan, the infamous leader of the PKK terrorist organisation, and it ended with the announcement of the European Union Summit held in Helsinki of Turkey's eligibility for candidacy. And there were many ground breaking developments in between.[79]

By the time of the Helsinki agreement, much of Gül's general vision for political reform, as outlined in his comments to PACE in January, had been adopted by Recai Kutan in his attempt to make Fazilet a credible party. By then, however, it was already too late. Since becoming party chair back in May 1998, Kutan had struggled against the perception that he was merely enacting Erbakan's will, regularly consulting in Ankara with Gül and other party members such as Cemil Çiçek, Ali Coşkun and Abdülkadir Aksu who were more moderate than Erbakan. With general elections coming up in early 1999, however, there was little he could achieve by way of shifting the powerful perception that Fazilet was merely Refah under a different name, and that it still spelled a vision of political Islam not very different from Erbakan's.

Suffering repeated harassment by the secular establishment – cases against mayors, economic boycotts of businesses associated with the party, even a petition filed by the State Security Courts (DGM) to close the party for crimes against the secular system – the party was constantly forced into defensive positions.[80] Early in February, Süleyman Demirel went so far as to accuse Fazilet of having 'two faces', thereby suggesting that they were an Islamist movement engaged in *takiyye*, dissembling and hiding their real intentions for religious purposes.[81] Despite Kutan's denials that such was the case, the perception proved impossible to shake. Meanwhile, a fully visible split was forming between Erbakan and his loyal followers, and the reformers.

In the run-up to the elections, Erbakan did the party's chances of holding on to Refah's former voters little good by putting his own name forward as an independent candidate for Konya. During his coalition with Tansu Çiller, he had learned to moderate his positions somewhat, and the FP election pamphlet abandoned familiar *Milli Görüş* slogans by declaring three goals: 'The state will be democratic; the government will be uncorrupted; and the society will be free.'[82] Erbakan may have allowed a different rhetoric into the campaign programme, but there were many – including party members – who were suspicious of the way he insisted on personally selecting party candidates. A month before the April elections, Erbakan's 'final effort' to control Fazilet policy was said to have 'brought the party to the edge of a break up'.[83] His stamp upon the selection of candidates was evident to all who were watching, including moderate conservatives who had formerly voted for Refah despite, rather than because of, Erbakan's pro-Islamic positions. At a time when opinion polls regularly showed that more than seventy percent of the population approved of lifting the headscarf ban in universities and public institutions, Erbakan saw an opening for promoting his version of

Islamic culture, insisting that eight of the seventeen women candidates being put forward for election were covered, knowing full well that their election would only cause trouble.

Although Fazilet did well in the municipal areas, the 18 April elections were a national disaster, dropping them into third place behind Bülent Ecevit's Democratic Left Party (DSP) and the Nationalist Action Party (MHP), now headed by Devlet Bahçeli, 'a veteran member of the violent "idealist" (*ülkücü*) movement' since the death of Alparslan Türkeş a year previously.[84] Formed from the bizarre coalition of Ecevit – considered by many at the time to be a socialist – and the extreme nationalist Bahçeli, the new government leaders were united in little except their opposition to Erbakan's party and their paranoid suspicions of Islamic conspiracies. Their great legacy would be leading the country into the worst and final recession of the decade within six months of being in power.

In the weeks following the 1999 elections, Abdullah Gül's name began appearing regularly in the Turkish press as a likely new party leader. He discouraged such rumours by ignoring them. A week after the election, however, Bülent Arınç was first among the reformist group to put his own name forward as a possible candidate for the new leadership, proposing changes to the structure of the party that would 'eliminate the influence of Erbakan'.[85] A lawyer who had represented the Aegean city of Manisa for Refah since 1995, Arınç was an obvious choice to begin announcing a future for Fazilet without Erbakan. While there were some within the group that thought Gül should step forward, his apparent diffidence at the time was no longer simply loyalty to Erbakan since there was a clear case that Arınç was the better man for the times. For one thing, with popular strongholds in Istanbul and Ankara, stretching the reformist group's footprint to the secular west coast was more than simply a good public relations tactic. Arınç was known to be well respected in a region traditionally loyal to the party and legacy of Atatürk, and his reputation was impeccable. The public prosecutor had brought cases against numerous FP deputies including Gül, but not Arınç. With Erdoğan on his way to prison, and Melih Gökçek holding the mayoralty of Ankara, Gül knew that careful planning for the future was his most important task.

The election results showed that disenchantment with Erbakan was a factor in the loss of support: the strong Islamists had defected, disappointed with what they considered his weakness while in power, while the 'famous hard-working party workers refused to make an extra effort to have Erbakan's

candidates elected'.[86] Fazilet had also lost substantial support from many conservative voters who were not Islamists but had supported Refah in the past
from disillusionment with the other parties. Reluctant to run against Erbakan,
Gül thought that his time would be better spent drafting a full-scale party
agenda setting out in detail his vision for achieving constitutional and other
reforms that would recapture the lost vote. This would eventually become
the AK Party Programme.

Abdullah Gül steered clear of the limelight through the early summer of
1999, refusing to join the well-publicized challenge to Erbakan inside the
party, where the fight against secularism was becoming a defining policy.
On 7 May, the public prosecutor Vural Savaş opened a court case against
Fazilet after Merve Kavakçı, one of the party's newly elected parliamentary
delegates, notoriously insisted on wearing her headscarf to the swearing-in
ceremonies. Demirel joined in the attack, accusing her of being 'an agent pro-
vocateur working for radical Islamic states'.[87] Immediately Kutan, Arınç and
Gül loudly defended Kavakçı and the party in the national press, declaring
that the headscarf was a human rights issue rather than a matter of religion. 'If
this country is a democratic state based on law,' announced Arınç, 'different
opinions will live freely', later in the year arguing that Turkey needed a new
civil constitution.[88] These were positions that Gül shared, but he was keeping such a low profile that one analyst presumed that this 'leading dissident'
voice in the party was now 'drifting in the wake of the traditionalists', silently
taking the 'same line as Erbakan's supporters', and thereby demonstrating that
'no discordant voice has a possibility of being heard in the party'.[89] Gül was
indeed busy doing other things; he was watching the economy while deliber-
ating future strategies for the party. Later in May, at a regional party meeting
in Kayseri, he did speak out on Kavakçı's behalf, using the occasion to attack
Ecevit, who was supporting the case against her, and his new government.
'Although this government has been formed,' he told party supporters in his
hometown, 'it's not going to last because it's doomed to failure. Why? Turkey
will get nowhere with Bülent Ecevit's economic policies and tax reform laws.
Turkey will get nowhere with a socialist mentality.'[90] Eager as ever to displace
religion from defining party political discourse, Gül was keen to keep other,
less tendentious issues to the fore. Ecevit's 'socialism' rightly promised better
income distribution but had no plans for sustaining and regulating the growth
that would be needed to pay for it all. Increasingly over the next few years, Gül
would keep his eyes on the economy, offering an international perspective
and advocating necessary reforms.

Meanwhile, with the Fazilet Party in near chaos, Abdullah Gül and Murat Mercan worked steadily organizing discussions with members of the reformist group, taking advice from visiting international academics, bankers and diplomats. They were debating how best to repackage and publicize the proposals for reform that Gül had outlined in Strasbourg into what became the AK Party Programme. Once it became known that Kavakçı was a US citizen with dual nationality and therefore not eligible for political office, Arınç and others simply abandoned her, turning the blame onto Erbakan for having insisted on her nomination in the first place. With Fazilet pursuing hard-line policies that were likely to result in its closure, keeping the reformist group together and focused was crucial, especially during those months that Erdoğan was in prison. Analysts had suggested that Erdoğan's popularity had encouraged many to vote for Fazilet on 18 April in order to protest the injustice against him. Shortly after his release from prison a poll conducted in Istanbul revealed that 'people from all walks of life and inclinations named Erdoğan as the most popular political leader',[91] Fehmi Koru, now a columnist for *Yeni Şafak*, reported in October. While drafting reform policies, Gül and Mercan kept in close dialogue with the imprisoned Erdoğan.

> Throughout these months we kept very close links with Tayyip Erdoğan. Abdullah Gül and I visited him while in prison almost twice a month after he was gaoled in April. We were busy running branches of the reform group, one in Istanbul and one in Ankara, and I spent a good deal of time keeping relations between them together, united against opposition from 'conspiracies' that were aimed at dividing the party. But relations between Tayyip Erdoğan and Abdullah Gül were always sound during this period. One of Abdullah Bey's main virtues is that he has always ignored critical comments against Tayyip Erdoğan. I have never known any instance of him listening to gossip from inside or outside the party. The Political Research Centre was the key to developing the new party's long-term strategies. When Tayyip Bey was released, Fazilet was falling apart, so we assembled in Ankara and discussed founding a new party. Abdullah Gül was working with the foreign ministry and bringing fresh ideas about democracy from Europe.[92]

Warding off suspicions of serious division within the party, Gül admitted that there was 'a "sweet" struggle within the party but [it] would never lead to disintegration'.[93]

In July, however, shortly after Erdoğan was released from prison, Gül together with Cemil Çiçek, Ali Coşkun and Abdülkadir Aksu all resigned from the party administrative committee, signalling suspicions that a leadership battle was about to break out. On 28 July, an anonymous party insider was reported to have said: 'Gül is one of the reformist's heavy guns. He is intelligent and has the support of the people.'[94] Speaking as deputy party chairman, Arınç responded to rumours that 'young reformers' were 'leaving home' to start their own party. 'We consider ourselves the house owners, not the lodgers,' he told the press, and denied gossip that the resignations of Gül and others had been inspired by Erdoğan during meetings while he was in prison. The resignations were, he explained, an internal matter of adjusting party administration to accommodate newly elected delegates onto the executive committee; no one had resigned from the party itself.[95] The following day, Gül himself confirmed that their resignations 'are not an effort to form a new party. We will continue to serve our party and our group.'[96] In Ankara that is just what he continued doing, serving both the party and the reformist group while advising Kutan on policies that were in line with the 'comments' he had presented earlier in the year at Strasbourg on the need to reform democracy and improve human rights. An unforeseeable disaster would give a tragic edge and new evidence for that need.

On 17 August 1999, critics of Turkey were temporarily silenced when an earthquake erupted east of Istanbul killing more than seventeen thousand people. During the summer parliamentary recess, Abdullah Gül with his wife and children was at his father-in-law's house in Gebze, the epicentre of the earthquake, when the earthquake struck, devastating an industrial region two hundred kilometres long and forty kilometres wide, and destroying the provinces of Kocaeli, Sakarya and Yalova.[97] The government's failure to organize relief operations immediately politicized the disaster. While the government stumbled over rescuing people and organizing relief, Gül was among the first volunteers to arrive in Sakarya. According to Sami Güçlü, 'he wanted to check on all his old colleagues at the university, make sure they were all okay, and to help in any way'. While government relief efforts continued to prove inadequate, thousands of volunteers set up impromptu rescue operations. Attempts by international relief organizations were sometimes delayed by red tape, but nationalist politics were laid aside as assistance from Greece and Israel was welcomed.

The government itself wasted further time and energy deflecting attention from their own failures. Suspicious that Islamist organizations would try to gain popular credit by stepping in with relief supplies, the government tried to prevent this from happening by sending police officers to raid Muslim foundations and to seize blankets, tents and any other relief supplies they might find. Fehmi Koru declared at the time that the government 'don't want Islamic groups or Islamic people to be able to take credit for helping anyone'.[98] For their part, extreme Islamists were busy making capital out of both the disaster and the government's failures by pronouncing startling and apocalyptic prophecies. Reporting to the *New York Times* ten days after the earthquake had struck, Stephen Kinzer quoted a columnist for an extreme paper who had written that: 'Earthquakes are brought on by adultery or oppression ... When people practice these sins, the earth rebels, prays to God and then shakes. This will continue until God deals a fatal blow to these people.' Kinzer, for his part, noted that 'such views ... are not widely shared even among devout Muslims in Turkey', and suggested that they reflected a division among the Muslim supporters of Erbakan's party. Asked for his opinion as a 'leader of the dissident faction' within Fazilet, Gül took the opportunity to demonstrate the calm, moderate and reasoned style he had developed in Strasbourg, deflecting any suspicion from Muslims like himself who had taken a hand in helping the victims, while admitting to party problems and reproving the government with ironic understatement rather than vitriol. He told Kinzer:

> Our party is not well organized now. Plenty of our people rushed to the earthquake area to help, but they did it as individuals. A lot of help also came from cities and towns where our people are mayors. But because of the party's internal problems, we haven't been able to act in any united way. The other problem is the pressure the state has been putting on us. They are very suspicious of our motives, and so they're preventing many of our groups from sending aid. That wouldn't be so bad if the state itself was perfectly organized, but as we have seen, that's not quite the case.[99]

When PACE met on 1 September, Gül was part of an international team that proposed establishing a 'world rescue organisation for natural disasters'.[100] But there was nothing natural about the disaster that soon would wreck the Turkish economy. Ecevit's government, having proved incompetent at handling earthquake relief, was incapable of halting the fourth recession of the decade that would see GDP decline by over six percent by year's end.[101]

Gül challenges Erbakan

An acknowledged leader of the reformist group within Fazilet, Abdullah Gül had become an international spokesman, using his reputation to advance the ideas he was developing for a new party to readers in the international media, while using his international experience and perspective to advise his party leader. In early November, he accompanied Recai Kutan and a Fazilet Party delegation to Washington, DC, where Kutan outlined their plans for Turkey, stating categorically that 'there is no danger of Sharia law in Turkey'.[102] On their return, Kutan arranged a press conference to 'launch the latest phase of his party's public relations crusade'. Even Fehmi Koru admitted that he was 'terribly surprised' when, 'from out of the blue', Kutan announced 'a "new constitution," radically different from the existing one in its approach to basic freedoms and institutions.'[103] The major features of the proposals followed the emphases of Gül's Strasbourg speech on necessary political reforms that would extend democracy and human rights. Clearly influenced by Gül's arguments, Kutan's key proposals included: reducing the military presence on the National Security Council to only one member; holding direct elections to the presidency, and allowing presidents a second term; judicial reforms that would free the courts from government control while widening the rights of detainees; abolishing the State Security Courts (DGM) thus putting the entire justice system under civilian control; lifting restrictions on the use of languages other than Turkish in the press and media; allowing right of assembly including the right of all workers to form unions and to strike; and, finally, freeing the Department of Religious Affairs (*Diyanet*) and the universities from government control. Kutan's 'democracy package' also proposed following international rather than domestic law in all cases where they conflicted, and striking clauses from the constitution regarding 'nationalization' in order to facilitate privatization.[104]

In December, even as Ecevit was signing a deal with the IMF that his government would prove incapable of following, Gül challenged Erbakan for leadership of the Fazilet Party.[105] By March 2000, there was no longer any doubt that in preparation for the party convention scheduled for 14 May, Gül would be standing as the reformist candidate against Recai Kutan. Still barred from political life, Erdoğan fully supported Gül's candidacy in what was reported as an attempt 'to confront Erbakan without any cracks in their ranks'. 'Reformists have been having talks among themselves since last February and, as a result, Arınç dropped from the race, and both Arınç and Şener have decided to back Gül's candidacy.'[106]

2000

At the beginning of the new millennium, Abdullah Gül found himself in the curious position of leading a reformist group within an opposition party for which he was a leading international spokesman but which was being threatened with closure on charges of promoting Islamic policies in which he had no belief. It was a position that enabled him to take the same message to Turkey that he had delivered in Europe. It was a message in which he had long believed, and one that he now had a chance to promote with realistic expectations: the need for fundamental reform to the Turkish constitution. Having learned from engaging in debates in Strasbourg how to set about establishing suitable institutions for guaranteeing rule of law, democracy and human rights, Gül was projecting how to apply these standards and measures to Turkey in reasonable, democratic and beneficial ways. Having listened to European critics of Turkey and quietly saying to himself 'you are right', he knew that the task ahead was a pragmatic one to find a way to bring about the necessary changes.

Following lengthy discussions on the topic of political reform at meetings of the Political Research Centre with Erdoğan, Şener and Arınç, Gül and Mercan had prepared a detailed speech outlining a programme of necessary reforms to the constitution. With this speech for a platform, Gül ran against Erbakan for party leadership at the 14 May 2000 congress.

> This search for reform was not on the agenda of the conservative nationalists or the Muslims on the right. It was the first time that reform has been on the agenda of the right! In his thinking and proposals, he was following Spain and other countries that were undergoing developments comparable to those in Turkey. He put great importance on taking realistic steps to democracy, using examples, in his challenge to Erbakan at the Fazilet congress. He didn't win, but this was an extraordinary moment to speak against the leader. In that speech he first laid out his reformist programme that would become the founding programme of the AKP.[107]

Scheduled to commemorate the first multiparty elections held back in 1950, the Fazilet Party congress of May 2000 was the stage for 'a competition unprecedented in the history of Turkish Islamist parties',[108] the first time that any political party had fielded two candidates in an election for its own leadership. Usually party administrative committees would nominate a single candidate for confirmation, so there was considerable interest in what would happen at the convention. Mehmet Ali Birand was impressed and claimed that the event heralded a new phase in Turkish democracy: 'There were no scuffles in the hall. There was no unpleasantness. Recai Kutan is to be given credit for the creation of such an atmosphere. He and Gül competed courteously with one another. In this respect the Virtue Party (FP) is the winner – along with Turkish democracy.'[109]

A new party is born

Abdullah Gül and the reformist group failed to capture control of the party, but they received a massive 521 votes against Kutan's 633: the reform movement was clearly a serious challenge. A split within the party seemed likely to all observers. Sami Güçlü confirmed that members of the reformist group recognized how 'forming a new party became inevitable' as soon as Gül and the proposals contained in his speech were turned down. 'Since a major problem with Fazilet had been over leadership, Gül was a natural choice given his background, popularity and easy manner; he represented a new kind of political leader unlike Erbakan who was no longer trusted by many within the party.'[110] With a court case pending against Fazilet, the reformists adopted the obvious tactic of awaiting the Court's decision. But there was no longer any reason to hide their plans. Murat Mercan continued to work with the national media, releasing press statements on behalf of the reformists. By December, their plans were stated publicly:

> If the Constitutional court rules not to dissolve the party, the reform-
> ists are resolved to wait a few months and, by avoiding accusations of
> 'disloyalty,' announce the forming of a new party. The preparations for
> a new party that the reformists have been working on for a year now
> have started to yield results. Even the declaration of establishment for
> the new party is ready.[111]

With the necessary initial documents all prepared, it would not be until August 2001, after the Constitutional Court had closed the Fazilet Party in June, that the new party declared itself. In the meantime, the Political Research Centre was seeking new members.

All were agreed that the new party needed a detailed approach to problems facing Turkish women. Gül and Erdoğan approached a number of possible candidates, including Ayşe Böhürler, a documentary film maker and journalist with Channel 7, and invited her to become a founding member of their new party. Known for reporting on the poverty, educational limitations and personal abuse facing many women in Turkey, Ayşe Böhürler was ideally suited to representing women within the party; she is smart, progressive and publicly engaged, and she wears a headscarf.

> I was invited to a meeting by Abdullah Gül and Tayyip Erdoğan. They were discussing the terms on which the new party was to be formed and they asked me who could be female founding members of the party. When they invited me to become a founding member I was very surprised and told them that I was an oppositional journalist! But Gül replied that this is why I was the kind of person they wanted – someone who was critical. This was intriguing to me because it is an unusual strategy for forming political parties since, in Turkey, being a party member requires devotion to the leader. So when they offered me the post, I said I would never be a fanatic or devoted member, but if that was okay then 'yes'. But you must understand, my husband is a former Marxist and my family are all MHP nationalists. I feel personally closer to the left, and had to tell all my friends, 'I didn't move from the left when I agreed to join the AKP.' But there is also a rumour that I never joined and am still not really a party member![112]

Ayşe Böhürler was actively engaged with women's organizations both inside and outside Turkey. Having recently filmed documentaries on women in Iran, central Anatolia and the Middle East, she knew where to go and who to contact. Travelling to promote the party in rural areas, she was again struck by rural underdevelopment and the particular problems facing Anatolian women. She reported back to the party leaders how, in the province of Ardahan in the extreme north east, there were no fewer than 167 villages that still had no electricity or running water. 'This was in 2000! And in other parts of Anatolia there were similar problems, so the women in all these places are part of the most underdeveloped society in the country.' While everyone in the party agreed that development was needed and would improve the lives of women, discussions about *women* – not 'society' or 'the family' – were not always so simple.

In all these targets the party as a whole accepted the general principles, but many were sometimes thinking differently from us. When I would say 'let's look from the woman's point of view,' they would say 'let's look from the family point of view'. Since they were conservative and many women in the party are conservative, we had to adjust our language. Abdullah Gül, however, was always supportive of the women's initiatives. When we were first building up the management of the party, I suggested a friend, who is a radical lawyer, become part of the central committee and they hesitated. But Gül came and asked her personally to join the central committee, and said to her 'if you don't demand you won't get your rights, and I will always support you'.[113]

When AKP later came to power, many of its earliest reforms to the judicial code would respond to demands made during discussions with women's organizations.

2001

Preoccupied as he was with setting up the new party, Abdullah Gül remained active at the Council of Europe where a decade's service had made him a highly respected senior member of the Parliamentary Assembly. During 2000 he took a lead on investigating conditions in Chechnya, while serving on committees looking into European banking, the global economy, projects for increasing stability in South East Europe, and Azerbaijan's application for membership of the Council.[114] In 2001, he joined a large multinational group protesting Armenia's continued occupation of Azeri territory in Nagorno-Karabakh, recommending that it be recognized as the latest phase in 'the genocide perpetrated by the Armenians against the Azeri population from the beginning of the 19th century'.[115]

In March 2001, Gül was appointed by the Political Affairs Committee to join a fact-finding team touring Israel and the Palestinian territories. It was less than six months previously that Ariel Sharon's visit to the Al-Aqsa mosque had sparked off the violent rebellion of the second Intifada, and only a month since Sharon had been elected prime minister of Israel. Sharon duly ignored the PACE team. But on 20 March, Abdullah Gül's first day in Jerusalem, after a morning visit to a Holocaust Memorial and an afternoon attending a special session of the Knesset, he met with Shimon Peres, then minister for foreign affairs.

I was with several deputies from Germany and some Palestinians. Peres was talking about the peace initiative at a time of failure. I asked him why he thought the initiative had failed and he said something. I said I wasn't satisfied. I said the problem was right here in Jerusalem. This was after the Camp David agreement had collapsed over the question of Jerusalem. So I told him Jerusalem was the problem, and Peres went silent. A German friend said, 'He is stuck!' Then Peres looked at me and asked me if I wanted to rule Jerusalem again. And I said 'Of course! Don't you remember that we handled it for several hundred years? We could do it again!' And he laughed and said, 'You Muslims, you all say the same things!'[116]

In Ramallah, Gül met with Yasser Arafat and Hanan Ashrawi before being taken on a tour of Gaza and the refugee camps there. Back in Strasbourg, the PACE team reported in April that 'both sides ... must stop immediately all forms of violence' and return to negotiations 'in the spirit of the Oslo Agreements'. But the violence and political killings would only intensify during the late spring and summer of 2001. A further recommendation of the PACE report stipulated that 'both sides should show a more flexible attitude in resolving the key issues and should refrain from outdated declarative rhetoric',[117] terms that Gül associated with the situation in Turkey, where, he believed, Erbakan's 'outdated declarative rhetoric' had provoked the closure of Refah and was about to close Fazilet.

Before that happened, Gül kept up the political pressure on the Ecevit government, using his position as a respected and leading spokesman for the young generation of moderates within the opposition party to make policy statements on foreign affairs, human rights problems and the government's mishandling of the economic crisis. By 2000, Turkey's economy was in a mess and about to become worse. Ecevit had taken over a crisis waiting to happen. Economic growth had picked up slowly after 1995, but inflation remained high, the trade deficit had grown dangerously, nothing was being done to end corruption, and Ecevit's economic policies during his spell in power had 'lacked credibility', creating enormous state debt.[118] Ecevit had celebrated his victory by increasing wages to government employees, but had failed to make good on proposals to pay for the shortfall from accelerating the privatization of state property and eradicating the black market, which Gül calculated to have become 'at least as big as half the GNP'.[119]

Economic crises

For over a decade, Turkey's financial institutions continued to fail at controlling the nature and extent of economic growth that Turgut Özal's neoliberal
reforms had introduced. In December 1999, Ecevit agreed with the IMF on
a programme of financial reforms that had led to a brief moment of optimism
as inflation and interest rates fell. But nothing was done to curb the black
market from cashing in as the lower interest rates led to people spending
more, causing the current account deficit to rise, and forcing the government 'to borrow at increasingly unfavourable rates'. By November 2000 the
IMF programme was in ruins as 'foreign banks, afraid of a sudden collapse,
stopped lending to Turkish banks', though 'a full-scale flight out of the lira was
narrowly avoided'. The brief reprieve did not last long: the highly publicized
row the following February when President Ahmet Sezer hurled a printed
copy of the constitution at Prime Minister Ecevit, accusing his government
of failing to tackle corruption, sparked a full-scale economic crisis leading to
the collapse of large sections of the banking sector, the loss of over a million
jobs, and the lira to halve in value.[120]

On 28 February, speaking at a press conference, Abdullah Gül responded
to the crisis by warning of hyper-inflation and calling for the government to
resign or implement 'urgent and serious measures'.[121] Having crunched the
numbers, he pointed out how 'during last November's financial crisis', failures at
the Central Bank had caused Turkey to lose 'some $7 billion in foreign capital'
creating a devaluation of the currency that made wages equivalent to those of
1980. He outlined an 'exit programme' that focused on ending corruption:

> Turkey has to implement a new economic policy using new staff. It is
> imperative that these people not be tainted in any way, not be involved
> in corruption in any way and that they be open, honest people who
> know what they are doing. The banks, which are the main source of the
> crisis, should be dealt with courageously and the banks made profitable.
> Reforms to remove political influence from the state banks must definitely
> be implemented. Corruption is at least as big as half the GNP and should
> also be tackled courageously and transparently in the public sector ...
> A growth model based on exports should be brought to life urgently.[122]

As if on cue, an emergency bail-out by the IMF of sixteen billion dollars
arrived, and it came with conditions. In March, Kemal Derviş was brought

in from the World Bank to serve as minister of the economy with the task of cleaning up Turkey's financial system. 'Over twenty ailing banks were seized by the state, to be sold, closed down or rehabilitated through mergers, and a complete overhaul of the financial sector was undertaken. Turkey's economy emerged transformed from this painful and costly process.'[123]

During his years in parliament, Gül had noticed the reluctance of the coalition governments to take a strong stand against corruption: too many politicians were benefiting personally. And he fully understood the need for engaging with 'the positive aspect of economic globalization based on active participation in the global market', while at the same time seeking to end the inflationary cycles and unemployment that adopting neoliberal policies had entailed since the 1980s.[124] Gül's call for ending corruption and reforming the banks would remain key elements of what he termed 'an economic philosophy', aimed at linking financial reforms with social policies designed to address the problems of high unemployment and 'an incredibly bad distribution of income' as part of a broader and integrated commitment to improving human rights in Turkey. Speaking on behalf of the reformist group in July 2001, he declared:

> We believe in the dynamism of the private sector and of the free market economy. We believe that development will not be able to happen using the state apparatus, or that if there is development, then it will be inadequate and ineffective. However, if there is one truth it is that social justice in Turkey is a mess. There is an economic picture that produces incredible unemployment. Not to foresee social policy in the light of this picture is simply to say 'Let the dying die and the survivors stay with us.' This is not going to be our position.[125]

This 'economic philosophy' indicated directions for economic reforms that, in line with Derviş's restructuring of the financial sector, Gül would put into practice once the AKP came to power in 2002. But until then, he could only keep pressuring the government while keeping a sharp and critical eye on how Derviş was handling the crisis.

Enter the AKP

In June 2001, the Constitutional Court closed the Fazilet Party. The next month Recai Kutan went off to form the *Saadet Partisi* ('Felicity Party' or

SP), while the reformists established the *Adalet ve Kalkınma Partisi* ('Justice and Development Party' or AKP) in August, with Recep Tayyip Erdoğan as party chair. Right from the start, the AKP presented themselves as a new kind of party, one that was 'not tightly-controlled … doing the bidding of its leader and manipulated by the elites'.[126] AKP was a team effort, one that had emerged from years of discussions among members of the Political Research Centre. Right from their inception, they had aimed to develop a comprehensive action plan, not based on meaningless slogans but on practical political and economic reforms that would recapture the majority vote once enjoyed by Refah while democratizing Turkish society. Murat Mercan explained:

> The initial AK Party Programme was the result of a group effort based on the experience of the Refah and Fazilet period, the failures and problems. The new party had young people in it who were keen to help the disadvantaged as well as the middling sorts and all who needed help. This came from the Refah days. The economy was very bad at the time, yet the mistakes of Refah and Fazilet were useful for learning about shortcomings of their policies. While in Fazilet, Abdullah Gül was always very critical of that party, and that experience directed the new Party Programme. AKP carried many key ideas over, but the underpinning philosophy was different. There were new people and ideas, especially in respect of style, new ideas and manners of presentation. The Party Programme outlined a different style of management and self-presentation to make clear that AK was distinct from what had come before, and to head off Western opposition that we were Islamists. We knew we needed to present a clearer face to the West and to the world, and that we needed to disassociate AK from Refah and Fazilet which had been directly inspired by, and hence continued the programmes of, *Milli Görüş* – and this was an association AK was keen to terminate. Much in Refah was unrealistic – economic plans, relations with foreign nations – so all these were changed in the new programme.[127]

Armed with their carefully developed Party Programme, the AKP won a landslide victory in the November elections of 2002 suggesting that 'the AKP appears to have successfully rebuilt the Özal–ANAP coalition'.[128]

Between the defeat of Özal's government in 1991 and the victory of the AKP in 2002, Turkey had suffered from too many weak coalition governments.

These had proved incapable of controlling the economy and of colluding in a disastrous war in the south east that had cost thousands of lives and intensified ethnic tensions as Turkish families who lost their sons in the fighting began confusing all Kurds with insurgent PKK fighters. The secular political classes had steadily fallen into disrepute as they formed short-lived political parties and unstable alliances, more interested in securing power than solving unemployment while at the same time enriching themselves rather than ending corruption. In the course of claiming to protect the secular state from a perceived threat from Islamic fundamentalists, they had alienated large sectors of the conservative population. Enforcing the ban on headscarves only made matters worse, while revelations of complicity between state officials and organized criminal organizations exacerbated distrust of the entire political system. It was time for a change.

After ten years of political life, Abdullah Gül and his reformist colleagues had brought a new party into being and into power, one that was committed to new styles of democratic organization and with plans for social, juridical and constitutional reforms. Gül and the Political Research Centre had prepared a comprehensive Party Programme, one that has continued to determine party policy ever since. The task in 2002 would be to begin putting that Programme into practice.

5

AKP and the 'New Turkey' 2002 to 2007

The year 2002 was one of increasing global uncertainties and would end with a factory-worker's son from Kayseri becoming Prime Minister of Turkey. When the AKP came to power, Abdullah Gül's party was little more than a year old, formally coming into being on 14 August 2001, mere weeks before the Twin Towers in New York were destroyed. Almost at once Turkey had achieved new importance to the US plans for a 'war on terror', a new status that opened up possibilities of rich financial benefits, not to mention regional and international prestige.[1] But handouts from the US always come at a price, and would do little to solve the long-term causes of the immediate economic crisis. Under the previous government and in line with IMF prescriptions, Kemal Derviş had set about privatization schemes to sell off the airlines, state-owned banks, petrol stations, oil refineries, and monopolies on tobacco and spirits. Feroz Ahmad succinctly describes the results: 'There was massive unemployment as plants shut down, and small businesses were squeezed out as a result of the reforms, which were marked by tight credit, slow production to bring down inflation and higher taxes.'[2] By November 2001, over a million people had lost their jobs since the start of the year. During protests held in Ankara that month, 'a mother of three set herself on fire, screaming "I am starving to death".'[3]

During the early weeks of 2002, Abdullah Gül kept a critical eye on Kemal Derviş's reform programme while pushing vigorously on behalf of EU accession reforms.[4] His experience in Strasbourg had provided him with new ideas and language needed for helping to draft the package of constitutional amendments that had already been adopted by the coalition parliament in

August 2001; but his efforts had so far failed to gain sufficient support for clauses abolishing capital punishment or extending human rights by permitting Kurds to learn and broadcast in their own language. His championing of these causes allied him with secular liberals from the CHP, much to the irritation of some AKP members, but it also enhanced his reputation in Europe by drawing attention to his independent position on these key problems.

At the same time, Abdullah Gül was pressing for improving human rights in Turkey, vocally condemning coalition government proposals to pass amendments to Article 312, which he claimed would endanger freedom of speech even further by giving judges the power to decide if a statement represented a 'clear and present danger' of inciting violence.[5] He strongly opposed US plans for invading Iraq. Following a visit to Ankara by Dick Cheney to find out if Turkey would support US military actions against Saddam Hussein, Gül boldly stated: 'When the TV stations and newspapers broadcast and publicize the stories of massacres in Palestine, it has become impossible for people of Muslim countries, especially the Arabic countries and Turkey, to accept an operation against Iraq.'[6] A year previously he had been a member of a European fact-finding mission to Israel and Palestine. On that visit he had met – and shared opinions with – Shimon Peres and Yasser Arafat, and later contributed to a PACE position paper critical of US and Israeli policies towards the Palestinian people.[7] He remained critical of US plans in Iraq, pointing out that polls taken at the time of Cheney's visit showed that ninety percent of the Turkish people opposed a US-led war against Iraq, which would, in any case, be an economic disaster for Turkey. Gül declared that Saddam Hussein had become a 'dictator' who 'had used chemical weapons against his own people', but believed that the UN should intervene to prevent a war against his army and people. At home, he insisted that Turkey's loans from the IMF 'should not hinder the government from giving a clear message to Cheney'.[8]

During the spring of 2002 the coalition government, fragile enough as it already was amid the economic crisis, ran into serious trouble when Bülent Ecevit became ill. Anticipating early elections, party executives looked about for future alliances and started campaigning.

Ankara and family life

During their first decade living in Ankara, Abdullah and Hayrünnisa Gül had struggled to find private time together at home amid an increasingly crowded diary of meetings. Abdullah was away most weekends and rarely saw the children, but once Ahmet Münir and Kübra had settled into their schools, Hayrünnisa and baby Mehmet Emre began joining him on his trips to Strasbourg, Paris, London, New York and Washington, DC.

In Jeddah, Hayrünnisa had paid particular attention to the selection not just of schools, but of individual teachers within them, and exercised the same diligence in choosing schools and teachers in Ankara. Although the family spoke Turkish at home, the children had learned to read and write in Arabic and English at school. 'When we came back to Turkey,' Hayrünnisa explained, 'the children had a hard time writing in Turkish. The first two years, we had a tutor coming to our house to teach them how to write in Turkish.'[9] Their early years in Jeddah had given both of them quiet and contemplative personalities; they were interested in reading books and discussing ideas and were encouraged to express their views at home.

> The children were very young then, Ahmet and Kübra. One was in second grade and the other one in third grade. We had a baby at home. I am happy now because I did not neglect them. Abdullah Bey was at the parliament during the week and would always go to Kayseri on the weekends. He also attended the Council of Europe meetings and travelled to Strasbourg frequently. He sometimes travelled to other cities, too.[10]

Within a year, both Ahmet and Kübra had adjusted to life in Turkey by focusing on their studies and spending time at home with the family. With baby Mehmet, Hayrünnisa began accompanying Abdullah on short trips to Europe.

> We regularly visited Strasbourg with Mehmet while he was still a baby. He was well behaved and travelled well. I must tell you a funny story. Once we had a long trip to Spain with a large group of European MPs – there must have been fifty of them – and there were meetings and so on. I would go along carrying Mehmet in the pushchair, and he would sit listening during meetings! We became friends with a British couple who were there and they asked me how Turkish babies are so well behaved! In Jeddah life was more comfortable but Mehmet never knew that, he was always moving with us so he never had that kind of family life. But his experience travelling with us has made him very interested in politics unlike his older brother. He likes to discuss politics with his father and knows more of the world. Maybe Ahmet

and Kübra grew up differently and became less interested in politics because they grew up knowing its problems and that there is an easier life. But none of them like to be visible or like being known by everyone because of their father.[11]

Both Ahmet and Kübra were doing well at school and would both win admission to, and graduate from, the prestigious industrial engineering programme at Bilkent University in Ankara.

> Upon our return to Turkey, Ahmet studied at a school teaching French and then went to Sabancı University for a year and then to Bilkent University to study industrial engineering. Kübra also studied industrial engineering ... Kübra was studying in English, so she caught up with her brother in school and studied in the same class. Students of industrial engineering go on an internship during the summer holidays. Let me also say that our children, during their junior and senior high school years, studied at schools which accepted students based on exam results. In other words, they experienced the same difficulties as all other children and received an education based on their hard work. Kübra first studied at the Anadolu High School, at Anadolu Imam Hatip School and then went to a science school. Ahmet studied at a college, but that school also accepted students based only on test results.[12]

Both remained shy of attracting public notice to who they were.

> Once Ahmet was on a distribution truck when he interned at a factory making biscuits. The driver was listening to the radio and there was some news about Abdullah Bey on the radio referring to what the foreign minister said and where he travelled and so on. The driver told Ahmet how he liked the foreign minister. Ahmet never told the driver he was his son.[13]

While Hayrünnisa and the young Mehmet Emre were becoming used to a certain amount of public notice from accompanying Abdullah Gül on international state visits, Ahmet Münir and Kübra shunned attention, finding Ankara and the remote Bilkent campus, with its international mix of students, professors and visiting experts, a relatively easy place to maintain a low profile. Life off campus, however, could prove a different matter, and make anonymity something of a challenge. Hayrünnisa recalled 'a number of similar incidents' when Ahmet avoided attention:

> Another time, Ahmet had a bad traffic accident: as he was coming back from school, thieves running from the police come from the wrong direction and hit Ahmet's car. Even in that moment of shock, when the police and the reporters standing there (the reporters were there because they were following the police during the chase) asked his name, he did not say his last name in that state of shock as he got out of the car. When they insisted on learning his last name, he said 'Ahmet Münir', using only his second name. Later on they recognized him when he had a medical check-up at the hospital.[14]

Hayrünnisa lives very much through the lives of her own children, but also holds strong opinions about improving life in Turkey, and was starting to use her new position in Ankara to promote chosen causes. Although strong-minded and determined to make her views known, Hayrünnisa remains modest by nature and found the 1990s to be a challenging period of finding ways to overcome her instinctive shyness before an intrusive media. When asked, she agreed that the cameras like her 'too much', and that 'it is not easy' when they are constantly pointing at you.

> At that time, I was hosting all the guests and participating in trips because Erbakan's wife did not go out in public much and Abdullah Bey was acting also like a foreign minister although he was minister of state. Over time, you end up learning a lot, no matter how young you are. Erbakan was the first prime minister who had a wife who covered her head but, as a wife covering her head, I was the first prime minis-ter's wife to be so visible … Those were difficult times. I was perhaps the first one to encounter these difficulties. I kept saying: please look inside my head and not outside. In other words, I kept saying that the headscarf did not cover my brain. As for now, the point of view of the press changed completely over time. They started to be positive as they began to see our work. This process was not easy at all. I never thought of occupying a position only to sit back and relax and enjoy that position. Believe me when I say that I worked hard to do many things by working till midnight and going to sleep much later than Abdullah Bey and waking up much before him. When you get involved,

you see how much time was lost and how much was neglected and feel bad about it … One grows very sad to see that many things were neglected. In the meantime, you travel to other countries, see all the beautiful things done there, compare and wonder why they should not happen in Turkey and you try to make them happen. So, this is a struggle … While our husbands work in their political life, we spend as much energy working behind the scenes to make things look better so that we can show the beauty of our house. When Abdullah Bey became prime minister, I could not find a place to host our guests and I had to host them at a hotel.[15]

There were problems being the wife of the prime minister. Having been hosted at international diplomatic events, Hayrünnisa found herself embarrassed by the low standards of diplomatic hospitality available to her through the government: there were, for example, no suitable buildings available for the new prime minister and his wife to host an international assembly.

In January 2003, Abdullah Gül called an emergency summit of regional political leaders – including Egypt and all neighbours of Iraq – to discuss a settlement that would avert US plans for military action against Saddam Hussain. This was a paradoxical moment for the wife of the Turkish prime minister: on government owned and secured properties, Hayrünnisa would be required to remove her headscarf in order to welcome heads of state from Saudi Arabia, Syria, Egypt, Jordan and Iraq. This was obviously out of the question. With only forty-eight hours to go before the summit was scheduled to open, the security problem was finally solved and the government informed the Kempinski Hotel group that they would be hosting the ninety delegates and all events at the Çırağan Palace Hotel. Once so many important heads of state had agreed to attend, outsourcing to Kempinski security was deemed the only reliable option. One journalist caught the sense of the last-minute rush while Hayrünnisa avoided the cameras.

Participants were starting to arrive even before the menus and details reached the hotel management. Add to their heroic efforts, the press conference scheduled for 6:45 pm was held up for three hours as the participants wrangled over the wording of the joint declaration. In other words, the dinner hosted by Prime Minster Gül started three hours late. Do you think the Çırağan Palace chefs tear their hair out in exasperation the way we see them do in the movies?[16]

On this occasion at least, journalists did not focus their gaze on Hayrünnisa, but she took the indignity of delay and confusion to heart and, as soon as Abdullah Gül became president in 2007, she set about improvements to the reception areas of the presidential palace at Çankaya which had been left shabbily undecorated since Atatürk's day.

Back in January 2003, Hayrünnisa found herself spectacularly 'in the spotlight' together with Emine Erdoğan while attending the World Economic Forum in Davos. On arrival, Emine Erdoğan quickly became the 'focus of attention with her showy clothes' which seemed to contradict wearing a headscarf. Observing that 'Mrs. Gül was plain and simple beside Mrs. Erdoğan', the Turkish media showed greater interest in the two leaders' wives and their clothing than in their husbands' activities, giving front-page coverage to debates over the tastefulness of Emine Erdoğan's fur coat.[17] Of special curiosity was how the two leaders' wives dressed for a Turkish fashion show staged one evening at the Hotel Seehof: 'Turkey's top models were on the catwalk with modern clothes but eyes were set once again on Emine Erdoğan who was wearing a black headscarf and Gül's wife Hayrünnisa Gül a *lamé* one.' Writers in the Islamic press such as Abdurrahman Dilipak directed their fury mostly at Emine Erdoğan for wearing high heels, thin stockings and make up: but the nationalist press was critical of them both, fearing their headscarves were damaging Turkey's 'secular and modern image'.[18] Noticing how previous leaders' wives who had worn headscarves had stayed entirely behind the scenes, one liberal commentator observed that, by stepping into the spotlight for the first time at Davos and declaring 'We are here too', Emine Erdoğan and Hayrünnisa Gül had 'painted a new picture of Turkey'; it was a new picture of a new Turkey where important and powerful women wore headscarves but were fashionable too.[19]

In the months and years ahead, with their different personalities and approaches to public life and performance, Hayrünnisa and Emine would sometimes find themselves competing for the spotlight, but official life also presented opportunities for developing projects without drawing undue attention. During 2003, with other women in the party, Hayrünnisa initiated a programme to encourage women to become more active in public and political life. 'This was an influential programme at a time when everything was very conservative; it helped women become more active,' recalls Ayşe Böhürler.[20] Official life also introduced Hayrünnisa to some new and lasting friendships. Abdullah Gül's strenuous political career had not stopped him from continuing his habit of seeking out smart people. On his first visit to New

York in the process of founding the AKP, he had contacted Salih Memecan, a political cartoonist whose satires on various aspects of Turkish life he much admired. In 1997, following the 28 February events, Salih Memecan and his family had left Turkey for the US in disgust at what was happening. They settled in Scarsdale, New York. Here Salih's wife, Mesude Nursuna, had set up a publishing company, Salih emailed his cartoons to press offices in Turkey, and the children were enjoying life in America. What had started as a one-year trip lasted for ten. Nursuna Memecan explained to me:

> We moved to New York being fed up with events in Turkey after 28 February. When we saw what was going on in the media, behind the media, and beyond, and all the things that the people were being told that were clearly not true and were dangerously misleading, we became so upset at the victimization and misinformation that we had to leave. While we were in New York, Abdullah Gül was elected. When he came to New York as prime minister, he contacted us, so we met over dinner a couple of times and we all liked each other. When we visited Turkey, we kept in touch and became friends. The first time I met Hayrünnisa at home, I told the driver to come back in half an hour, but we talked for over four and a half hours! Hayrünnisa asked me to stay overnight, and I insisted that she must visit us in New York. So when they did come to the States, there were regular family visits.
>
> I mentioned the school system in Scarsdale where we were living and Abdullah Gül said this was just what his youngest son Mehmet needed, he was in need of this sort of school, so he came to stay with us in New York and he attended Scarsdale School. I soon realized that I would not have the courage to leave my son with another family for a semester or a year, but this showed me how Abdullah Gül is so open and confident in his judgements. He knows that I am not religious or practising, but they were happy to leave their son with us after asking Mehmet if he would like to stay and let him choose. So Mehmet stayed on and his clothes had to be shipped over later. I had two children at the time – both older than Mehmet – and they were all supportive and friendly and knew how to take care of Mehmet. Hayrünnisa came over and stayed with us in New York and we enrolled her in English classes – she was diligent and didn't miss a class and did all her homework. Mehmet Emre stayed with us for two semesters over two years, spending his first semester in the US and the second in Turkey.[21]

As the two families saw more and more of each other, Abdullah Gül invited both Salih and Nursuna to consider returning to Turkey and joining the AKP. Salih, eager to maintain his credibility as a political satirist, declined and remains reluctant to associate himself with any party. In 2007, however, Nursuna would become an AKP parliamentary delegate for Istanbul, a post she held while representing the government at the PACE in Strasbourg. Meanwhile for the Gül family, the rhythms and routines of domestic life had taken a sharp turn away from the idyllic togetherness of Jeddah, but with their roots in traditional family values and their prospects opened by educational opportunities, the children were all flourishing. 'The kids were encouraged to be outspoken with their own ideas,' Nursuna observed, 'so the family as a whole is involved in expressing ideas and they criticize their father if they don't like what he is doing. They also insist that he keep in touch with young people, their ideas and interests, and this keeps him alive and alert. They make him stay in touch with technology; these days, Abdullah Gül twitters personally because of pressure from his kids and other young people.'[22]

The AKP takes over

Abdullah Gül and the new AKP had faced serious opposition right from the time the party was founded, mostly from those who were suspicious that it was an Islamist party, a continuation of Erbakan's *Milli Görüş* with little more than a new public relations strategy. Gül has commented that 'all the other party leaders at the time accused AKP of seeking an Islamist state, claiming that we were radical and fundamentalists. But we were not: and if we look at their standards on human rights, on democracy, on economic transparency – all of that is on record – we can see the hypocrisy.'[23]

Proclaimed by the media since their formation as 'Erdoğan's party', the AKP found its charismatic leader's life and every word held up to scrutiny as keys to the party's 'real' intentions. Observing that the party name – *Adalet ve Kalkınma Partisi* – had appeared as 'Ak Partisi' on banners, one journalist quibbled that they had 'misspelt' their own name, 'because, being part of the party initials, the letter 'k' should be capitalized as well'.[24] This was, surely, deliberately to miss the point that had been obvious enough to others, that 'ak' – meaning white or clean – signalled the party's intention of being a 'clean party'.[25] Critics were not convinced, and seem to have taken special pleasure in vilifying Erdoğan for his background. *Hürriyet* called him 'a major contender for the leadership of political Islam in Turkey', insisting that AKP was simply another Islamist party in disguise. Meanwhile *Cumhuriyet* went further, confidently declaring that: 'The AK Party founded under Erdoğan's leadership is under the influence of the Iskenderpaşa *dergah* [dervish lodge] and the Süleymancis.'[26] National television stations joined in, broadcasting video footage of Erdoğan speaking at a rally in 1994 when he called on Muslims to rebel against state secularism. On behalf of the party, Bülent Arınç conceded that 'if he said the same words recently, it might be possible to accuse him', but 'the speech was made ten years ago'.[27]

Within a week of the party's founding, hostile prosecutors were already applying to ban Erdoğan and six of AKP's women delegates, all of whom wore headscarves, from holding office within the party.[28] But as journalist Kemal Balcı astutely observed at the time:

> The all-out offensive by the mainstream media against Erdoğan is regarded as a golden opportunity for the former mayor and his party. The criticism levelled against the AK Party and Erdoğan coming from the media, which has lost public credibility and confidence, is only an advantage for the new political movement. The party gets its support from the peasants and Anatolia as well as the deprived and poor people trapped in the suburbs of major cities. These masses clearly do not have any positive views about the mainstream press. If the papers say something is 'black' they tend to believe it is 'white', which is 'Ak' in Turkish. 'Ak' is used for a clean society and it seems that that was why it was chosen as the name of the new party.[29]

On 3 November 2002, despite the criticism levelled at the new party, the Turkish voters showed that many of them were persuaded: AKP received a massive 34.3% of the vote to take 363 parliamentary seats out of 550; the CHP took only 19.4%, while Recai Kutan's SP took a meagre 2.5%. One think-tank in Washington, DC called it a 'political earthquake'.[30] There was, however, a snag. While everyone in the party unanimously agreed that the charismatic Erdoğan was the natural party leader, his spell in prison disqualified him from holding ministerial office: Gül would serve as prime minister while steps were taken to amend the law blocking Erdoğan's appointment.

Prime Minister Gül, November 2002 to March 2003

By contesting Erbakan's wishes at the Virtue convention back in May 1998 and running for party leadership, Abdullah Gül had opened a new chapter in the history of democracy within Turkish party politics. With their care-fully prepared programme leading to their election victory of 2002, Gül and the AKP opened another one, not only by winning the election but also by establishing a new model of party accountability and then actually setting about doing what they had promised to do. Among colleagues from the Political Research Centre who entered Gül's Cabinet, Abdüllatif Şener served as deputy prime minister, and Beşir Atalay as minister of state, posts they continued to hold during Erdoğan's first Cabinet. Party founders Murat Mercan and Nursuna Memecan were elected to represent AKP for Eskişehir and Istanbul respectively, while Sami Güçlü joined Gül's Cabinet as minister of agriculture. For the post of foreign minister, Gül appointed Yaşar Yakış, a widely experienced career diplomat who was ambassador to Saudi Arabia during Gül's time at the Islamic Development Bank. Once elected, instead of holding lengthy victory celebrations to give themselves time to figure out what to do next, they went straight to work.

In his first public statement as prime minister, Abdullah Gül sought to make some things clear; they were not Islamists practising *irtica* or 'religious reaction' aimed at ending the secular state.

> We have no secret agenda. I will take care to ensure transparency and accountability ... We are not going to spring any surprises ... We are not elitist. We are children of the people, people who come from the middle class and poor segments of society. Our priority is to give them some relief. We will work hard. First of all, we will deal with the State Security Courts and the detention period.[31]

Not everyone was, or is, convinced by this. But the party machinery was in place and running right from the start to bring about a series of democratiz-ing constitutional reforms, including abolishing the State Security Courts (*Devlet Güvenlik Mahkemeleri*).[32]

Unlike critics in Turkey, some foreign correspondents were sanguine about Abdullah Gül and the new AKP government. On 17 November, Dexter Filkins, writing in the *New York Times*, perceptively noticed the class angle and presented Gül as if his were an all-American success story, noting how the new prime minister was 'a former economics professor and son of a machinist', whose party had 'swept aside much of Turkey's governing class' thereby marking 'a historic moment' in the history of the Turkish Republic: truly an inspiring tale of upward mobility through education and from there into the history books.[33] A few days later, Nicole Pope, writing for *Middle East International*, praised Gül's first Cabinet, noticing that most spoke foreign languages, had higher degrees earned at foreign universities, and represented new ideas. 'A daring but welcome appointment,' Pope noted, 'was that of Ali Babacan, a 35-year old US-educated former financial adviser who was part of the team that drew up the AKP's economic plan. He enjoys the confidence of the financial markets and has already announced that he will continue to cooperate with the IMF, which has pledged a total of $31bn in loans since 1999.'[34] By February, Mehmet Ali Birand joined in the chorus, praising Gül for having 'chosen competent people capable of presenting to him new, different views – rather than picking up some of his "comrades" from among the AK Party ranks out of consideration for the sensitivities of the AK Party rank and file.' Gül had, Birand observed, 'surrounded himself with talented people' such as Ahmet Sever to advise on EU accession, Professor Ahmet Davutoğlu, and Gürcan Türkoğlu 'who has a Foreign Ministry background'.[35] This was a government whose first priorities at home were economic and judicial reforms, while maintaining excellent relations with both the US and the EU – most often an impossible balancing act – continued to dominate foreign policy.

Abdullah Gül's months as prime minister – from the outset it was well known that he would stand aside once Tayyip Erdoğan was cleared to hold office – began amid a continuing economic crisis, crucial stages in promoting Turkey's application to Europe, with daily mounting pressure from the White House and Pentagon to support military action against Saddam Hussein. His final days in the prime minister's office would be marked by the notorious refusal, on 1 March, of the Turkish parliament to ratify a government bill permitting the US to use Turkey as a base for their planned invasion of Iraq. On 11 March, he would hand over the prime minister's office to Erdoğan, who had recently been cleared to re-enter the political arena.

These were busy months for Abdullah Gül, who in addition to running the prime ministry, was taking an active role in steering new directions in foreign affairs. No one was surprised when he took over as foreign minister under Erdoğan. The founders of the party had long agreed that theirs was a team effort, that Erdoğan was the obvious charismatic leader, and that the programme of reforms on which they had all agreed would define and determine their policies and direction. Gül would endeavour to deliver the Party Programme.

Common sense said we would rule the country from the first day in a very serious way. When establishing the new party and its agenda, we worked very hard for a long time, holding long discussions and debates of a high academic standard. The most crucial time for AKP's success was the preparation – the many debates. It was the think-tank in Ankara that brought us all together and we criticized what was wrong in the existing party in order to learn from that and how not to be a burden on religion, people or history – we knew we had to study everything. We started with the economy, then questions of religion and secularism, the judiciary and human rights, and then we settled down and wrote the programme of the party. We announced our declaration of intent before the election in a very carefully written programme. It was better than any previous declaration before an election. Usually these were written by the best writer in the party and had nothing to do with a real programme: that would only be drafted once the party got into power. We didn't do that. We worked hard and based our programme on real debates, including the question of EU accession and thinking about that helped us to understand what we needed to do. So our minds were clear from the start – democracy and a free market economy were key standards in our plan – we made this clear.

I was leading all of this. We all agreed that Erdoğan was to visit different places for finding support, and the real intellectual work was in Ankara. When we declared our plan, the interest rates dropped because people knew we would win. And we had made our economic policy clear. I had sent Ali Babacan to New York and London to contact and talk with the financial institutions and to find out what we would need to do if we won. We didn't write our individuality or personal opinions when we were laying down our road map, but we all worked on it together and that is why we won the election. I was asked to form a government since the chair was not eligible.[36]

In the run up to the elections, hostile elements in the media had cast doubt on AKP's financial policies, despite reasoned reassurances from Ali Babacan that they were planning 'improvements' but 'absolutely no changes to the main framework of the [IMF] programme'.[37] And such would be their economic policy now they were in government.

The economy

Once in office, Abdullah Gül began by unrolling the party's plans for reform and economic recovery based on rigorous fiscal discipline, on tax reforms that would encourage increased production of marketable goods thereby attracting foreign investment, and on plans to reduce the public debt and government spending.[38] 'Ah yes' – President Gül paused when I asked him about taking power at a time of financial crisis – 'then the economy was very fragile.'

> In our action-plan we had called for certain things, and in 2003 we had to make good on what we had said. The economy was a turning point. We managed to be realistic. In the past, governments prepared the budget by exaggerating incomes and depressing costs to show how everything is balanced. Everyone knew it was a joke, but a bad one because you fool only yourself. We were realistic with full transparency and realistic projects. So for the budget; we increased tax income and trimmed expenses. After we declared our budget, everyone saw that the maths was convincing because it was realistic without the classical mistake of artificial balance. So we laid down lines and the government is still following that policy; Babacan is still in charge. He was young at that time, only thirty-three, when the economy was the key project. When we declared him minister in charge of the economy, everyone called him the 'baby minister' – 'babycan' – and said, 'This boy is going to save the nation.' He is so good at working with other countries' financial circles.[39]

Ali Babacan had done his work among Western bankers. Within two weeks of Gül announcing a number of measures that would ease the way for attracting direct foreign investment, Lehman Brothers raised Turkey on their Eurasia Group Stability Index to tenth place, earning the new government a vote of confidence in parliament, and stimulating foreign capital investment.[40]

One of the party's more surprising initial moves at reform was to demonstrate good will by setting a good example and cutting government costs by reducing the number of government ministers – and their ministries – from thirty-seven to twenty-three.

> My first action was to reduce the number of ministers in the cabinet. Imagine, giving up so many ministers when everyone in the party

wanted a job! But we had declared our action plan, the real road-map for Turkey that is still active for today. It has economy, foreign affairs, human rights and domestic issues that concern people, all things that we decided were important. Before us, when governments were formed, they would try to force their new ideas and tell people to do things the way they wanted them to. When we came to power, people were shocked because they simply wanted to know if we meant what we had laid out. We told them it was our plan to save our country, not just to please the political elites but the people.[41]

Starting out by streamlining the government set a bold precedent for the levels of fiscal responsibility and transparency that Gül and the Party Programme were demanding at all levels. In January, the government set about making further cuts in government spending alongside a tax-reform package aimed at increasing social security and subsidies to the agricultural sector.[42]

Such moves showed how the party was living up to its image as a 'clean party' with ambitions to 'save the country'. Shutting down so many ministries certainly struck a blow against one form of corruption that had been popular since the 1980s. Export tax subsidies introduced under Turgut Özal's neo-liberalization of the economy had introduced a lucrative practice involving four elements: members of government ministries, private-sector export-ers, inflated export vouchers, and equally inflated government payments. Writing two years after the AKP came to power, political economist Ziya Öniş observed that the 'government has been making a concerted effort for the first time to deal with the pervasive problem of corruption ... by taking legal action against key businessmen and politicians who are accused of having been involved in corruption during the recent era'. Economic recovery was gradual, but by 2004, the Turkish economy was outperforming expectations. Professor Öniş writes:

> After a few months in office ... it was quite clear that the fears and misgivings concerning the JDP [i.e. AKP] government were rather exaggerated and lacked a serious base. The government, by and large, displayed a strong commitment to the basic principles of fiscal stabi-lization and structural reforms embodied in the IMF program. Judged in terms of broad macroeconomic indicators, the JDP's performance could be classified as a significant success. Over the period of the past two years economic growth has been stronger than even the most

optimistic forecasts and inflation lower than IMF-agreed end-of-the-year targets ... during the first quarter of 2004, the Turkish economy recorded an astonishing growth of 12 percent in real GNP, which could, in part, be interpreted as a concrete sign of rising investor confidence ... At the heart of this process of rapid recovery was a single-minded commitment to fiscal discipline.[43]

Reforming the tax regime in order to achieve greater social equity proved easier to legislate than to enforce: achieving compliance among high-earning professionals, unregistered workers and businesses such as 'travel agents, restaurant owners, clothing workshop owners and dentists' who were accustomed to paying 'only about 10–15 per cent of their estimated tax liabilities', could not be achieved overnight.[44] Abdullah Gül told me: 'We were under economic pressure, and my hair went white back then – I used to have very dark hair, but just four months in that office and my hair changed. Those days were very difficult days. With the destiny of your nation in your hands; your responsibility to your people, to history, to the next generation ...'[45]

Not improving matters, the early AKP reforms were coming under suspicion from right-wing think-tanks in Washington DC, perhaps because of their success with the economy and policy of introducing fuller transparency. Writing for Daniel Pipes's *Middle East Quarterly* at the end of 2005, Michael Rubin wondered what to make of 'as much as $5bn' that had 'entered the system since the AKP took power', pondering misreported tourism revenues, money laundering and legitimate investments, without recognizing that the new government was, for the first time, obliging the Central Bank to publish actual figures that revealed the extent of the black economy: this was a key tactic in their war against corruption. Instead, Rubin assembled masses of what he calls 'circumstantial evidence' to suggest irregularities behind the economic success of the AKP government. He drew attention to how Erdoğan's family had become rich from business deals with companies such as Ülker that were known to have supported Islamic causes. And he linked rumours about suitcases full of cash arriving at Turkish airports with anonymous gossip about how the AKP was receiving Saudi and Malaysian funding in exchange for 'readjusting its position toward Israel'. Rubin cited several 'Turkish officials' who told him that 'the money could only come from wealthy Arab countries like Saudi Arabia where Gül lived for so long'.[46] Rubin withheld further comment, and seemed blithely unaware of the curious irony that it was the AKP that had forced the banks to reveal the anomalies in the first place, or that relations with Israel had been generally good and remained stable for some time.

The economy was invariably linked with other major problems facing the new government. Together, they were helping to turn Abdullah Gül's hair grey. European accession and US plans to invade Iraq were both urgent issues that were putting pressure on the limits of governmental power over other state institutions, most especially the military. Feroz Ahmad described the predicament in 2005 when he wrote that 'the government ... know that while they control parliament and the cabinet, they do not control the state, that is to say the armed forces and the bureaucracy'.[47] Or, as Gül put it to me: 'Of course we owned the government but we were not in charge of everything.'[48] Not even, as it would turn out in March 2003, the parliamentary vote.

Foreign policy

While drafting the language of the AKP programme and when later developing its foreign policy provisions with specific plans, Abdullah Gül was in constant conversation with Ahmet Davutoğlu whom he assigned as his chief advisor with the title of Ambassador. In his 2001 book, *Stratejik Derinlik*,[49] Davutoğlu elaborated a model of how Turkey enjoys 'strategic depth', a fact of geography and history that made it not a bridge between East and West – as Western journalists and politicians continue to think – but rather the focal point of a massive Eurasian region of global importance.[50] Davutoğlu argues how this position made Turkey 'a central country', one that should take a lead in promoting common prosperity and contributing to 'global and regional peace'.[51]

Abdullah Gül was ever willing to listen to and learn from clever people who are experts in their fields. In drafting the final version of the AKP Programme, he paid special attention to ensuring that its language clearly emphasized how the party's goal was to transform Turkey into 'an attraction zone' through cooperation rather than competition – military, commercial or otherwise – with countries adjoining Turkey or linked by history. Acknowledging the 'dynamic circumstances brought about by the post-Cold War period', AKP foreign policy was clearly outlined in terms of following 'a realistic foreign policy befitting the history and geographical position of Turkey'. This was not limited to improving relations with the US and Europe, but also included 'cooperation rather than competition' with Russia, improving ties with Greece, helping the new Turkic republics in efforts to 'turn the region into a wide area of cooperation', increasing 'bilateral relations' with 'Islamic countries',

while 'reshaping the policy of Turkey in the Balkans, in light of our historical, cultural and economic relations with the region's countries'. Also on the
AKP foreign policy agenda was seeking better relations with China and 'the
dynamic economies of South East Asia'.[52] Here, in summary, were the outlines
of an ambitious globalized vision for Turkey's future that Gül energetically put
in place throughout his time as foreign minister and that has largely defined
AKP policy ever since. Becoming 'an attraction zone' set Turkey the task of
'resolving regional disputes' and of taking a lead 'in attempts to overcome
the supposed clash between the West and the Muslim world' by making
'greater use of "soft power" – economic, political and cultural – in place of
the alternative heavily securitized approaches, especially in relations with its
Middle Eastern neighbours'.[53]

In September 2002, in anticipation of the forthcoming November elections, Abdullah Gül gave an 'exclusive' interview to the English-language
Turkish Daily News in which he elaborated on the outline of AKP foreign policy
by adding contemporary details and his own rhetorical stamp. He emphasized
his 'realistic' approach to political responsibility, arguing that Turkey can and
should only go so far in taking up its new leadership role in world affairs. He
was bold in attributing and apportioning responsibility for solving problems.
Admitting that Turkey had so far failed in Cyprus, he said that it was now up
to the Greek Cypriots to recognize the rights of Turkish Cypriots, and for
Europe to stop 'treating Greek Cypriots as the sole government on the island'.
Turkey was, he said, very keen to improve relations with Armenia, but the
Armenians first needed to leave the occupied territories of Azerbaijan, and
he insisted that Europe should take a leading role in resolving the problem.
This was a move characteristic of Gül's practical approach to political difficulties: when negotiations deadlock or fail, challenge those responsible for the
deadlock to find an answer and involve international organizations as much
as possible. At the same time, he warned against expecting any political party
to act alone in solving international crises: again, responsibility needs to be
shared proportionally. Since a solution to Iraq 'concerns the vital interests
of the state, a party cannot have its own approach ... If we establish the
government and if this problem persists we would ask the Foreign Ministry,
Turkish military and some institutions in connection with Iraqi affairs for
their opinion [and] devise an approach accordingly.' Iraq was a national and
even international problem, not a party problem. Insisting throughout on
the right of nations to determine their own political systems, and therefore
opposing unilateral attempts at forcing regime change in Iraq or anywhere

else, he sternly declared: 'no country should say, "I can do whatever I want", ignoring the laws and people. This goes for the US as well as the European Union.' Calling to mind the continuing damage caused by US interventions in Latin America, he reflected on how 'The last Gulf Crisis cost Turkey more than $40 billion for which we have not been compensated despite all the pledges.'[54]

During the interview, Abdullah Gül was openly bullish about party plans to acknowledge Turkey's responsibility to take a leading role in regional affairs. The aim, he explained, was not to seek regime change anywhere, but to promote mutually beneficial commercial and cultural joint projects. Turkey's responsibility towards 'the Central Asian and Caucasian Turkic republics,' he announced, was 'to set an example' of how 'a Muslim democratic country can become a developed country'. He clearly recalled how hard he and Sami Güçlü had struggled in 1997 to finance, publish and deliver books to Turkmenistan without any support from the government. He blamed Turkey for neglecting relations with the Central Asian republics 'for the past four years', and for failing to deliver on 'projects and promises' that were unrealistic. 'This will have to change fast. We are not saying Turkey should play a "big brother" like role in the region; on the contrary, a web of relations between equals should be developed for our mutual benefit.' On Turkey's duty to take an active role in the Middle East, Gül was emphatic: 'Turkey has to be an influence in the region. Turkey controlled the region … Under Ottoman rule, the region lived the longest uninterrupted peace.' With the second Intifada still underway, he observed how 'Israel under the Sharon administration … gave strength to anti-Semitic movements', and how it was Turkey's duty to help bring about peace in no uncertain terms: 'An Independent Palestine state should be established. Israel should withdraw from the invaded territories and Israel's security must be provided.'[55]

Abdullah Gül has always loathed violence, and the carnage in Iraq and violence in Israel and the Palestinian territories appalled him. A close advisor from the time told me: 'Normally there are many double standards; people feel bad about terror or war in one place but not others. Gül feels bad whatever the case, he feels personally about the attacks whether in Israel or against the Palestinians.'[56] Gül still held true to his maxim that 'the killing had to stop', wherever it might be taking place. On the topic of terrorism, he presented the interviewers with his own views, which he still holds:

There is no way to support terror. We do not welcome suicide attacks. There is no difference between an innocent Palestinian child and an innocent Israeli child. However, this is not the end of the issue. You have to look at Palestine and the Gaza territories under occupation. Then you may understand how people reach such a level of madness. I repeat it, this does not mean we approve of such things. I do not approve of suicide attacks. Neither Muslim nor Jew, I do not want any blood or teardrops. This has to be stopped but we also think that we first have to know the reason for the problem. If a girl at the age of eighteen becomes a suicide attacker, you have to find the reasons behind this. You have to solve the problem, and then you can end the attacks. There is no way to reach a solution by bombing. The world is full of examples of this.[57]

When speaking to the press a year after the 11 September attacks on New York, Abdullah Gül showed a better understanding of the systemic problems that were generating the threat of terrorism than many political leaders elsewhere. He reported how the AKP leaders had realized the same day that the attacks began a new era of 'international terrorism' and marked a 'turning point in world politics'. That evening, the party executive wrote to the US ambassador declaring 'common ground for fighting with terror'. For Gül and for Turkey, the old slogan of 'peace at home and peace abroad' took a new turn with the arrival of international terrorism and its direct product: Islamophobia.

For his first foreign policy speech as prime minister, Abdullah Gül put his international credentials once more to the forefront by speaking in English, announcing that 'Turkey will maintain its focus on both its strategic partnerships with the US and its candidacy for EU membership.'[58] With his ambitions set on moving Turkey closer to the EU, Gül was perhaps alone among AKP parliamentarians in fully appreciating the nature of the challenges ahead, having been personally briefed by the military on options for supporting US military actions in Iraq, and having held private discussions with the EU representative in Turkey – Hans-Joerg Kretschmer – within days of AKP's election victory.[59] Gül was also acutely aware that Kofi Annan had recently proposed a UN solution to the Cyprus problem that would require Turkey's assent. With the EU about to meet in Copenhagen to set the timetable for future accessions, the decision was critical. Gül could see that there would be objections to the plan from the military and the Turkish Cypriot leader Rauf Denktash, but also knew that accepting was the only way forward for Turkey's EU ambitions. On taking office, he gave initial government backing to the plan, despite his own doubts about certain of its terms, but very soon ran into opposition from within the party as well as from the military General Staff who, in early 2003, joined with Denktash to block formal acceptance.

> There was Cyprus at the time and this was urgent because the Copenhagen summit was looming. Cyprus was a key issue for Turkey. Kofi Annan came with a map. But he didn't know the place, he wasn't familiar with it. When he asked me if I supported his plan or not, I didn't know what to say. He told me that if we did not support it, there was no other way for us to go, but if we did, then the whole island would join the EU. Erdoğan agreed not to refuse the plan because we were sure the Greeks would reject it. But I couldn't convince my people; so at the time, I followed their advice and President Denktash who had his own independence and solidarity with their objections. Later on I realized I was correct.[60]

As early as January 2003, the army had made its position clear when General Aytaç Yalman, commander of land forces, 'publicly claimed that "the UN Cyprus Plan was unacceptable"'.[61] But Gül and Erdoğan would continue to lobby on behalf of the Annan Plan, and were helped in this when Mehmet Ali Talat replaced Denktash as prime minister of the Turkish Republic of North Cyprus in January 2004. That same month, Gül and Erdoğan met with Kofi Annan at Davos and agreed on a scheme to allow the UN to solve any detailed problems once the overall plan had been accepted. 'In effect, the Turkish government agreed to hand the authority for pushing through a solution over to Kofi Annan and the Cypriot people.'[62] On 23 January at a meeting of the National Security Council, despite continuing opposition from many within the armed forces, the military high command agreed to support the Annan Plan under these conditions. Three months later, just as Gül and Erdoğan had all along cynically suspected, the Greek Cypriots turned it down.[63] But their achievement had been, in only a few months, to bring the General Staff and the National Security Council onto their side, and to show they were a party seeking to solve rather than fuel disputes.

Dealings with the military

Relations with the military were daily on the calendar throughout the months that Abdullah Gül was prime minister. Although the AKP had declared itself to be a conservative, not religious, party and that it was dedicated to Kemalist democratic ideals, many senior officers whose lives were devoted to protecting their version of state secularism, and who saw creeping Islamism behind every headscarf, beard and moustache, remained highly suspicious. General Hilmi Özkök, head of the General Staff since August 2002, was quick to register offence when, a few weeks after AKP's victory, Bülent Arınç appeared at a state occasion in his role as speaker of parliament accompanied by his wife Münevver who was wearing a headscarf. On 28 November, a few days after the episode, 'Turkey's force commanders, headed by Özkök, delivered a wordless warning to Arınç by visiting him in his office in Parliament, where they sat in complete silence for three minutes before leaving.'[64] Headscarves scared some soldiers so much that the issue remained more than a public-relations problem: Emine Erdoğan and Hayrünnisa Gül joined with Münevver Arınç and agreed to stay covered and avoid appearing at public events organized by the state.

On some issues, though, the military high command was curiously in agreement with AKP policies, though perhaps for different reasons. They too favoured Turkey joining the EU since it would ensure checks on the spread of religious politics, and they were equally eager to preserve strong relations with NATO and the US, the primary source of their military hardware and up-to-date training. With one eye on politicians' wives who challenged their version of secularism, and another on AKP's dealings with the US over the impending war in Iraq, the General Staff were keeping a close watch on the new government. They had had plenty of practice at this. Now, under insistent pressure from the US to declare support for a war that was massively unpopular throughout Turkey, the generals – like Gül – suspected that war was inevitable and that Turkey had little choice in the matter, only in the details of Turkey's role; an especially irksome problem was raised by the US refusal to allow Turkey unilaterally to send its own troops into northern Iraq.[65] Although they would not openly admit to it, the General Staff were eager to go into northern Iraq in order to secure the border from Kurdish guerrillas and take control of the valuable oil and gas fields in Kirkuk for exploitation by Turkish companies. Gül understood the pressures from Washington and the potential advantages to Turkey, but was strongly opposed to initiating military actions, especially against fellow Muslims. So both Gül and the generals hedged their bets, stayed quiet and refused to take a lead in favouring unconditional support for Bush's plans: neither wanted to ignite massive popular opposition.

War in Iraq, 2003

On the day Abdullah Gül was appointed prime minister, Bülent Ecevit had personally warned him to avoid involvement in Iraq.[66] For his own part, Gül was personally against a war in Iraq or any neighbouring country. Ever opposed to using military violence to solve political problems, he was also aware that supporting a Western-led action against Muslims would lose the government credibility among neighbouring Muslim countries, not to mention voters at home. As early as March 2002, while still in opposition, Gül had outlined his views at a press conference, arguing that Saddam's regime 'had used chemical weapons against its own people', but while there was no reason to have 'sympathy' for Saddam, a peaceful solution still needed to be found. On the same occasion, he warned the US that President Bush's plans would turn the US into a regional enemy, so 'the immediate restoration of peace in the region would be in the United States' interests'. As with Cyprus, Gül believed the best way forward in such situations was to trust to democratic arbitration through international organizations, such as the UN, and that is just what he advised Saddam to do. He told reporters: 'What Iraq should do is to start talks with the United Nations and prevent a new war. Iraq should make this move.'[67] This was a suggestion that he would repeat in personal letters to Saddam over the next months; but to no avail.

While in the prime minister's office, Abdullah Gül struggled to prevent a war in Iraq in line with promoting the party's new vision of Turkey's foreign policy. Early on he insisted that Turkey's priorities were maintaining a 'strategic partnership with the US and … candidacy for EU membership'. Acknowledging US pressure over Iraq, he sought to show that this was a question not just for Turkey but for Europe as a whole and called for 'the establishment of a NATO–EU strategic partnership and the development of the European Security and Defence Policy'. If, Gül argued, the EU wanted to be 'a credible actor in the new security environment' then it surely realized the need to include 'non-EU NATO countries like Turkey' within its strategic planning.[68] Such an arrangement would usefully shift the burden of responsibility away from Ankara, undermining US military and political control by involving both the EU and NATO. For Abdullah Gül and Ahmet Davutoğlu, his chief foreign policy advisor, the Iraq question was a key element of a larger-scale vision of the future of Turkish foreign policy, one that, for example, involved behaving as if Turkey were already an equal member of the EU with sufficient confidence in its own authority to tell

Bush that Turkey was not, like certain Gulf states, simply a base for US military purposes.

Days after the AKP victory in November 2002, Abdullah Gül had announced: 'We believe Turkey can play a big role for world peace. This is a built-in factor. History gives the chance to us, geography gives the chance to us.'[69] He has continued to push this agenda throughout his political career since the AKP came to power. On 3 December he had the opportunity to put this view of Turkey's 'role for world peace' into practice when US Deputy Defence Secretary Paul Wolfowitz arrived in Ankara to outline the Pentagon's plans for Turkey. Wolfowitz explained how US military inspectors would arrive to assess existing US bases in Turkey; next, military technicians would arrive to improve bases and communication networks; finally, over sixty thousand US troops and over two hundred military planes would arrive to form a northern front against Iraq. At that meeting, 'Gül agreed to implement only the first stage (which did not require parliamentary approval) without committing Turkey to the other two', although Wolfowitz later claimed otherwise.[70] In an unusual move, clearly aimed at flattering the AKP government, President George Bush invited Erdoğan for talks in Washington on 10 December, knowing full well that, at the time, he held influence but no official government position.

At a summit on Iraq held at the presidential residence in Ankara on 18 December, Gül and Davutoğlu both spoke on Turkey's need to be more active in regional and international affairs. Rather than continuing to accept a peripheral position in the world, they argued, Turkey should take note of its geopolitical position and historical legacy and assume a leading role in regional and international affairs.[71] While General Özkök and the General Staff were becoming increasingly impatient to sign a deal with the US, Abdullah Gül was eager that Turkey should prove itself ready to take a leading role that would prevent the war. He stalled the US by setting the price of Turkey's support at $92 billion, a figure that included compensation for the massive financial losses the Turkish economy had suffered following the 1991 Gulf War, but far more than the White House would ever approve.[72]

Despite increasing pressures, including a strong personal letter sent by President George Bush on 20 December, Abdullah Gül, the interim prime minister from Kayseri, haggled into the New Year over the terms of US financial compensation while attempting to find a regional solution for peace. Before the month was over, he held further meetings with General Özkök and the General Staff – who on 23 December went so far as to announce that Turkey 'should not stand aside' from the inevitable invasion.[73] He also met with the Kurdish leaders Jalal Talabani and Massoud Barzani, with the Iraqi Turkmen leader Sanan Ahmed,[74] and held secret meetings with Saddam Hussain's deputy, Taha Ramadan, and his foreign minister, Naji Sabri.[75]

In the early days of January, Abdullah Gül and Tayyip Erdoğan set off on separate missions to consult with Middle East and Central Asian leaders. When Gül returned from meetings with the leaders of Syria, Egypt, Jordan, Saudi Arabia and Iran to face hostile criticism at home and outrage from US spokespeople for delaying Turkey's declaration of support for the US, he boldly defended his party's position in terms of the new agenda for Turkish foreign policy. 'Turkey has taken the initiative and is making great efforts for the end of the current crisis without a war. A new era is beginning with the visit I paid to the region's countries in this respect.' On 11 January, Gül's trade ambassador Kürşad Tüzmen arrived in Baghdad and delivered the last of the personal letters to Saddam in which Gül pleaded with the Iraqi leader to be a hero to his people and open direct talks with the UN.[76] An insider told me: 'He wrote to Saddam as a friendly neighbour and said that, rhetoric aside, this is the last chance for a debate in the United Nations on disarmament, warning that otherwise your country will be ravaged as if the Mongols had come again. He felt a moral obligation to his neighbouring countries. Saddam wrote back politely.'[77]

Abdullah Gül's firm belief that, even this late, the US war machine could be stopped, has usefully been characterized since as 'strategic fantasizing' by political scientist Saban Kardaş. Speaking and behaving as if Turkey was already in fact the world leader it should aspire to be, was a key to Gül's rhetorical positioning when promoting the Party Programme in foreign affairs. 'If there was a unique [AKP] stamp on Turkey's policy during this period,' Kardaş argues, 'it was the regional diplomacy formulated by the main figure on Gül's foreign policy team, Ahmet Davutoğlu.'[78] Quickly following on from his Middle East tour in January, Gül called a summit of leaders from Syria, Saudi Arabia, Iran, Jordan and Egypt that would be held at the Çırağan Palace Hotel. The arrival of Joschka Fischer, the German foreign minister, lent considerable weight to Gül's earnest call to prevent war and to view regional security from a regional and a European, not just a US, point of view. But from the start, the delegates mostly disagreed, taking such a long time refusing even to agree among themselves on their opening statement that, as already mentioned, the protocol dinner being hosted by Hayrünnisa in her role as the prime minister's wife was delayed by over three hours.[79]

By 31 January, unable to achieve regional agreement over Iraq, Abdullah Gül met with the chiefs of staff, President Ahmet Sezer and other government leaders and agreed to come to final terms with the US, drafting a bill to be debated in parliament. 'I still think there's a chance for peace,' Gül told the press at the time, 'but Turkey has to take steps to protect its national interests.'[80] Washington was not happy. By now he had received two strongly worded letters from President Bush, 'a long telephone call' from Vice President Dick Cheney, and a personal visit by the chairman of the US Joint Chiefs, General Richard Myers.[81] On 6 February, parliament approved the second stage of the Pentagon's plan for a northern front in Turkey, allowing the US to upgrade existing facilities. But they did not agree on permitting foreign troops to enter Turkey; for this to happen, the constitution demanded a special resolution. A further parliamentary vote was duly scheduled for 1 March, providing Gül with a chance to obtain public endorsement from the General Staff before the debate. Political historians William Hale and Ergun Özbudun remind us that even this late in the day, 'the military were as reluctant as the politicians to shoulder the responsibility'.[82] At a meeting of the National Security Council the day before parliament was to meet, instead of endorsing the proposal, General Özkök once again remained significantly silent and ignored the topic. Everything now hinged on the parliamentary debate. Approval of phase two, however, was clearly 'a decision that made no sense unless Parliament also voted to allow the troops into the country', as commentator Gareth Jenkins observed.[83]

These were among the tensest hours of Abdullah Gül's period as prime minister. Might a Turkish refusal help sway US policy and prevent a war? That seemed hardly likely since the Americans – even more than the Europeans he had debated with in Strasbourg – had outdated expectations about democratic power in the Turkish Republic.

> The Americans were not knocking on the door but beating on it, demanding that we join the war. Every day someone came from the US government, and every day CNN came and asked what we were going to do. CNN thought that I had no option since previous governments always listened to other voices, not the Turkish people. I was telling them they must ask the people. I am an elected prime minister who will listen to his people. The Americans were shocked because they had seen in the past how, when serious issues arise in Turkey, decisions were not about the people or parliament. They expected me to be powerful

and simply take charge of this matter. Anyway we handled it nicely and democratically, I think, and we showed our system worked.[84]

On 1 March, parliament went to the vote even as national television networks broadcast live feeds of more than ten thousand anti-war protestors demonstrating in Ankara. Parliament's decision, once public, was widely pronounced a great surprise and even a shock. So many AKP delegates had voted against the government's bill that hostile critics became immediately enthusiastic at discovering a split within the party, one that surely foretold that its days were numbered. Ismet Berkan writing in *Radikal* gleefully prophesied that now, unless the government renewed and passed the bill within a week, they 'will be the shortest-term single-party government of the republican era'. Writing in *Hürriyet,* Oktay Ekşi agreed, calling on Gül to 'withdraw from office' and for Erdoğan to 'set up a new government' and use it to muscle approval through by 'using party discipline'. But Ekşi stretched for ironic detachment too, observing how 'the entire world was probably shocked' by the vote, then knowingly observed how in this case, the 'entire world' really only consisted of 'the White House, Baghdad, British Premier Tony Blair, French President Jacques Chirac, Tayyip Erdoğan and the Turkish General Staff'.[85]

    Abdullah Gül confirmed that he was not surprised by the vote. 'Yes, that's right,' he told me shaking his head, 'the world was very surprised, but I knew that our delegates were representing the people and what they wanted was always clear. I think that Colin Powell was a decent man but I don't know if he was shocked or even surprised because he too was also very realistic then.'[86] When Colin Powell phoned him that day, Gül was able to persuade him to agree on a 'wait and see' policy: Powell later appeared on national television in the US and 'said he did not think Turkey had anything to apologize for'.[87] There was little else for Gül to do except reassure the US ambassador, Robert Pearson, that the vote showed the truly democratic nature of his party and should not be interpreted 'as if we burnt the bridges'. The Embassy quickly responded by announcing that they 'respect the decision' and consider that 'Turkey is still our friend'.[88] Paul Wolfowitz thought otherwise and declared that Turkey had made 'a big, big mistake'.[89]

    Abdullah Gül had tried right to the last minute to do everything he could to avert war in Iraq, knowing full well that 'once the great powers get moving it is very hard to stop them', so that 'whatever there is to be done we must do it to stop a war'.[90] So while parliament's decision went along with his personal conviction, he understood the full range of challenges now facing the party. The vote had showed that the AKP delegates were not to be bullied into adopting an unpopular decision. Gül, Erdoğan, Arınç and other party leaders agreed not to renew the bill to allow armed US troops heading for Iraq to travel into, and out of, Turkey. But in June, parliament conceded to allow the US to use the NATO base at Incirlik 'for logistical support for US forces in Iraq, with a land bridge to the Iraqi frontier'.[91] By October the government went further and 'attempted to achieve a more active involvement in operations in Iraq' by passing a resolution allowing ten to twelve thousand Turkish soldiers to join the 'stabilization force'.[92] Throughout the summer, the Pentagon and US State Department had been pressuring Turkey to do just that, send troops; but when the offer finally came, it was rejected by the US-appointed Provisional Governing Council of Iraq.

Critics of the AKP, and of Turkey, continued to complain of the government's irresolution in the lead-up to the US invasion of Iraq, blaming its failure to push the vote on 1 March and its subsequent delaying tactics. While right-wing pundit Michael Rubin was describing 'American–Turkish Diplomacy and the Iraq War' as a 'Comedy of Errors', other commentators started taking a different view, sensing that something had usefully changed in Turkish political life.[93] Feroz Ahmad describes it thus: 'Unlike earlier parties in government, the AKP was not a tightly-controlled political party doing the bidding of its leaders ... It was responsive to popular opinion and the anti-war demonstration had been significant in directing the negative vote. As some Turks noted, the concept of democracy had changed as a result.'[94] Others observed that a 'new Turkey' was being born.[95]

Foreign Ministry and political reforms, 2003–07

The planned handover of the prime minister's office to Recep Tayyip Erdoğan in March 2003 proved seamless, despite the pronouncements of critics eager to disclose behind-the-scenes conflicts between the two men. The party leaders were fully in agreement on how to proceed. Abdullah Gül had activated the party's 'action plan' during his months in office, putting in place a series of economic and foreign policy reforms, including constitutional amendments starting with the one permitting Erdoğan to resume his political career. Later constitutional reforms enacted that July, notably those curtailing the power of the military authority over the National Security Council and the abolition of the State Security Courts, were put into action during Gül's term as prime minister. On 18 August, Mehmet Yiğit Alpogan – a career diplomat – became the first civilian head of the National Security Council, marking a key moment in the formation of the 'new Turkey', one that was loosening the power of the military Chiefs of Staff. Feroz Ahmad speculates on whether 'the wings of the powerful military establishment' were finally 'clipped by these reforms', or whether the military establishment had shifted its public relations policy while secretly relying on 'the so-called "deep state", a state within the state which was out of the control of its political masters and responsible to no higher authorities'.[96] Throughout its ranks, the military felt it had already suffered more than enough humiliation from parliament's vote over Iraq, but matters got worse. On 4 July US troops arrested a small contingent of Turkish armed forces at their station near Süleymaniye in northern Iraq, notoriously marching them to prison with sacks over their heads. Turks everywhere were furious. This incident, the *Çuval Olayı* ('Sack Incident'), inspired a 2006 action film, *The Valley of the Wolves: Iraq*, in which a group of 'deep state' agents from a recently popular television series set about seeking revenge on the ignoble US perpetrators. A fan of cowboy films as a child, Abdullah Gül had never developed a taste for the violence of 'action films', but that year, and again in 2010, as we shall see, he would be confronted by diplomatic crises arising from this series, which had swiftly developed into a widely popular and internationally distributed television franchise.

While prime minister and as foreign minister, Abdullah Gül pushed the AK Party Programme of constitutional reforms with his eyes only partly on the views of the US and EU. He had now been in political life long enough to understand that some changes took a long time: patience is key. Another that he knew from Kayseri is that it is always better to persuade an adversary into a workable agreement than to accept unprofitable terms or resort to violence. Some have criticized him for what they see as his 'failure' over the Iraq vote. Yet the premise of one commentator, that 'Turkey's inability to successfully conclude the negotiations with the United States on the eve of the Iraq war', might just as usefully be inverted to speak of the US inability to justify its plans for war in Iraq to its international allies such as Turkey.[97] As Hale and Özbudun put it, 'US policy-makers, especially those in the Pentagon, were also to blame.'[98] In Turkey at the time, some critics argued that the 1 March vote proved there was a serious split between followers of Gül and followers of Erdoğan that would destroy the AKP if attempts to close the party failed. Erdoğan and Gül simply got on with advancing the AK Party Programme. But the Turkish press remained preoccupied with diagnosing underlying conflicts among the two leaders, failing to recognize the coherency of their

Programme and its relative autonomy from the opinions of any individual leaders.

As soon as AKP came to power, journalists looked to find and exaggerate differences between Abdullah Gül and Recep Tayyip Erdoğan, eager to discover disagreements. Nicole Pope quickly observed that 'Gül and Erdoğan have been political companions for many years, although there is a rivalry between the two', but offered no details.[99] Kemal Balcı was certain there would be problems ahead for AKP because of its 'double-headed administration', admitting he was confused by party procedures.[100] Ilnur Çevik more perceptively noticed how they had 'established a viable partnership', adopting a crucial division of labour by which Gül's talents as 'an economic technician' with foreign experience and an international reputation were proving a perfect complement to Erdoğan's 'exceptional leadership qualities' which had 'won millions of votes for the AK Party'.[101] Such, indeed, had been the party plan; Gül and his research team designed the Party Programme while Erdoğan took it to the voters. Ayşe Böhürler describes the early years of the AKP government as a 'consensus of two things: Abdullah Gül and Tayyip Erdoğan. Gül knows how the state works. He had been in international political life and is very cautious, while knowing Ankara very well. Erdoğan knows Istanbul and the Turkish public, so he was able to motivate mass movements. The party was a mix of Gül's inner knowledge and Erdoğan's motivational spirit. Abdullah Gül was the architect; Tayyip Erdoğan was the engineer.'[102]

Abdullah Gül's time as prime minister was never simply one of service as a caretaker for Erdoğan, as Mehmet Ali Birand recognized as early as February 2003: 'As time went by it was seen that Gül was not a caretaker … The most important asset he has is the nature of his approach. He has a smiling face and he takes care not to hurt people's feelings. His approach is reconciliatory rather than confrontational.'[103] One highly experienced career diplomat, who served as ambassador and foreign policy advisor during the first AKP government, confirmed that Gül's single most important contribution in those early years was bringing a new style into Turkish political life, not only by his manner towards colleagues but also by his clearly defined and dedicated approach to solving problems through consultation and cooperation. 'Some politicians can be manipulated,' he explained, 'but Gül listens to everyone, including his wife.'

He is open to being corrected. When I was at first his advisor, I delivered a brief early one morning. Then in the afternoon we went to another briefing on the same topic and I watched him listening as if for the first time. At first I was angry; it was as if I had not already troubled to brief him on this matter. Then I realized it was good because the second presentation might be from a different point of view and that Gül was listening for the differences, and he seeks to have a solid basis for decisions. The professional civil servants in the Foreign Ministry were very happy to have him in control because he is easy to work with and because he listens – which is not always the case. He listens and he takes advice. In 2002 when he arrived in power, he wanted to create a forum over Iraq with a view to making sure there would be no war. This was his first target as prime minister, to eliminate Saddam by peaceful means because he could see the disastrous consequences of war in Iraq. But once the war started, he set out to create a forum of neighbouring countries with common agenda – he phoned Mubarak [of Egypt], Assad [of Syria], Abdullah [of Jordan], and visited all the neighbouring countries. These leaders like to be flattered and so the first thing Abdullah Gül said to Mubarak was 'my purpose is to bring these countries together, but it should not be centred in Turkey. It should be in your country with you as president!' So he was focused on achieving the purpose of the forum not his personal prestige. His focus on the purpose at hand makes life easy for us advisors and bureaucrats![104]

Unlike previous Turkish politicians who, once in power, tended to become authoritarian in their manner and even fickle in their decisions, Gül listened to advice while keeping to the Party Programme he had spent so much energy devising, asking expert advisors for practical solutions to impossible problems and taking their answers, however partial, into account. With Arınç in the post of speaker of parliament, Erdoğan as prime minister with Şener his deputy, Çiçek minister of justice, and Gül foreign minister, the key players were all in place to continue pushing through their programme of reforms.

Islamophobia strikes

Perhaps the biggest unexpected challenge Abdullah Gül faced during the early years of the AKP government was dealing with the 'globalization of Islamophobia' that followed the World Trade Center attacks in September 2001 because it seriously complicated relations with the US, with Europe, and with the EU.[105] Since many in the US felt betrayed on discovering that

Turkey was not a pliable ally for the invasion of Iraq, the new Turkey started being viewed with certain misgivings. 'Islam' and 'democracy' quickly became favourite buzzwords in discussions and debates of how and in what ways Turkey fitted into the picture being drawn by Bush's allies in the 'war on terror'. Barely three weeks after the AKP had come to power, on 25 November 2002, Bush passed the Homeland Security Act, and there were very few gullible enough to mistake how 'terrorist' most often meant 'Muslim'. His invasion of Iraq the following March, and subsequent May Day claim of 'Mission Accomplished', provoked Islamic violence throughout the world. It reached Istanbul on 15 and 20 November 2003 when synagogues, banks and the UK consular offices were bombed, killing twenty-five including the British consul Roger Short.[106] Despite the attacks, which if anything indicated Islamist hostility towards the government, the AKP leaders remained suspect. They had come to power from an openly Islamist party background and, despite widely declared differences from the political Islam of Erbakan – now back in political life and leading the *Saadet* Party (SP) – remained targets of mistrust among anxious European democrats and neoconservative commentators in Washington, not to forget the military, political elite and secular nationalists at home.

Even as the AKP pushed through constitutional reforms to meet EU standards – most of which Gül had helped draft under the previous government – Erdoğan's early involvement with the Iskenderpaşa congregation of Mehmet Zahid Kotku continued to cast doubts on the party's connections to Islamic organizations. The community of businessmen who had helped bring the party to power also came under renewed scrutiny. Political leaders in France and Germany began using scare tactics to oppose Turkey's entry into the EU. In April 2003, the German-based *Milli Görüş* organization was put under scrutiny, despite never having been involved in any known forms of terrorism, Islamist or otherwise. In order to allay the possible threat to Turkish communities in Europe, Gül sent out a memo to Turkish ambassadors asking them to assist expatriate organizations. Meanwhile, the secular establishment was certain that the government was finally revealing its Islamic intentions: Chief of Staff General Hilmi Özkök told reporters that the military 'are closely following the developments'.[107]

At home, the AKP had promised, and set about delivering, 'conservative democracy', but in Washington think-tanks it would soon become clear that Gül and Erdoğan represented a new and different kind of political power in Turkey that was challenging expectations. Ideas about a 'Turkish model' needed to be remodelled and recast with the AKP leaders given the preferred role of 'moderate Islamists' and what that might mean for US interests.[108] The European Commission adopted a slightly more nuanced language than this, suggesting that Turkey under the AKP 'combines secularism within a Muslim social and cultural environment to offer a good example for other countries in the region.'[109] Yet the notion that Turkey represented a 'model' of anything directly connected to Islam was, reasonably enough, anathema to President Ahmet Sezer, to the military high command and the secular establishment, as much as it was to many of the AKP leaders themselves. Early on, Erdoğan insisted that 'Islam is my personal reference. My political reference is democracy',[110] while Gül also rejected the role of 'moderate Islamist' from the start. His favourite term in this context remains 'conservative reform', which describes bringing Turkey into line with EU standards and has nothing to do with introducing *shariat* law.

'Conservative reform' is clearly a paradoxical formula, but Abdullah Gül points to how by 2002, ten years of AKP mayors had cleaned up Istanbul and developed Kayseri – by then a city of over 600,000 people – into a global economic power. Yet reforms introduced in a conservative way, however they might succeed in being passed, are bound to involve compromises. Thanks to Gül's efforts, the death penalty in times of peace had been abolished, and legislation to curtail the use of torture enacted. He had worked diligently on improving human rights to EU standards and, despite strong opposition from nationalists, the ban on broadcasting and teaching in Kurdish was finally lifted in June 2003. However, as political scientist Kerem Öktem notes, 'pro-Kurdish politicians as well as liberals were enraged by the strings attached to these reforms: Kurdish and other language broadcasts would be allowed only on state radio and TV and limited to less than an hour daily. The language courses would have to fulfil high technical specifications and would be closed to schoolchildren.' But Öktem also observes how such 'criticisms ignored the symbolical importance of these steps, which effectively gave Kurdish the official recognition it had been denied during the entire history of the Turkish Republic'.[111]

By the summer of 2004, even neoconservative commentators in the US were noticing that 'much to the surprise of its critics, Erdoğan's administration has pushed harder (and more successfully) for liberal and democratic reforms than any previous Turkish government' and that in doing so 'it has strengthened Turkey's relations with both Europe and the United States'.[112] Yet neoconservative approval came wrapped with the belief that the new

Turkey was ready to become a 'model for democratic Islam' because the early months of the AKP government had shown 'that external pressure for political reform can achieve results': a belief, that is to say, that the 'new' Turkey was ready to be shaped by US 'pressure'. When I asked him about coming to power at a time when Turkey's foreign relations were so complicated, with the US seeking to make Turkey into a 'model' of 'moderate Islam', Gül recalled elements of an earlier discussion about the failure of history teaching during his days at school to address the Ottoman legacy:

Yes, Turkey became a 'model' after 2002 when we came to power, but in a different way from what the US was thinking. Before us, the politicians who ruled the country always distinguished themselves from old Ottoman power and this meant that they always blamed the people, who were Muslims, for everything that was wrong. In this they ignored the past. They also thought we were Islamists. For myself I tried to make it clear that I am a pious Muslim and this is part of my identity, but I don't go about showing this as I once did, and also for me being a Muslim means believing in universal standards. The real change that we brought to politics in this country is that now the people and the state can embrace each other: we listen to them and follow the people's advice when we can. In the same way Turkey and other Muslim countries have embraced. This is the real change we brought, not political Islam.

In the past there were old Muslim politicians and leaders who used rhetoric but didn't follow actual political events. We brought real political answers and were not just using rhetoric. We listened to the people and at the same time were showing that we can be Muslims and democrats. Equality, accountability, transparency – I can give you all the historical key words. We are making them real, not just rhetoric. For Muslims many of these ideas are obvious and were always part of the system. Turkey is showing everyone that we are allowing people to speak up and defend their rights. We have introduced equality, accountability, rights of the person, individual rights, rule of law, respect to others and their religions, and all these are in the Qur'an. But no religion can be enforced. These principles are clear and were practised in Ottoman times. Human rights were practised under the Ottomans. But people were not used to this debate until us; the republic ignored the past, and we didn't know about it.

We are looking beyond religious questions as such, but still want to show how Muslim people can be comfortable with others, working with developed countries with different religions. We have shown this and have made it clear since 2002. We brought all these issues into politics for the first time. So our movement was really about studying the world.[113]

Now that the AKP was in power, for Gül the imperatives were clear: 'We listened to the people and at the same time were showing that we can be Muslims and democrats.'[114]

Domestic reforms

Within eight months, the AKP launched four sets of constitutional reforms aimed at bringing Turkey into conformity with the EU. None of them showed a trace of an Islamic political agenda, though the views and values of conservative Muslims were certainly being taken into account for the first time. Following the practice that Gül had initiated in the 1991 Kayseri elections, the government set out to find out what people thought. In accordance with policies outlined in the Party Programme, the AKP's early constitutional and juridical reforms were drafted after seeking the 'opinions and suggestions of the volunteer establishments, non-governmental organizations active in the area of human rights'.[115] Kerem Öktem puts it thus: 'In a measure considered as one of the benchmarks of Turkey's transition towards European norms and procedures, the government consulted – and more importantly listened to – civil society representatives.'[116] Compromise with the military and educational authorities, however, limited the cultural and human rights being granted to the Kurds: penal code reforms concerning women's rights and conditions were, on the other hand, swiftly broadened in response to debates with women's organizations and women party members.

Initial drafts of what would become the AK Party Programme made a commitment to 'universal standards for rights and freedoms of women, children and labour',[117] but Ayşe Böhürler and other women among the party founders had already developed a more detailed position for the party on tackling problems facing Turkish women in terms that were generated after numerous meetings with various women's groups. Ayşe Böhürler recalled:

During the early years, women in the party always felt Gül was fully supportive of their efforts and initiatives. We made stronger efforts in the early years because women had so far to go. I was very active working with other women's organizations from outside Turkey. It was easy for us to introduce all the feminist projects into the Party Programme. The Turkish mainstream might not like what we were doing, but the party leaders always supported gender equality. [118]

As a result, the Party Programme was revised to include preventing 'violence, sexual and economic exploitation against women' among its 'priority policies', specifying that: 'In regions where women commit suicide, or honour killings take place, preventative and educational work shall be carried out towards orienting the women and their families.'[119] This was the first time such matters had been openly introduced into the programme of any Turkish political party. Following further consultations with women's rights groups, plans to educate families were backed up with laws to protect women. Political scientist Ayşe Kadioğlu recalls her surprise at just how serious the men of the AKP were at listening to, and taking advice from, women's groups.

The debates on the penal code were quite amazing. The women's organisations insisted on revising the articles dealing with violence against women. They ensured that the issue of 'honour killings' and sexual violence was dealt with in the interests of women rather than society. And the government took their advice. This was a true case of deliberative democracy.[120]

Democratic legislation can target and set penalties, but not so easily end violence against women. What AKP achieved was to make the problems visible for the first time, putting them directly on their immediate political agenda, which was aimed at improving the life of all Turkish citizens. Men in Turkey continue to abuse their female relatives, but no longer can anyone claim there is a legal defence for 'honour killing', or that they thought it was lawful for a man to beat his wife.

Going global in 2003

Abdullah Gül's years as Turkey's foreign minister would be shadowed by persistent concerns over US and EU attitudes to Turkey, by the rise of

Islamophobia globally and a resurgence of religious–political violence at home. At the same time, they were animated by the improving economy and by strenuous attempts to achieve for Turkey a central place and leading role in regional and international affairs. Yet these were also years of global terrorism when Turkey could not help but be caught up in repercussions following the US invasions of Afghanistan and Iraq. The reprisals began in November 2003 with the Al-Qaeda bombings of British and Jewish people and institutions in Istanbul, and ended with the assassination of Hrant Dink in January 2007. These years were framed by strenuous attempts to enter the European Community. Hopes were raised in 2004, only to be dashed at the end of 2006 as a consequence of increasing European anti-Turkish chauvinism. These were also years when Turkey was enjoying unprecedented economic growth and stability, and the country began assuming an active role in world affairs, developing regional and international initiatives. These moves were in line with the party's declared ambition to make Turkey into a 'pioneer within its own borders, in its region and the whole world, of innovation, development, peace and welfare'.[121]

Having ever been opposed to violence and the use of military force, Abdullah Gül set about promoting Turkey's 'soft power' in line with the Party Programme's general aim, while shaping it to suit times and audiences. His early months as foreign minister, dominated as they were by the US-coalition invasion of Iraq, also entailed a full calendar of international meetings that provided opportunities for him to explore, develop and explain Turkey's new policies in greater detail. For his official speeches, he was armed with ideas and notes from discussions with advisors and from group meetings in addition to his years of experience in Strasbourg where he had learned to develop workable solutions based on international and democratic principles and practices. Confident from the exemplary success of Kayseri at demonstrating how modernization and economic development were not merely compatible with, but actively promoted by, Muslim values, Gül was well prepared to advance his ideas beyond Turkey.

He began in the Balkans. On 8 April, Gül addressed a meeting of South East European nations in Belgrade on how the 'radically altered political geography in South East Europe' meant that the region is now 'steering towards European and Euro-Atlantic structures and resolved to anchor there for good'. This was, he insisted, 'the correct vision, a vision for lasting peace, stability and prosperity', and would best be fully served by the countries involved agreeing to work together. Insisting that '"coordination" should be an equally important key word as "cooperation", he advocated setting up an email network to keep all parties equally informed at all times.[122] On 12 May, in Bulgaria, he argued that NATO and Atlantic–European diplomacy would be crucial for promoting trade and security in the Black Sea region, whose governments should welcome and support the 'road-map' for peace in the Middle East being proposed by the US, Russia, the UN and the EU.[123] In neither of these speeches did he indicate that Turkey, rather than the EU or UN or NATO, should take a lead role in the political affairs of other nations.

Although he was only too aware of how the US and the UK had entered Iraq without a legitimate UN mandate, his years in Turkish politics had hardened his conviction that democracy developed best in concert with multilateral international organizations.

On 28 May in Tehran, a month after President George W. Bush had announced 'Mission Accomplished' in Iraq, Abdullah Gül made his first bid to persuade other Muslim countries that Iraq had shown how 'we as the Muslim world' were still facing 'strategic risks' and that 'we should first put our house in order'.[124] Speaking before the annual assembly of the Organization of the Islamic Conference (OIC), Foreign Minister Gül adopted a more forceful tone than when he had addressed regional leaders in Istanbul back in January. With the Iraq war formally over, but peace hardly achieved, Gül recalled the Istanbul summit and how he had then called on 'the Iraqi leadership of the time to heed the calls of Iraq's friends and show the level of cooperation to the United Nations that would have allowed no leeway for any military move'.[125] Implicitly reprimanding 'the Muslim world' for having failed to rally and prevent the bloodshed, he declared that 'we must act with a refreshed vision', and that vision was based on principles he had learned from Europe and introduced into his party's agenda for Turkey. It was, he explained,

> a vision in which good governance, transparency and accountability will reign, the fundamental rights and freedoms as well as gender equality are upheld, and there would be no place for blunting rhetoric and slogans. In short, we should first put our house in order. Rational thinking should be our divining force, as we draw our strength from our spiritual values. Creating a synergy from these values inherent in our being will be our test as well as our contribution to our modern age.[126]

Gül spoke in English, but even in translation 'rational thinking' was clearly a challenge to states founded in terms of faith and Islamic law – such as Iran,

Pakistan and Saudi Arabia – and frowns broke out on the faces of many in his audience. But he meant every word. A close colleague of the time recalls that the Foreign Ministry had originally provided him with a speech, but he worked until three in the morning revising the entire text. His aim was to put the need for reform among the Islamic nations right to the forefront rather than leaving it as a formula at the end.[127] With memories of Jeddah and what he had learned of the economies and social conditions in many oil-rich states, Gül generated a series of barely muted accusations in the form of a list of things needing to be done, though here too the terms applied fully to his plans for reform in Turkey:

> We should start by eradicating illiteracy, corruption, waste of human natural and material resources. We should address the underlying causes of violence. We must promote higher living standards for all, and reduce income disparities and the urban–rural divide. We must be cognizant of the fact that the absence of economic rationality and perpetual political instability in our societies prevent us from fully benefiting from our resources as well as our capabilities.[128]

In Tehran, Gül called upon the OIC to adopt a message of 'unity in diversity' while urging member states to encourage and pursue democracy and development, since doing so would challenge 'those who speak of the clash of civilizations', while reviving the Muslim world's 'spiritual heritage of peace, harmony, tolerance and affection' in order to 'strengthen our inspiration for achieving freedom, peace, prosperity and democracy'.[129] The secular Turkish press was enthusiastic. *Milliyet* called it 'the most radical speech in the history of the OIC', praising Gül's 'new vision based on gender equality'; even *Radikal* approved of his call for democratizing 'the Islamic world'.[130] In June, Colin Powell applauded Gül's speech and his call for gender equality, marking a relaxation in diplomatic tensions between Turkey and the USA.[131] The Arab world took longer to respond, but when it did, Gül's lecture 'telling Islamic nations to reform in terms of human rights, gender equality, transparency, accountability, and the rational use of resources instead of squandering wealth alongside poverty' generated controversy in the Arab countries and among the Arab diaspora. 'When he began instituting these reforms in Turkey, people in Arab countries finally took notice of what he was up to,' a colleague recalls. 'I remember Arab waiters in Brussels applauding him when we entered a restaurant.'[132]

Looking west in 2003

Following his approaches to the Balkans and Muslim world, Abdullah Gül spent the summer of 2003 representing Turkey's 'new vision' in London and the USA. In London on 3 July, he told members of the Royal Institute of International Affairs at Chatham House that 2004 was going to be a 'momentous year' for Turkey with a forthcoming meeting of the OIC foreign ministers and a NATO summit scheduled to take place in Istanbul. He spoke confidently of how Turkey's economic stability and reform packages were satisfying the criteria for admission to the EU, and that admission would promote greater stability and prosperity. But he also emphasized how Turkey was now in a position to take a leading role as an agent of peace in the Middle East, recalling how 'the peoples of this region could live together in peace and harmony also during the Ottoman times'. Noticing how the 'road-map' recently agreed on by both Israel and Palestine provided a way forward for peace in the region, Gül again tuned his vision of Turkey's future to its historical mission: 'I believe that it is Turkey's responsibility to work towards the goal of a good future for the Middle East. This is not only based on economic and political interests. There is also a humanitarian and moral imperative rooted in history.' But he also drew attention to the need for reform in Turkey and throughout the Muslim world, recalling how he had personally 'contributed to this call on various occasions', and was a reliable witness. 'I have been able to speak as a representative of the government of a Muslim country that is successfully undertaking major political, social and economic reforms to attain the highest standards of democracy and modernity while preserving its identity.' Here, for the London audience, was the same message he had delivered to Muslim leaders in Tehran concerning the need for them to follow Turkey and embrace modernity, advance democratic standards, and seek what he called 'unity and diversity' among themselves.[133]

   In July, mere weeks after US armed forces had seized and put sacks over the heads of Turkish soldiers in Süleymaniye, Abdullah Gül travelled to Washington, DC. Although many in Turkey regarded the insult to the Turkish military as an insult to the nation as a whole, Gül was eager to improve relations with the US and ignored the incident. Instead, and in line with the general directions outlined in the AKP programme, he elaborated on his key ambitions for Turkey's future while broadcasting his government's early successes. On 23 July he reassured the Turkish business community in Washington, DC that the AKP had already achieved a 'stable macroeconomic environment' with declining inflation, growing exports, and a significant drop in the public debt.[134] Two days later, addressing the Washington Institute on Near East Policy, he more aggressively advertised his government's success at achieving their mission of proving 'that a Muslim society is capable of changing and renovating itself, attaining contemporary standards, while preserving its values, traditions and identity'. He subtly boasted of how, in only eight months, the AKP government had achieved so much that it seemed to many to be 'a paradox':

> A government that was formed by a party known to be based on moral and traditional values, wrongly branded by some as an 'Islamist' Party, was implementing a most spectacular economic and political reform campaign in Turkey; reforms that even astonished the liberals and the skeptics at home, causing surprise in some of them and admiration in others.[135]

Turkey, he pronounced, was leading reform at home and in the Muslim world, and was proud to enjoy a history of strong strategic relations with NATO and the US, recalling the Korean and Cold War eras of US–Turkish collaboration. With Secretary of State Colin Powell, he was even now working on humanitarian assistance and peacekeeping efforts in Iraq, and was in dialogue with Israel and the Palestinian Authority, assisting both in fulfilling the 'road-map' for peace. 'Being the only Muslim country with historical and close ties with both of them,' he reminded his audience,

> Turkey is in a position to play an important role to facilitate a better understanding between the two parties … It is gratifying to see that both parties are giving the Turkish views due consideration. Our joint efforts with the parties are aimed at freeing the Holy Land from violence, terror, hatred, injustice and poverty first; establishing peace and cooperation second. The Road Map is the only viable way to achieve this. It is very much necessary and desirable that the Syrian and Lebanese tracks are also revived in a similar manner.[136]

Gül reiterated this confident vision of Turkey's special role in a number of speeches delivered in New York.

On 22 and 24 September, Abdullah Gül presented himself to the Turkish business and labour communities of New York as one who was 'proud' to be 'a representative of a reformist Government in Turkey', reporting on his party's economic achievements and advising on new opportunities for Turkish businesses in Afghanistan and Iraq, the Balkans and Central Asia.[137] On Wednesday 24 September he addressed the second annual Eurasia Summit by reflecting on how the ancient Silk Road was 'an example of early globalization, linking up different cultures, beliefs and centres of knowledge', while 'fostering cultural creativity and economic growth'. Shut down during the Cold War, the Eurasian Silk Road 'stretching from Madrid to Vladivostok, from Stockholm to Singapore' was open once again, providing new opportunities for peace, stability, trade and development.[138]

He elaborated on this historical theme three days later, arguing this time that his government's economic and domestic reforms were part of 'our vision to create a more prosperous and stronger Turkey' that included a major shift in foreign policy. 'During the long days of the Cold War,' he pronounced, 'Turkey was primarily known for her military-strategic contribution to NATO … Now, besides that, we are increasingly known for our regional ties, economic dynamism and secular democracy.' In language doubtless recalling discussions with Ahmet Davutoğlu, he declared that 'Turkey lies at the hub of a vast region which beholds the weight of the past, the many challenges of the present, along with the many promises of the future.'[139] Under the new government, Turkey was already exercising considerable 'soft-power' through peacekeeping, business investment and promoting a newly assertive style of diplomacy designed to make the most of Turkey's strategic importance in the post-Cold War era. Gone was the 'inward-looking' foreign policy inherited from Atatürk's time that, even under Özal, had sought to maintain 'the international status quo', to be replaced in favour of independent foreign policies and initiatives aimed to promote 'Turkish national interests'.[140] For Abdullah Gül, diplomacy was the means, and his government was dedicated to 'demonstrating a culture of win-win solutions and a commitment to problem solving'. In short, he assured his New York audience that Turkey was setting an 'example [that] can be inspiring to those societies which are at the threshold of profound change'.[141] Since US policy makers would continue thinking in terms of the 'Turkish model', the best plan for the moment was to take the initiative and set the terms of exactly what that might mean and not leave it up to the Pentagon or White House to define Turkey's role. Interviewed by William Safire for the *New York Times*, Gül reported how 'public opinion is changing' over Turkish involvement in Iraq, and that the parliament and military leaders now all supported 'going down there'. Safire assured his readers that 'Mr Gül … strikes me as a real statesman.'[142]

Going global, 2004–06

From the beginning of his term as foreign minister, Abdullah Gül developed policy speeches that elaborated and refined the foreign policy aims of the AK Party Programme, which involved energetically promoting Turkey's engagement with regional and global politics as well as domestic reforms aimed at satisfying EU admission standards. Characteristically tuning his observations to different audiences, he developed and pursued policies in keeping with his vision of Turkey's new role in the world. During these years he developed principled views on major political ambitions for Turkey about which he has avoided compromise: 'democracy, rule of law, human rights, good governance, transparency, accountability, gender equality, the rejection of violence, and economic structures that function more effectively and freely'.[143] At the same time, and unparalleled among his political colleagues, Gül's international experience made him a prime actor in foreign policy. While keeping his eyes ever directed at the EU accession talks, Gül actively sought better economic and diplomatic relations with China,[144] and took a lead in early diplomacy with Syria, persuading them to withdraw from Lebanon.[145] Peace in the Middle East was also a key goal. Following the assassination of Sheikh Yassin, the founder of Hamas, in March 2004, Prime Minister Erdoğan had horrified the Israeli press by branding Israel a 'terrorist' state, but Gül continued to promote trade and diplomacy between Turkey and Israel.[146] While in New York, he made a point of reminding Turkish businessmen there that Turkey and Israel were 'the two democracies in the region', and how 'the friendship between the Turkish and Jewish peoples, dating back half a millennium, has served as a sound basis upon which Turkey and Israel have developed close relations'.[147]

For Gül, preserving that 'sound basis' was essential if Turkey hoped to have any influence on Israel that would help bring about a just peace for the Palestinians. In January 2005, he returned from a short visit to Israel and the Palestinian Authority, critical of President Sharon's plan to withdraw from Gaza.[148] A month later, Gül praised Sharon for the peace agreement he signed with Palestinian leader Mahmoud Abbas at Sharm el-Sheikh, and announced that Turkey was assisting the Palestinian authority by providing police uniforms and training for Palestinian security forces.[149] According to Alon Liel, Israel's ambassador to Turkey at the time, Gül enthusiastically pursued strengthening trade and diplomatic ties with Israel and was well received. Liel recalls Gül visiting Jerusalem in March 2005 for a meeting at the King David Hotel at which he withdrew earlier criticism to declare that

Turkey favoured the withdrawal from Gaza. From this moment on, according to Liel, diplomatic relations between the two countries continued to improve for several years, despite criticism of Israel over Palestinian rights and occasional indiscreet comments by AKP government ministers, but could not survive Israel's invasion of Gaza in December 2008.[150]

Abdullah Gül opposed violence, whether state-approved or otherwise. In London, and later in Washington and New York, he had already announced Turkey's commitment to eradicating terrorism, insisting that 'terrorism was a global problem' that 'cannot be associated with any religion, culture or geography' since it is a 'crime against humanity'.[151] The Al-Qaeda sponsored bombs that went off in Istanbul a little over a month after his return from New York provided gruesome and deadly evidence of his position: the targets were British and Jewish, but it was also an attack on the people and sovereignty of a Muslim country. It could, he insisted, only be considered a criminal rather than a religious act. Turkey was a victim too with undeniable stakes in rebuilding Iraq, promoting just peace throughout the Middle East, and sponsoring regional cooperation.

In the early months of 2004 after the Istanbul bombings, Turkey's new status as a victim helped Abdullah Gül's efforts to ease relations with the Western powers. It also provided further edge to his call on the Muslim world to follow Turkey's lead in challenging the growth of Islamophobia.[152] Unlike Necmettin Erbakan who had pursued personal and unilateral deals with Muslim states, Gül deliberately sought out multilateral organizations such as the OIC to present his ideas on how his government's reforms in Turkey would benefit Muslims everywhere. By 4 October 2005, when the EU formally began talks on Turkey's accession, Gül had been busy developing and refining his case for democratic reform within the Muslim world and had presented it to audiences of government and business leaders at OIC assemblies in Azerbaijan, Jordan, Kuwait, Palestine, Malaysia, Yemen and Iran. In Kuala Lumpur, he declared that his government's 'mission was to prove that a Muslim society is capable of changing and renovating itself ... while preserving its values, traditions and identity'. He insisted that modern democratic values – such as 'gender equality, free markets, civil society' and rule of law – were all 'universal expectations' that conformed to Muslim values'. 'These values are "universal" because no one can claim monopoly over humanistic values that are the common inheritance of civilization. Islam has made highly significant contributions to this common civilization.'[153] Development, democracy and modernization: in addition to these key directions for reform in Muslim countries, he also continued to argue for the need for improved diplomacy in the new contexts of globalization.

While in charge of the Foreign Ministry, Abdullah Gül continually pressed the case for social and democratic reform to other Muslim nations. Before an economic forum in Jeddah held on 11 February 2006, he argued that since globalization had produced uneven development, promoting tolerance of cultural differences via improving diplomatic relations and communications was the only way forward for nations to 'live together on this planet in peace and harmony'. The Danish 'cartoon scandal' was still a hot issue among Muslims everywhere, but Gül urged his audience to bear in mind European standards on the issue. He recalled Article 10 of the European Convention on Human Rights which 'explicitly states that identities and religious values cannot be degraded, let alone attacked!' Freedom of speech and of the press, he insisted, were complements of 'respect for cultural and religious values', not opposites: 'There is no right on earth that is boundless.' Muslim countries, he argued, both among themselves, and in their relations with other countries, needed to revise their diplomacy in terms of 'tolerance and mutual respect'. Doing so was urgent since 'Islamophobia is on the rise, almost replacing anti-Semitism as a menace.'[154] To an audience the next day at King Abdul-Aziz University, he elaborated by arguing that there are key Muslim aspirational values – 'knowing one's limits, humility; hard work rewarded by spiritual richness as much as by material riches' – that urgently needed to be made more active in closing what he termed the 'gap of mutual understanding' that was threatening the world. 'If modernity,' he proclaimed, 'is built on rule of law, human rights, transparency, and accountability, let me say ... these also are our values! Look at our history, and find them there, among us!'[155]

Encouraging Muslim countries to embrace 'rule of law, human rights, transparency, and accountability', however, was doing little to allay continuing suspicions among hard-line secularists at home that the AKP were up to no good; nor did it help to persuade extreme Islamist groups that working alongside the US in Iraq was the right thing for a country with a majority Muslim population to be doing. At home, headscarves continued to cause disproportionate amounts of trouble, while Erdoğan-inspired plans for building new mosques, banning the sale of alcohol in certain neighbourhoods, and proposals to reform the adultery laws in 2004 were all touted as continuing evidence of an Islamist agenda. Diplomatically, the NATO summit held in Istanbul that summer had been a great success: security arrangements had kept President George Bush and others safe amid massive anti-NATO demonstrations. The government and General Staff had shown they were able to agree, if only on assuming a common front for the international press.

That summer Abdullah Gül renewed his friendship with Condoleezza Rice, soon to replace Colin Powell as Bush's secretary of state. Rice recalls meeting Gül previously in Ankara, and rather liked him. 'Although,' Rice observes in her memoirs, 'one should always be on guard against reacting to a foreign colleague based on personality, we're all human. Chemistry matters, and with Gül it was immediately good. As we talked in the car about the future of Turkey, I was convinced that he was a democrat at heart.'[156] It was on the morning of the first meeting of the Istanbul–NATO summit on 28 June that Rice passed Bush a note: 'Mr President, Iraq is sovereign. Letter was passed from Bremer at 10:26 AM Iraq time – Condi.' The occupation of Iraq had, formally at least, come to an end. 'President Bush sent the note back to me,' Rice recalls, 'with a line written across it: 'Let Freedom Reign!'[157] But the violence in Iraq was not over, and in Turkey, a new cycle of political killings was about to break out, exposing how covert operatives of the 'deep state' were just as active as those Islamist extremists who had bombed Istanbul back in November 2003.

Domestic problems, 2005–06

By the time EU accession talks opened in October 2005, 'an unprecedented nationalist backlash against Europe and the idea of European Union membership' had broken out in Turkey, fuelled among Turkish Muslims by the rise of Islamophobia in Europe, and shared by secular nationalists who were equally alarmed at relinquishing authority to Brussels.[158] A group of extreme nationalists within the judiciary, calling themselves the *Büyük Hukukçular Birliği* ('Great Union of Jurists') led by a lawyer named Kemal Kerinçsiz, set about deliberately embarrassing the government and its EU ambitions by bringing charges under Article 301 of the constitution against journalists, writers, academics and even visiting EU representatives for insulting the Kemalist ideals of 'Turkishness'. In September they had nearly prevented an academic conference on 'Ottoman Armenians' from taking place. Gül's party colleague Cemil Çiçek, who was justice minister at the time, joined in the protest against the conference, accusing the organizers of 'backstabbing the Turkish nation'.[159] But Gül was strongly in favour of academic conferences whatever their ostensive political aims and orientations might be: 'I was working hard at the time of the 2005 Ottoman–Armenian conference to make overtures to Armenia. I supported the project of the conference and wanted to attend but I had to be in New York and so I sent a message supporting them.'[160] With cases to prosecute well-known writers including Orhan Pamuk, Elif Shafak, Murat Bilge and Hrant Dink waiting to go to trial under Article 301, Gül held a press conference at which he told reporters that the government was 'watching closely how the existing laws are being implemented' and that 'there may be need for a new law'.[161]

Other attempts to embarrass the government and put a brake on EU accession were both covert and violent. On 9 November, news arrived from the remote and mountainous Kurdish district of Şemdinli that made it seem as if Susurluk had happened all over again. Word got out that two bombings earlier that week, initially attributed to the PKK, had been carried out by members of a local unit of state-appointed gendarmes; 'two were military officers', the other 'an ex-PKK informant ... Once again, the deep state had been caught red handed, but this time it was harder to deny.'[162]

During those early weeks of 2006, even as Abdullah Gül was preparing his speeches for an OIC summit in Jeddah, the Şemdinli bombings made regular headlines for providing evidence of 'deep state' opposition to AKP power; though journalists found details were hard to come by since the local military authorities were keeping the investigation to themselves.[163] But it was also becoming clear that religious nationalists were close to breaking point too, as they watched what they believed to be increasing evidence of Islamophobia threatening their beliefs and rights. In November 2005 the European Court of Human Rights had defended the ban on headscarves in universities to the dismay of Muslims and liberals alike, and to the fury of paranoid fundamentalists.[164] On 5 February, a week before Abdullah Gül was due to fly to Jeddah, a sixteen-year-old schoolboy in Trabzon shot and killed a local Catholic priest, Andrea Santoro. When Gül returned from Jeddah, Turkey's relations with the US were being set back once again as the ultra-nationalist action film *The Valley of the Wolves: Iraq* was released, setting new box office records throughout Turkey and inflaming anti-US feeling. Gül met again with Condoleezza Rice – now secretary of state – that summer and was able to improve formal relations, putting the strategic partnership 'back on track'.[165]

But at home the violence had returned. On 17 May, an influential judge who opposed lifting the headscarf ban, Yücel Özbilgin, was murdered by an extreme Islamic-nationalist Alparslan Aslan.[166] Nearby, the summer brought war to the Middle East in June when Israel launched 'Operation Summer Rains' against militants in Gaza, and followed with attacks against Hezbollah in Lebanon during July. Muslim nationalists in Turkey found more cause for anger; the government deplored these actions but it was otherwise business as usual with Israel. Turkish Islamists who had expected AKP to push a religious agenda were greatly disappointed by their first years in power,[167] but were doubtless just as pleased as the secular nationalists when, in December, President Sarkozy froze Turkey's admission talks at the EU.

Turkey's reputation in Europe already soiled, the murder of Armenian journalist Hrant Dink in Istanbul on 19 January 2007 was a horrible new stain to begin an election year, and it was one that only spread as the courts dragged out the case against the killer, turning him into a local hero among extreme nationalists. But the massive civil society demonstrations, culminating in a procession of '100,000 mourners ... holding placards with the slogans "We are all Armenians," and "We are all Hrant Dink" in Armenian, Turkish and Kurdish' also showed that Turkish society was starting to recognize ethnic difference as an issue of human rights: at least in metropolitan Istanbul.[168] On 4 February, angry nationalists held a smaller counterdemonstration in the same city, shouting 'We are all Turks. We are all Mustafa Kemal.'[169] A year of new political dramas had begun.

Spring 2007

With both general and presidential elections on the horizon, the spring of 2007 was a time for campaigns, demonstrations and protests. When he was named as party nominee for the president's office on 24 April, Abdullah Gül knew he was facing organized opposition that soon became a series of 'constitutional battles' over his candidacy.[170] Earlier in the year, outgoing president Ahmet Sezer had warned the nation about the dangers of re-electing an AKP government, declaring: 'The political regime of Turkey has not faced such danger since the founding of the Republic.'[171] The first protest marches against the possibility of a president from the AKP had already taken place in Ankara on 14 April. When Gül's name was announced, market analysts were, however, generally optimistic that his nomination, and likely election, would be good for the Turkish economy.[172] But secular hackles bristled at the news: 'Millions took to the streets to show their anger and fear about Gül being elected as president, mainly because his wife wears a headscarf.'[173] During April, thousands protested against Gül's candidacy on the streets of Ankara, Manisa, Çanakkale, Bodrum, Izmir, Denizli, even Samsun.[174]

Encouraged by popular outbursts and eager to back President Sezer, the military joined the attack. They needed to distract attention from recent embarrassments in any case. In March, *Nokta* magazine had published revelations – based on an electronic diary inadvertently left on a laptop by a former admiral – that revealed how since 2004 there had been plans for a military coup to overthrow the AKP government. The operation was suitably code-named 'Blond Girl'. The military authorities never denied the claims, and might well have left the matter there, a silent warning. Instead, they set about raiding the offices of *Nokta* magazine and arrested the editor, Alper Görmüş, for violating Article 301, thereby confirming belief that the 'deep state' was alive, well and acting without legitimate authority.[175] Using the internet to flex their secularist muscles virtually, on 27 April the General Staff joined the protest against Gül's candidacy, publishing a memorandum on their website implying that the election of a 'non-secular' president – one, that is, with a wife who wears a headscarf – would justify military intervention.[176] Nothing daunted, Gül put his name forward, but the first two rounds of presidential voting at which he received massive support were annulled.

> To the shock of some of the most eminent constitutional jurists in the country, and at the request of the main opposition party, the Constitutional Court decided that Gül's election was indeed null and void because of the lack of a two-thirds quorum, which no legal scholar of any standing had ever heard before. It was clear that the court's decision was political and responded to the military's preferences.[177]

After the second annulled vote of 6 May, Gül withdrew his candidacy even as the government faced a deadlock over the constitutional timetable for general and presidential elections. With President Sezer's appointment due to expire, Erdoğan was obliged to call an early general election.

The July general elections showed that the AKP was capable of continuing to shock secular nationalists and generals alike, increasing their 2002 vote from 34.3% to a massive 46.7%. From now on, it was clear that the AKP was 'the only political party that could justifiably claim to represent all regions of Turkey'.[178] Within the AKP, electoral victory left the presidential question open. Earlier in the year, before the protesting began, Erdoğan had considered himself a possible candidate. With three rounds of voting scheduled for August, the discussion reopened within the party: Erdoğan's charisma had clearly attracted the voters, while Gül had the obvious advantages of knowledge based on international experience and language skills suited to the presidency.[179] Erdoğan's public statements in late July that he was prepared to 'compromise' on the presidency made little sense if he were interested in the position for himself.[180] But if Erdoğan did caution against re-nominating Gül because of controversies surrounding his previous candidacy, on 13 August, a week before the first of three rounds of voting, Gül nevertheless declared his return to candidacy. With the newly enforced two-thirds policy in place, it was only after the third round of votes held on 28 August that Gül became eleventh President of the Republic of Turkey. The next day, in his first public speech as president, Abdullah Gül loudly declared his allegiances to secularism and democracy. 'The Turkish Republic,' he said, 'is a democratic, secular and social state governed by the rule of law.'[181] There was no place for the military. The secularist opposition were furious at the prospect of a president with a covered wife, but this time the generals knew better than to intervene any further.

As William Hale and Ergun Özbudun have observed, the 2007 constitutional crisis sparked by Gül's candidacy arose from two reasons: 'the threat perception of the secularist state elites' for whom the presidency is 'a symbol and "the last citadel" of the secular republic', and the nature and extent of presidential power. Since 1982, the president held 'broad discretionary powers, especially in the fields of high-level judicial appointments and in the appointment of university administrators'. There were fears that 'presidential powers may be used to infiltrate the judiciary, the universities and the public administration in general with Islamist elements'.[182] These fears continue to haunt secular analysts in and beyond Turkey.

For the second time in his political career, Abdullah Gül had stepped forward and taken up the challenge of leadership. Although he had failed in his bid for leadership of Fazilet back in 2000, this time he had challenged a far greater opponent than Erbakan, the military establishment, and won. During the AKP's first term in office, Gül had diligently set about implementing the AK Party Programme, tuning foreign policy and encouraging domestic reforms to promote European standards of democracy within the 'universal' values taught by Islam while eschewing an Islamic agenda. In line with that programme, the government had enacted a range of constitutional and juridical reforms bringing Turkey into line with EU requirements, challenged the military, opened up a political debate over women's rights and gender equality, and started to loosen restrictions on the Kurdish language. Islamophobia in the world and political violence at home put new obstacles and challenges in the way, but under the AKP the state of the economy surpassed strict IMF regulations. The government had shown little sign of making serious efforts to Islamize Turkish society as many continued to fear. Despite occasional lapses when pandering to populist sentiment, as party leader, Erdoğan could rightly take credit for the modernization and reforms that had been taking place in Turkey since 2002. Through it all, Gül had proclaimed and proved himself committed to secular and democratic political reform, whatever his personal beliefs and past history in Islamic parties, and his election to the presidency was widely praised internationally for promising future democratic developments.[183]

At the time, scholars looking back at the time over the AKP's first term in office regularly commented on their record of successful reforms in the contexts of the questions concerning the particular convergence of Islam and democracy to produce what had come to be called the 'new Turkey'. Introducing a volume of academic studies on *The Emergence of a New Turkey: Democracy and the AK Parti* published in 2006, Hakan Yavuz observed that the 'new Turkey' had two defining characteristics: 'the curtailing of the power of the military', and 'the evolution of a new political discourse'. According to Yavuz, 'this discourse consists of democracy, civil society, human rights, and freedom of speech. This new discourse empowers the marginalized sectors of Turkish society and opens new ways of imagining state-society relations.'[184] At the heart of the AK Party Programme, the terms of this 'new political discourse' defined both Gül's abiding political vision and the policies of the party during their first term: extending democracy by removing the military from government while liberalizing civil society.

Not all scholars were as sanguine as Yavuz[185] – who is by no means a fan of the AKP – pointing to 'Turkey's failure' under the AKP to tackle some of its more difficult challenges, such as dealing with the US over the invasion of Iraq, or failing to 'establish cordial and cooperative relations with the Kurds of Iraq' in the aftermath of the invasion, or even to satisfy the reasonable demands of 'its own Kurdish population'.[186] Industrial relations expert Engin Yıldırım pointed to the rising unemployment and continuing labour problems left unresolved by the first term of AKP government, leading to the suspicion that the party 'leadership and cadres are of the view that traditional patterns of patrimonial relations are enough to address industrial relations issues'.[187] He was not alone in wondering about the party's future as it entered its second term. While scholars debated the party's relation to Islam, Graham Fuller – former chair of the National Intelligence Council for the CIA – fulsomely praised the new Turkey that had come into being under the AKP for democratizing at home while demonstrating 'capability to resolve the leading challenge to the Muslim world today: the management and political integration of Islam'.[188] As William Hale observed in 2006, what remained to be seen was whether the AKP could 'remain an invigorating as well as dominant force in Turkish politics in the years ahead'.[189] There are many who believe that some within the secular establishment were already making plans to prevent any such thing.

6

Presidency

A bdullah Gül's election to the presidency in August 2007 was no
simple personal achievement. Elected despite his well-known though
distant background in Islamic politics, his origins placed him outside
the ranks of the political elite. But it was religion, not class, that caught the
international headlines. The *New York Times* boldly announced 'Turk With
Islamic Ties Is Elected President', while the BBC noticed that 'his election as
president makes him the first politician with an Islamist background to become
head of state since the Turkish Republic was established in 1923'.[1] His election
was the deeply symbolic victory of conservative Muslims from provincial,
non-elite backgrounds, the skilled workers and local business communities
that were producing and benefitting most from economic development and
democratic representation under the AKP. But Gül's appointment was also
welcomed from outside the community of his supporters. Yaşar Kemal wrote
personally congratulating the new president, and was not alone: other well-
known left commentators, including Mehmet Ali Birand and Murat Belge,
publicly welcomed the new president.[2]

Yet Gül's move into the presidential office was also a personal achievement, just recognition of his efforts on behalf of the country's democratic
and economic progress. In Turkey, his election was greeted from a variety
of different constituencies, often in personal terms. Novelist Elif Shafak
was enthusiastic about the new president, noticing that 'he has been a successful, pro-EU diplomat and a mild and moderate voice within his party.
His public support for journalists and writers on trial has also brought him
close to intellectuals. Today, in addition to his own electorate, he has the
empathy and support of many in the intelligentsia and business circles.'[3] As
if to reassure the *New York Times* and BBC, former ANAP prime minister

Mesut Yılmaz – a staunch defender of secularism throughout his career – observed: 'It would be wrong to evaluate Gül on the basis of his past views. He had ties to a political party then, but now he has none with any party. If he keeps his pledges, he could play a major role in bringing about social peace.'[4] Now that Gül was in the president's office, he was out of the party and out of parliament, but held final veto over parliamentary bills. In the words of a European Stability Initiative briefing, 2007 would prove to be 'a dramatic year for Turkish politics and society, even by the standards of a country used to political drama.'[5]

The move to Çankaya: Madame Gül, first lady

Confronting the military and making them stand down in the name of democracy, Abdullah Gül's campaign and victory set in process a chain of events that would remove the military from political life in Turkey. And of crucially symbolic importance in the political drama of that year, Hayrünnisa Gül defied secular ire to become the first first lady to enter the presidential palace at Çankaya wearing a headscarf. Keeping out of the public eye was not an option.

> Consider the presidential elections. The opposition to Abdullah Bey was pursued through me. Those who wanted to prevent him from becoming president always presented my headscarf as an issue. Put yourself in my shoes and think: the political career of my husband and destiny of the country were subject to my headscarf.[6]

Having returned from exile in New York to run for election as an AKP candidate, Nursuna Memecan recalls the hostile media campaigns of early 2007:

> During the debates over the presidential nomination about whether she deserved to be first lady because she wore a scarf, there were things on TV insulting her personally, her appearance, her education, her family. It was terrible; she was being torn apart by reporters, both men and women.[7]

Ayşe Böhürler too remembers the vicious media attacks, and how reports generated confusions, backbiting and divisions within the party.

During the presidential elections in 2007 the headscarf issue divided the party into different camps. I thought there were more important issues than the scarf at this time and wrote an article asking: should we work for a civil constitution or spend time on the debate over a president's wife with a scarf? I said that a president having a wife who wore a scarf would be a step forward since it would defuse the debate. There were lots of reactions to this. I received lots of criticism and insults. Some even said that this was aimed at Abdullah Gül! It was not, but at that time it created a sense in the party that I was against his running for president. But I was saying something different.[8]

Finding herself being blamed for creating rifts within the party and constantly the focus of television debates, Hayrünnisa was by no means pleased by the attention but managed to stay detached. Nursuna Memecan told me:

> Someone else would not have been able to cope but because she believes and has faith and because of her background she was able to take all of this. Several evenings we would sit and watch TV and Hayrünnisa would laugh, and I thought I could never have laughed like that at such public humiliation if it were me. Now we joke about those bad old days. She started out as a strong woman and has become stronger since then. Hardly anything fazes her these days.[9]

At the time, however, public humiliation took another form once it became clear that there would be protocol problems. Outgoing President Sezer refused to conduct handover ceremonies at Çankaya since that would entail inviting Madame Gül, nor would she be invited to attend the inauguration ceremonies.[10] Compromises had to be reached.

To avoid undue difficulties, President Gül held initial meetings with state officials and bureaucrats over working breakfasts, rather than evening receptions to which wives would traditionally be invited.[11] The formal, evening receptions that the new president was obliged to hold in 'public' areas within Çankaya still banned to covered women were, in the event, boycotted by the CHP and many – but not all – of the top military leaders.[12] Since avoiding constant attention was impossible, Hayrünnisa was determined to set the stage on which she would be expected to appear and insisted that they stay on in the residence of the foreign minister where they had lived for the last five years. Here headscarves would not violate the space that had once been home to

Atatürk. More importantly, the children had grown up here and Hayrünnisa
had set up the household to run as she wanted it to. Moving into the presidential residence, even after restoration, would be needlessly disruptive. But
there was more to it than simply creating a comfort zone where dignitaries
might also be received and entertained. For Madame Gül, becoming first lady
was an active engagement: 'I always say that God has given us roles to play in
this world,' she told me in a different context: 'This is a theatre stage and we
act our roles. We try to do our best and move along.'[13]

On 29 August, Madame Hayrünnisa Gül formally visited the presidential
palace and grounds at Çankaya for the first time, not to start living there but
to assume her position as first lady. She was relieved that the family would not
have to live there.[14] She found all the buildings, especially public offices and
reception rooms, decrepit, disordered, and furnished in an eclectic mixture
of styles, with lots of 'fading kitsch' everywhere. Everything was old, worn out
and disorganized; a shame to the state. An obsolete air-conditioning system
blew smelly air from the kitchens directly into the important meeting rooms.
In the hot summer months, hosting meetings of international guests would
be to insult them with air-conditioned cooking smells. The corridors and
receptions halls were drab and dingy with mismatched curtains, and there
were cellar rooms piled with decades of gifts to former presidents, many of
them beautiful and valuable.

> There was a lot that was inherited from Atatürk in the warehouses. We
> took them all out and put them in display cases. While repairing old
> sculptures and paintings, we are getting new sculptures that will be
> inherited by future generations. We also established systems for the
> protection of these pieces and work to make these systems permanent.[15]

In short order, Madame Gül became a practical archivist as she set about
reorganizing and redecorating, cataloguing the presidential collection of gifts,
carpets, plates and awards, and having them repaired and restored.

With the same care and energy that she used when she renovated the
presidential buildings in Çankaya and Tarabya, Istanbul – where visiting
foreign diplomats are increasingly welcomed – Hayrünnisa 'took command
of branding the presidential office'. When she arrived, the styles of writing
paper used within the presidential offices – for letterheads, memos and formal
invitations for various occasions – were all different, reflecting disparate periods and tates. Hayrünnisa hired a design company and worked closely with

them, 'learning how corporate identity works and why it is important'. They developed a booklet for all the different offices, bringing everything within 'a uniform concept'.[16] With considerable experience hosting international guests, as first lady Hayrünnisa continued to supervise every detail, designing menus featuring traditional Turkish dishes that are tuned to the season, and even, it is said, upgrading the quality of wine served to international guests.

Besides improving, branding and reforming the presidential offices, Hayrünnisa took control of media perceptions of her appearance, resisting attempts, both hostile and otherwise, to tell her what she should wear. Since 2003 in Davos when, together with Emine Erdoğan, she had come under close media scrutiny for wearing a fashionable headscarf decorated with gold thread at an international event, Hayrünnisa had done her best to avoid publicity. Withdrawing her case at the European Court of Human Rights against Ankara University in 2004 had briefly made headlines, but otherwise she had managed to carry on her educational and family projects without drawing too much attention to herself. Since the beginning of 2007, however, Hayrünnisa Gül had been back in the news and the target of attack from the secularist establishment. By August, in the days before Abdullah Gül was confirmed in the president's office, the 'intense scrutiny' of 'the role played by his wife' led Hayrünnisa to make a public statement about 'how extremely uncomfortable the attention and scrutiny being paid to her personal life choices is making her'.[17] But she recognized and accepted the symbolic importance of her new position as Turkey's first lady.

While it was unsurprising that media attention was directed at her clothing, it was none the less frustrating: 'I kept saying: please look inside my head and not outside. In other words, I kept saying that the headscarf did not cover my brain.'[18] But no one in the media was listening, and while not all of the attention being drawn to her clothing was critical, it could prove just as alarming for other reasons. Even the BBC carried reports about how Turkey's new first lady was consulting with various designers including Atil Kutoğlu – a young and dynamic Turkish designer who had taken Vienna by storm, dressing sundry Habsburg princesses as well as international celebrities such as Catherine Zeta-Jones and Naomi Campbell. Kutoğlu himself appears to have claimed that Madame Gül asked him 'to modernize her look and to have some new ideas for the headscarf', and to design a wardrobe for her that would bring a 'Hollywood look' to conservative style: 'I am imagining like Romy Schneider or Catherine Deneuve wearing some turban looks in their movies,' he enthused.[19]

Other Turkish designers were also quick to express great excitement imagining the new styles that, they were confident, Hayrünnisa was destined to promote among covered women throughout the world. Istanbul-based fashion designer Neslihan Yargıcı announced that there was a new era opening up for fashion-conscious conservative women. With the new first lady presiding in Çankaya, Yargıcı called on Turkish designers to take a world lead in creating the new styles. Equally enthusiastic at the prospect of Hayrünnisa becoming a new style icon was Barbaros Şandal, founding member of the 'Pink Life' (*Pembe Hayat*) movement in Turkey and famous for designing gowns for the transgender pop singer and film star Bülent Ersoy.[20] Much to her shocked surprise, Hayrünnisa discovered that her new role as first lady meant she had inadvertently become something of a gay icon: like it or not, her public role meant constant scrutiny and dressing for the part could not be more important. But against all the rumours and gossip, she insists that she takes entire responsibility for her own wardrobe, and has never fulfilled the dreams of excitable and fanciful designers. 'Turkish designers designed things, but I never wore just a single designer's clothes,' she told me in 2013, and denied that she ever 'worked with' Kutoğlu exclusively.[21]

> From this point of view, the first Republic Day reception was important. In that case, I worked with a woman fashion designer. I did work with other designers, too, but I do not want to be the topic of discussion because of my clothes or the designers I work with because I take care of my own wardrobe as well. For example, we made what I am wearing today here at home. In other words, it was sewn here. I am personally involved in this, so I do not expect someone to make them for me. In any case, we do not have that luxury in Turkey. Our life is very busy and one needs many clothes, but I never had a single designer or just one place where I got my clothes from.[22]

Madame Gül energetically assumed the possibilities of her new role in national life, not simply by renovating the interiors of presidential buildings and displaying a flair for stylish modesty in her costume, but also using her status to promote improvements in education, child care and family welfare. She has initiated and promoted a number of social responsibility projects aimed at improving educational opportunities and health care facilities in non-metropolitan areas, especially the south east. Her colleagues assure me that she is actively and personally engaged, and not simply a figurehead making speeches. 'In her children's campaigns, she knows the names of the kids.'[23] Among these, the '81 Stars' project provides financial support for talented students nominated by the governors of each of the eighty-one provinces.

> Although many things have been done in health and education, there is still more to do ... I am ambitious in projects. There are children we look after in cities as part of our '81 Stars from 81 Provinces Project'. I have five children in each province at the moment. I take care of them, I try to go to day-care centres, I visit families of martyrs and I get to see the development in Turkey perhaps more closely than anyone else.[24]

Hayrünnisa also became actively engaged in improving existing child welfare institutions. In 2008, Sarah, Duchess of York, the former wife of Prince Andrew, had visited Turkey and made an undercover film that was shown on British television exposing the appalling conditions inside a state-run orphanage.[25]

> I went to Saray Çocuk Evleri ... The Sarah Ferguson incident took place at Saray. I visited without informing the minister, the provincial director or even the governor. It was an unannounced visit. The first house we entered was inhabited by children with disabilities. Everything is running well now including their healthcare and education ... I was very worried when I went there wondering what I would see, but to see everything running smoothly even during an unannounced visit impressed me a lot. I thank Allah to have granted us the possibility to see and experience all this.[26]

Hayrünnisa was relieved to find that any such conditions as were reported in the film were not to be found now. In her new position as Turkey's first lady, Madame Gül began taking her duties and responsibilities very seriously from the start, using her new authority to promote her chosen causes while entering the ceremonial world of international political life with a new status and increasing confidence.

Meanwhile, presidential office removed Abdullah Gül from governmental politics and the direct running of the country, but provided increasing opportunities for representing the 'new' Turkey in the international arena.

The move to Çankaya: President Gül

For Abdullah Gül, the year 2007 began rather badly. Quietly upset by the constant personal attacks on himself and his family, he was suffering from continuing difficulties recovering his full hearing after an operation the previous year for an ear infection that, given the numerous hours he spent on aeroplanes, had become deeply embedded. If his months as prime minister trying to solve the economic problems and dealing with US plans to invade Iraq had turned his hair grey, his years in the presidency would be marked by recurrent hearing loss. Politically, becoming president meant formally relinquishing his leading position in the AKP team and hence his ability to press for continuing the democratic reforms laid out in the Party Programme and initiated in 2004. Some within the party were initially hesitant about Gül's presidential candidacy since his was among the most influential voices continuing to push for democratic reforms. There were fears he would have less influence over government policy from the presidential office. At the same time, it was also clear that Gül was the only member of the AKP with the international experience and language skills suited for that position. 'He has good contacts in all countries and on all sides, and he has a strong reputation for problem solving working with different kinds of leader from all around the world. No one in the AKP can do this kind of work as well as him.'[27] Any hesitations within the party concerning Gül leaving governmental office for the presidency were eventually put aside, though the constitutional crisis stirred up by the CHP over the nature of the presidential office that raged throughout the election campaigns continued well after his August election.

Over the summer, while the elections were still underway and deadlock over the presidential vote yet to be resolved, Erdoğan's government proposed constitutional amendments that would introduce popular elections to the presidency rather than parliamentary appointment, and establish a maximum of two terms of five years. CHP opponents argued that popular elections would 'create a semi-presidential system' by increasing 'the political weight of the President already endowed with broad constitutional powers', a system that 'had long been advocated by such centre-right leaders as Turgut Özal and Süleyman Demirel'.[28] Nevertheless, the CHP fought the amendments through the Constitutional Court all summer and it was not until October that the amendments were adopted by referendum: 'the long drawn-out battle over the question of the presidency seemed to be finally over, but not quite'.[29] These amendments were in line with more general AKP proposals for an entirely new constitution. In June, Erdoğan had assembled a team of constitutional lawyers to prepare a 'draft constitution within the parameters of the party's election manifesto' that would alter the powers of the president. [30] Following the July parliamentary elections, party leaders met to debate the draft, 'which is incomparably more democratic and liberal than the present Turkish Constitution'.[31] Once made public, the draft proposal was nevertheless received with suspicions of Islamist intent and drew noisy objections from the Turkish Bar Association. Plans to publish the draft and invite a long period of public debate over the new constitution, to be followed by an eventual referendum, were 'silently shelved', perhaps following 'some differences of opinion within the AKP itself'.[32] A substantial set of further constitutional amendments would be passed by referendum in 2010, while efforts to produce a completely new constitution continue.

Presidential soft power

Once Abdullah Gül was installed in the presidency and away from AKP and parliamentary meetings, his direct engagement with the engines of social and democratic reform was reduced. Gül found that his distance from the party combined with the very achievements of AKP's first term in power made it more difficult for him to contribute to the reforms. Although committed throughout his political life to the need for a new constitution that would protect the democratic rights of minorities, his new position removed him from direct influence over party debates. Another problem was that the impetus of the party's success had attracted new members who were not always in tune with the original Party Programme and its directions for reform. New agendas arose as circumstances globally and at home demanded attention. The AKP's success increasingly encouraged Prime Minister Erdoğan to promote social policies beyond the original Programme, listening to advisors who already tended to agree with him rather than challenge his tendency to tell people what they should do. With a great deal of his time now devoted to international protocol, Gül focused on promoting what had come to be called Turkey's 'soft power'.

From the beginning of his presidency, Abdullah Gül took a leading role in numerous foreign policy initiatives.[33] He quickly proved good at the job, opening direct and personal diplomatic relations with heads of state in the new Balkan and Central Asian countries, and encouraging improved relations with Brazil, China, Spain, Syria and Pakistan. From Kayseri he brought a talent for making a good deal against the odds, and for staying on good terms with opponents afterwards, whatever the outcome. To this he added a vision of a democratic Turkey inspired by his years in England and nearly a decade in international banking observing the needless problems endemic to political Islam. And he also brought experience of a decade in political office working to advance democratic reforms in Europe and endeavouring to bring those reforms to Turkey. Since the 1990s and the Refah years, he had kept to his practice of commissioning and absorbing expert briefs, sometimes asking for two or more reports on the same topic, so that he fully understood the issues at stake in any important meeting. President Gül was an informed negotiator who proved especially persuasive in direct dealings with other heads of state because of his open and genial manner. During his first weeks in office, Gül hosted President Bashar al-Assad of Syria on 16 October and, a month later, brought Israeli president Shimon Peres together with Palestinian president Mahmoud Abbas at a forum in Ankara on 13 November.[34] After a year in office, Gül addressed the General Assembly of the United Nations and was rightly able to boast 'that Turkey has been actively contributing to the advancement of peace as a facilitator of dialogue'.[35]

The Armenia initiative, 2007–09

In early November 2011, shortly after elections that brought the AKP to power for a third term, I asked President Gül what he considered to be the most urgent tasks facing the remaining years of his presidency. Without hesitation he replied: 'Cyprus, Armenia and the Kurdish issue'. Since Cyprus and the Kurdish problem are political scenarios involving numerous crucial actors representing entrenched and inflexible positions, the influence of any individual Turkish politician can only be minimal. Certainly Cyprus, as Gül had been insisting since the Greek-Cypriot rejection of the Annan Plan in 2004, can only be resolved through the United Nations.[36] Armenia is a different matter. In direct and personal negotiations with the president's office in Yerevan, Gül was able to use his skills at achieving workable answers to seemingly intractable problems by personal intervention. He recalled his early diplomatic initiatives:

> I believe if Turkey is to be an important country in the region then we must have peaceful, normal relations with all our neighbours including Armenia. Keeping apart makes no sense. We made strong overtures to Armenia. When I was foreign minister, I worked hard, and still work hard, and I haven't given up this. We opened our archives and sent a challenge to the whole of the Caucasus to open theirs, and we said to

any interested Turkish- or Armenian-Americans that together we can form a committee and go through the old archives. This was a real and serious challenge. We called out to all Armenians saying that we are ready to meet, and will accept anyone into the group. This could have made a family among American-Armenians who are divided. People in many countries supported this project. When Sarkisian became president, I sent him a warm letter of congratulations and showed my reasons to work to solve the problems. I was the first to take this step; later on he sent me a message; it was warm and friendly and I replied that we needed to normalize.[37]

During their first term, the AKP government had faced continued campaigns by Armenian nationalist groups 'to persuade parliaments in third countries to pass resolutions classifying the deaths of the Ottoman Armenians during the First World War as an act of "genocide".[38] As recently as January 2001, the French National Assembly had passed just such a resolution, joining a number of other European countries. When Gül became foreign minister the following year, he tried to rectify matters by courting the powers in Yerevan directly, opening flights between the two countries and offering some trade incentives. But the stand-off was destined to continue so long as the two countries remained in dispute over the status of the Nagorno-Karabakh Republic, a land-locked enclave within Azerbaijan. Turkey kept its land border with Armenia closed and continued to hesitate over establishing formal diplomatic relations.

In April 2005, Prime Minister Erdoğan and Foreign Minister Gül had initiated government proposals for an international commission to examine the historical archives and settle the 'genocide' question accordingly: President George W. Bush was among those in favour of the proposal. When, a week later, the Turkish state archives 'issued a list of more than 523,000 Turks it said were killed by Armenians in Turkey from 1910 to 1922', the *New York Times* declared treachery. Rather than exploring the chain of command that had led to the expulsions of Armenians, a countermove was being played in order to deflect charges against Turkey.[39] Erdoğan's proposals for an international commission had, in any case, been rejected by Robert Kocharian, the Armenian president at the time, who wanted to leave Bush out of the deal, insisting that only the two countries concerned should be involved in solving their problems, and that their meetings should address all disputes, including the closed border.[40] Involving other countries with complex legal positions on the genocide question would needlessly complicate the possibility of

Armenia and Turkey coming to terms. Kocharian was prepared to deal with Gül, but not with Bush's White House.

While still foreign minister, Abdullah Gül had publicly declared his support for open debate on the 'genocide' question, announcing that, if he had not had UN meetings in New York, he would have attended the scholarly conference on 'Ottoman Armenia' eventually held at Istanbul's Bilgi University on 24 September 2005.[41] By 2007, during the first months of his presidency, Gül faced a new challenge in the form of a bill being proposed in the US Congress referring to 'the Armenian Genocide'. President Bush and his military advisors were all too aware of how aggravating US–Turkish relations in this way would 'cause great harm to the American war effort in Iraq', recalling how Turkey had broken off military ties with France in 2001 after France recognized the 'genocide'.[42] The White House and Pentagon understood just how eager the Turkish military were to go into northern Iraq and take control of Kirkuk and its oil on the pretext of attacking the PKK. Provoking Turkey in this way did not seem a good option at the time, and by October when the bill came up for debate in Congress, several key sponsors had been persuaded to withdraw their support and request a delay: supporters of the bill have still not been successful.

In April 2008, the election of Serzh Sarkisian to the Armenian presidency provided President Gül with an ideal opportunity for improving diplomatic relations further between the two countries, one that caused great excitement in the international press, the Armenian diaspora and even the White House.[43] An advisor to President Gül's office at the time explained: 'When there are elections, Gül like other presidents congratulates the winner as a protocol matter and usually the individuals have no idea these messages have been sent. But Gül wrote Sarkisian a substantial message of congratulations, not simply a formal document.'[44] In reply, Sarkisian invited Gül to a soccer match. He announced the invitation in a speech before the Armenian community in Moscow on 23 June. Two weeks later, he repeated it for a wider, international audience in an op-ed article published by the *Wall Street Journal* which outlined plans for a 'fresh start' in relations with Turkey, even hinting at reversing his predecessor's refusal to form a commission to look into the historical archives. 'Just as the people of China and the United States shared enthusiasm for ping pong before their governments fully normalized relations,' Sarkisian wrote, 'the people of Armenia and Turkey are united in their love for football ... I hereby invite President Gül to visit Armenia to enjoy the match together with me in the stadium.'[45] Doubtless flattered by the comparison,

George Bush and the US State Department liked the idea, but nationalists in Turkey, Armenia and Azerbaijan were hostile.

Under attack by the opposition parties in Ankara, Abdullah Gül delayed his reply until almost the very last moment. A senior Turkish diplomat recalled:

> Imagine: two countries that have never had an official ministerial meeting, with no diplomatic relations – though Turkey formally recognizes Armenia. Normally meetings between the two countries are at minor events, music or culture, or something in a third country. But soccer among thousands, including hooligans and so on, this was a big risk. The day the invitation arrived Gül was excited and thought it was very important. Many advised him not to go for political or security reasons. This was one of the most symbolic examples of Gül's courage and problem-solving attitude – it was a big risk, personal and in terms of political prestige.[46]

Since there were no diplomatic relations between Turkey and Armenia, Abdullah Gül could not use normal channels to communicate directly and personally with Sarkisian, so he took the imaginative step of enlisting the help of Murat Yetkin, a journalist writing for the left-liberal paper *Radikal*.

Murat Yetkin had arranged to interview President Sarkisian in Yerevan, later describing how 'a high-ranking official from the Çankaya Presidential Palace phoned me on August 26 to ask if I could deliver a message from Gül. In the message, Gül delivered his greetings and good will and said he would be glad to meet Sarkisian in Astana. So the two presidents met in the Kazakh capital Astana.'[47] As Yetkin observes, using a journalist as a go-between on affairs of state was no reliable 'indication of a decision' regarding the soccer match, but 'showed that the mutual good will was understood'. On hearing Yetkin's report of his meeting with Sarkisian, Gül announced he would accept the invitation. While first meeting in Kazakhstan avoided breaking any of the rules regarding borders, the decision horrified Turkish nationalists at home and risked offending President Ilham Aliyev of Azerbaijan, who relied on Turkish support over reclaiming Nagorno-Karabakh and might fear he was being abandoned. Even 'as Gül took a bold step in relations with Armenia', giving 'Yerevan a chance to make certain corrections in its foreign policy', he needed to reassure Aliyev and arranged a press conference in Baku 'to dispel the Azeri public's doubts about Turkey's politics'. To avoid the closed border on his visit to Armenia, Gül's official car and security vehicles took a '600-kilometre detour' through Georgia.[48] The match itself, which Turkey won 2 – 0, was played on 6 September and was, by all accounts, a great public relations success for all concerned. Gül recalled the visit clearly:

> When we landed at Yerevan there were thousands of people and they were demonstrating peacefully. When we went to President Sarkisian's office for lunch, there was a well-known musician who played. We knew all the songs, the food was the same food, the bread was the same, and nothing was strange to us there. Then we went to the football match and it was exciting. There were fourteen Turkish tourists in the audience, with 140 police protecting us! All the time we were in a bullet-proof cabinet. We didn't ask for it but they did it. In Armenia they had killed many of their own deputies, so they were very careful of us when we visited. Then I invited Sarkisian to Turkey for the return match in Bursa. He came and we had dinner. [49]

Sarkisian's visit to Turkey for the return match in Bursa, played on 14 October 2009, was no less contested by nationalists on both sides, and by Azerbaijan. The previous April, Turkey and Armenia had announced an agreement to establish diplomatic relations and, by August, had agreed on terms that would be signed in advance of the match. Sarkisian infuriated nationalists at home and members of the Armenian diaspora by suggesting that Turkey's acceptance of the events of 1915 as 'genocide' should no longer be a condition for establishing diplomatic relations. [50] Protocols were signed and the Bursa football match was another public relations success, but with the problem over Armenia's support for the Nagorno-Karabakh Republic left unsolved, the 'stand-off continued', [51] and still continues, despite the best efforts of the two presidents.

When I pressed him on the 'genocide' question, Abdullah Gül elaborated – as he likes to do – on the historical contexts that are still shaping the limitations on public opinion in Turkey today:

> I think that in this region you cannot always survive by maintaining hostilities. All of us should not underestimate the sufferings – not only Armenians, but Turks and others – over 500 years. That's why there are now more Bozniaks and Chechnians living here in Turkey than in their homelands. Historians know what happened; the documents are all there. I am not underestimating the pains and suffering. If you asked me to move from my house to go somewhere else – and all the rest – I just can't imagine. It isn't easy to understand these things happening

in modern times, or what happened to so many of those people and to so many people in the Balkans. We are still living with the First War. So we understand the pains. But saying there was genocide is too much for the Turkish people to accept. We don't impose any ideas on people. We represent people's thoughts.[52]

In October 2009, following Sarkisian's visit, the two nations' foreign ministers met in Geneva and signed protocols aimed at improving relations, but their respective parliaments refused to agree. Gül had been optimistic, demonstrating how in direct negotiations with equal political partners, he knew how to listen to an opponent and find terms on which a deal could be made. Although progress would necessarily be slow while disagreements over Azerbaijan continued, the protocols proved a dead-end. Nevertheless, throughout the deadlock over Nagorno-Karabakh, Gül has maintained good diplomatic relations with President Aliyev: one of his first state visits as president in the autumn of 2007 was to Azerbaijan, and he has kept up annual visits and reciprocal invitations ever since. Perhaps of more significance for Gül, the failure of his Armenia initiative also emphasized a crucial problem with the current state of democracy and public opinion in Turkey: he could not always share the uninformed views of many whose ideas he was dedicated to represent, and he sometimes disagreed with parliamentary decisions. The Armenia episode exemplifies how, throughout his presidency, and indeed political career, Gül has often found himself hostage to his own principles however eager he is to bring about reform.

If President Gül is disappointed by the inability of his early years in Çankaya to solve the Cyprus and Kurdish problems, it is worth observing how Armenia represents a different scenario and opportunity. In personal dialogue with the Armenian and Azerbaijani presidents, his political equivalents, Gül was able to display his understanding and develop a convincing opening, while the Cyprus and Kurdish problems field too many competing political actors and interest groups. If Gül's Armenia initiative has achieved less than many hoped for, it showed him able to engage convincingly with international political leaders across important differences, and marks one of his signal qualities as an international statesman.

Soft power: Syria and the Middle East

Armenia was not President Gül's only promising foreign policy initiative that would be derailed. Befriending President al-Assad from early in his presidency,

Gül energetically pursued efforts to bring Syria in from the cold of President George W. Bush's 'axis of evil', leading to the opening of the border between the two countries in October 2009 and a boom in regional trade. His personal ties and formal meetings with President al-Assad made other diplomatic encounters possible and opened informal channels of communication with the US and Israel over plans for setting the stage that would improve the chances of a settlement in the Middle East. As early as May, 'indirect peace talks' between Syria and Israel were being held in Istanbul.[53] In the aftermath of Israel's assault on Gaza at the end of 2008, it was rumoured that Syria had pressured Lebanese Hezbollah not to retaliate as a result of strenuous Turkish diplomacy. Gül had established close contacts with al-Assad, engaging in reciprocal visits and becoming the first Turkish president to visit Aleppo in May 2009.[54] As with neighbouring Syria, so with next-door Iran, Gül set out to promote diplomatic dialogue. In pursuing 'the quest for peace in the Middle East', in 2009 Gül made a state visit to Tehran and was disappointed the next year when the UN rejected Turkey and Brazil's proposals for the 'Tehran Declaration', which Gül defended as 'an important confidence-building step that aims to pave the way towards the peaceful resolution of Iran's nuclear file.'[55]

When anti-government rioting broke out in Syria in March 2011, Gül was hopeful that his discussions with President al-Assad about democracy and the place of civil society would lead him in the right direction. On 4 August, he wrote to al-Assad in much the way he had written in a 'friendly' manner to Saddam Hussain, encouraging him to consider the global and historical situation and decide what he should do that would be best for the Syrian people as well as an Arab-Islamic world that was currently undergoing massive historical change. Gül insisted that the current historical moment was not to be mistaken for a foreign conspiracy; with his habit of historicizing, he suggested that the 'Arab Spring' and events in Syria were more akin to the political upheavals that characterized the European revolutions of 1848. What was unfolding at present was a new and 'belated' historical movement shaking the region out of its 'chronic democratic deficits'. It was time, Gül urged, to 'keep promises and take actions' that would progress with, not stand against, 'the course of history'.[56] Whatever Gül's personal disappointments that al-Assad has continued to resist the new historical dynamism advancing democratization, he joined the government in opposing direct military action, yet was more hesitant about breaking with the 'no problems with neighbours' policy than Davutoğlu and Erdoğan, who proved eager early on to assist the armed struggle of the anti-government movement.

Technology, NGOs and political change

Watching the political upheavals in Tunisia, Libya and Egypt, President Gül was not greatly surprised by the place of modern telephone and online-networking in the early days of opposition to al-Assad. Two years before, he had pointed out that modern communications systems, notably the internet, were destabilizing traditional political systems: and he approved, recognizing that the challenge would advance democratic reform. In a speech before the International Conference of Islamic Civil Society Organizations, Gül declared that 'Muslim countries' needed to find 'their own solutions for their problems' in order 'to pave the way for positive change'. He emphasized how civil society movements were essential to this process of addressing the historical and developmental problems confronting 'the Islamic world' in an age of globalized economics and communications. As events had shown, the telephone had challenged the traditional dominance of the mosque.

> In today's world, technological and scientific advances affect our lives in all fields. Through television and the internet, events in far away corners of the world can be watched. Access to information has become ever easier. As information becomes globalized, everyone can follow everyone else. Consequently, with the phenomenon of globalization, the classical notion of sovereignty has also changed. States are now responsible for their actions not only to their people, but to the whole international community.[57]

On entering the president's office, Gül set up a team to use the internet to record and catalogue events in his official calendar, including speeches and addresses often in English, a selection of YouTube clips, and a photo-record of ceremonies both domestic and international. Madame Gül has her own site within the presidency website. Encouraged by his children, Gül became the first president – of Turkey at least – to become a regular 'tweeter'. During 2011, he held occasional live-feed conversations on television via web-cam with people throughout Turkey. Understanding that attempts to control the internet could not succeed, he ignored early calls for restrictions on social-networking that accompanied the Gezi Park demonstrations, convinced that telecommunications could assist the democratic process. Since first campaigning on behalf of Refah in Kayseri back in 1991, Gül held firm to his principle that democratically elected representatives should find out what people want by listening to their views. Democracy for President Gül has ever been a 'process of change ... responsive to the expectations of our societies and must be owned by them'. Civil society organizations and freedom of public discussion are, for him, 'indispensable' agents of this process, and modern communications technology an equally 'indispensable' means.[58]

Abdullah Gül quickly recognized how communications technology was creating new forms of civil society in Turkey, as in the world, and they were changing the rules of foreign as well as domestic policy. While the AKP government managed to survive the 2008 global crisis and bring Turkey out of recession by 2010, 'new forms of politics and civil society activism' were emerging as significant political actors that were strenuously critical and independent of the government.[59] Under the AKP, historian William Hale observes, NGOs 'began to have a significant impact on Turkey's international relations', citing the 'Foundation for Human Rights and Freedoms and Humanitarian Relief' (IHH), a Turkish relief charity which organized an aid ship, the *Mavi Marmara*, to lead an international effort to bring humanitarian aid to Gaza in May 2010.[60] Conspiracy theorists, especially those writing in the Israeli press, sensationalized links between the IHH and Erkaban's Islamic *Saadet Partisi* ('Felicity Party', or SP), suggesting that the government was promoting Islamist causes.[61]

Since the beginning of 2009, Ankara's relations with Israel had already been thrown into reverse thanks to several factors: Israel's attacks on Gaza in December 2008 and January 2009, the confrontational, rather than diplomatic approaches of the prime ministers of both countries, and the modern miracle of YouTube. Thanks to modern telecommunications, the whole world was watching when, at a Davos conference in January 2009, Erdoğan demanded 'one minute' in which time he berated Israeli president Shimon Peres, declaring: 'You know well how to kill people.' A video clip of the incident went viral; 'one minute' became a catchphrase in Turkey and Erdoğan became a hero among critics of the state of Israel's policies throughout the world. Gül too had felt shocked, dismayed and personally betrayed by Israel's attacks on Gaza. He had rather liked Peres when they first met in 2000, and one of his very first presidential acts had been to write personally to the Israeli president, inviting him to Ankara to become the first Israeli statesman to address the Grand National Assembly.

In response to Israel's invasion, President Gül diplomatically avoided inflammatory rhetoric even while harshly condemning the use of military force in Gaza. Public sentiment throughout Turkey had become markedly hostile to Israel, aroused by Turkish television companies producing programmes depicting Israel's attack on Gaza. When the *Mavi Marmara* set out on 10 May, 'most AKP supporters were almost certainly sympathetic to the aims of the blockade-runners, as were many supporters of other parties'.[62] Israel's attack killing nine Turkish activists and Tel Aviv's belligerent defence brought a diplomatic crisis that was contained from escalating by 'continuing bilateral trade, family relations between the Turkey-based Jewish community and Israel as well as intensive behind-the-scenes diplomacy on the part of the United States'.[63] It was also important that Erdoğan and his government ministers managed to avoid saying anything at the time about the Israeli government that might be construed as anti-Semitic. The enemy in this case was Israel's militarized government, not the Israeli people. For his part, Gül took an unusually strong position, declaring that relations with Israel would never be the same. Commenting on the attack on the *Mavi Marmara*, he declared: 'Israel has made a mistake that it will regret a lot. It will understand this fact better in the future.'[64] In condemning the attack, he emphasized the international implications, asserting that 'Israel has deeply injured the international public conscience with this act', and that 'the Gaza blockade is not an issue directly between Turkey and Israel but rather a huge international human tragedy. We expect,' he continued, 'this inhumane blockade lifted right away.'[65] He declared that the incident should be subject to an international trial, not the internal inquiry initially conducted by Prime Minister Benjamin Netanyahu's government. As Foreign Minister Davutoğlu argued: 'A defendant of a case cannot be the prosecutor of that case at the same time.'[66]

When the UN Palmer Commission report was finally published on 1 September 2011, after many delays and interim reports rejected by both sides,[67] President Gül dismissed it for finding Israel's blockade legal and declared it 'null and void'. He confirmed Davutoğlu's earlier statements that 'Turkey will be imposing sanctions that are well known by Israel and some other international parties', including continuing to support humanitarian efforts on behalf of the Palestinians.[68] Turkey had made the terms of its demand for an apology from Israel clear to all concerned.[69] On 2 September, the Israeli ambassador was expelled from Ankara and has not been replaced.[70] After more than a year of strenuous lobbying by President Obama, Netanyahu phoned Erdoğan to apologize on 22 March 2013, and the terms of the apology were formally accepted.[71] Although relations with Israel are set to improve, in its announcement concerning ambassadorial appointments on 28 June 2013, the Ankara government left the posting to Israel vacant for the next three years.[72]

When I asked him in November 2011, President Gül insisted that, despite major dead-ends that had not been of Turkey's making, Ankara's soft-power initiatives were continuing to pursue the goal of achieving zero-problems with neighbouring countries. Beyond diplomacy, he pointed out that Turkish cultural producers had become especially important.

> In the Balkans there are villages where the most popular cultural events are watching Turkish soap operas on TV. They are so popular because we have the same background, and even the Turkish characters' names are maintained. These shows are also popular in Greece, Hungary and Croatia. No one should worry about this because we have no hidden 'neo-Ottoman' agenda. In fact, Turkey is supporting democracy and improvements in living standards in those countries. So maybe the best contribution we are making is through culture. Why we are seeing Turkey becoming an inspiration is clear – they see us from the point of view of Muslims. They are achieving more and they see us here. Since the Muslim population here is now so successful, they ask 'why not us?' They are now used to questioning their rulers and we think that is a good thing.[73]

Ergenekon and the Kurdish initiative

As well as an early move to close down the AKP government, Abdullah Gül's early years as president were marked by the Ergenekon trials, and the 'Kurdish opening' of 2009. Having survived the hostility of the press during and after the presidential elections, Gül viewed the attempt to close the AKP and remove him from office that had begun in April 2008 – only to be rejected by the Constitutional Court in July – as the final anger of a defeated opposition wasting time, and so yet further evidence of the need for major judicial and constitutional reforms. Meanwhile, with the judicial system still empowered by the 1982 constitution, the Istanbul prosecutor's office had opened investigations into circumstances involving a case of grenades discovered in June 2007 in possession of a clandestine security force, the *Özel Harekat Dairesi* ('Special Forces Command'). Political scientist Kerem Öktem observes:

> the prosecutors in charge were probably aware that their investigation would change the course of Turkey's history: named after Ergenekon – the mythical Turkish homeland in Central Asia, as it has been imagined by Turkish nationalists since the 1920s – the investigation set in motion a court case that would see hundreds of

retired and serving military personnel, including high-ranking officers, nationalist academics and Kemalist activists, being charged for
membership of a terrorist organisation attempting to subvert the
democratically elected government.[74]

As the arrests and unconfirmed reports of mass graves continued to accu-
mulate, President Gül maintained silence on the affair in conformity with
the neutrality demanded by his office. A year into the investigations, he met
with the retired former chief of General Staff, Hilmi Özkök, who had made
headlines by declaring that the Ergenekon investigation was dragging the country into 'chaos', and suggesting 'that Gül become involved in the Ergenekon
dispute without naming him directly'.[75] Neither revealed the upshot of their
two-and-a-half hour luncheon meeting. Gül reiterated that he was holding
'open as well as closed meetings to calm political tensions', but has otherwise
avoided interfering in the Ergenekon affair.[76]

Meddling directly in the Ergenekon investigation was not an option.
Abdullah Gül had achieved a strong reputation throughout his political career
for honesty and meaning what he said, and he was determined to bring dignity
to the presidential office in keeping with his belief in Turkey's place in the
world. While avoiding attempts to involve him in the Ergenekon investigations
and controversies, what came to be known as the 'Kurdish opening' (*Kürt
açılımı*) of 2009, was a different matter. Gül's personal commitment to a democratic solution to the problems confronting Turkey's Kurdish population had
been well known since his disagreements with Erbakan over this very issue,
and his public statements ever since. In campaigning speeches on behalf of
constitutional and judicial reform during his presidency, Gül had indicated
principles for necessary democratic reforms that the CHP opposition rightly
observed would enfranchise Turkey's Kurdish population.

Symbolically, the Kurdish opening of 2009 began the first day of the
year when television broadcasting in Kurdish began. Within days, Gül
went on record declaring that 'a modern democracy' is only 'successful
as long as it provides a political, cultural and legal system to guarantee
the freedom and rights of those who think different from the majority'. 'A
democratic state,' he continued, 'does not fuse different features to get one
standard nor embrace an attitude of alienation', and insisted that for the
modern democracy of Turkey 'our existing diversity [is] our richness'.[77]
Devlet Bahçeli, leader of the right-wing nationalist MHP and Deniz Baykal,
leader of the CHP, responded with muted fury over the clearly implicit

threat to what they considered the meaning of being a 'Turk'. So during 2009, as the Kurdish opening developed into what many hoped would be a major advance, President Gül was already in the frame, though formally uninvolved in government activities.

Back in 2004, the PKK had renewed armed activities in protest at what they considered parliamentary delays in implementing agreed reforms. Bombings spread throughout the country, from tourist resorts to metropolitan centres. These attacks were not always claimed by Abdullah Öcalan and the PKK military command, who formally announced a ceasefire in 2006 that was quickly disregarded by all sides. Whether sanctioned by Öcalan and the PKK or not, bombings continued as did the consequent 'counter-insurgency operations' by the military throughout the south east – with a brief ceasefire in late 2010 – until early 2013. But in October 2008, anticipating local elections the following March, Prime Minister Erdoğan visited Diyarbakır, in many ways the political capital for Turkish Kurds, with hopes of winning votes. Backing up his promises of democratic reforms by pointing to the Kurdish language television channel about to open – as it did on 1 January 2009 – he caused a riot only moments later by calling the pro-Kurdish *Demokratik Toplum Partisi* ('Democratic Society Party', or DTP) a terrorist organization with links to the PKK. Since more than half of the voters in Diyarbakır had voted DTP candidates into municipal government, this was not an obvious way to win votes.[78]

The AKP did poorly in the March elections, but Erdoğan's indication that the party acknowledged the existence of Kurdish rights was nevertheless heard and taken seriously as a possible opening. In April, from his prison on Imralı island in the sea of Marmara, Abdullah Öcalan called on armed PKK forces to cease fire and promised that in August he would present Ankara with a 'road-map' for resolving the conflict. By July, the AKP government began leaking reports that its own plans for a peaceful settlement would soon be made public, ever aware that there would be massive opposition in parliament to anything that looked like direct negotiations with Öcalan.[79] At the end of the month, Beşir Atalay publicly announced that the government was 'working very meticulously, very sensitively' on a plan for democratic reforms that would provide a solution to the Kurdish problem. President Gül used the occasion to declare his confidence that the Turkish state would solve the issue without foreign interference while asserting the need for change, declaring: 'Problems will automatically be solved once the democratic standards are raised. What's important is to strengthen every citizen's identity toward the

Turkish Republic.'[80] Bahçeli and Baykal continued to criticize any plans that might involve negotiating with Öcalan.[81]

During September 2009, AKP plans to address the grievances of the Kurdish population began to be leaked. A spokesman for the Kurdish DTP, Sırı Sakık, welcomed Erdoğan's initiatives, which included restoring the original Kurdish names of villages, restoring citizenship to Kurdish refugees, and a negotiable amnesty for PKK fighters, calling it 'late but promising'. Sakık also picked up on Atalay's earlier declaration that 'the government expected contributions from everyone' and insisted that Öcalan should be directly included in negotiations.[82] It would be more than a year before the government acknowledged that it was, and had been, conducting 'indirect' talks with Öcalan.[83] But during the early months of 2009 Abdullah Öcalan, the jailed leader of the PKK, was evidently aware of, and impressed by, President Gül's public statements, and Leader Apo's opinion was evidently important to the Executive Council of the *Koma Civaken Kurdistan* ('Union of Communities of Kurdistan' or KCK), Öcalan's outlawed political movement. At least, according to an online English-language transcript of a KCK executive statement dated 1 June 2009, Öcalan and council members agreed to an extension of the ceasefire, due to expire that day, because of their confidence in Abdullah Gül's public commitment to the peace process. The KCK statement reads:

> the process of discussion of a resolution to the Kurdish question has gained momentum amongst the public opinion in Turkey and abroad upon the explanations of our Leader and Movement. Turkish President Abdullah Gül has also made explanations in terms of the definition of Kurdish question as the most important issue of Turkey, of which the resolution should not be postponed... Leader Apo called for the continuity of non-aggression, which ends on 1st June, also taking into consideration explanations of the President Abdullah Gül in terms of the resolution of the question, discussions amongst the public, invitations by various intellectuals, democratic parties and civilian society organisations, and the expectations of our people in terms of the resolution of the issue.[84]

On 8 May, three weeks before the purported date of this statement, Madame Hayrünnisa Gül had visited the Kurdish village of Zangirt, renamed Bilge, where days before a family feud had caused the deaths of forty-four men, women and children, in order to commiserate with the suffering women.[85]

Though initially feared to be a major threat to negotiations, the incident was swiftly shown to be domestic, not political, and her visit was much publicized.

The president and first lady were demonstrating that they recognized and were listening to and acting on the specific problems of the Kurdish public in Turkey. Their personal efforts were, at least in the early months of the 'Kurdish opening', gaining influential respect. Confidence in the integrity of Gül's public views had gained and held the esteem of his opponents, but once again to little avail beyond the short term. Faced with increasing evidence that there was too much anti-Kurdish feeling in the country, the government started to lose its initial energy and enthusiasm.[86] In May 2010 Öcalan broke off attempts to negotiate with Ankara. The AKP's Kurdish opening was declared a 'failure' or, at best 'losing steam'.[87] Over the summer, PKK armed attacks increased until an autumn ceasefire that held, but only just, through the June 2011 elections. In July, even as Öcalan declared himself 'the only person who can end terrorism in Turkey',[88] PKK attacks resumed. In an unusually strong public statement, President Gül condemned the deaths of thirteen soldiers killed in Diyarbakır province, declaring that 'the very ongoing effective struggle against terrorism will resolutely continue with all its dimensions', and calling on 'all the political actors to act responsibly and to eradicate terrorism and violence'.[89] By August, Turkish military operations against armed Kurdish rebels extended into northern Iraq.[90] Violence continued into the spring of 2013.

President Gül, international statesman

Throughout the Ergenekon trials and continued outbreaks of violence interrupting government attempts at a Kurdish opening, Abdullah Gül continued to speak out on the need for constitutional and judicial reforms in Turkey that would directly address the rights of Kurds in Turkey in his wider vision of democratic reforms that would broaden the base of civil society. To international audiences, he repeated calls for similar reforms throughout the Islamic world, a major theme he had first elaborated in 2003 in Tehran.[91] Gül introduced the annual habit of making speeches to celebrate Christian and Jewish holidays – Easter, Christmas and Hanukkah – in addition to major Islamic feasts and festivals. He broadcast his vision of the new Turkey to the West in speeches to the Woodrow Wilson Center in Washington, DC, (8 January 2008) and in his welcome speech to HM Queen Elizabeth (13 June 2008), and his vision of Turkey's place in the world in speeches to the World Leadership Forum (24 September 2008), the Turkey–Africa Summit

(19 August 2008) and the Global Relations Forum (18 November 2009). In April 2009, 'Barack Obama chose to visit Turkey on his first bilateral trip overseas as president, clearly hoping to mend fences damaged during the Bush presidency.'[92] A further indicator of the international prestige that President Gül brought to Turkey is the list of countries with universities that awarded him honorary doctorates between 2003 and 2010: Bulgaria, the UK, Azerbaijan, Romania, Russia, China (two), India, Pakistan and Bangladesh. He has also been awarded state honours by the UK, Portugal, the Netherlands, Sweden, Italy, Qatar, Kuwait, Cameroon, Saudi Arabia and Pakistan.[93] In 2010 he was awarded the Chatham House Prize by the Royal Institute of International Affairs, London, marking his historical contribution to international diplomacy.

Abdullah Gül has always rather liked England, and admires the Commonwealth as a model for establishing links across nations with a common imperial past. He maintains a sentimental attachment to favourable memories of his student years in England. Learning the language and discovering how life was lived there greatly challenged his preconceptions about the West. His time in England had fully convinced him that European standards of democracy and development were necessary goals for Turkey. He is also a great fan of Queen Elizabeth II, and recalls joining the crowds cheering her motorcade when it passed through Istanbul during her first state visit to Turkey in October 1971, and later going to watch her public appearances coming and going from Buckingham Palace while he was living in London.[94] Madame Gül admits to preferring shopping in Paris and Rome to London, but they were both personally delighted at the prestige of hosting Queen Elizabeth II in May 2008. 'She came twice to Turkey during my time, and this was exceptional!' he proudly declared.[95] In his welcome speech in 2008, Gül flatteringly recalled the Queen's Christmas broadcast of 1957 – the first to be broadcast via television – in which she had promised 'my heart and my devotion to these old islands and to all the peoples of our brotherhood of nations'.[96] Elaborating on the theme of 'our brotherhood of nations', Gül recalled how Turkey and the UK share an 'inextricably interwoven' history that has 'defined the course of events in Europe for centuries'. In more recent times, the two nations have pursued common goals, Gül observed, quoting Atatürk on the imperative of seeking 'the peace and welfare of all nations'.[97] For Hayrünnisa, the visit was the fifth time she had hosted presidential dinners at Çankaya since becoming Turkey's first lady,[98] and she enjoyed accompanying Queen Elizabeth on tours to Bursa and Istanbul. The visit to

England in November 2010 to receive the Chatham House Prize would be an occasion to meet again.

In Abdullah Gül's eyes, the granting of this prestigious award for international diplomacy recognized his achievements and efforts not only for advancing democracy in Turkey, but also in Europe and the Islamic world. In an unusual and diplomatically significant move, Queen Elizabeth herself presented the award – most often presented by other members of the royal family – and recalled the 'kind hospitality' with which she had been received during her 2008 visit to Turkey. Adding a personal note to her brief award speech, the queen observed that Gül had 'provided notable leadership and international statesmanship over many years'.[99] In a slightly longer reply, Gül declared himself 'truly enchanted' by the Queen's presence, and that he accepted the award on behalf of 'the people of Turkey' who had proved victorious in the face of an 'unprecedented economic crisis', who were pursuing a 'silent revolution in democratic, social and economic standards', who had 'opposed an unjust war in Iraq' and 'are united in the fight against terrorism'. 'The award,' he concluded, 'signifies the role played by Turkey in its multidimensional neighbourhood and beyond, where she nurtures peace, stability and welfare.'[100]

Earlier in the day, he had elaborated on these themes to describe Turkey's emergence as a principal international player. At a breakfast meeting with top UK business leaders, he eloquently described the conditions that had brought Turkey substantial economic growth, making it a prime site for international investment. In the afternoon before the award ceremonies, he delivered a formal speech on Turkey, Europe and the 'international system' in the first quarter of the twenty-first century. He recalled that Britain had appointed its first embassy to the Ottoman Empire in the sixteenth century, since which time the 'international system' had changed, most recently following the end of the Cold War. Today, he observed, a new 'harmony of powers' led by the US, the EU, Russia, China, India and Brazil had come into being. Among these, Gül confidently proclaimed, Turkey 'will certainly take its rightful place'. A long-term and loyal NATO partner, Turkey was rapidly democratizing to European standards. Given a continuing 'shift towards the East and Asia' in the international balance of power, Gül concluded that it was 'a strategic imperative for the EU to have Turkey as a member'.[101]

Coming to England to accept the award provided opportunities for other engagements. While in the UK, President Gül formally opened the Yunus Emre Cultural Centre in London, and addressed the Oxford Centre for

Islamic Studies on 'The Islamic World, Democracy and Development'. In his Oxford talk he reiterated key arguments concerning the need for reform within Islamic countries that he had first announced in Tehran in 2003: 'We have to put our house in order.' Democracy and development, he argued, were essential and 'enlightened' values within Islam that had become contaminated by association with the European 'enlightenment' and its legacy of colonialism. 'Our main task,' he stated, was 'breaking this deep-rooted alienation of the Islamic world as far as democracy and development are concerned.' As the Islamic world looked to bring order to its own house, uneven development, education, poverty and health care were key problems needing to be solved: 'we must aim at higher living standards for all as well as reducing income disparities and the urban–rural divide … Gender equality is a must.' There were, he noticed, hopeful signs and Turkey was becoming a 'source of inspiration … in the Islamic world of a vibrant democracy and a flourishing free-market economy'. Nor was the Islamic world entirely at fault for current problems. The 'political economy of the global system' continued to treat many Muslim countries in unfair and unjust ways: 'The plight of Palestine and the war in Iraq are the two recent examples in point.' He concluded by insisting that 'the prime method for tackling complex challenges actually boils down to one simple word: "Dialogue".'[102] Only talking can resolve conflicts. The visit to England to receive the Chatham House Prize in 2010 was clearly a success, both diplomatic and personal. A year later, Queen Elizabeth invited the Güls back to stay at Buckingham Palace.

In general elections held in June 2011, Recep Tayyip Erdoğan led the AKP to an unprecedented third-term victory, taking 49.8% of the vote, while the CHP with just under 26% and the MHP with 13% performed above the threshold to form what everyone recognized would be a feeble parliamentary opposition. In August, Abdullah Gül was invited to pay a formal state visit to the UK in November. The Güls arrived in London a bit early, on Sunday, 20 November, giving Abdullah Gül the opportunity to deliver a keynote address at the annual conference of the Confederation of British Industry the next day, before the formal state visit began on Tuesday. That morning, President and Madame Gül were received by the Queen and the Duke of Edinburgh at Horse Guards Parade, and then carried in a stately horse-drawn procession to Buckingham Palace. After lunch, Abdullah Gül met with Prime Minister Cameron while Madame Hayrünnisa visited the Royal Collection and discussed one of her favourite topics, preservation and restoration techniques, with experts working in the Royal Archives.

In the minds of the British public, First Lady Hayrünnisa was an appealing figure, earning the teasing adulation of a *Daily Mail* headline in that paper's characteristic style of ventriloquizing the beloved queen: '"You might find the stairs tricky, my dear": Queen's astonishment as Turkish President's wife turns up at the Palace in a pair of killer heels.'[103] The accompanying photograph caught the Queen's astonished gaze perfectly. Unlike the undue and usually critical attentions of the Turkish press, this is just the kind of amusing moment that the British popular media loves to report of those it most admires; and there can be few better ad-hoc indexes of the views of 'ordinary' British people than the *Daily Mail*. Hayrünnisa was a hit. That same day, 23 November, President Gül delivered the inaugural annual address at Wilton Park, a think-tank founded by Winston Churchill in 1946 and dedicated to conflict resolution. His speech, 'Historic Transition in the Middle East and Its Impact on Global Politics', reiterated how 'Turkey's political and economic development is seen as inspirational by people in countries of the Middle East' while 'fragile democratic transitions [are] underway across the Middle East and North Africa'.[104] After banquets and protocol meetings with various dignitaries, the Güls bid farewell to Queen Elizabeth on Thursday before setting off to be hosted at the Royal Naval Base in Portsmouth. Here they visited the nearby cemetery of the nineteenth-century Turkish mariners who died during an outbreak of cholera while their ships were stationed in the English port. They flew home from Southampton that evening.[105]

Gül and Erdoğan: future speculation

Throughout his presidency, Abdullah Gül has made his political vision for Turkey clear many times, pursuing basic principles that informed the AK Party Programme. They entail a new constitution and a continuing process of democratic reforms to attain European standards that would respect religious freedom, bring rule of law, transparency and accountability to government, encourage the development of strong civil society organizations, and achieve gender equality and an end to violence. He developed these principles in numerous public statements and in speeches to international audiences, on one hand seeking to encourage Europe to recognize that Turkey was pursuing democratic reforms while, on the other, seeking to persuade nations in the Islamic world to follow suit. And it was during the course of his presidency that Gül's political style, experience, knowledge and international vision for Turkey started becoming more clearly distinct from those of Prime Minister Erdoğan.

Although the media have regularly looked for a split between the two, and differences in style and manner were apparent early on to close observers, party practice demanded team agreement. Party meetings were regularly marked by often fierce disagreements among ranking members, but projecting a common front was also a founding rule. Erdoğan's charisma continued to captivate the conservative voters whose values he embraced, personified, and often helped shape. Internationally, his strong personal stand against Israel had made him 'the new hero of the Palestinian cause' and an idol throughout the Arab world.[106] His early prison time on charges of Islamism had brought him popular acclaim at home as a *mazlum*, a hero who has suffered oppression for his faith. While mayor, he had famously cleaned up Istanbul. He was good at being a local hero who looked after the folks in the neighbourhood, taking care of the infirm and making the streets safe for conservative consumers to stroll in without confronting alcohol.[107] With Gül in the presidency and no longer in parliament, commentators noticed changes in the ways the AKP was going about its business.

By late 2009, complaints had started appearing about the 'gross majoritarian and alienating political style of the prime minister and the AKP'.[108] During his second term in power, Prime Minister Erdoğan began leading from the front, treating development as a way of growing the economy but also as a form of social engineering, not unlike the state tutelage of the republic before 1950. Gül, meanwhile, remained constant to his principle: 'We don't impose any ideas on people. We represent people's thoughts.'[109] One international commentator observed in the spring of 2013: 'Only after Gül left government to become president in 2007 did Erdoğan begin to consolidate his now near-total control over the AKP.'[110]

Public criticism of the AKP government and policies during Gül's presidency were seldom directed personally at him. Turkish satirical cartoon magazines, such as *Penguen* and *Uykusuz*, have shown remarkably little interest in making fun of the president from Kayseri, though legal cases have been brought against several individuals for sending email and text messages that insult the presidential office.[111] In numerous interviews and informal conversations, I have met no one who doubts that Gül is remarkably honest, especially among Turkish politicians, and that he means what he says when projecting democratic reforms for Turkey. A controversial poll taken in September 2012 and often cited by Erdoğan's critics indicated how, in a contest for the presidential vote, 50.9% would choose Gül while only 22.7% would vote for Erdoğan. But not all popular support for President Gül comes in the form of opposition to Prime Minister Erdoğan.[112] In April 2013, when the Kurdish opening was going well and the withdrawal of armed forces on both sides was imminent, I asked a hotel waiter in the southeastern city of Mardin what he thought of Erdoğan, and he immediately smiled and declared that the prime minister was a good man for agreeing to the conversation with Leader Apo. And what of *Cumhurbaşkan* Gül, I then asked. He smiled even more enthusiastically and exclaimed '*Mükemmel!*' ('excellent, splendid') before continuing excitedly in a dialect beyond my ability to understand.

But the AKP government continues to face criticism, most notably from secularist members of the traditional political classes who, increasingly bereft of power and confronting a government ruled by a party with a massive majority, remain certain that Erdoğan and Gül are inseparable from their past associations with political Islam. The new visibility of religious Muslims in Turkey, an 'Eastward' turn in foreign policy, and Erdoğan's often misguided moves to control social life according to popular quasi-religious beliefs; for some commentators all these provide reason to look for a scarcely concealed Islamic agenda. One scholar exploring the 'mobilization of political Islam in Turkey' observes that Gül's presidency 'opened up an additional political opportunity enabling the party to mobilize the Islamist social movement'. Banu Eligur provides evidence: 'Unlike his prosecular predecessor Sezer, President Gül approved most of the [AKP's] bills and appointment of high-ranking bureaucrats into key state institutions' from religious backgrounds, individuals whom Sezer had previously blocked.[113] By supporting efforts to lift the headscarf ban and promoting the careers of those previously discriminated against because of their religious beliefs, by this reckoning, Gül has shown evidence of an Islamic agenda since the early years of his presidency.[114] There are some who are evidently eager to agree, despite lack of evidence. In a study published in a collection of essays pre-emptively titled *Islamization of Turkey under the AKP Rule* (2011), Nur Bilge Criss writes: 'Since 1980, Islamists professionally entrenched themselves in all state institutions ... theirs is not a frontal attack but a siege policy ... The election of Abdullah Gül, an ardent Islamist, as president was one of the first coups' that will 'finally transform Turkey into an Islamic republic'.[115] Such beliefs carry weight outside Turkey, as William Hale points out, feeding 'neo-conservative commentators such as Michael Rubin and Daniel Pipes' with the conviction that, 'under the AKP, Turkey had fallen into the grip of Islamist extremists'. However, as Hale continues, 'other observers felt little difficulty in refuting these views'.[116]

Those fearful that Gül's presidency heralded a new reign of Islamism also found evidence in his personal support for the IHH, the NGO which had

organized the *Mavi Marmara*, with their links to the Islamic *Saadet Partisi* (SP).
More significantly, however, a different Turkish NGO, 'with clearly Islamist
sympathies' that has direct 'impact on Turkey's international relations' and
thereby encourages fears among secularists about the complicity of Gül's
presidency in a religious political movement, is the international media and
educational foundation of the religious leader Fethullah Gülen.[117] Gül himself disavows any direct or personal links to the Gülen movement. However,
speculations continue to feed the doubts of those inclined to be suspicious.
Gülen's movement, the self-styled Hizmet ('Service') certainly encourages
assumptions of grand designs, not only in Turkey but also globally, and has
promoted the legend of a rivalry between Gül and Erdoğan.

A 'charismatic preacher hailing from the brotherhood of Bediüzzaman
Said-i Nursi', Fethullah Gülen separated from the national Nur brotherhood
to found his own religious movement. It now has 'millions of members and
powerful educational and media institutions'.[118] Gülen split with the national
brotherhood by publicly approving the military action against Erbakan back
in 1997, calling on his government to resign at the time, and has since been
living in self-imposed exile in Pennsylvania. 'One of the most influential
and most liberal Nurcu Communities, the Fethullah Gülen community ...
tried to maintain good relations with the secular state establishment',[119] but
continues to arouse serious qualms among secularists. Gülen-sponsored
schools and colleges, teaching Turkish and Turkish culture, have spread from
'south-east Europe to Central Asia, Africa and even the United States'. During
the 1990s, as William Hale notes, the Gülen 'movement' had been treated
with distrust by Turkish governments, 'but under the AKP it achieved a far
wider degree of acceptance, and even moral support, as a unique attempt to
promote Turkey's image on a global scale'.[120] The Gülen 'movement' is not
so much a centralized organization as a complex network of independent
charitable foundations, schools, colleges, universities, newspapers and other
media outlets, all claiming allegiance to the ideas and beliefs of their leader,
Fethullah Gülen. In Turkey, for example, the owners of the mass-circulation
daily newspaper *Zaman* are followers of Gülen, and editorial policies promote
his ideas, but the paper is otherwise independently owned. Asya Finans, an
early participation bank, was founded by supporters of Gülen. In England,
to take a single instance, the Wisdom School in Harringay, North London,
is an independent school that makes no reference to Gülen on its website,
[121] but which is owned by Axis Educational Trust which does, defining the
Trust as having been: 'set up by parents and teachers inspired by Fethullah

Gülen's teachings that emphasize the importance of providing comprehensive and inclusive education for children.'[122] Gülen schools also serve to promote Turkey and Turkish culture internationally, making them unavoidable for a president who is keen on assisting developing countries.

When opening up diplomatic links with Congo and Cameroon in 2010, President Gül visited schools in Kinshasa and Yaoundé that receive Gülen funding.[123] Journalist Ece Temelkuran, who accompanied the presidential entourage, told me that Gül was particularly attentive to her harsh criticism of the welcoming ceremonies performed at Şafak School in Kinshasa on 15 March. Did he not agree, she recalled asking, that the spectacle of young African children dressed in varieties of 'Turkish' national costume in order to sing the Turkish national anthem was objectionably 'neocolonial', an attempt to produce 'new Turks' beyond the scope of ceremonial welcome? After pondering this, Gül agreed. Temelkuran offered this anecdote as an example of Gül's unusual openness to criticism and new ideas, and it may not have been by chance that the students from Amity International College in Yaoundé, who ceremonially performed to welcome the president of the Turkish Republic two days later, did so in their own school uniform.[124]

For a president keen to broaden Turkey's international links through diplomacy and trade, visiting overseas Turkish schools that receive Gülen funding is all part of the job. Neither of the two schools in question is reputedly a nursery of political Islam, though many look askance at anything connected to Gülen: Russia closed down Gülen schools for fear they were CIA operations.[125] Although Gül disavows any links with Gülen and his supporters, suspicion, rumour and the politics of Islam in Turkey make the issue a little more complicated since, where the blogosphere opens up global communications, eccentric ideas and self-contradictory conspiracy theories thrive: on the internet one can find reports that Gül is a 'protégé' of, variously, the Gülen movement, Saudi Arabia, and even a global US–Zionist conspiracy, while Erdoğan is fancied to be in the pay of the Muslim Brotherhood.[126]

Conspiracy theories aside, a possible split between the two founders of the AKP has continued to be pondered by informed and responsible commentators. Writing in May 2013, Amberin Zaman observed there might be some reason to think in such terms: 'Tensions between Erdoğan (a fellow imam) and Gülen have been simmering for some time.'[127] As well they might, since Erdoğan takes his orientation into the politics of religion from the more conservative İskenderpaşa community and the Milli Görüs movement, making 'the pair unlikely bedfellows.' Such being the case, the logic of suspicion goes, it follows that if Gülen is hostile to Erdoğan, he must be supporting Gül. If, Zaman speculated, the Gülen movement were to put their weight behind a rival to Erdoğan in the 2014 presidential elections – and 'only if that candidate were the highly popular President Gül' – then Erdoğan would be in trouble. But even in 2013, when Erdoğan's intentions regarding the presidency were still unclear, Zaman admitted that 'sources close to the president' told her that Gül 'has absolutely no interest in being drawn into a fight',[128] while rivalry between the two AKP founders remains wishful thinking on the part of those opposed to Erdoğan.

The future remains unwritten. From the point of view of the presidential office, assisting developing countries with Muslim populations is no secret policy; promoting teaching of the Turkish language in such countries with a view to developing a population able and likely to conduct business with Turkey as part of their own modernization programmes has been on the party agenda from the start. Supporters of Gülen may well prefer Gül's style and political vision over Erdoğan's, yet President Gül's interactions with the *Hizmet* movement by visiting schools in countries where Turkey is opening diplomatic channels remains slender evidence of his support either for the Gülen movement or an Islamist agenda.

Speculations over an impending split between Gül and Erdoğan have continued to spread and, as many observe, evident differences between the two politicians in background, education, range of experience, political style and choice of advisors encourage such thoughts. Erdoğan and Gül come from and represent different constituencies; they appoint and listen to their advisory teams differently; they have different ways of seeking to promote Turkey's place in the world; and they approach the questions of democracy and social justice from different perspectives and with different ambitions. They have significantly different attitudes towards press freedom and modern communications technology. Erdoğan has supported and even instigated the imprisonment of journalists who are critical of his rule. Gül, on the other hand, has supported ending such cases, though some have criticized him for failing to back up that position. Although he has since disclaimed believing it, Erdoğan has often been quoted as saying that democracy is like a bus that takes you somewhere, then you get off at your destination. During his third term in government, some journalists claim, Erdoğan seems to have convinced himself that he knows what the future should be like, and has set about constructing it. His plans for conspicuous new mosques in Istanbul and his project to cut a new canal between the Black Sea and the Sea of Marmara horrify secularists and the ecologically aware. While Erdoğan boasts of having fifty percent of the Turkish electorate backing up everything he does, Gül continues to insist that 'democracy is not only about elections'.[129] From his years working with PACE in Strasbourg, Gül understands that democracy is not an achieved state but rather a condition of continual revision and reform, a process of constantly putting the house in order, listening to people's views and respecting the rights of minorities. And, as he told his audience at the Graduate Business School at Stanford in May 2012, leaders must themselves be similarly open to revision: 'Effective leaders must love to learn, change and expand. If you are not learning, maturing, changing or expanding, then you cannot expect the people to believe in you, and follow you.'[130]

Among senior AKP members and the reformist cadres within government, the evident differences between Gül and Erdoğan continue to be considered central to the party's vision, success and vitality, but the international media continues to see things differently. Within weeks of the 2011 elections, readers of the *New York Times* were warned of 'a creeping authoritarianism engineered by Prime Minister Recep Tayyip Erdoğan, who has governed since 2003'.[131] The world was watching as Erdoğan began acting on the belief he had received a personal mandate to rule. The general perception that Erdoğan 'is punch-drunk with power' occasioned Istanbul-based journalist Andrew Finkel to suggest that, after two terms of AKP government, only Abdullah Gül could revive 'the embers of the reforming zeal' that had first brought the party to power in 2002. Noting how Gül had urged parliament at its opening session in October 2012 to be swift in producing a new constitution and other reforms that would kick-start the EU bid, Finkel contrasts how Erdoğan entirely ignored Europe in his parliamentary address that year and 'immediately' snubbed Gül's proposal to release elected – mainly Kurdish – MPs being held on charges of conspiring against the government. In anticipation of the 2014 presidential elections, Finkel observed that while some presume that Gül will, as in 2002, step aside for Erdoğan, others 'say that like Vladimir Putin and Dmitry Medvedev, Gül and Erdoğan might just swap jobs. Then again, Gül might try to stay put; after all, lately he has become the government's most effective critic.'[132]

In 2013, Finkel was by no means alone in wondering 'how much longer' Gül will 'continue to be so obliging' to Erdoğan. Other journalists I spoke with that year also said they thought that Gül should act more forcefully in line with his own statements, especially regarding imprisoned Kurdish MPs and journalists, and in pressing harder for a diplomatic solution in Syria in contrast to Erdoğan's aggressive stance in favour of forcing regime change. A scholar of the Turkish media comments: 'If Gül really wanted to strengthen freedom of speech in Turkey, he could work to persuade Erdoğan to support amendments on the articles in question. Maybe he is sincerely for changes to a better democracy but he is not able to change Erdoğan's mind. As Erdoğan is getting more powerful day by day, some people are even saying that Gül is one of Erdoğan's officers!'[133]

The 'government's most effective critic' or 'one of Erdoğan's officers'? Neither seems entirely accurate, yet such entirely contradictory speculations continue to appear in support of predictions of a forthcoming split between the two AKP founders. Noticing in April 2013 that Gül was becoming more vocally distant from Erdoğan, international analyst Svante Cornell observed that 'while it may be too early to talk of a rupture' between the two, nevertheless 'the trenches separating the Gül and Erdoğan camps are growing deeper, and more open'.[134] For Cornell, 'Gül's credentials are arguably stronger' than Erdoğan's for leading the party, so he argues that while Gül taking the lead 'would cause short-term instability, it would in all likelihood be a positive force for Turkey's continued democratization and European integration. Erdoğan's increasingly personality-centred system would be thwarted; and the Islamic conservative movement would be pulled back increasingly to the centre, just as it was in the early 2000s.' To support his suggestion, Cornell rightly emphasizes the importance of differences between 'the Gül and Erdoğan camps', suggesting that 'the growing consolidation of the Fethullah Gülen movement's support for Gül' provides crucial evidence, given Erdoğan's open hostility to Gülen, of a deepening divide. But however popular Gül might have become among Gülen's followers, there is no evidence that he is in league with Gülen. Yet such insinuations remain common. A contributor to such neoconservative journals as Daniel Pipes's *Middle East Quarterly*, Cornell might have been expected to be in search of an Islamist agenda, if not an Islamist conspiracy, and has been encouraged by listening to gossip in Ankara that Gül and his advisors were 'building a political organisation that could be turned into a political party at short notice'.[135] Cornell believes that Gül would attract formidable support, not only from Gülen's followers, but also from those in the AKP 'who have tired of Erdoğan' and are 'more pro-European and democratically minded' as well as 'former politicians aligned with the center-right ANAP and DYP parties'. Such an alliance would 'for all practical purposes resemble Turgut Özal's

ANAP, which unified religious conservatives, liberals and Turkish nation-alists. Özal may be an example in more than one way,' Cornell continues, 'just like Gül but unlike Erdoğan, Özal was conciliatory and brought people together, and was strongly pro-Western.'

Here, in placing Abdullah Gül's political vision and achievements in line with the exemplary figure of Turgut Özal, the neoconservative observer Svante Cornell finds common ground with a host of other commentators with perspectives quite different from his. I have already quoted the socialist sociologist Mehmet Ali Dikerdem's observation that 'Özal opened the gate from which Erdoğan and Gül would pass.'[136] There is also general agreement among liberal observers that the success of the AKP has depended greatly on applying and developing Özal's pro-Western and pro-business initiatives and managing to do so without alienating religious and nationalist sympathies. Similarly, William Hale and Ergun Özbudun have documented continuities in AKP attitudes and policies towards secularity and religious freedom, for-eign policy and plans for a semi-presidential system, suggesting that many key policies and strategies have been inherited from Özal's years in power.[137] One of Gül's oldest colleagues from the planning days of AKP and before, current deputy prime minister Beşir Atalay, is similarly keen to link Gül with Özal. When I spoke with him in April 2013, Atalay strenuously insisted that throughout his political career, Abdullah Gül had not compromised on the principles from which they worked when planning the AK Party Programme back in the early 1990s, and how much these had been influenced by Özal's 'wider perception' of Turkey's place in the world.[138] Amid speculation and scrutiny, Gül's supporters remain loyal, while his political future remains as yet unscripted.

As of 2011, Abdullah Gül became an established and highly respected inter-national statesman. Even as EU accession talks stumbled, he had remained in friendly contact with major European figures – European Commission president José Barroso, Jack Straw, even Daniel Cohn-Bendit – and had earned the personal respect of Ann Dismorr, Swedish ambassador to Turkey during a period when her government was passing legislation condemning the Armenian 'genocide'. Being awarded the Chatham House Prize, and following the remarkable return visit to London at the invitation of Queen Elizabeth, he gained Turkey the international recognition that he long believed it deserved and for which he had worked. Alone among the heads of state of Muslim countries, Gül has considerable experience of working with, and even on behalf of, Western democratic institutions. His informed speeches and statements on international occasions showed a consistent commitment to democratic reform and ending war in the cause of developments aimed at improving living standards globally: these are topics he addressed forcefully in 2010 before the UN Assembly in New York.[139] He was later invited to speak at the Chicago Council on Global Affairs on 22 May 2012, where he linked Turkey's economic success and 'visible role' in international affairs to democratic reforms that were successfully promoting both 'religious freedom and secularism' in pursuit of 'an ultimate assurance of democratic pluralism and harmony between the state and society'.[140] The next day he was hosted by Condoleezza Rice before delivering his lecture on leadership at Stanford University.[141] Throughout his tenure in Çankaya, President Abdullah Gül's energy and international reputation have kept Turkey firmly on the stage among the leading international players.

EPILOGUE

E arly on the morning of Friday, 31 May 2013, police used tear gas to
disperse protesters who had recently occupied Gezi Park in central
Istanbul. The protests were aimed at plans to develop the park into an
Ottoman-themed shopping mall with mosque. Adjacent to Istanbul's central
Taksim Square, the park was the last remaining public space with grass and
trees in an area already crowded with recently constructed hotels. On 27
May, activists had first confronted bulldozers about to tear down the trees.
The next day, Sırrı Süreyya Önder, a parliamentary deputy for the Kurdish
Barış ve Demokrasi Partisi ('Peace and Democracy Party', or BDP), used his
parliamentary authority to halt the bulldozers and persuade police to remove
barriers around the park. Later in the day, the picture of police spraying a
woman protestor with tear gas went viral on social media. The picture of 'the
woman in red' quickly came to represent the excessive use of force against
the protesters even as the protests continued to bring together a number of
otherwise unconnected groups who were finding common cause. As news
of the tear-gas attack on the Friday morning circulated through social media,
thousands more protesters arrived in Beyoğlu and other neighbourhoods
around Taksim. The police responded with water cannons, rubber bullets and
more tear gas. Over the weekend, as demonstrations spread nationwide, Prime
Minister Erdoğan dismissed the protestors, calling them *çapulcu*, 'marauders',
a term quickly adopted by protestors with pride.[1]

The Gezi Park protests erupted at a delicate time for Turkey and the government, providing occasion for, and evidence of, yet further differences between
President Gül and Prime Minister Erdoğan. With Syria still in chaos, a delicate
agreement involving a withdrawal of PKK military forces into Northern Iraq
underway, plans for a new constitution still being held up in parliament, some

hopes that EU relations might improve, and the US-sponsored reconciliation with Israel only recently in place, the government needed to act carefully and with delicacy both at home and on the world stage. While Gül called for conciliation and dialogue, Erdoğan continued to rely on his popular mandate and took a strong position against the demonstrators.

The prime minister had reason to be confident. He can rightly claim credit for the PKK initiative and for the new phase of what President Obama termed a 'model relationship' with the US. In 2011, Obama 'was reported to have placed more telephone calls in that year to Tayyip Erdoğan than to any other world leader except the British prime minister David Cameron'.[2] Certainly Israel's grudging and much belated apology to Turkey over the *Mavi Marmara* seems to have been brokered by Obama during his visit to Israel in March 2013. The trade-off, it has been suggested, was over Syria. Since Obama was keen to avoid direct US interference, Erdoğan proved eager to take a leading role by supporting military force to bring about regime change in Damascus, marking a break with Turkish foreign policy since the founding of the republic. He has been criticized for it.

Further trouble came once it was revealed that Erdoğan's government was in direct dialogue with Abdullah Öcalan and other PKK leaders, news that provoked fierce opposition in parliament and from the public. Families who had suffered losses in the years of fighting rallied to protest engaging in dialogue with terrorists, but negotiations continued and were achieving results. In March 2013, even as timetables were being negotiated for the release of prisoners and the withdrawal of armed PKK units from Turkey, President Gül hailed the direct dialogues as 'well intentioned and sincere endeavours to put an end to the terror'. He welcomed these hopeful negotiations alongside an urgent call for 'a constitution that includes all the characteristics of developed democracies'.[3] Later that month, Erdoğan was praised by PKK leaders for taking the risk of seeking peace, but the CHP continued to object. By late April, with withdrawal of PKK armed forces from Turkish territory set for the first week of May, opposition leaders continued to accuse the government of 'undisclosed concessions' to the outlawed organization.[4] However, on 8 May, right on schedule, 'Kurdish militants began withdrawing from Turkey into their stronghold in northern Iraq ... a major step towards ending a decades-long conflict that has left tens of thousands of people dead.'[5] Amid general anxiety that something might go wrong at any moment, the withdrawal has so far proved a successful step, though some BDP deputies complain that the summer protests delayed subsequent progress.

Meanwhile, back on Friday 31 May, even as protestors were being tear-gassed in Gezi Park, President Gül was in Ashkhabad on the final day of a state visit to Turkmenistan being presented with a pure-bred golden-coloured Akhal-Teke horse named *Arkadaş* ('Friend') by President Gurbanguly Berdimuhamedov.[6] Before arriving back in Ankara, with international news services picking up on social media reports and broadcasting scenes of excessive police violence before him, Gül was on the phone to Istanbul governor Hüseyin Mutlu, Interior Minister Muammer Güler and Prime Minister Erdoğan. He urged them all that the best policy was 'moderation' over this 'very sensitive' situation. Gül followed up that afternoon with a written statement repeating his insistence that 'the security forces should act more carefully than usual, should be sensitive while dealing with protesters, and should not let "saddening" scenes emerge'. He also reported 'that he had shared these thoughts with state and government officials, including Erdoğan'.[7] After receiving Gül's telephone call, Interior Minister Güler ordered the police forces to withdraw from Taksim, but clashes broke out again the next night.[8]

Within days, the protests spread to other cities as 'crowds of mostly youthful demonstrators in Istanbul, Ankara and Izmir' gathered and united in a call 'for an end to Mr. Erdoğan's more than 10 years in power'.[9] A survey conducted on 3 and 4 June showed that the majority of those protesting were under thirty, and that over ninety percent of them were protesting three issues: the 'disproportionate' police response to the Gezi Park occupation, 'the violation of democratic rights', and Erdoğan's 'authoritarian attitude'. Perhaps most significantly, a number of the protestors identified as 'conservative'. While the mainstream conservative elements of Turkish society – a big majority – have yet to support the Gezi cause, images of fashionable young Muslim women protesting alongside members of secular civil rights organizations suggest new attitudes are emerging among the new generation of practising Muslims. Amid the gatherings, the police use of water cannons and tear gas continued with the prime minister's approval.

On Sunday, 2 June, by which time two protestors had been killed, Erdoğan issued a press statement even as he was preparing for a state visit to Morocco, Algeria and Tunisia. 'There is a menace called Twitter,' he pronounced, 'social media is a troublemaker in society today.'[10] The protests, he said, 'were the work of extremists led by political opponents trying to overthrow his government', and he even suggested 'the possibility of foreign provocation'.[11] With Erdoğan's confrontational style becoming part of the problem, Gül contacted CHP leader Kemal Kılıçdaroğlu, Nationalist Action Party (MHP) leader

Devlet Bahçeli, and Peace and Democracy Party (BDP) co-chair Selahattin Demirtaş.[12] Kemal Kılıçdaroğlu agreed to meet later that day, and was highly critical of Erdoğan's attitude and response. After their discussion, Gül released his own statement that 'the message of the protestors was received'.[13] The next day, Gül spoke out in Izmir, continued his call 'for calm from all sides' and declared 'the protests and demonstrations were a natural part of democracy'.[14] Erdoğan, however, would not be convinced that protesting was a democratic right. Commenting on their different responses, the *New York Times* observed: 'While Mr. Erdoğan referred to his electoral victories and his parliamentary majority as a license to carry out policies as he saw fit, Mr. Gül stressed that true democracy "does not only mean elections."'[15] Later on Monday, with Erdoğan out of the country, Gül met with Deputy Prime Minister Bülent Arınç to work out a way to calm the violence and restore peace by addressing immediate and longer term problems.[16] Following that meeting, Arınç formally apologized for the excessive use of police violence and announced government plans to hold meetings with representatives of the protesters. Existing plans to develop the park into a mall were temporarily shelved, though by then the protest movement had expanded beyond the future of Gezi Park.

Through the early days of June, President Gül was keeping one eye on the growing demonstrations in Brazil as he set out to reassure world leaders that events in Turkey were unlike uprisings in the Middle East; they were, he observed, more akin to the London riots of 2011, and the Occupy Wall Street movement. 'What happens in Turkey,' he declared on Tuesday 4 June, 'is similar to these countries,' where people protest 'about trees and because of fears the government was interfering in their lifestyles.' But he also understood and recalled the political history of Turkey, where authoritarian state power had oppressed significant minorities for generations. 'There may be those,' Gül observed, 'who don't approve of the government's actions. There are times when politics in Turkey can hurt feelings, so they may get hurt.'[17] Only too aware of the struggle to enfranchise the conservative Muslims who were prospering under the AKP, Gül viewed democracy as a condition in which the state should listen to people's criticisms and feelings rather than ignore or seek to control them. Generating tensions between different sectors of the public was a moral and political error that denied the lessons of recent Turkish history and turned the clock back on progressive democratic reform. The Ergenekon investigations and trials had already brought the government under suspicion of seeking vengeance, not justice, and this was no time for needless provocation. The next day, he indicated that he 'might not approve a controversial bill restricting alcohol use and sales', a measure that Erdoğan had pushed through parliament towards the end of May.[18] Along the way, Erdoğan had defended the new alcohol laws for being in line with regulations in European countries, but then caused outrage by declaring that Turkey's current laws had been written by drunks, thereby insulting both Atatürk and Inönü. For his part, Gül understood how the new restrictions would damage the livelihood of a significant group of retailers. For his part, Gül approved of restricting the sale of alcohol, but remained concerned about needlessly infuriating the secular opposition at a time when the government should be listening to and openly recognising the rights of significant and minority sectors of the population. Having ensured that the bill met constitutional requirements, he announced his approval on 10 June.[19]

Before returning to Turkey, Erdoğan began generating personal support for his hostile approach to the protesters and foreign critics. Observers were commenting that Gül and Erdoğan 'were at loggerheads' with each other over the protests. 'Gül's remark that democracy is not just about elections, and that the message of the streets has been received, clearly annoyed Erdoğan,' suggested one Turkish reporter. 'Commenting on these remarks, Erdoğan responded curtly from Morocco that he was not aware what the message referred to was.'[20] The day before Erdoğan's return, Gül met with the head of the Turkish Bar Association, Metin Feyzioğlu, to discuss the recent release of over thirty people who had been arrested in Izmir for 'inciting riots and conducting propaganda' by means of social media. Even before the Arab Spring, Gül had often declared his enthusiastic approval of the way global telecommunications was shaping the future of democracy on the world stage as well as in Turkey. Social media, he saw, had become a fact of life that served to advance freedom of speech and foster a stronger civil society. These were matters on which he had been elaborating for some years in major speeches and his own approach to public broadcasting. Insisting that he would not allow a 'witch hunt' to break out over the use of Twitter, Gül called on everyone 'in this process ... to act responsibly' and with restraint,[21] remarks clearly directed both at the protesters and the state authorities. The prime minister was not convinced.

On his arrival back in Istanbul late on Sunday night, Erdoğan found thousands of supporters assembled to welcome him at the airport. At 2.45 a.m., Erdoğan spoke out to enthusiastic crowds, energetically criticized those responsible for the protests and ensuing violence, pointing the finger at specific 'artists' and 'foreign guests' who were using social media to provoke the protests that were bringing the nation into ill repute. Later that day, he responded to international criticism of the Turkish police for using excessive violence by borrowing Gül's comparison with the protests in New York, but elaborated fancifully. 'Those who try to lecture us,' he is reported to have said, 'what did they do about the Wall Street incidents? Tear gas, the death of seventeen people happened there.' Within an hour, the US embassy responded through an official Twitter account that 'Reports related to the U.S. Occupy Wall Street movement are inaccurate. No U.S. deaths resulted from police actions in OWS.' While the prime minister was striking out on his own and getting his facts wrong, a group of protesters, the *Antikapitalist Müslümanlar* ('Anti-Capitalist Muslim Collective'), were holding Friday prayers inside Taksim Square, 'while other protesters "stood guard" against any kind of provocation'.[22] No longer simply about the trees of Gezi Park, the protests had mobilized the next generation of voters from across different social and religious backgrounds in opposition to what they perceived to be Erdoğan's authoritarian style of rule. Some observers recalled recent precedents of leaders who stayed too long in power: Adnan Menderes and Süleyman Demirel, even Margaret Thatcher, provided comparisons.

Quick off the mark, veteran Turkey analyst Hugh Pope unpacked the political moment of Erdoğan's return. 'Every turn confirms,' Pope wrote, 'that this protest is mainly about Erdoğan's increasingly take-it-or-leave-it style, the excessive brutality of the police, and a slew of huge projects and initiatives that threaten to limit secular lifestyles and to concrete over not just Istanbul's Gezi Park, but also whole forests and city districts.' Within days, the Taksim Solidarity Platform, which had organized the initial protests, had grown into a network of 'more than 35 professional bodies, civil-society organizations, environmentalist groups, secularists, community associations and trade unions.' 'So far,' Pope observed of Erdoğan's response, 'he has mishandled the situation, and on June 6 showed no sign of backing down. That's a mistake, because he has the ability to turn the protests to his advantage and the country's.'[23] For Erdoğan, doing so would simply involve 'one of those famous U-turns for which he has become famous.' Erdoğan has pushed forward several unpopular plans: a new Istanbul airport that will destroy vast tracts of forestry, a conspicuous new mosque to dominate the city, a new Bosporus bridge 'with associated highways that would plow through yet more woodland', not to mention a new shipping canal into the Sea of Marmara.[24] Like most powerful and charismatic political leaders, Erdoğan has come in for his share of criticism, not all of it reasonable or justifiable.[25]

Nevertheless, despite the different kinds of criticism directed at Erdoğan, as Hugh Pope shrewdly noted, the demand of 'Tayyip, resign!' was 'to be taken with a grain of salt' even as it was spreading nationwide. 'Turks are well aware that municipal elections in March, a presidential poll in August 2014 and parliamentary elections in June 2015 will give ample opportunity for change.' Journalists in New York and London observed that President Gül was adopting a 'conciliatory' position and making 'his mark on Turkey's Taksim uprising'.[26] Pope emphasized Erdoğan's increasing isolation from the party that had put him in power. 'Luckily for the ruling party,' he commented,

> it still has a strand of idealism that harks back to the reformist agenda that it pressed so successfully in the early 2000s. President Gül has spoken out during the protests to support freedom of expression, noting that democracy isn't just about winning elections. Deputy Prime Minister Bülent Arınç made a refreshingly empathetic speech, in which he apologized for police excesses and held talks with the Taksim Solidarity Platform about their demands.[27]

Pope's comments appeared on 7 June, since which time events have continued to complicate matters further. Yet his early recognition remains sound: that the broadening of the protests provides a welcome opportunity for the government to restart stalled reforms and speed through revisions to the constitution that would address 'the grievances of the protesters, Kurds and other minority communities' while 'fixing Turkey's judiciary system, state tenders and the transparency of government'.[28] If Prime Minister Erdoğan's Kurdish initiative succeeds – and I have met no one who wishes otherwise – then he will have used his position and power to solve the most pointless ethno-political crisis to have bloodied the history of the Turkish Republic.

For President Gül and those close to him, the protest movements that began in Gezi Park are evidence that popular democracy is increasing its purchase on political life in Turkey and that there are new opportunities to be pursued. For them, the widening of civil society activities in Turkey – especially those bringing young people together with a common purpose for their future – proves that the right to freedom of speech is respected. It is perhaps worth noting that the character of incidents of violence – so far – has been unlike that in Turkey during the early 1980s and 1990s. Attacks on members of protest groups not only by police but also by men with sticks and even machetes that have appeared on YouTube, horrific as they clearly are, nevertheless differ in kind and scope from the days when municipal police openly collaborated with the organized violence of militants among the Grey Wolves. Turkey has a long and unfortunate history of self-appointed guardians prepared to act violently and against the law. Turkey is still very much an 'angry nation', in Kerem Öktem's phrase, where anger quickly turns to violence. Clearly there are problems in any national culture that over values military virtues and attitudes among its young men, but democratic standards have advanced significantly in Turkey.

Gül pointed out early on that the Gezi Park and other protests are directed at an elected and responsive government, unlike those of the 'Arab spring', which were aimed at governments in 'countries where there are no free elections ... and the courts are not up to Western standards'.[29] On 15 June he celebrated Turkey's current democratic standards as evidence of past achievement and future promise by using Twitter to address representatives of the Gezi Park protests on their continuing talks with government officials: 'The meeting and the opening of dialogue channels is the sign of democratic maturity. I believe that this process will produce good results'.[30] He also encouraged the protesters to end the occupation of the park, more in hope than expectation. On 23 June, amid fears that the wave of protests might derail the PKK withdrawal, demonstrations were held nationwide to commemorate the arson attack in 1993 on a hotel in Sivas that killed thirty-five people, mostly Alevi intellectuals. What had begun in Gezi Park had, by the end of June, firmly established the ethno-political parameters of the protests alongside unsolved democratic business as the 'new Turkey' enters its third decade.

The 2013 protests bring into focus a number of urgent political matters on which Abdullah Gül has made his general principles clear on several occasions, many of them in sympathy with the demands of the protestors, while holding firm to a defence of neoliberal development. When we spoke in April 2013, just before the riots broke out, he admitted that economic and social developments came at a price. I asked him his thoughts on urban development and the cultural shifts taking place as new generations continue to leave the social world of traditional villages with public tea- and coffee-houses for concrete apartment blocks in suburban projects lacking social facilities. He employed the scholar's evasion, insisting on the need for more research: 'People are becoming more wealthy and less shy and afraid than before. Development distances people from traditional cultures and the global influences today take over within popular culture, and these can be unfortunate. There are always new changes in all segments of life that need careful examination.'[31]

I pressed on other kinds of development project that would cause, or already were causing, massive ecological damage, such as a new Bosporus bridge that would predictably exacerbate existing traffic chaos, or the new Istanbul airport that would destroy forestry, or a shipping canal linking the Black Sea and the Sea of Marmara. I mentioned that I had recently visited the Ilısu dam project in the south east that was set to flood the ancient city of Hasankeyf in order to fulfil plans for hydro-electric power and irrigation systems designed in the 1950s and known to be outdated.[32] Gül sat back before acknowledging 'some mistakes have been made. As for the dam ... as far as I can see there are problems but utmost care is being taken to minimize them. These efforts are for irrigation and energy to combat rural poverty. They are aimed at generating prosperity in the region. It is very difficult to find balance.' Since this was intended to be our last scheduled interview before I submitted this book to the publisher, I thought it best not to press the point that the Ilısu dam project was going ahead without a proper environmental risk analysis, in violation of UN regulations protecting the ancient heritage site at Hasankeyf. After all, what more could he say?

We discussed other matters. President Gül once more confirmed his long-held belief that a new constitution remains urgently needed to advance democracy and guarantee freedom of speech while assuring the rights of ethnic and religious communities, notably the Kurds but also the Alevi and Jewish communities. Noting that Turkey's 'current achievements' in welfare, business and education were already in line 'with Europe and with developed democracies', he observed how 'the lack of consensus among the parties makes me not very hopeful that this round [of constitutional amendments] will solve the remaining problems'. Among the problems, he suggested, were the different rates at which 'people are willing to change', not simply parliamentarians and jurists, but the Turkish people themselves. In some cases, reforms introduced in 2004, such as gender equality, have yet to become fully enforceable so long as traditional values and attitudes continue to hold sway over large areas of society. Similarly, efforts at ethno-political reconciliation can only move slowly while racial and religious hostility and anger persist in such violent and divisive forms as they do. Promoting democracy throughout Turkey through constitutional reforms would help resolve the Kurdish issue, but as he has often said, it is not the task of the constitution to define the identity of its citizens.[33] Although laws must 'remove anything undermining people's rights', he insisted that raising 'awareness' was equally important. 'I remain confident that the solution can be achieved by following these two approaches – encouraging democracy and awareness of the need to respect human rights – so I am encouraging recent initiatives being pressed by the prime minister in the discussions with the PKK.'[34]

Of plans for the end of his presidential term in July 2014, Abdullah Gül was predictably circumspect: 'I hope to be at the service of this state and people. I will definitely be occupied with something useful, but as for the form, it is too early to say anything. I will never be retired in the sense that all I do is sit and read! They have named a new university after me in Kayseri, and I want it to become a top-class university in central Anatolia. I will help work to raise funds for students and other projects. So I will never retire but become involved in academia.' Prompted by this declaration, he told me he was currently reading Salih Tuğ's Turkish translation of Philip Hitti's *History of the Arabs*, and a history of the Balkan wars.[35] That was in April 2013, before Gezi Park.

Later in the year, fears that nationwide protests would resume in October once students returned to campuses proved largely unfounded, though in Ankara demonstrations against destroying the METU forest for a new highway continued with some nasty confrontations. The lifting of the ban on women wearing headscarves – with exceptions for those in the military, police and judiciary – on 8 October was a historic achievement of Erdoğan's government. Hardline secularists may have been horrified, but – remarkably enough – within weeks the headscarf question had clearly ceased being a serious issue. Recalling the massive protests of early 2007, First Lady Hayrünnisa Gül can only have felt that her personal struggles against the ban had finally been vindicated.

On 17 December, however, Prime Minister Erdoğan and members of his government came under direct and personal attack when financial crime prosecutors arrested a number of leading figures on corruption charges: those arrested included the AKP 'Mayor of Istanbul's Fatih district ... and the sons of three cabinet ministers.'[36] With municipal elections coming up in March, Erdoğan was directly embarrassed when the implicated Cabinet ministers resigned a week later: one of them calling on Erdoğan himself to resign. In characteristic manner, Erdoğan went on the offensive, finding the hand of the Gülen movement and international conspirators at work. His government promptly set about purging the Police Department and Finance Ministry of suspected Gülen supporters.[37] Against fierce opposition, the government then muscled through two pieces of controversial legislation. The first was designed to give the government increased control over the Supreme Board of Judges and Prosecutors (HSYK), the second – more ambitiously – aimed to give them control over the internet.

In the early weeks of January 2014, fights broke out in parliament during debates over the proposed bill of judicial reforms, while fears of a political crisis were seriously damaging the Turkish economy. On 14 January, President Gül intervened, meeting with the leaders of the opposition parties to reach a compromise on the justice bill. All were in general agreement on the need for changes to the judicial system, which was still marked by anomalies left over from the 1980s reforms, but the current bill was clearly aimed at distracting attention from the corruption allegations. Four days later, Gül met with Erdoğan and attempted to persuade him to 'freeze' the current proposals for reshaping the HYSK in order to gain multiparty support for broader constitutional reforms that would, among other matters, tackle wider problems with the justice system.[38] Those talks proved inconclusive, but Gül continued to meet and discuss the reforms with Erdoğan and Justice Minister Bekir Bozdağ.[39] Meanwhile, Erdoğan's government was already busily launching a second frontal assault, this time against social media and the internet.

The 17 December arrests had depended on evidence gathered from years of eavesdropping on the telephone calls of leading businessmen and politicians. Erdoğan and his supporters here found evidence of a secret state operation aimed at the prime minister and his party and justification not only for reshaping the prosecutor's office but also seizing greater control of communications technology. Since the Gezi protests, Erdoğan had become a figure of popular scorn on certain social media, and did little to hide his anger. In early January his government started drafting a bill enabling authorities to monitor and limit internet access. The outcry was instantaneous and international: Erdoğan's Turkey, it seemed, was attacking freedom of speech. On 18 January, even as President Gül was meeting with Prime Minister Erdoğan to discuss judicial reforms, protestors against the internet legislation were gathering in Istanbul; they would later be dispersed by tear gas and water cannon, as would subsequent protestors in later weeks.

For President Gül, the dilemma was acute. His own views on both the need for judicial transparency through constitutional reform and communications technology were too well known for it not to be clear he opposed both pieces of legislation. However, as president, his options were limited. To use his one-time right of veto would most certainly result in parliament sending the bill back, untouched, at which point he would have no option but to sign. Instead, he had experts advise him on the proposals with special attention to their constitutionality and conformity with European standards and returned them to parliament with changes that he insisted had to be made before he would sign off. In the twelve articles of the bill reforming the Supreme Board of Judges and Prosecutors, Gül stipulated the need for no fewer than fifteen crucial changes in order to bring the legislation into conformity with 'the constitution and globally accepted democratic standards.'[40] All these changes were adopted in the law that Gül eventually passed on 26 February.[41]

Outside Turkey, the passage of the new laws went largely unobserved, though President Gül himself had recently become the target of international scrutiny. The week before, on Tuesday 18 February, he had signed off on the parliament's bill seeking to control the internet. In this case, he fully understood the futility of the attempt to control social media by laws of this kind, and nevertheless insisted on crucial revisions that made the controlling agencies more responsible and transparent: these revisions too were adopted. The *New York Times* was not sufficiently impressed, however, declaring in an editorial of 21 February that President Gül had 'joined Prime Minister Recep Tayyip Erdoğan in the government's assault on free speech.'[42] At a press conference held three days later, Gül called the accusation 'unfair', explaining once again that he recognized the futility of attempting to control the internet and how his stipulations protected both due process and internet privacy. But the headlines in Turkey that day, 24 February, were taken up with breaking news that recordings of wiretaps on Erdoğan and leading journalists, bankers, businessmen and academics had been 'found in the Istanbul public prosecutor's office by the new prosecutors who were assigned following mass purges in the judiciary'.[43] If the discovery of these illegal documents might seem to have helped Erdoğan's case that there was a 'parallel structure' of Gülen supporters within the police and judiciary that was out to get him, the problem was that the recordings included conversations between himself and his son Bilal after the 17 December arrests discussing how to hide 'dirty' money. Erdoğan swiftly retorted that the recordings uploaded onto YouTube were no more than a 'montage' of different conversations, but few can have been convinced.[44] The important question was rather whether the electorate would hold the allegations against AKP candidates in the forthcoming elections.

On 6 March, with three weeks to go before the municipal elections, Erdoğan once again made international headlines when he threatened to close down YouTube and Facebook.[45] Then, with only a week to go, late in the evening of 20 March, the Turkish Telecommunications Authority blocked access to Twitter, only hours after Erdoğan had promised to do so: 'We'll eradicate Twitter,' he had announced that afternoon in Bursa. The outcry was immediate and international: it included President Gül who broke the ban on 21 March by tweeting 'A total shutdown of social media platforms cannot be approved.'[46] Going in to the crucial municipal elections, the positions were clear and the stakes remained as they had been for some time. A significant drop in the number of votes the AKP had received in local elections in 2011 would reduce Erdoğan's chances if he ran for the presidency, while marginally improving Gül's chances were he to stand for reappointment. Without compromising his office, President Gül continued to avoid any form of direct statement that would challenge the party he had helped to found while making his differences from current policies as clear as possible.

On 30 March, despite months of anti-government protests since the Gezi Park demonstrations, and despite the corruption investigations, the AKP emerged victorious, taking a little over forty-five percent of the vote. In his victory speech, Prime Minister Erdoğan declared that 'the new Turkey won today', triumphing over 'the politics of lies, slander, blackmail and montage' and delivering 'an Ottoman slap' to his political opponents. He also promised that the AKP would immediately turn to finding ways to increase support 'to fifty or sixty [percent].'[47] In the aftermath of elections, the numbers count for everything. 'Some 45 percent is enough to win an eighth poll since 2002 for Erdoğan,' observed Murat Yetkin, 'but it will not be enough for the presidency, for which 50 percent plus one vote will be needed.'[48] Others disagreed: 'After these figures, Mr. Erdoğan's presidential nomination and election are almost guaranteed,' claimed the director of an 'Ankara-based pollster' as cited in the *New York Times*.[49] On 1 July, the AKP publicly declared Erdoğan their presidential candidate. As this book goes into production, the results of the August election remain to be seen, but Abdullah Gül and AKP leaders have all supported Prime Minister Erdoğan's candidacy.

What remains to be said of Abdullah Gül and the 'new Turkey' of the twenty-first century? Hakan Yavuz rightly observed that 'Gül's political life summarizes the evolution of the new actors of transformation in Anatolia', and that he has been 'the window of his party to the outside world'.[50] Gül's early years in provincial Kayseri, interrupted by regular visits to cosmopolitan Izmir, provided him with an unusually wide experience and perspective on the social and political events that followed the democratic opening of the 1950 elections. The 'Islamic Calvinism' of Kayseri provided cultural values – at once conservative, religious and provincial, yet rapidly embracing modernization and economic development – while regular visits to Izmir provided experience of the different values and lifestyles of Turkey's secular and cosmopolitan west. From his pious Muslim father, he learned to listen to apparently opposing views and discover how Muslims share many values with non-Muslim cultures and religions. During his years of student activism, Gül's early instinct to stand up and tell leaders where they were going wrong re-emerged when he denounced violence and promoted Turkish culture as a meeting ground for political opponents. Necip Fazıl had taught him to put culture, not religion, in charge of politics; life in England and Jeddah confirmed his belief that this was the right direction and emphasis. Living among the benefits and limitations of both secular and Islamic states, he became firmly committed to European-style democracy over political Islam. Witnessing the globalization of the 1980s from the perspective of Islamic banking theory and practices, Gül recognized how Özal's opening of the economy to global markets was the key to Turkey's future prosperity. And Özal was not only westward-looking but also a Muslim who sensibly advocated replacing Turkey's religious laws with a US model of religious freedom.

By the end of the 1980s, new forms of development and democratization were underway in Turkey. Kayseri was now leading an economic boom, but all was not well. Erbakan's Refah Party provided Gül with a political opportunity for taking a direct role in the future of his home city and nation, confident that religious rights and sensibilities could be protected amid neoliberal reforms. Through the 'lost decade' he learned the skills of an international politician while working with European politicians in Strasbourg, and alongside Erbakan in Ankara, never fully embracing his leader's *Milli Görüş* nationalism but remaining certain that states should be based on democratic, not religious, principles. When founding the AKP, Gül set out to ensure that Turkey's government became more democratic, more transparent and accountable according to European standards, while its economy developed in line with neoliberal global trends. Throughout his political career, close colleagues have continued to admire Gül for his personal style of leadership, combining a constant eagerness to seek out expert advice with an unusual willingness to listen to it, especially when experts contradict each other. And they admire him for his remarkable talent for subsequently coming up with pragmatic solutions to problems in a manner that causes no one offence.

The Turkish language, especially in its rural colloquialisms, is rich in colourful terms for describing different forms of men and masculinity, and these are sometimes applied to politicians both critically and as markers of admiration or respect. Coming from the Black Sea, Bülent Ecevit was often called a *karaoğlan* – the same term Gül's father used to describe Yaşar Kemal – literally a 'black boy', someone who stood out from the crowd.[51] In contrast, Recep Tayyip Erdoğan has been called a '*kabadayı* from Kasımpaşa', linking him with the notoriously 'rough, macho neighbourhood' in which he grew up, and attributing him with the qualities of being a tough guy who refuses to compromise.[52] Later, earning respect for serving time in prison over his beliefs, Erdoğan was greeted by supporters as a *mazlum*, a 'wronged one'. Following his election to the presidency in 2007, Gül too was welcomed as a *mazlum*, but also as a *mağdur*: he was both a 'wronged one' and a 'victim', who had suffered from a campaign of personal attacks on his family during the election campaigns. But perhaps more relevant for this most recent period of his presidency is the style of manliness he imagined for himself while still a boy. Early in his life, it will be recalled, young Abdullah Gül cast himself in a slightly different heroic role, that of *babayiğit*, not a victim but a 'brave-heart' prepared to stand up for what he believed in when those in power are going wrong. He may never have attained the intimidating physical size most often associated with the *babayiğit*: in Hollywood terms we might think of the painted Scottish warrior played by Mel Gibson in the film entitled *Braveheart*. But throughout his life and career, Gül has upheld the moral values – collectively termed *mert* in Turkish – that are essential qualities of the *babayiğit*: a man who earns renown for being brave, honest, courageous, trustworthy, dependable, reliable and responsible.

NOTES

Foreword

1   Kinross, *Atatürk* (1964) and Mango, *Atatürk* (1999).
2   For an early use of the term 'new Turkey', see Mehmet Ali Birand, 'The New Turkey perception of Turkey, *Hürriyet Daily News*, 19 September 2003, and see Morris, *New Turkey*.
3   Kinross, *Atatürk*, 473–4.
4   Mango, *Atatürk*, 61–4.
5   For this and the next paragraph, I have relied on Kinross, *Atatürk,* 208–30, and Lewis, *Turkey*, 58–78.
6   See MacLean, 'Motoring with Mehmet'.
7   MacLean, 'Strolling in Seventeenth-Century Syria', and *The Rise of Oriental Travel*.
8   Finkel, Clow and Landry, *The Evliya Çelebi Way*.
9   Among obituaries, see for example, Joost Lagendijk, 'Mehmet Ali Birand in a Class of His Own', *Today's Zaman*, 20 January 2013.
10 Printed books such as Yavuz Selim, *Gül'ün Adı…* (2002), Fatih Bayhan, *Kayseri'den Cankaya Köşkü'ne* (2007), and Hasan Taşkin, *11. Başkomutan Abdullah Gül* (2007), are summary collections of details – often inaccurate – from previous newspaper reports, as is the online biography by M. Hasan Uncular, 'Abdullah Gül's Unknown Sides.' Can Dündar's more detailed biographical sketch, 'Bir Gül Portresi', was serialized in *Milliyet* from 29 August 2007, and reissued in full at (www.candundar.com.tr).
11 For Gül's thoughts on this observation, see *Hürriyet*, 3 October 2007.
12 *Hürriyet*, 19 November 2011; my thanks to Dr Alaadin Paksoy for the summary translation of this and other pieces from the Turkish-language press cited in this book.
13 Alaadin Paksoy, personal communication, 16 July 2013.
14 Yusuf Yerli, 'Gül'ün Adı', *Kayseri Haber* website at (www.kayserihaber.com.tr/yazar-59-), 5 December 2011.

1   The Early Years, Kayseri: 1950s and 1960s

1   Interview with Abdullah Gül, Tarabya, 3 November 2011; hereafter AG2.

2   Interview with Mehmet Özhaseki, Kayseri, 28 November 2011.

3   Abdullah Satoğlu interview, 18 December 2009, online at: *525-ci Gazet* website (www. old.525.az/view.php?lang=en&menu=12&id=23696&type=1).

4   Interview with Abdullah Gül, Ankara, 3 December 2011; hereafter AG3.

5   Faroqhi, *Towns*, 42.

6   Ibid., 43.

7   European Stabilization Initiative, *Islamic Calvinists*, this passage from section 111.A, 'Max Weber in Kayseri,' 23.

8   Faroqhi, *Towns*, 43.

9   Davis, *Life in Asiatic Turkey*, 292.

10   Ibid., 300.

11   Mango, *Turks Today*, 316–17.

12   Clark, *Twice a Stranger*, 100, 103–4.

13   *Hürriyet*, 3 August 2009.

14   Kevorkian, *Extermination* (www.massviolence.org/Article?id_article=110), 21–2, 28, 35, 36; and see Kevorkian, *Le Génocide*, 640–8, republished in English, *Armenian Genocide*, 513–22.

15   Zürcher, *Turkey*, 102. In 1909, Yakub Cemil had been sent to assassinate Mustafa Kemal, but was already one of Kemal's staunchest supporters in the struggles for power within the Committee of Union and Progress: he was later executed in 1916 for leading a failed coup aimed at replacing Enver with Kemal; see Kinross, *Atatürk*, 39, 48, 102–3.

16   See Kevorkian, *Armenian Genocide*, 514, and the Foundation of Kayseri Surp Krikor Lusavoriç Armenian Church website (www.kayserikilisesi.org/en/kayseri-and-armenians).

17   Kevorkian, *Armenian Genocide*, 515.

18   See Kevorkian, *Extermination*, 31; Neyzi and Kharatyan-Araqelyan, *Speaking*, 59–61.

19   Mehmet Özhaseki interview.

20   Kevorkian, *Extermination*, 41; Kevorkian, *Le Génocide*, 648; Kevorkian, *Armenian Genocide*, 520.

21   Neyzi and Kharatyan-Araqelyan, *Speaking*, 48.

22   Ibid., 51.

23   AG2.

24   AG3.

25   Lewis, *Turkey*, 101.

26   Sağlam, *Dağı Dağa Kavuşturan*, trans. Nancy F. Öztürk with Adnan Tonguç as *Embracing the Mountains* (2004).

27   Ibid., 74.

28 Ibid., 28, 29.
29 AG3.
30 Sağlam, *Embracing*, 74.
31 van Velsen, *Peripheral Production*, 26.
32 See 'Kayseri Tayyare Fabrikasi (KTF)' at The Turkish Aircraft Production website (www.tuncay-deniz.com/ENGLISH/KTF/ktf.html).
33 Webster, *Turkey*, 134, 249.
34 Ibid., 249.
35 Naval Intelligence Division of the British Admiralty, *Geographical Handbook: Turkey*, 2: 205; hereafter 'Admiralty, *Turkey*'.
36 Admiralty, *Turkey*, 2: 205 and 1: 365.
37 Webster, *Turkey*, 249, 250.
38 On Orhan Kemal, see: Kemal, *In Jail with Nazim Hikmet*; Narli, *Orhan Kemal*; Bezirci, *Orhan Kemal*; Findley, *Turkey*, 341–8; and http://orhankemal.org. Kemal's *Bereketli Topraklar Üzerinde* ['On These Bountiful Lands'] of 1954, has not appeared in English translation.
39 Webster, *Turkey*, 250.
40 Lewis, *Turkey*, 101.
41 Linke, *Allah Dethroned*, 314.
42 Ibid., 312.
43 Ibid., 307.
44 Lewis, *Turkey*, 112.
45 Webster, *Turkey*, 248–9.
46 Linke, *Allah Dethroned*, 305–6, 307.
47 Ibid., 303–4.
48 *Zaman*, 1 November 2008.
49 Interview with Turkish diplomat who wished to remain anonymous, Paris, 14 November 2011; hereafter Paris interview.
50 AG3.
51 Zürcher, *Turkey*, 200; and Uncular, 'Abdullah Gül's Unknown Sides/Exclusive', *World Bulletin*, 12 August 2007.
52 According to Taner Timur: 'inflationary policies designed to finance wartime military expenditures had led to a 400% increase in prices in five years, causing great hardship among the populace; moreover, this had been accompanied by widespread profiteering, and the creation of a new class of war-rich'; see 'The Ottoman Heritage', 7.
53 Zürcher, *Turkey*, 207.
54 Ibid., 206–18. See also Eroğul, *Demokrat Parti*; Karpat, *Turkey's Politics*; and Ahmad, *Turkish Experiment*.
55 Mango, *Turks Today*, 45.
56 'When the DP came to power in 1950, at a time when the majority of the Turkish people lived under medieval conditions, it launched the slogan of "unprecedented

development" promising to make Turkey a little America'; Timur, 'Ottoman Heritage', 21–2.

57 On the sugar factory, see European Stabilization Initiative, *Islamic Calvinists*, 17–19.

58 van Velsen, *Peripheral Production*, 50, 27, 38.

59 Mango, *Turks Today*, 44, 45; and see Karpat, 'Social Effects of Farm Mechanization'.

60 AG3.

61 van Velsen, *Peripheral Production*, 26.

62 Interview with Abdullah Gül, Tarabya, 3 November 2011; hereafter AG1.

63 Interview with Mesude Nursuna Memecan, Ankara, 18 October 2011; hereafter Nursuna Memecan interview.

64 Interview with Abdullah Gül, Ankara, 19 April 2012; hereafter AG4.

65 Interview with Macit Gül, Kayseri, 28 November 2011; hereafter Macit Gül interview.

66 AG4.

67 *Ilk okulu diploma kayit defteri* ('Primary School Report Card') Gazi Paşa Ilk Okulu, dated 16 July 1962; copy kindly supplied through the offices of Mehmet Özhaseki: with special thanks to Kasım Akçil, press manager for Kocasinan Belediyesi for this and other kindnesses offered during my visit to Kayseri in November 2011.

68 AG3.

69 Macit Gül interview.

70 I heard this story in Kayseri from a middle-aged taxi driver in May 2013; Abdullah Gül interview, Tarabya Residence, 17 August 2013, hereafter AG6.

71 Macit Gül interview.

72 AG1.

73 Ibid.

74 Interview with Bekir Yıldız, Kayseri, 28 November 2011; hereafter Bekir Yıldız interview.

75 Interview with Fehmi Koru, Istanbul, 3 November 2011; hereafter Fehmi Koru interview.

76 *Ilk okulu diploma kayit defteri*, see note 67 above. On the primary school curriculum at the time, its aims and objectives, see Kazamias, *Education*, 142–5.

77 AG2.

78 Ibid.

79 AG1.

80 Interview with Nurşen Özdamar, Kayseri, 28 November 2011; hereafter Nurşen Özdamar interview.

81 Bekir Yıldız interview.

82 See Eroğul, 'The Establishment of Multiparty Rule,' 118–24.

83 See Ahmad, *Turkish Experiment*, 147–76.

84 AG3.

85 Ibid.

86 Hale, *Political and Economic Development*, 89–90.

87 Zürcher, *Turkey*, 224; Lewis, *Turkey*, 131.

88 Mango, *Turks Today*, 47.

89 Zürcher, *Turkey*, 224.

90 See Hirsch, *Poverty and Plenty*.

91 Hale, *Political and Economic Development*, 96. On the well-documented impact of radios, see Ahiska, *Occidentalism*.

92 Zürcher, *Turkey*, 223.

93 Ibid., 230.

94 Dodd, *History and Politics*, 19.

95 Ibid., 21.

96 Ibid., 23.

97 Hale, *Political and Economic Development*, 88.

98 Zürcher, *Turkey*, 229.

99 Ibid., 240, and see Hale, *Political and Economic Development*, 87.

100 AG3.

101 Eroğul, 'Establishment of Multiparty Rule', 101.

102 'Kayseri Lisesi'ni müdürü ile muallimleri ile bütün talebesi ile cumhuriyetin ateşli, feyizli bir ocağı bulduk' Abdullah Muradoğlu, '68'li Başbakan'. English translation, Alaadin Paksoy.

103 Ibid.

104 AG3.

105 Nurşen Özdamar interview.

106 Zürcher, *Turkey*, 250.

107 Akşin, *Turkey*; and Ahmad, *Quest*, 198.

108 Szyliowicz, 'Turkish Elections: 1965', 473.

109 AG3.

110 Zürcher, *Turkey*, 245.

111 Hale notes that the number of registered university students rose from about 25,000 in 1950 to over 54,000 in 1960, *Political and Economic Development*, 101.

112 See ibid., 108–10.

113 Zürcher, *Turkey*, 250.

114 Ahmad, *Making of Modern Turkey*, 142.

115 AG1. One scholar agrees and argues that little has changed: 'The teaching of history in pre-university schools in Turkey is very inadequate. Little world history is taught, and the teaching of Turkish history is also inadequate. The treatment of twentieth-century Turkish history is particularly sketchy and superficial, and generally ends with the death of Atatürk in 1938 ... It is not easy to describe this situation as accidental: probably it is a consequence of the unfortunate policy of governments unfriendly to enlightenment, which spread its shadow over Turkey after 1950.' Akşin, *Turkey*, v. On the curricular aims of secondary education at the time, and the failure to achieve them, see Kazamias, *Education*, 145–51.

116 AG1.

117 Bekir Yıldız interview.

118 See Mardin, *Religion and Social Change.*

119 Ibid., 13.

120 Ibid., 96.

121 Yavuz, *Islamic Political Identity,* 151.

122 Yavuz, *Secularism,* 137, citing interview from 8 August 2005.

123 Ibid.

124 Findley, *Turkey,* 340.

125 *Yeni Şafak,* 18 November 2002.

126 Findley, *Turkey,* 340.

127 Yavuz, *Secularism,* 138. Elsewhere Yavuz observes: 'Necip Fazıl elucidated the search for a deeper self and an Islamic cognitive map of meaning and action for himself and his society. He dealt with the lack of shared primordial language and emotions that led to the deep existential pain of his generation.' *Islamic Political Identity,* 116.

128 Paris interview.

129 Translated from 'O ve Ben', in Tezcür, *Muslim Reformers,* 185.

130 Mardin, 'Culture Change', 208–10.

131 Ibid., 185.

132 Ibid., 200.

133 AG3.

134 Muradoğlu, '68'li Başbakan'.

135 Mardin, 'Culture Change', 210.

136 Şükrü Karatepe interview.

137 Bekir Yıldız interview.

2   Istanbul, England and Saudi Arabia: 1969 to 1991

1 In 2011, the OIC renamed itself; see Organization of the Islamic Cooperation website (www.oic-oci.org/home.asp).

2 *New York Times,* 23 January 1968.

3 The Israeli submarine, *INS Dakar,* disappeared on 25 January; see Dunmore, *Lost Subs,* 152–3. The French submarine, *Minerve,* disappeared two days later; see (www.netmarine.net/bat/smarins/minerve/index.html).

4 On the disappearance of the *USS Scorpion* on 22 May, see Offley, *Scorpion Down.*

5 See Zürcher, *Turkey,* 275, and Dodd, *History,* 67–8.

6 Ahmad, *Making of Modern Turkey,* 139. Contemporary US accounts of anti-Americanism in Turkey include Lawson, 'New Regime in Turkey', and Giritli, 'Turkey since the 1965 Elections'.

7 Szyliowicz, 'Students and Politics', 150; Roos, Roos and Field, 'Students and Politics in Turkey'; and Zürcher, *Turkey,* 240.

8 Macit Gül interview.

9   Ibid.

10 Samim, 'The Left', 174 n. 23.

11 Ağaoğulları, 'The Ultranationalist Right'.

12 Zürcher, *Turkey*, 257.

13 Türkeş, 'Komando Kampları', *Milli Hareket* 27 (October 1968), 13; cited and translated in Ağaoğulları, 'The Ultranationalist Right', 214 n. 113.

14 Öktem, *Angry Nation*, 48.

15 See Landau, *Radical Politics* for a detailed account written close to the events. Apaydın, *Kim Öldürüyor, Niçin Öldürüyor* ['Who Is Killing, and Why'], provides a detailed account of political assassinations up to 1978.

16 See Ergil, *Türkiye'de Terör ve Şiddet*. Quantitative analysis of the violence and terrorism of these years can be found in Keleş and Ünsal, *Kent ve Siyasal Şiddet*.

17 On Türkeş, see Ağaoğulları, 'The Ultranationalist Right', 193–5, and passim.

18 Szyliowicz, 'Students and Politics', 152–4.

19 Bekir Yıldız interview.

20 Mehmet Ali Dikerdem, personal communication, 21 September 2011.

21 Fehmi Koru interview.

22 Interview with Sami Güçlü, Cankaya, 1 November 2011; hereafter Sami Güçlü interview.

23 Ibid.

24 AG4.

25 See MTTB website (www.mttb.org.tr).

26 See Calvert, *Sayyid Qutb*.

27 See Momin, 'Dr Muhammad Hamidullah (1909–2002)' online at (www.renaissance.com.pk/Febobti2y4.html).

28 Interview with Mehmet Tekelioğlu, Meclis, Ankara, 19 October 2011; hereafter Mehmet Tekelioğlu interview; also Sami Güçlü and Bekir Yıldız interviews.

29 Fehmi Koru interview.

30 Can Dündar, 'Bir Gül Portresi' (www.candundar.com.tr/_old/index.php?Did=5289).

31 Bekir Yıldız interview.

32 Dodd, *History*, 18; and Sami Güçlü and Bekir Yıldız interviews.

33 Sami Güçlü interview.

34 Mehmet Tekelioğlu interview.

35 Öktem, *Angry Nation*, 49.

36 Ahmad, *Making of Modern Turkey*, 147.

37 Mehmet Tekelioğlu interview.

38 See 1961 constitution, articles 35 to 53; article 53 is here cited in translation from Hale, *Political and Economic Development*, 117–18.

39 Ahmad, *Making of Modern Turkey*, 129.

40 Ibid., 135.

41 Ibid., 142.

42 Ibid., 144.

43 Ibid., 134, 146; and see Arınır and Öztürk, *Işçi Sınıfı* ['The Working Class...'], for a detailed analysis of the strikes.
44 See Vaner, 'The Army'; and Hale, *Turkish Politics*, 88–214.
45 Ahmad, *Quest*, 123.
46 Ahmad, *Making of Modern Turkey*, 130.
47 Ibid., 147.
48 Referring to guardianship of the Turkish Republic, Atatürk had declared: 'This holy treasure I lay in the hands of the youth of Turkey. Turkish Youth! Your primary duty is ever to preserve and defend the National Independence, the Turkish Republic.' Kemal, *Nutuk-Söylev*, 724–5. By 1931, however, Atatürk shifted his emphasis, praising the army as 'the permanent vanguard' of the revolution; cited Hale, *Turkish Politics*, 81.
49 See Timur, 'Ottoman Heritage', 19.
50 Mehmet Tekelioğlu interview.
51 Hale, *Political and Economic Development*, 124, 125.
52 See Landau, 'The National Salvation Party in Turkey', and Heper, 'Islam, Polity'.
53 Şükrü Karatepe (b. 1949) served as mayor of Kayseri Büyükşehir from 1994 to 1998; Bekir Yıldız (b. 1951), has been mayor of Kocasinan municipality in Kayseri since 1994; Irfan Gündüz (b. 1950), professor of religious atudies at Marmara University, served as MP representing Istanbul from 1999 until 2007.
54 Şükrü Karatepe interview.
55 See Özbudun, 'State Elites', 247–68.
56 Mehmet Tekelioğlu interview.
57 Eligür, *Mobilization*, 24; and see Zürcher, *Turkey*, 288–90.
58 See Kafesoğlu, *Türk-Islam Sentezi*; for an English introduction, see Poulton, *Top Hat*, 170–87. A useful introduction is provided in Kurt, 'The Doctrine'.
59 See Eligür, *Mobilization*, 3, 48; Yavuz, *Islamic Political Identity*, 69–70; and Yavuz, *Secularism*, 140.
60 Sami Güçlü interview.
61 AG4.
62 AG4.
63 Mehmet Tekelioğlu and Bekir Yıldız interviews.
64 On Cemil Meriç, see Köksal, 'The Dilemmas'.
65 Erbakan, *Milli Görüş*.
66 Paris interview.
67 Ibid.
68 Ibid.
69 Tahir worked with directors including Metin Erksan, Halit Refiğ and Atıf Yılmaz; see 'Kemal Tahir', in Pirim, ed., *Tanzimat'tan Bugüne*, 2: 591–4.
70 Paris interview.
71 Sami Güçlü interview.
72 Ibid.

73   Paris interview.

74   See the Foundation's website (www.tmkv.org.tr).

75   Şükrü Karatepe interview.

76   According to Alma, Baroness Birk, when proposing the 'Drought Bill' to the House
      of Lords on 20 July; see Hansard website (http://hansard.millbanksystems.com/
      lords/1976/jul/20/drought-bill.hl).

77   See (www.london-weather.eu/article.115.html).

78   See FOSIS website (http://fosis.org.uk).

79   AG1.

80   AG3.

81   AG1.

82   AG2.

83   Fehmi Koru interview.

84   AG2.

85   Fehmi Koru interview.

86   AG2.

87   See Wiegers, 'Dr Sayyid Mutwalli ad-Darsh's *fatwas.*'

88   Ibid., 181.

89   Fehmi Koru interview; to which I also owe much of this discussion of visits to Speakers'
      Corner.

90   AG1.

91   AG6.

92   Fehmi Koru interview.

93   Ibid.

94   Ibid.

95   AG4.

96   AG1.

97   AG6.

98   Selim, *Gül'ün Adı...*, 48.

99   Fehmi Koru interview.

100   Şükrü Karatepe interview.

101   Fehmi Koru interview.

102   AG1.

103   No one is certain how the old pub got its name. Some suggest that an Ottoman sea-
      captain was once captured and brought here to be held prisoner: certainly, the cellars
      were once used as dungeons. Others suggest that, as with many other pubs of the same
      name throughout the country, it recalls a once popular jousting game from the time
      of the Crusades that involves a player striking a stuffed 'Saracen's Head' mounted on a
      swivelled boom that swings around to hit the player who is too slow on his feet.

104   AG1.

105   AG2.

106 Fehmi Koru interview.

107 Macit Gül interview.

108 Nasr, *Forces of Fortune*, 246.

109 Yavuz, *Islamic Political Identity*, 68.

110 Birand, *The Generals' Coup*, 31.

111 Yavuz, *Islamic Political Identity*, 68.

112 Amnesty International, *Turkey*.

113 Birand, *Generals' Coup*, 48.

114 Zürcher, *Turkey*, 263.

115 Abdullah Gül, personal email to author, 10 January 2014.

116 Taner Timur has observed how the three coups followed periods of similar economic and social patterns of mismanagement, a process that was repeated three times with ten-year intervals: 'Elected governments always resisted antipopular austerity measures until the bitter end, while economic instability led each time to political instability and created regime crises. The army was forced, willingly or otherwise, to take over power.' See Timur, 'Ottoman Heritage', 21.

117 *Milliyet*, 1 August 1980.

118 Hale, *Political and Economic Development*, 120.

119 Birand, *General's Coup*, 173.

120 Ibid., 143.

121 Nevşehir interview with former Grey Wolf, 19 April 2012.

122 Admiralty, *Turkey*, 2: 520.

123 Sami Güçlü interview.

124 Interview with Hayrünnisa Gül, Ankara Residence, 25 April 2013; hereafter Hayrünnisa Gül interview 2013.

125 Hayrünnisa Gül interview 2013.

126 Interview with Hayrünnisa Gül, Ankara Residence, 4 April 2012; hereafter Hayrünnisa Gül interview 2012.

127 Ibid.

128 AG3.

129 Ibid.

130 Ibid.

131 Hayrünnisa Gül interview 2012.

132 AG3.

133 Nursuna Memecan interview.

134 Hayrünnisa Gül interview 2012.

135 AG3.

136 Ibid.

137 Zürcher, *Turkey*, 279.

138 Birand, *Generals' Coup*, 163.

139 Zürcher, *Turkey*, 279.

140 Ibid., 279–80.

141 Ibid., 280, 288; and see Copeaux, *Türk Tarihi Tezinden.*

142 AG4.

143 AG3.

144 Ibid.

145 Ibid.

146 'When the government, at the end of 1981, tried to impose some order on the market and introduced minimum standards of credit worthiness, over 300 brokerage firms collapsed … even *Banker Kastelli*, the eleventh largest bank in Turkey, collapsed.' Zürcher, *Turkey*, 307.

147 AG3.

148 Ibid.

149 Ibid.

150 Şükrü Karatepe interview.

151 Hayrünnisa Gul interview 2012.

152 Ibid.

153 See Kalaycıoğlu, 'The Motherland Party', 45.

154 Findley, *Turkey*, 354.

155 Mehmet Ali Dikerdem, personal communication, 20 September 2011.

156 Hakan Yavuz describes Özal's political career in terms of occupying and controlling a 'new opportunity space' in the Turkish political system; Yavuz, *Islamic Political Identity*, 75.

157 Pearson, 'Turkey's Gulf War Gamble', *Businessweek* website.

158 Selim, *Gül'ün Adı…*, 49.

159 AG3.

160 Ibid.

161 Ibid.

162 Hayrünnisa Gül interview 2012.

163 AG3.

164 Hayrünnisa Gül interview 2012.

165 Ibid.

166 Paris interview.

167 Macit Gül interview.

168 AG3.

169 Ibid. Timur Kuran has forcefully and controversially questioned 'whether the traditional sources of Islam do, in fact, prohibit *all* forms of interest', and has gone on to assert that 'Islamic banks do not even avoid interest, except in name', and that 'half a century after the birth of Islamic economics, nowhere has interest been purged from economic transactions'; see Kuran, *Islam and Mammon*, ix, xi, xvi–xvii.

170 See Henry and Wilson, eds, *Politics of Islamic Finance*, 2–3.

171 Mehmet Tekelioğlu interview.

172 Muhammad Iqbal (1877-1938), was an influential Urdu poet and Muslim political philosopher.

173 Paris interview.

174 Mehmet Tekelioğlu interview.

175 AG1.

3   The Refah Years, Ankara: 1991 to 1997

1   On the history of the Islamic Development Bank and other initiatives to develop 'Islamic' banking, see Kahf, 'Islamic Banks', and Kuran, *Islam and Mammon.*

2   Yavuz, *Secularism*, 136–7.

3   Zürcher, *Turkey*, 283–4.

4   Ibid., 284.

5   Ibid., 285.

6   Interview with Beşir Atalay, Çankaya, Ankara, 25 April 2013; hereafter Beşir Atalay interview.

7   Karasipahi, *Muslims in Modern Turkey*, 1, 2, 7.

8   Paris interview.

9   Zürcher, *Turkey*, 286.

10 See Henry and Wilson, eds, *Politics of Islamic Finance*, 8, 23.

11 Öniş and Şenses, 'New Phase', 1.

12 Ibid.

13 Macit Gül interview.

14 AG1.

15 Ibid.

16 AG1, and Muradoğlu, '68'li Başbakan'.

17 AG1.

18 Interview with Mustafa Boydak, Kayseri, 27 November 2011; hereafter Mustafa Boydak interview.

19 AG1.

20 AG1. In the general elections that year, Refah took seventeen percent: Zürcher, *Turkey*, 292.

21 Hayrünnisa Gül interview 2012.

22 Ibid.

23 AG4.

24 Hayrünnisa Gül interview 2012.

25 Ibid.

26 Ibid.

27 Ibid.

28 Pope and Pope, *Turkey Unveiled*, 313.

29 *Hürriyet Daily News*, 9 September 1998.

30 *Hürriyet Daily News*, 2 March 2004.

31 *Hürriyet Daily News*, 3 March 2004.

32 Mango, *Atatürk*, 436.

33 Zürcher, *Turkey*, 292.

34 Öktem, *Angry Nation*, 89.

35 Zürcher, *Turkey*, 313.

36 Gülalp, 'Political Islam', 26, citing Erbakan, *Adil Ekonomik Düzen*. On Erbakan's 'Just Order', see Yavuz, *Islamic Political Identity*, 220–5, and 310 n. 47.

37 Zürcher, *Turkey*, 295.

38 On women's activism on behalf of Refah, see White, *Islamist Mobilization*, 19 and passim, and Sözen, 'Gender Politics', 261–3.

39 Zürcher, *Turkey*, 298.

40 Açikgöz, 'Kelimlerin Büyüsü', 147, cited in Gülalp, 'Political Islam', 27 n. 19.

41 Zürcher, *Turkey*, 298.

42 AG4.

43 Tansu Çiller, television interview on Kanal 7 (27 October 1996), cited in Gülalp, 'Political Islam', 36.

44 AG4.

45 Ibid.

46 Mustafa Boydak interview.

47 Ibid.

48 See Öniş, 'Evolution of Privatization', and the same author's *State and Market*.

49 See Tokatli and Kızılgün, 'Upgrading', esp. 230–40.

50 Zürcher, *Turkey*, 307, 311–12.

51 The others, all of increasing intensity and impact, were 1994, 1997 and 2000/1. Among the many English-language studies written on the economic situation in Turkey during the 1990s leading to the major crisis of 2000/1, I have found the following especially useful: Alper and Öniş, 'Financial Globalization', Altunbaş, Kara and Oğlu, *Turkish Banking*, and the recent essays collected by Çetin and Oğuz, eds, *Regulation and Competition*.

52 See Wilson, 'Capital Flight', especially 132–6.

53 ESI, *Islamic Calvinists*, 11. By 2007, the Boydak furniture factory was making sofa-beds and upholstered armchairs worth over a billion dollars a year in export revenues alone: see Nasr, *Forces of Fortune*, 245; and more generally, Gülalp, 'Globalization'.

54 ESI, *Islamic Calvinists*, 27.

55 See ESI, *Islamic Calvinists*, 27, and Altunbaş, Kara and Oğlu, *Turkish Banking*, 166–7. In 1985, two 'special finance houses' had been established in Turkey that were joint ventures between Saudi and Turkish investors. In 1991, *Anadolu Finans* was the first participation bank to be founded entirely by Turkish private investors. See Henry, 'Financial Performances', 119, and Başkan, 'Political Economy', 226–34.

56 Mustafa Boydak interview.

57   ESI, *Islamic Calvinists*, 11.

58   Ibid., 9.

59   Zürcher, *Turkey*, 315; on the banking sector during the 2000–2 crisis, see Akcay, 'The Turkish Banking Sector'.

60   Mustafa Boydak interview.

61   The committee was made up of MPs Salih Kapusuz and Abdullah Gül (RP), Husamettin Özkan (DSP), Mesut Yılmaz and Sevket Bülent Yağnıcı (MHP).

62   Mustafa Boydak interview.

63   Türkiye Finans website (http://www.turkiyefinans.com.tr/en/about_us/history.aspx).

64   See reports on the 'Anadalou Kaplanları' appearing in *Millyet* during June 1996.

65   ESI, *Islamic Calvinists*, 6 n. 8.

66   AG1.

67   ESI, *Islamic Calvinists*, citing *Suddeutsche Zeitung* (13 June 2006) in prefatory materials.

68   Zürcher, *Turkey*, 312.

69   Öktem, *Angry Nation*, 90.

70   For this, and other incidents noted in this paragraph, see ibid., 88–91.

71   Yavuz, *Secularism*, 137.

72   AG4.

73   Document 6564 (4 February 1992), PACE website.

74   Documents 6788, 6790, 6789 (March 1993), PACE website.

75   Recommendation 1212 (11 May 1993), PACE website.

76   See Robins, *Suits and Uniforms*, 61–3.

77   Document 6671 (17 September 1992), PACE website.

78   Document 6616 (7 May 1992), PACE website.

79   Document 6628 (10 June 1992), citing the 'Interim reply by the Committee of Ministers' (21 May 1992), PACE website.

80   Resolution 984 (30 June 1992), PACE website.

81   Ibid.

82   Recommendation 1189 (1 July 1992), PACE website.

83   Document 7654 (1 February 1993), PACE website.

84   Resolution 994 (3 February 1993), PACE website.

85   Ibid.

86   See Resolutions 1010 and 1011 (28 September 1993), PACE website.

87   Recommendation 1218 (27 September 1993), PACE website.

88   See the Tribunal's website (http://www.icty.org).

89   Document 6889 (1 July 1993), PACE website.

90   Document 6758 (3 February 1993), PACE website.

91   Resolution 984 (30 June 1992), PACE website.

92   Document 6712 (16 October 1992), PACE website.

93   Document 6713 (19 October 1992), PACE website.

94   Document 6722 (18 November 1922), PACE website.

95 Documents 6618 (8 May 1992), 6643 (30 June 1992) and 6645 (8 July 1992), PACE website.

96 Documents 6732 (12 January 1993), 6766 (8 February 1993) and 6890 (1 July 1993). See also Recommendation 1222 (29 September 1993), PACE website.

97 Documents 6850 (28 May 1993) and 6854 (17 June 1993), PACE website.

98 Documents 6665 (16 September 1992) and 6733 (11 January 1993), PACE website.

99 Paris interview.

100 See Resolution 1030 (13 April 1994) and Document 7112 (28 June 1994), PACE website.

101 See Güney, 'The People's Democratic Party', and Judgement 25141/94 (10 December 2002), in French, at European Court of Human Rights website at (www.hudoc.echr.coe.int).

102 Alper and Öniş, 'Financial Globalization', 6.

103 Zürcher, *Turkey*, 313.

104 See Şen, *Refah Partisi'nin*, 61–5, and Bulaç, *Modern Ulus Devlet*, 43–8.

105 AG2.

106 AG1.

107 Şükrü Karatepe interview.

108 Ibid.

109 Mehmet Özhaseki interview.

110 Interview with Murat Mercan, Balgat, Ankara, 17 October 2011.

111 Ibid.

112 See *Hürriyet*, 28 December 2002, and 'Antisemitism in the Turkish Media, Part 3: Targeting Turkey's Jewish Citizens', Middle East Media Research Institute website (http://memri.org).

113 AG4.

114 Erdoğan had been head of Refah's Istanbul branch since 1985, but his 1991 election victory was cancelled because of a now obsolete technicality; see Zafer Özcan, 'Küllerinden doğan siyasetçiler', *Aksiyon*, 31 April 2007 at (www.aksiyon.com.tr/aksiyon/haber-16419-33-kullerinden-dogan-siyasetciler.html).

115 *Guardian*, 27 November 1995.

116 The Turkish press picked up these comments and used them against him in 2007: see *Milliyet*, 1 May 2007, and the next day's editorial in *Hürriyet*.

117 Şükrü Karatepe interview.

118 AG2.

119 Mehmet Tekelioğlu interview; and see *Hürriyet Daily News*, 1 January 1997.

120 *Hürriyet Daily News*, 8 August 1996.

121 *Hürriyet Daily News*, 19 November 1996.

122 *Hürriyet Daily News*, 1 April 1997.

123 Sami Güçlü interview.

124 *Hürriyet Daily News*, 10 November 1997.

125 *Hürriyet Daily News*, 31 October 1997.

126 *Hürriyet Daily News*, 3 November 1998.

127 Robins, *Suits and Uniforms*, 52.

128 Ibid., 69.

129 *Hürriyet Daily News*, 8 August 1996.

130 AG1.

131 Robins, *Suits and Uniforms*, 80.

132 Ibid., 148.

133 Quoted from a speech made on 8 March 1995 by Emin Cölaşan, 'Bay Gül'ün Dünü ve Bugünü', *Hürriyet*, 23 November 2006, cited in Yavuz, *Secularism*, 136.

134 By 1997, the deal had gone wrong: Robins, *Suits and Uniforms*, 262.

135 AG4.

136 *Hürriyet Daily News*, 6 January 1997.

137 Robins, *Suits and Uniforms*, 158; citing *Hürriyet*, 24 September 1996.

138 *New York Times*, 7 October 1996. For the Turkish press see, for example, *Hürriyet Daily News,* 10 September 1996.

139 *New York Times*, 7 October 1996.

140 'It was only through the combined efforts of Abdullah Gül and senior members of the foreign ministry that Erbakan was persuaded not to press ahead with his intention to visit Islamist Sudan.' Robins, *Suits and Uniforms*, 158.

141 Barkey, 'Turkey and the Great Powers', 251.

142 'Brief History of D-8', D-8 Organization for Economic Cooperation website at (www.developing8.org).

143 *Hürriyet Daily News,* 14 October 1996.

144 Cited in Gülalp, 'Political Islam', 38.

145 *Hürriyet Daily News,* 5 November 1996.

4 From Refah to AKP: 1997 to 2001

1 *Hürriyet Daily News*, 5 November 1996; and see Öktem, *Angry Nation*, 102–3.

2 *Hürriyet Daily News*, 5 November 1996.

3 Ibid.

4 Öktem, *Angry Nation*, 102.

5 *Hürriyet Daily News*, 5 November 1996.

6 *Today's Zaman*, 5 March 2004, and *Hürriyet Daily News*, 14 November 2006.

7 Ibid.

8 Quoted in *Milliyet*, 27 November 1996.

9 Quoted in *New York Times*, 31 December 1996.

10 *Hürriyet Daily News*, 6 December 1996.

11 *New York Times*, 31 December 1996.

12 AG2.

13 On Sincan, see Öktem, *Angry Nation*, 106.

14 See Gülalp, 'The Poverty of Democracy'.

15 'Turkey: The Western Study Group', UNHCR Document TUR38370.E (7 February 2002), online at (www.unhcr.org).

16 Gülalp, 'Political Islam', 40.

17 Sami Güçlü interview. I have been unable to date this meeting; in October, Turkey and Kyrgyzstan would sign an 'Eternal Friendship and Cooperation Agreement' outlining conditions for diplomatic and trade cooperation. *Hürriyet Daily News*, 25 October 1997.

18 Gülalp, 'Political Islam', 29.

19 Ibid., 27 n. 19.

20 Paris interview.

21 See, among other accounts, Eligür, *Mobilization*, 226–7.

22 Thus Zürcher, *Turkey*, 301, though charges were brought in terms of anti-secular rather than criminal activities.

23 Ibid., and see Eligür, *Mobilization*, 234.

24 Eligür, *Mobilization*, 228.

25 *New York Times*, 14 June 1997.

26 Eligür, *Mobilization*, 235.

27 Gülalp, 'Political Islam', 41.

28 Sami Güçlü interview.

29 Murat Mercan interview.

30 Beşir Atalay and Murat Mercan interviews.

31 *Hürriyet Daily News*, 21 July 1997. The case against Refah had been filed by prosecutor Vural Savaş back in May 1996, but was brought forward following Erbakan's resignation on 30 June 1997.

32 *Hürriyet Daily News*, 29 August 1997.

33 *Hürriyet Daily News*, 1 and 5 August, and 2 September 1997.

34 *Hürriyet Daily News*, 19 September 1997.

35 *Hürriyet Daily News*, 9 November 1997.

36 *Hürriyet Daily News*, 11 December 1997.

37 *Washington Post*, 20 December 1997.

38 *Hürriyet Daily News*, 11 November 1996.

39 *Hürriyet Daily News*, 10 October 1997.

40 *Washington Post*, 20 December 1997.

41 *Hürriyet Daily News*, 22 December 1997.

42 *Hürriyet Daily News*, 24 December 1997. The article attributes this statement to 'the young RPs', though the language and arguments suggest a press release prepared by the Political Research Centre.

43 Ibid.

44 Ibid.

45 Ibid.

46   Ibid.

47   *New York Times*, 17 January 1998.

48   *Hürriyet Daily News*, 25 April 1998.

49   Among numerous accounts, see Jenkins, 'Muslim Democrats', 52.

50   Beşir Atalay interview.

51   AG2.

52   *Hürriyet Daily News*, 24 December 1997.

53   *Hürriyet Daily News*, 16 January 1998.

54   Scott Peterson, 'Can Miniskirts and Veils Walk Amid Mosques?', *Christian Science Monitor*, 20 January 1998.

55   *Hürriyet Daily News*, 15 February 1998.

56   Cited Eligür, *Mobilization*, 162.

57   *Hürriyet Daily News*, 25 January 1998.

58   *Hürriyet Daily News*, 13 May 1998.

59   See Document 8000 (29 January 1998) and Motion 8002 (5 February 1998): see also Communication 8079 (21 April 1998), PACE website.

60   *Hürriyet Daily News*, 13 May 1998.

61   *Hürriyet Daily News*, 16 May 1998.

62   Nazlı Ilıcak was among journalists threatened by the National Security Council for publicly declaring that the 28 February coup-by-memorandum was illegal; see Öktem, *Angry Nation*, 108–9.

63   Ibid., 109.

64   *Hürriyet Daily News*, 11 March 1999.

65   *Hürriyet Daily News*, 11 October 1998.

66   *Hürriyet Daily News*, 28 February 1999.

67   AG4.

68   Murat Mercan interview.

69   Document 8183 (3 June 1998), PACE website.

70   AG4.

71   *Hürriyet Daily News*, 6 July 1998.

72   Document 1377 (25 June 1998), PACE website.

73   *Hürriyet Daily News*, 6 July 1998.

74   Ibid.

75   AG2.

76   Document 8212 (24 September 1998), PACE website.

77   Document 8300 (15 January 1999), with links to relevant previous documentation involving monitoring of human rights in Turkey, PACE website.

78   Document 8300 (15 January 1999), PACE website.

79   Koru, 'Preface', *One Column Ahead*, 9.

80   *Hürriyet Daily News*, 25 April 1999.

81   *Hürriyet Daily News*, 5 February 1999.

82   Translated in Eligür, *Mobilization*, 236, citing the Fazilet election programme, *Günışığında Türkiye*, 6.

83   *Hürriyet Daily News*, 11 March 1999.

84   Zürcher, *Turkey*, 303. Hakan Yavuz suggests that 'the outcome of the April 1999 elections can be viewed as the institutionalization of the politics of fear', since the two dominant parties 'both espoused a militant and particularistic version of nationalism that is hostile to Turkey's diverse ethnic and religious groups'. Since 28 February, according to this view, the military 'with the help of the major media cartels, successfully "convinced" part of the public of internal threats ... By concentrating all forces on hammering the pro-Islamic FP, the powerful military prepared the ground for the nationalistic takeover.' See Yavuz, *Islamic Political Identity*, 250–1.

85   *Hürriyet Daily News*, 24 April 1999.

86   *Hürriyet Daily News*, 25 April 1999.

87   Yavuz, *Islamic Political Identity*, 249.

88   Cited in Eligür, *Mobilization*, 240; and see 240–1 for statements by Recai Kutan.

89   *Hürriyet Daily News*, 9 May 1999.

90   *Hürriyet Daily News*, 24 May 1999.

91   Koru, 'A new beginning or an end?', *Yeni Şafak* (27 October 1999), rpt. in *One Column Ahead*, 70–3, this passage 71.

92   Murat Mercan interview.

93   *Hürriyet Daily News*, 27 May 1999.

94   *Hürriyet Daily News*, 28 July 1999.

95   *Hürriyet Daily News*, 30 July 1999.

96   *Hürriyet Daily News*, 31 July 1999.

97   '17 August 1999 Kocaeli Earthquake', Bosphorus University Earthquake Centre Report at ⟨www.eaee.boun.edu.tr/bulletins/v18n1/kocaeli.htm⟩.

98   *New York Times*, 27 August 1999.

99   Abdullah Gül, cited in *New York Times*, 27 August 1999.

100 Document 8492 (1 September 1999), PACE website.

101 Zürcher, *Turkey*, 315.

102 *Hürriyet Daily News*, 1 November 1999.

103 Koru, 'Guess who is crusading for democracy?' (12 November 1999), rpt. *One Column Ahead*, 86–9, this passage 86–7.

104 Ibid., 87–8.

105 *Hürriyet Daily News*, 13 December 1999.

106 *Hürriyet Daily News*, 12 March 2000.

107 Paris interview.

108 Hale and Özbudun, *Islamism*, 5, citing Dagi and Çalmuk, *Recep Tayyip Erdoğan*, 92–6.

109 *Hürriyet Daily News*, 16 May 2000.

110 Sami Güçlü interview.

111 *Hürriyet Daily News*, 18 December 2000.

112 Interview with Ayşe Böhürler, Istanbul, 4 November 2011; hereafter Ayşe Böhürler interview.

113 Ibid.

114 See, for example: Documents 8697 (4 April 2000), 8748 (23 May 2000), 8758 (7 June 2000) and 8804 (10 June 2000), PACE website. Both Armenia and Azerbaijan were admitted to the Council of Europe in early 2001.

115 Document 9066 (14 May 2001), revising the original version of 26 April, PACE website.

116 AG2.

117 Document 9032 (11 April 2001), PACE website.

118 Zürcher, *Turkey*, 314.

119 *Hürriyet Daily News*, 1 March 2001.

120 Zürcher, *Turkey*, 315.

121 *Hürriyet Daily News*, 1 March 2001.

122 Ibid.

123 Pope and Pope, *Turkey Unveiled*, 320–1.

124 Öniş, 'Political Economy', 209, and see Öniş, 'Domestic Politics'.

125 *Hürriyet Daily News*, 23 July 2001.

126 Ahmad, *Turkey*, 184.

127 Murat Mercan interview.

128 Hale and Özbudun, *Islamism*, 37.

5   AKP and the 'New Turkey': 2002 to 2007

1   On the visit of a US delegation that visited at the start of October, see *Hürriyet Daily News*, 2 October 2001.

2   Ahmad, *Turkey*, 177.

3   Ibid., 178.

4   See *Hürriyet Daily News*, 22 December 2001, 3 January 2002.

5   *Hürriyet Daily News*, 22 January 2002.

6   *Hürriyet Daily News*, 19 March 2002.

7   See Document 9032 (11 April 2001), PACE website.

8   *Hürriyet Daily News*, 19 March 2002.

9   Hayrünnisa Gül interview 2012.

10   Ibid.

11   Ibid.

12   Ibid.

13   Ibid.

14   Ibid.

15   Ibid.

16   *Hürriyet Daily News*, 25 January 2003.

17   *Hürriyet Daily News*, 2 February 2003.

18   *Hürriyet Daily News*, 30 January 2003.

19   *Hürriyet Daily News*, 2 February 2003.

20   Ayşe Böhürler interview.

21   Nursuna Memecan interview.

22   Ibid.

23   AG2.

24   *Hürriyet Daily News*, 16 August 2001.

25   See, for example, Ilnur Çevik in *Hürriyet Daily News*, 15 August 2001.

26   *Hürriyet Daily News*, 16 August 2001.

27   *Hürriyet Daily News*, 23 August 2001.

28   *Hürriyet Daily News*, 22 August 2001.

29   Kemal Balcı writing in *Hürriyet Daily News*, 20 August 2001.

30   Bülent Alırıza and Seda Çiftçi, *Turkey Update* (8 November 2002), Center for Strategic and International Studies website (www.csis.org).

31   Cited in Ahmad, *Turkey*, 183.

32   See Hale and Özbudun, *Islamism*, 55–62.

33   *New York Times*, 17 November 2002.

34   Pope, 'Breaking with the Past?', 18.

35   Mehmet Ali Birand, 'Gül Carries Prime Ministry Well', *Hürriyet Daily News*, 8 February 2003.

36   AG2.

37   *Hürriyet Daily News*, 11 September 2002.

38   *Hürriyet Daily News*, 25 November 2002.

39   AG2.

40   See *Hürriyet Daily News*, 10 and 21 December 2002.

41   AG2, and see *Hürriyet Daily News*, 14 November 2002.

42   *Hürriyet Daily News*, 21 January 2002.

43   Öniş, 'Political Economy', 215–16; and see Hale and Özbudun, *Islamism*, 99–114 for a more detailed assessment from a slightly later perspective.

44   Hale and Özbudun, *Islamism*, 109.

45   AG2.

46   Rubin, 'Green Money', citing an anonymous 'national security correspondent', Middle East Forum website (www.meforum.org).

47   Ahmad, *Turkey*, 182.

48   AG2.

49   Davutoğlu, *Stratejik Derinlik*.

50   See Davutoğlu, 'Türkiye merkez ülke olmalı', *Radikal* (26 February 2004), online at (www.radikal.com.tr).

51   Hale and Özbudun, *Islamism*, 120.

52   'Foreign Policy', AK Party Programme, section 6; online at (www.akparti.org.tr/english/akparti/parti-programme).

53   Hale and Özbudun, *Islamism*, 121.

54   Kanli and Eksi, 'Exclusive Interview', *Hürriyet Daily News*, 2 September 2002.

55   Ibid.

56   Paris interview.

57   Kanli and Eksi, 'Exclusive Interview'.

58   *Hürriyet Daily News*, 20 November 2002.

59   See Sedat Ergin, 'Bizden Saklananlar – IV', *Hürriyet*, 20 September 2003, and *Hürriyet Daily News*, 7 November 2002.

60   AG2.

61   Hale and Özbudun, *Islamism*, 83.

62   Ibid., 123.

63   Ibid., 123–4; see also Dodd, 'Constitutional Features', and Çelenk, 'The Restructuring of Turkey's Policy'.

64   Jenkins, 'Symbols', 195.

65   See Hale and Özbudun, *Islamism*, 130–2 for a detailed account of negotiations, starting with Paul Wolfowitz visiting Ankara on 3 December 2002.

66   Ibid., 129.

67   *Hürriyet Daily News*, 19 March 2002.

68   *Hürriyet Daily News*, 20 November 2002.

69   *Hürriyet Daily News*, 8 November 2002.

70   Hale and Özbudun, *Islamism*, 130.

71   On the summit, see *Hürriyet Daily News*, 20 December 2002; on Davutoğlu's foreign policies in this context, see Kardaş, 'Turkey and the Iraqi Crisis', esp. 318–21.

72   Hale and Özbudun, *Islamism*, 131–2.

73   Ibid., 131.

74   *Hürriyet Daily News*, 24 December 2002.

75   Hale and Özbudun, *Islamism*, 131.

76   See *Hürriyet Daily News*, 15 January 2003 and AG3.

77   Paris interview.

78   Kardaş, 'Turkey and the Iraqi Crisis', 325, 316.

79   *Hürriyet Daily News*, 25 January 2003.

80   *Hürriyet Daily News*, 4 February 2003.

81   Bülent Alırıza and Seda Çiftçi, *Turkey Update*, 14 February 2003, Center for Strategic and International Studies website (www.csis.org).

82   Hale and Özbudun, *Islamism*, 84.

83   Jenkins, 'Symbols', 205 n. 42.

84   AG2.

85   *Hürriyet Daily News*, 3 March 2003.

86   AG2.

87   Ibid.; Colin Powell, interview on NTV, 7 May 2003, cited in Hale and Özbudun, *Islamism*, 185 n. 68.

88   *Hürriyet Daily News*, 3 March 2003.

89   Hale and Özbudun, *Islamism*, 133.

90   *Hürriyet Daily News*, 29 January 2003.

91   Hale and Özbudun, *Islamism*, 133.

92   Ibid.

93   Rubin, 'Comedy of Errors'.

94   Ahmad, *Turkey*, 184.

95   See Mehmet Ali Birand, 'The new Turkey perception of Turkey', *Hürriyet Daily News*, 19 September 2003.

96   Ahmad, *Turkey*, 185.

97   Kardaş, 'Turkey and the Iraqi Crisis', 306.

98   Hale and Özbudun, *Islamism*, 130.

99   Pope, 'Breaking'. So too Jenny White writes of 'fierce internal battles over party leadership in 2001' with no direct evidence; *Islamist Mobilization*, 147.

100 *Hürriyet Daily News*, 25 December 2002.

101 *Hürriyet Daily News*, 18 November 2002.

102 Ayşe Böhürler interview.

103 Mehmet Ali Birand, 'Gül carries prime ministry well', *Hürriyet Daily News*, 8 February 2003.

104 Paris interview.

105 Öktem, *Angry Nation*, 122.

106 'Istanbul rocked by double bombing', BBC News online, 20 November 2003. Abdullah Gül was in Stockholm on 20 November; Dismorr, *Turkey Decoded*, 61.

107 *Hürriyet Daily News*, 24 April 2003.

108 Öktem, *Angry Nation*, 123.

109 European Commission Working Paper (6 October 2004), cited in Ümit Cizre, 'Introduction', to Cizre, ed., *Secular and Islamic Politics*, 7.

110 Cited by Yıldız, 'Problematizing the Intellectual', 57.

111 Öktem, *Angry Nation*, 136,

112 Carroll, 'Turkey's Justice and Development Party.'

113 AG2.

114 Ibid.

115 'Fundamental Rights and Freedoms', AK Party Programme section 2.1, online at AKP website (www.akparti.org.tr).

116 Öktem, *Angry Nation*, 135.

117 'Fundamental Rights and Freedoms', AK Party Programme, section 2.1.

118 Ayşe Böhürler interview.

119 'Women', AK Party Programme, section 5.7.

120 Cited in Öktem, *Angry Nation*, 135.

121 'Introduction', AK Party Programme, section 1.

122 Gül, speech delivered in Belgrade (8 April 2003), in Gül, *Horizons*, 591, 592.

123   Gül, *Horizons*, 594–8.

124   Gül, speech delivered in Tehran (28 May 2003), in Gül, *Horizons*, 528.

125   Ibid., 529.

126   Ibid., 528.

127   Paris interview.

128   Gül, *Horizons*, 528.

129   Ibid.

130   *Hürriyet Daily News*, 30 May 2003. Plans to hold a future OIC conference on women's rights in Turkey were proposed following that meeting, and eventually announced in 2005; the meeting eventually took place in March 2011; see *Hürriyet Daily News*, 8 December 2005.

131   *Hürriyet Daily News*, 12 June 2003.

132   Paris interview.

133   Gül, speech delivered in London (3 July 2003), in *Horizons*, 31, 32–3.

134   Gül, speech delivered in Washington, DC (23 July 2003), in *Horizons*, 404–5.

135   Gül, speech delivered in Washington, DC (25 July 2003), in *Horizons*, 40–1.

136   Ibid.

137   Gül, speeches delivered in New York (22 and 24 September 2003), in *Horizons*, 407–9 and 410–13.

138   Gül, speech delivered in New York (24 September 2003), in *Horizons*, 43.

139   Gül, 'Strategic Interests of Turkey and US–Turkish Relations', speech delivered in New York (27 September 2003), in *Horizons*, 415, 416.

140   Duran, 'JDP and Foreign Policy', 290.

141   Gül, *Horizons*, 416, 417.

142   William Safire, 'The Turkish Card', *New York Times*, 24 September 2003.

143   Gül, speech to the 'International Conference of Islamic Civil Society' in Istanbul (1 May 2005), in Gül, *Horizons*, 345; the Turkish original appears in Gül, *Horizons*, 562–7.

144   *Hürriyet Daily News*, 2 March 2005.

145   *Hürriyet Daily News*, 17 March 2005.

146   See, for example, Dismorr, *Turkey Decoded*, 177–8, on 'genuine efforts' by Erdoğan and Gül to solve 'the Israel–Palestine conflict'.

147   Gül, *Horizons*, 416.

148   *Hürriyet Daily News*, 6 January 2005.

149   *Hürriyet Daily News*, 10 February 2005.

150   Alon Liel, 'Turkish–Israeli Relations: Is the Story Ending?', the 2013 John Martin lecture, Turkish Area Study Group, delivered at the Brunei Gallery, SOAS, London, 22 February 2013. Liel reported that Turkey was engaged in 'secret talks' with Syria during the period February 2007 until November 2007, news of which was 'exposed' in May 2008, causing a cooling in relations with Israel. According to Liel, Israel's invasion of Gaza in December 2008 ended a golden age of Turkish–Israeli relations that Gül had brought about.

151   Gül, speech delivered in London (3 July 2003), in *Horizons*, 33.

152 For a contemporary analysis of the effect of the Istanbul bombings on EU views of Turkey, see Öğüzlü, 'Changing Dynamics', 101.

153 Gül, 'Address to OIC Business Forum', delivered in Kuala Lumpur (15 October 2003), in *Horizons*, 540, 542.

154 Gül, 'Finding Common Grounds in Diversity', speech delivered in Jeddah (11 February 2006), in *Horizons*, 570.

155 Gül, 'Islam and the Twenty-First Century', speech delivered at King Abdul-Aziz University, Jeddah (12 February 2006), in *Horizons*, 574.

156 Rice, *No Higher Honour*, 330.

157 Ibid., 278.

158 Öktem, *Angry Nation*, 125.

159 Ibid., 149.

160 AG2.

161 Zerin Elci, Reuters Report (28 December 2005), courtesy of David Barchard.

162 Öktem, *Angry Nation*, 141.

163 The bombers were eventually released on appeal and the case was transferred to a military court; see ibid., 142.

164 Ibid., 136.

165 *Today's Zaman*, 30 December 2006.

166 Öktem, *Angry Nation*, 150.

167 On the early disappointment of conservative Muslims, see Duran, 'JDP and Foreign Policy', 299.

168 Öktem, *Angry Nation*, 151; Gül was in Paris on UN business at the time and not at the march that day, as Öktem reports.

169 Cited in European Stabilization Initiative, 'Turkey's Dark Side', 3.

170 Hale and Özbudun, *Islamism*, 65.

171 ESI, *Turkey's Dark Side*, 5.

172 See the summary of international responses, *Hürriyet Daily News*, 25 April 2007.

173 Lagendijk, 'Turkey's Accession', 174.

174 See Öktem, *Angry Nation*, 152–4 and *Hürriyet Daily News* reports, 27–30 April 2007.

175 On the *Nokta* affair, see Hale and Özbudun, *Islamism*, 88–9.

176 See ESI, *Turkey's Dark Side*, 5.

177 Öktem, *Angry Nation*, 153.

178 Ibid., 155.

179 Swedish ambassador Ann Dismorr observes: 'surprisingly, the pro-Kurdish DTP abstained from supporting Gül, disappointing many moderate Kurds and fuelling speculation that it was taking instructions from the jailed PKK leader Öcalan', *Turkey Decoded*, 222.

180 As reported internationally; see BBC News online, 25 July 2007.

181 BBC News online, 29 August 2007.

182 Hale and Özbudun, *Islamism*, 40.

183   BBC News online, 28 July 2007.

184   Yavuz, 'Introduction', *Emergence*, 15.

185   See, for example, the thorough critique in Lagendijk, 'Turkey's Accession'.

186   Öğüzlü, 'Changing Dynamics', 104; and see Kardaş, 'Turkey and the Iraqi Crisis', 306, and Jenkins, 'Symbols', 197.

187   Yıldırım, 'Labor Pains', 253–4.

188   Graham Fuller writing in 2004, cited by Duran, 'JDP and Foreign Policy', 302 n. 36.

189   Hale, 'Christian Democracy', 83.

6   Presidency

1   *New York Times*, 29 August 2007; BBC News online, 28 August 2007.

2   See Mehmet Ali Birand's op-ed columns in *Hürriyet Daily News*, esp. 9, 15, 29, 30 August 2007. In anticipation of the elections, Belge avowed his preference for Gül over Erdoğan for the presidency and held that AKP was the only party that 'belongs to civil society'. See *Radikal* website, 27 April 2007 and NTV/MSNBC website, 19 July 2007.

3   Shafak, 'Turkey's Soul Unveiled', BBC News online, 29 August 2011.

4   BBC News online, 28 August 2007.

5   ESI, *Turkey's Dark Side*, 1.

6   Hayrünnisa Gül interview 2012.

7   Nursuna Memecan interview.

8   Ayşe Böhürler interview.

9   Nursuna Memecan interview.

10   *Hürriyet Daily News*, 24 August 2007.

11   *Hürriyet Daily News*, 1 September 2007.

12   *Hürriyet Daily News*, 5 and 6 September 2007.

13   Hayrünnisa Gül interview 2012.

14   *Hürriyet Daily News*, 30 August 2007.

15   Interview with Hayrünnisa Gül, Ankara Residence, 25 April 2013; hereafter Hayrünnisa Gül interview 2013.

16   Nursuna Memecan interview.

17   *Hürriyet Daily News*, 23 August 2007.

18   Hayrünnisa Gül interview 2012.

19   BBC News online, 21 August 2007, and Taşkın, *11 Başkomutan*, 249.

20   Taşkın, *11 Başkomutan*, 249–50.

21   'I never worked with Atıl Bey', Hayrünnisa Gül interview 2013.

22   Ibid.

23   Nursuna Memecan interview.

24   Hayrünnisa Gül interview 2012.

25   In January 2012, a case was opened against Sarah Ferguson in an Ankara court on

charges of entering the country under false pretences; see *Daily Mail* website (www. dailymail.co.uk), 13 January 2012.

26 Hayrünnisa Gül interview 2012.

27 Paris interview.

28 Hale and Özbudun, *Islamism*, 63.

29 Ibid., 65.

30 Ibid., 66.

31 Ibid., 66.

32 Ibid., 67.

33 Hale, *Turkish Foreign Policy*, 254.

34 See 'Visits', Presidency website.

35 Abdullah Gül, address to United Nations, 'Turkey: Emerging Donor Country', *Hürriyet Daily News*, 25 September 2008.

36 See, for example, Gül's speech to the UN, *Hürriyet Daily News*, 25 September 2008.

37 AG2.

38 Hale and Özbudun, *Islamism*, 139.

39 *New York Times*, 18 April 2001.

40 Hale and Özbudun, *Islamism*, 139.

41 Elif Shafak, 'In Istanbul, a Crack in the Wall of Denial', *Washington Post*, 25 September 2005.

42 *New York Times*, 17 October 2007.

43 See, for example, 'Gül in landmark visit to Armenia', BBC News online, 6 September 2008. For sample coverage of the initial excitement in the Armenian diaspora media see: 'US Keen on Gül Accepting Sarkisian Soccer Invitation', 14 July 2008, Asbarez Armenian News website (http://Asbarez.com); and 'Armenia, Turkey "in Secret Talks"', 21 July 2008, at European Armenian Federation website (http://eafjd.eu).

44 Paris interview.

45 Tarek Hohberg, 'When Diplomats Score: The Role of Football in the Turkish-Armenian Rapprochement', at Heinrich Böll Foundation website (http://georgien.boell-net. de). See also Serzh Sarkisian, 'We Are Ready to Talk to Turkey', *Wall Street Journal*, 9 July 2008, reprinted on the Asbarez website (asbarez.com/57719/sarkisian-discusses-turkey-relations-in-wall-street-journal).

46 Paris interview.

47 Murat Yetkin, 'Restoring Trust with Azerbaijan', first published in Turkish in *Radikal*, 10 September 2008, here translated at (www.turkishpress.com/news.asp?id=251391). Yetkin's original interview with Sarkisian appeared in *Radikal*, 28 August 2008. An English translation was published in the *Azerbaijan Development Bulletin* of the United Nations Development Programme at (www.un-az.org/undp/bulnews63).

48 Yetkin, 'Restoring Trust'.

49 AG2.

50 *Hürriyet Daily News*, 31 August 2009.

51   Hale and Özbudun, *Islamism*, 139.

52   AG2.

53   Ibid.

54   Presidency website and interview with anonymous European diplomat, Brussels, 12 December 2011.

55   Quotations are from Gül's defence of Turkey's position before the Council on Foreign Relations delivered in New York on 24 September 2010; Presidency website. Turkey's position briefly set back relations with President Obama; see Hale, *Turkish Foreign Policy*, 171, and Finkel, *Turkey*, 83–4.

56   Key phrases from a summary translation of Abdullah Gül's letter of 4 August 2011 to President Bashar al-Assad provided by Yusuf Müftüoğlu, Ankara, 23 April 2013.

57   In Yavuz, ed., *Emergence*, 342.

58   Ibid., 341.

59   Öktem's phrase, *Angry Nation*, 183.

60   Hale, *Turkish Foreign Policy*, 150.

61   See references cited throughout Lombardi, 'Turkey and Israel'.

62   Hale, *Turkish Foreign Policy*, 151.

63   Öktem, *Angry Nation*, 177.

64   *Hürriyet Daily News*, 4 June 2010.

65   'H.E. President Gül's Statement on the Attack on the Humanitarian Aid Flotilla to Gaza', 31 May 2010, Presidency website.

66   *Hürriyet Daily News*, 9 June 2010.

67   See Hale, *Turkish Foreign Policy*, 231–2.

68   'H.E. President Gul's Statement on the Attack on the Humanitarian Aid Flotilla to Gaza', 31 May 2010, Presidency website. 'President Gül Pronounces the Palmer Report as Void', *Hürriyet Daily News*, 9 June 2010; Davutoğlu, interview in *Today's Zaman*, 1 September 2011.

69   Ben Lombardi, a strategic analyst for the Canadian government, curiously writes that 'when Turkish president Abdullah Gül declared the Palmer Report "null and void" and stated that his country "will not only protect its own rights but also those of all people in need"' he was making a veiled reference to Turkey's intention to continue to pursue a larger regional profile', 'Turkey and Israel', 14. There was of course nothing 'veiled' about Gül's remarks, or in Turkey's ambitions for a larger regional profile.

70   *New York Times*, 2 September 2011.

71   *Washington Post*, 22 March 2013.

72   *Today's Zaman*, 28 June 2013.

73   AG2.

74   Öktem, *Angry Nation*, 159–60.

75   *Today's Zaman*, 10 July 2008.

76   *Hürriyet Daily News*, 11 July 2008.

77   *Hürriyet Daily News*, 10 January 2009.

78   Öktem, *Angry Nation*, 164–5.

79   *Hürriyet Daily News*, 25 July 2009.

80   *Hürriyet Daily News*, 29 July 2009.

81   *Hürriyet Daily News*, 30 September 2009.

82   *Hürriyet Daily News*, 29 July 2009.

83   Öktem, *Angry Nation*, 169.

84   'Kurds-Barzani-KCK-Amnesty', 2 June 2009, online at (http://gilgamish.org/printarticle.php?id=18782), accessed 5 July 2013.

85   Presidency website.

86   Interview with Ayşe Kadioğlu, Şişli, Istanbul, 19 November 2011.

87   *Hürriyet Daily News*, 30 and 31 May 2010, and 18 June 2010.

88   *Hürriyet Daily News*, 20 July 2011.

89   14 July 2011, Presidency website.

90   *Hürriyet Daily News*, 14 and 15 July 2011, 18 August 2011.

91   See, for example, speeches made in Pakistan (December 2007), to the OIC (13 March 2008), the D-B (7 August 2010), and in Indonesia (6 April 2011); Presidency website.

92   On Obama's visit, see Finkel, *Turkey*, 83.

93   For honorary doctorates and honours, see Presidency website.

94   AG6.

95   Ibid.

96   Queen Elizabeth, Christmas Broadcast 1957, online at (www.royal.gov.uk/ImagesandBroadcasts/TheQueensChristmasBroadcasts).

97   'Speech by H.E. Abdullah Gül President of the Republic of Turkey, on the Occasion of the Dinner Hosted in Honour of Her Majesty Elizabeth II the Queen of the United Kingdom and His Royal Highness the Duke of Edinburgh', 13 May 2008, Presidency website.

98   Madame Gül hosted heads of state from Syria, North Cyprus and Sudan in 2007, and José Barroso representing the EU in April 2008; Presidency website.

99   Queen Elizabeth's speech, 8 November 2010; Chatham House website (www.chathamhouse.org).

100 Gül's acceptance speech, 8 November 2010; Chatham House website.

101 Gül, 'International System, Europe and Turkey in the First Quarter of the 21st Century', 8 November 2010; Presidency website.

102 Gül, 'The Islamic World, Democracy and Development', Oxford Centre for Islamic Studies, 8 November 2010; Presidency website.

103 *Daily Mail* website (www.dailymail.co.uk), 23 November 2011.

104 'President Abdullah Gül of Turkey delivers our inaugural Annual Address', Wilton Park website (www.wiltonpark.org), 23 November 2011.

105 See reports on the state visit 22 to 24 November 2011 at (www.royal.gov.uk) and Hayrünnisa's page, Presidency website.

106 Al Jazeera English website, 20 June 2010.

107 Yavuz writes of Erdoğan: 'Erdoğan is not a thinker but rather a pragmatic politician.

This lack of introspectiveness may be responsible for his apparent lack of general vision … He is always in tune with the popular will to figure out what his views ought to be.' *Secularism*, 134.

108 *Hürriyet Daily News,* 31 December 2009.

109 AG6. In this 2013 interview, Gül quoted this formula, which had first appeared in a 1997 press release; see chapter 4 n 42.

110 Cornell, 'Diverging Paths'.

111 See *Hürriyet Daily News,* 25 September 2012.

112 *Hürriyet Daily News,* 26 September 2012.

113 Eligur, *Mobilization*, 261–2.

114 Ibid., 263, and see 271 on Gül's appointment of university rectors who favour removing the headscarf ban.

115 Criss, 'Dismantling Turkey', 46–7.

116 Hale, *Turkish Foreign Policy*, 257.

117 Ibid., 258.

118 Öktem, *Angry Nation*, 128.

119 Hale and Özbudun, *Islamism*, 15.

120 Hale, *Turkish Foreign Policy*, 150.

121 Wisdom School website (www.wisdomschool.org.uk).

122 'About Us', Axis Educational Trust website (http://axiseducationaltrust.org).

123 See 'Foreign Visits' on the Presidency website.

124 Interview with Ece Temelkuran, Istanbul, 21 November 2011. Video clips of Gül's two visits are available on the 'Foreign Visits' links on the Presidency website.

125 Zaman, 'Looming Power Struggle'.

126 Various blogsites and Poyraz, *Musa'nin Gül'ü.*

127 Zaman, 'Looming Power Struggle'.

128 Ibid.

129 Gül, 'Crisis and Transformation'.

130 'Speeches', Presidency website.

131 *New York Times,* 30 July 2011.

132 Finkel, 'Gül Unleashed', *New York Times* website, 19 October 2012.

133 Alaadin Paksoy, personal email, 8 July 2013.

134 Cornell, 'Diverging Paths'.

135 The story appeared in Orhan Bursalı, 'Gül'den Parti Resti', *Cumhuriyet,* 11 March 2013.

136 Mehmet Ali Dikerdem, personal email, 10 June 2012.

137 See Hale and Özbudun, *Islamism,* xxi, 63, 120.

138 Beşir Atalay interview.

139 'Speeches', Presidency website.

140 Ibid.

141 Ibid. Rice's discussion with Gül is posted on YouTube.

Epilogue

1   Noam Chomsky is reported to have called himself a '*çapulcu*' in support of the protests; *Hürriyet Daily News*, 6 June 2013.

2   Hale, *Turkish Foreign Policy*, 170, 258.

3   *Hürriyet Daily News*, 11 March 2013.

4   *Hürriyet Daily News*, 28 March and 25 April 2013.

5   *Hürriyet Daily News*, 8 May 2013.

6   *Hürriyet Daily News*, 1 June 2013.

7   Ibid.

8   *Hürriyet Daily News*, 3 June 2012.

9   *New York Times*, 3 June 2013.

10   *Hürriyet Daily News*, 7 June 2013.

11   Ibid.

12   *Hürriyet Daily News*, 3 June 2013.

13   'Timeline of Gezi Park Protests', *Hürriyet Daily News*, 6 June 2013.

14   *New York Times*, 3 June 2013.

15   Ibid.

16   *Hürriyet Daily News*, 3 June 2013.

17   *Hürriyet Daily News*, 4 June 2013.

18   See Al Jazeera English website, 24 May 2013, and *Hürriyet Daily News*, 5 June 2013.

19   *Hürriyet Daily News*, 10 June 2013.

20   *Hürriyet Daily News*, 6 June 2013.

21   *Hürriyet Daily News*, 7 June 2013.

22   Ibid.

23   Hugh Pope, 'Erdoğan Can Win by Engaging Turkey's Park Protesters', International Crisis group website (www.crisisgroup.org), 7 June 2013.

24   Ibid.

25   Reports circulate in the Turkish public media that billionaire Rahmi Koç once claimed that Erdoğan had millions of dollars in a Swiss account; in Ankara and Istanbul and on the blogosphere, hostile rumours circulate of his involvement in dubious practices involving state tenders for construction contracts. One informed Turkish journalist laughed and told me that while everyone says Erdoğan wants money and to be personally rich, they also say that Gül wants to be comfortable and for everyone to have a better standard of living in Turkey. Interview with an anonymous Turkish journalist, Istanbul, 4 April 2013. The next day, a different but equally informed journalist told me that there was a moment when there were tales, at least, circulating in Ankara hotel lobbies of a price list for being given government construction contracts; Istanbul, 5 April 2013.

26   *Financial Times*, 6 June 2013; see also *New York Times*, 6 June 2013.

27   Pope, 'Erdoğan Can Win'.

28   Ibid.

29   *Hürriyet Daily News*, 4 June 2013.

30   *Hürriyet Daily News*, 15 June 2013.

31   Interview with Abdullah Gül, Çankaya, 23 April 2013, hereafter AG5.

32   On the Ilısu project and Hasankeyf, see 'Damocracy', Doğa website (www.dogadernegi. net).

33   See, for example, Andrew Finkel, 'The Curse of Atatürk', *New York Times* website, 5 April 2013.

34   AG5.

35   Hitti, *Siyasi ve Kültürel Islam Tarihi*, trans. Salih Tuğ.

36   *Hürriyet Daily News*, 18 December 2013.

37   *Hürriyet Daily News*, 1 January 2014.

38   *Hürriyet Daily News*, 9, 14, 18 January 2014.

39   Personal email from Ambassador Sadik Arslan and Yusuf Müftüoğlu, 22 March 2014.

40   Ibid.

41   *Hürriyet Daily News*, 27 February 2014.

42   'Turkey's Internet Crackdown', *New York Times*, website, 21 February 2014.

43   *Hürriyet Daily News*, 24 February 2014.

44   *Hürriyet Daily News*, 25 February 2014.

45   *Hürriyet Daily News*, 7 March 2014.

46   *Hürriyet Daily News*, 21 March 2014.

47   'Turkish PM Erdoğan's post-election "balcony speech"', *Hürriyet Daily News*, 31 March 2014.

48   *Hürriyet Daily News*, 31 March 2014.

49   *New York Times*, 31 March 2014.

50   Yavuz, *Secularism*, 137.

51   Pope and Pope, *Turkey Unveiled*, illustration 12.

52   Yavuz, *Secularism*, 118.

WORKS CITED

Interviews

Anonymous Turkish journalists, Istanbul, 4 and 5 April 2013.

Anonymous former Grey Wolf, Nevşehir, 19 April 2012.

Anonymous European diplomat, Brussels, 12 December 2011.

Anonymous Turkish diplomat, Paris, 14 November 2011.

Beşir Atalay, Çankaya, 25 April 2013.

Ayşe Böhürler, Istanbul, 4 November 2011.

Mustafa Boydak, Kayseri, 27 November 2011.

Sami Güçlü, Çankaya, 1 November 2011.

Abdullah Gül, Tarabya Residence, 3 November 2011 (AG1).

Abdullah Gül, Tarabya Residence, 3 November 2011 (AG2).

Abdullah Gül, Çankaya, 3 December 2011 (AG3).

Abdullah Gül, Çankaya, 19 April 2012 (AG4).

Abdullah Gül, Çankaya, 23 April 2013 (AG5).

Abdullah Gül, Tarabya Residence, 17 August 2013 (AG6).

Hayrünnisa Gül, Ankara Residence, 4 April 2012.

Hayrünnisa Gül, Ankara Residence, 25 April 2013.

Macit Gül, Kayseri, 28 November 2011.

Şükrü Karatepe, Çankaya, 2 April 2012.

Ayşe Kadioğlu, Şişli, Istanbul, 19 November 2011.

Mesude Nursuna Memecan, Meclis, Ankara, 18 October 2011.

Murat Mercan, Balgat, Ankara, 17 October 2011.

Nurşen Özdamar, Kayseri, 28 November 2011.

Mehmet Özhaseki, Kayseri, 28 November 2011.

Ece Temelkuran, Istanbul, 21 November 2011.

Mehmet Tekelioğlu, Meclis, Ankara, 19 October 2011.

Bekir Yıldız, Kayseri, 28 November 2011.

Turkish-language newspapers, TV and news magazine websites

Aksiyon website: www.aksiyon.com.tr

Cumhuriyet website: www.cumhuriyet.com.tr

Hürriyet website: www.hurriyet.com.tr

Kayseri Haber website: www.kayserihaber.com.tr

Milliyet Haber website: www.millyet.com.tr

NTV/MSNBC website: www.ntvmsnbc.com

Radikal website: www.radikal.com.tr

Yeni Şafak website: http://yenisafak.com.tr

Zaman website: www.zaman.com.tr

English-language newspapers, TV and news magazine websites

Aljazeera English website: www.aljazeera.com

Asbarez Armenian News website: http://Asbarez.com

Azerbaijan Development Bulletin of the United Nations Development Programme website: www.un-az.org

BBC News online: http://www.bbc.co.uk/news

Businessweek website: http://www.businessweek.com

Center for Strategic and International Studies website: www.csis.org

Christian Science Monitor website: www.cs.monitor.com

Daily Mail website: www.dailymail.co.uk

Guardian website: www.guardian.co.uk

Hürriyet Daily News (*The Turkish Daily News* until December 2008) website: www.hurriyetdailynews.com

International Herald Tribune website: global.nytimes.com/?iht

New York Times website: www.nytimes.com

Today's Zaman website: www.todayszaman.com

Washington Post website: www.washingtonpost.com

World Bulletin website: www.worldbulletin.net

Other websites

Axis Educational Trust website: http://axiseducationaltrust.org

The British Monarchy website: www.royal.gov.uk

Center for Strategic and International Studies website: www.csis.org

Chatham House website: www.chathamhouse.org

D-8 Organization for Economic Cooperation website: www.developing8.org

Doğa website: www.dogadernegi.net

European Armenian Federation for Justice and Democracy website: http://eafjd.eu

European Court of Human Rights website: www.echr.coe.int

European Court of Human Rights document database: hudoc.echr.coe.int/sites/eng

Federation of Student Islamic Societies website: www.fosis.org.uk

Foundation of Kayseri Surp Krikor Lusavoriç Armenian Church website: www.kayserikilisesi.org/en/

Heinrich Böll Foundation, South Caucasus, website at: http://georgien.boell-net.de

Hansard 1803–2005 (official reports of debates in UK parliament) website: http://hansard.millbanksystems.com

Koma Civaken Kurdistan (KCK) website: http://gilgamish.org

London-Weather website: www.london-weather.eu

Middle East Forum website: www.meforum.org

Middle East Media Research Institute website: http://memri.org

Milli Türk Talebe Birliği (National Turkish Student Association) website: www.mttb.org.tr

Ofsted website: www.ofsted.gov.uk

Online Encyclopedia of Mass Violence website: www.massviolence.org

Organisation of Islamic Cooperation website: www.oic-oci.org/home.asp

Orhan Kemal website: http://orhankemal.org

Net Marine (Unofficial French Navy) website: www.netmarine.net/eng

Parliamentary Assembly of the Council of Europe (PACE) website: assembly.coe.int/defaultE.asp

Presidency of the Republic of Turkey website: www.tccb.gov.tr

TurkishPress.com website: www.turkishpress.com

Türkiye Finans website: http://www.turkiyefinans.com.tr

Türkiye Milli Kültür Vakfi (Turkish National Culture Foundation) website: www.tmkv.org.tr

United Nations Development Programme in Azerbaijan website: www.az.undp.org/azerbaijan/en/home.html

United Nations High Commissioner for Refugees website: www.unhcr.org

United Nations International Criminal Tribunal for Yugoslavia website: http://www.icty.org

Wilton Park website: www.wiltonpark.org

Wisdom School website: www.wisdomschool.org.uk

Published books and articles

Açikgöz, Namik. 'Kelimlerin Büyüsü ve 24 Aralik Seçimleri', *Türkiye Günlüğü* 38 (1996), 45–7.

Ağaoğulları, Mehmet Ali. 'The Ultranationalist Right', in Schick and Tonak, eds, *Turkey In Transition*, 177–217.

Ahiska, Meltem. *Occidentalism in Turkey: Questions of Modernity and National Identity in Turkish Radio Broadcasting*. London: I. B. Tauris, 2010.

Ahmad, Feroz. *The Making of Modern Turkey*. London: Routledge, 1993.

Ahmad, Feroz. *Turkey: The Quest for Identity*. 2003; rpt. Oxford: Oneworld, 2005.

Ahmad, Feroz. *The Turkish Experiment in Democracy: 1950–1975*. Boulder, CO: Westview, 1977.

AK Parti Programme, at: www.akparti.org.tr/english/akparti/parti-programme

Akcay, Cevdat. 'The Turkish Banking Sector Two Years after the Crisis', in Öniş and Rubin, eds, *The Turkish Economy,* 169–87.

Akşin, Sina. *Turkey: From Empire to Revolutionary Republic: The Emergence of the Turkish Nation from 1789 to the Present.* Trans. Dexter Mursaloğlu. London: Hurst, 2007.

Alper, C. Emre and Ziya Öniş, 'Financial Globalization, the Democratic Deficit, and Recurrent Crises in Emerging Markets: The Turkish Experience in the Aftermath of Capital Account Liberalization', *Emerging Markets Finance and Trade* 39: 3 (May–June 2003), 5–26.

Altunbaş, Yener, Alper Kara and Özlem Oğlu. *Turkish Banking: Banking Under Political Instability and Chronic High Inflation.* Basingstoke: PalgraveMacmillan, 2009.

Amnesty International. *Turkey: Human Rights Denied.* London: Amnesty International, 1988.

Apaydın, Orhan. *Kim Öldürüyor, Niçin Öldürüyor* ['Who is Killing, and Why']. Istanbul: Çağdaş Yayınları, 1978.

Arınır, Turgan and Sırrı Öztürk. *Işçi Sınıfı, Sendikalar, ve 15-16 Haziran* ['The Working Class, the Unions, and the 15–16 June']. Istanbul: Sorun Yayınları, 1976.

Barkey, Henri J. 'Turkey and the Great Powers', in Kerslake, Öktem and Robins, eds, *Turkey's Engagement,* 239–57.

Baskan, Filiz. 'The Political Economy of Islamic Finance in Turkey: The Role of Fethullah Gülen and Asya Finans', in Henry and Clement, eds, *Politics of Islamic Finance,* 216–39.

Bayhan, Fatih. *Kayseri'den Cankaya Köşkü'ne Abdullah Gül.* Istanbul: Pegasus, 2007.

Bezirci, Asim. *Orhan Kemal: Hayat, Sanat Analyisi, Hikayeleri, Romanlari, Oyunlari, Raportajlari, Anilari.* Ankara: Tekin, 1984.

Birand, Mehmet Ali. *The Generals' Coup in Turkey. An Inside Story of 12 September 1980.* Trans. Mehmet Ali Dikerdem. London: Brassey's, 1987.

Bosphorus University Earthquake Centre Report at: www.eaee.boun.edu.tr/bulletins/v18n1/kocaeli.htm

Bulaç, Ali. *Modern Ulus Devlet.* Istanbul: Iz, 1995.

Calvert, John. *Sayyid Qutb and the Origins of Radical Islam.* London: Hurst, 2010.

Carroll, Thomas Patrick. 'Turkey's Justice and Development Party: A Model for Democratic Islam?' *Middle East Forum* 6: 6–7 (June/July 2004), at (www.meforum.org).

Çelenk, Ayşe Aslıhan. 'The Restructuring of Turkey's Policy towards Cyprus: The Justice and Development Party's Struggle for Power', *Turkish Studies* 8: 3 (2007) 349–63.

Çetin, Tamer and Fuat Oğuz, eds, *Regulation and Competition in the Turkish Banking and Financial Markets.* New York: Nova, 2012.

Cizre, Ümit, ed. *Secular and Islamic Politics in Turkey: The Making of the Justice and Development Party.* London: Routledge, 2008.

Clark, Bruce. *Twice a Stranger: How Mass Expulsion Forged Modern Greece and Turkey.* London: Granta, 2006.

Copeaux, Etienne. *Türk Tarihi Tezinden Türk-Islam Sentezine.* Istanbul: Tarih Vakfı, 1998.

Cornell, Svante E. 'The Diverging Paths of Abdullah Gül and Tayyip Erdoğan', *Turkey Analyst* 6: 8 (24 April 2013) at (www.turkeyanalyst.org).

Criss, Nur Bilge. 'Dismantling Turkey: The Will of the People?' in Yeşilada and Rubin, eds, *Islamization*, 43–56.

Dagi, Ruşen and Fehmi Çalmuk. *Recep Tayyip Erdoğan: Bir Donusumun Oykusu* ['The Story of a Transformation']. Istanbul: Metis, 2001.

Davis, E. J. *Life in Asiatic Turkey. A Journal of Travel*. London: Stanford, 1879.

Davutoğlu, Ahmet. *Stratejik Derinlik: Türkiye'nin Uluslararası Konumu* ['Strategic Depth: Turkey's International Position']. Istanbul: Küre Yayınları, 2001.

Davutoğlu, Ahmet. 'Türkiye merkez ülke olmalı', *Radikal*, 26 February 2004, at (www.radikal.com.tr).

Diamond, Larry, ed. *Political Culture and Democracy in Developing Countries*. Boulder, CO: Reiner, 1993.

Dodd, Clement. 'Constitutional Features of the UN Plan for Cyprus', *Turkish Studies* 6: 1 (2005), 39–51.

Dodd, Clement. *The History and Politics of the Cyprus Conflict*. Basingstoke: PalgraveMacmillan, 2010.

Dismorr, Ann. *Turkey Decoded*. London: Saqi, 2008.

Dündar, Can. 'Bir Gül Portresi', *Milliyet* (29–31 August 2007); reissued at (www.candundar.com.tr/_old/index.php?Did=5289).

Dunmore, Spencer. *Lost Subs: From the Huntley to the Kursk*. Oxford: Perseus, 2002.

Duran, Burhanettin. 'JDP and Foreign Policy as an Agent of Transformation', in Yavuz, ed., *Emergence*, 281–305.

Eligür, Banu. *The Mobilization of Political Islam in Turkey*. Cambridge: Cambridge University Press, 2010.

Erbakan, Necmettin. *Adil Ekonomik Düzen*. Ankara: Refah Partisi, 1991.

Erbakan, Necmettin. *Milli Görüş*. Istanbul: Dergah Yayınları, 1975.

Ergil, Doğu. *Türkiye'de Terör ve Şiddet: Yapısal ve Kültürel Kaynakları*. Ankara: Turhan Kitabevi, 1980.

Eroğul, Cem. *Demokrat Parti (Tarihi ve Ideolojisi)*. Ankara: Ankara Universitesi Siyasel Bilgiler Fakültesi Yayınları, 1970.

Eroğul, Cem. 'The Establishment of Multiparty Rule: 1945–71'. Trans. Rezan Benatar and Irvin Schick, in Schick and Tonak, eds, *Turkey in Transition*, 101–43.

European Stabilization Initiative. *Islamic Calvinists: Change and Conservatism in Central Anatolia* (Berlin and Istanbul: ESI, 2005) at (www.esiweb.org/pdf/esi_document_id_69.pdf).

European Stabilization Initiative. *Turkey's Dark Side: Party Closures, Conspiracies and the Future of Democracy* (Berlin and Istanbul: ESI, 2008), at (www.esiweb.org/pdf/esi_document_id_104.pdf).

Faroqhi, Suraiya. *Towns and Townsmen of Ottoman Anatolia, 1520–1650*. Cambridge: Cambridge University Press, 1984.

Fazilet Partisi. *Günışığında Türkiye* ['Turkey in Daylight']. Ankara: Fazilet Partisi, 1999.

Findley, Carter Vaughn. *Turkey, Islam, Nationalism, and Modernity: A History, 1789–2007.* New Haven: Yale University Press, 2010.

Finkel, Andrew. 'The Curse of Ataturk', *New York Times* website, 5 April 2013.

Finkel, Andrew. 'Gül Unleashed', *New York Times* website, 19 October 2012.

Finkel, Andrew. *Turkey: What Everyone Needs to Know.* New York: Oxford University Press, 2012.

Finkel, Caroline, Kate Clow, with Donna Landry. *The Evliya Çelebi Way: Turkey's First Long-Distance Walking and Riding Route.* [Istanbul]: Upcountry, 2011.

Giritli, Ismet. 'Turkey since the 1965 Elections', *Middle East Journal*, 23: 3 (Summer 1969), 351–63.

Gül, Abdullah. *Horizons of Turkish Foreign Policy in the New Century.* Ankara: Government Foreign Office, 2007.

Gül, Abdullah. Speech to the 'International Conference of Islamic Civil Society Organizations: In Search of a New Vision in a Changing World', Istanbul (1 May 2005), in Yavuz, ed., *Emergence*, 341–5.

Gül, Abdullah. 'Crisis and Transformation', Project Syndicate website (www.project-syndicate. org), 31 December 2012; Turkish translation on Presidency website.

Gülalp, Haldun. 'Globalization and Political Islam: The Social Bases of Turkey's Refah Party', *International Journal of Middle East Studies* 33: 3 (August 2001), 433–48.

Gülalp, Haldun. 'Political Islam in Turkey: The Rise and Fall of the Refah Party', *The Muslim World* 89: 1 (1999), 22–41.

Gülalp, Haldun. 'The Poverty of Democracy in Turkey: The Refah Party Episode', *New Perspectives on Turkey* 21 (Fall 1999), 35–59.

Güney, Aylin. 'The People's Democratic Party', *Turkish Studies* 3: 1 (2002), 122–37.

Hale, William. 'Christian Democracy and the JDP: Parallels and Contrasts', in Yavuz, ed., *Emergence*, 66–87.

Hale, William. *The Political and Economic Development of Modern Turkey.* London: Croom Helm, 1981.

Hale, William. *Turkish Foreign Policy Since 1774, Third Edition.* London: Routledge, 2013.

Hale, William. *Turkish Politics and the Military.* London: Routledge, 1994.

Hale, William and Ergun Özbudun. *Islamism, Democracy and Liberalism in Turkey: The Case of the AKP.* London: Routledge, 2010.

Henry, Clement. 'Financial Performances of Islamic *versus* Conventional Banks', in Henry and Wilson, eds, *Politics of Islamic Finance*, 104–28.

Henry, Clement and Rodney Wilson, eds. *The Politics of Islamic Finance.* Edinburgh: Edinburgh University Press, 2004.

Heper, Metin. 'Islam, Polity and Society in Turkey: A Middle Eastern Perspective', *Middle East Journal* 35: 3 (Summer 1981), 345–63.

Hirsch, Eva. *Poverty and Plenty on the Turkish Farm: A Study of Income Distribution in Turkish Agriculture.* New York: Columbia University Press, 1970.

Hitti, Philip. *Siyasi ve Kültürel Islam Tarihi*, Turkish translation of *The History of the Arabs* (1937) by Salih Tuğ. Istanbul: Boğaziçi Yayınları, 1980.

Jenkins, Gareth. 'Muslim Democrats in Turkey', *Survival* 45: 1 (Spring 2003), 45–66.

Jenkins, Gareth. 'Symbols and Shadow Play: Military-JDP Relations', in Yavuz, ed., *Emergence*, 185–206.

Kafesoğlu, Ibrahim. *Türk-Islam Sentezi*. Istanbul: Aydınlar Ocağı, 1985.

Kahf, Monzer. 'Islamic Banks: The Rise of a New Power Alliance of Wealth and *Shari'a* Scholarship', in Henry and Wilson, eds, *Politics of Islamic Finance*, 17–36.

Kalaycıoğlu, Ersin. 'The Motherland Party: The Challenge of Institutionalization in a Charismatic Leader Party', in Rubin and Heper, eds, *Political Parties*, 41–61.

Kanli, Yusuf and Ozgur Eksi. 'Exclusive Interview with Abdullah Gül, the Foreign Policy Expert of the AK Party', *Hürriyet Daily News*, 2 September 2002.

Karasipahi, Sena. *Muslims in Modern Turkey: Kemalism, Modernism and the Revolt of the Islamic Intellectuals*. London: I. B. Tauris, 2009.

Kardaş, Saban. 'Turkey and the Iraqi Crisis: JDP Between Identity and Interest', in Yavus, ed., *Emergence*, 306–30.

Karpat, Kemal. 'The Social Effects of Farm Mechanization in Turkish Villages', *Social Research* 27: 1 (1960), 83–103.

Karpat, Kemal. *Turkey's Politics: the Transition to a Multi-Party System*. Princeton: Princeton University Press, 1959.

Karpat, Kemal. *Turkey's Politics: the Transition to a Multi-Party System*. Princeton: Princeton University Press, 1959.

'Kayseri Tayyare Fabrikasi (KTF)' at The Turkish Aircraft Production website (www.tuncay-deniz.com/ENGLISH/KTF/ktf.html).

Kazamias, Andreas. *Education and the Quest for Modernity in Turkey*. London: Allen and Unwin, 1966.

Keleş, Ruşen and Artun Ünsal. *Kent ve Siyasal Şiddet*. Ankara: Ankara Üniversitesi Siyasal Bilgiler Fakültesi Yayınları, 1982.

Kemal, Mustafa. *Nutuk-Söylev*, 2 vols. Ankara: Türk Tarih Kurumu, 1984.

Kemal, Orhan. *Bereketli Topraklar Üzerinde* ['On These Bountiful Lands']. 1954; rpt. Istanbul: Remzi Kitabevi, 1964.

Kemal, Orhan. *In Jail with Nazim Hikmet*. Trans. Bengisu Rona. London: Saqi, 2010.

Kemal, Yasar. *Memed My Hawk* (1955). Trans. Edouard Roditi. London: Collins, 1961.

Kerslake, Celia, Kerem Öktem and Philip Robins, eds. *Turkey's Engagement with Modernity: Conflict and Change in the Twentieth Century*. Basingstoke: Palgrave, 2010.

Kevorkian, Raymond. *The Extermination of Ottoman Armenians by the Young Turk Regime (1915-1916)* (2008), online at (www.massviolence.org/The-Extermination-of-Ottoman-Armenians-by-the-Young-Turk-Regime?artpage=17).

Kevorkian, Raymond. *Le Génocide des Arméniens*. Paris: Odile Jacob, 2006. Republished in an English version as *The Armenian Genocide: A Complete History*. London: I. B. Tauris, 2011.

Kinross, Patrick. *Atatürk: The Rebirth of a Nation*. 1964; rpt. London: Weidenfeld, 1993.

Köksal, Duygu. 'The Dilemmas of a Search for Cultural Synthesis: A Portrait of Cemil Meriç as a Conservative Intellectual', *New Perspectives on Turkey* 21 (Fall 1999), 79–102.

Koru, Fehmi. *One Column Ahead*. Istanbul: Timaş, 2000.

Kuran, Timur. *Islam and Mammon: The Economic Predicaments of Islamism*. Princeton, NJ: Princeton University Press, 2004.

Kurt, Umit. 'The Doctrine of "Turkish-Islamic Synthesis" as Official Ideology of the September 12 and the "Intellectuals' Hearth – Aydınlar Ocağı" as the Ideological Apparatus of the State', *European Journal of Economic and Political Studies* 3: 2 (2010), online at (http://ejeps.fatih.edu.tr/docs/articles/110.pdf).

Kuru, Ahmet and Alfred Stepan, eds. *Democracy, Islam, and Secularism in Turkey*. New York: Columbia University Press, 2012.

Lagendijk, Joost. 'Mehmet Ali Birand in a Class of His Own.' *Today's Zaman*, 20 January 2013.

Lagendijk, Joost. 'Turkey's Accession to the European Union and the Role of the Justice and Development Party'. In Kuru and Stepan, eds, *Democracy*, 166–88.

Landau, Jacob. *Radical Politics in Turkey*. Leiden: Brill, 1974.

Landau, Jacob. 'The National Salvation Party in Turkey', *Asian and African Studies* 11: 1 (1976), 1–57.

Lawson, Ruth C. 'New Regime in Turkey', *Current History* 52: 306 (February 1967), 105–10.

Lewis, Geoffrey. *Turkey*. London: Benn, 1955.

Linke, Lilo. *Allah Dethroned: A Journey Through Modern Turkey*. London: Constable, 1937.

Lombardi, Ben. 'Turkey and Israel: Brinkmanship and the Grand Strategy of the Erdoğan Government', *The Levantine Review* 1: 1 (Spring 2012), 7–22.

MacLean, Gerald, ed. *Britain and the Muslim World: Historical Perspectives*. Newcastle: Cambridge Scholars, 2011.

MacLean, Gerald. 'Strolling in Seventeenth-Century Syria'. In Marius Kociejowski, ed., *Syria Through Travellers' Eyes*. London: Eland, 2006, 227–35.

MacLean, Gerald. 'Motoring with Mehmet'. In Barnaby Rogerson and Rose Baring, eds, *Meetings with Remarkable Muslims*. London: Eland, 2005, 106–22.

MacLean, Gerald. *The Rise of Oriental Travel: English Visitors to the Ottoman Empire, 1580–1720*. Basingstoke: PalgraveMacmillan, 2004. Turkish translation by Dilek Şendil, *Doğu'ya Yolculuğun Yükselişi: Osmanlı İmparatorluğun İngiliz Konuları (1580–1720)*. Istanbul: Yapı Kredi Yayınları, 2006.

Mango, Andrew. *Atatürk*. London: Murray, 1999.

Mango, Andrew. *The Turks Today*. London: Murray, 2004.

Mardin, Şerif. *Religion and Social Change in Modern Turkey: The Case of Bediüzzaman Said Nursi*. Albany, New York: SUNY Press, 1989.

Mardin, Şerif. 'Culture Change and the Intellectual: A Study of the Effects of Secularization in Modern Turkey: Necip Fazıl and the Nakşibendi.' In Mardin, ed., *Cultural Transitions*, 189–213.

Mardin, Şerif, ed. *Cultural Transitions in the Middle East*. Leiden: Brill, 1994.

Momin, A. R. 'Dr Muhammad Hamidullah (1909–2002)', at (www.renaissance.com.pk/
Febobti2y4.html).

Morris, Chris. *The New Turkey: The Quiet Revolution on the Edge of Europe*. London: Granta,
2005.

Muradoğlu, Abdullah. '68'li Başbakan,' at Yeni Şafak website (http://yenisafak.com.tr/
diziler/agul/index.html).

Narli, Mehmet. *Orhan Kemal'in Romanlari Uzerine Bir Inceleme*. Ankara: T. C. Kültür Bakanlığı,
2002.

Nasr, Seyyed Vali Reza. *Forces of Fortune: The Rise of the New Muslim Middle Class and What
It Will Mean for Our World*. London: Free Press, 2009.

Naval Intelligence Division of the British Admiralty. *Geographical Handbook Series, Turkey*,
2 vols. [London]: HMSO, 1942, 1943.

Neyzi, Leyla and Hranush Kharatyan-Araqelyan. *Speaking to One Another*. Bonn: DVV
International, 2010.

Offley, Ed. *Scorpion Down: Sunk by the Soviets, Buried by the Pentagon*. New York: Basic
Books, 2007.

Öğüzlü, H. Tarik. 'Changing Dynamics of Turkey's US and EU Relations', *Middle East Policy*
11: 1 (Spring 2004), 98–105.

Öktem, Kerem. *Angry Nation; Turkey Since 1989*. London: Zed, 2011.

Öniş, Ziya. 'Domestic Politics versus Global Dynamics: Towards a Political Economy
of the 2000 and 2001 Financial Crisis in Turkey', in Öniş and Rubin, eds, *Turkish
Economy*, 1–30.

Öniş, Ziya. 'The Evolution of Privatization in Turkey: The Institutional Context of Public-
Enterprise Reform', *IJMES* 23: 2 (May 1991), 163–76.

Öniş, Ziya. 'The Political Economy of Turkey's JDP', in Yavuz, ed., *Emergence*, 207–34.

Öniş, Ziya. *State and Market: The Political Economy of Turkey in Comparative Perspective*.
Istanbul: Boğaziçi University Press, 2008.

Öniş, Ziya and Barry Rubin, eds. *The Turkish Economy in Crisis*. London: Cass, 2003.

Öniş, Ziya and Fikret Şenses. 'The New Phase of Neo-Liberal Restructuring in Turkey: An
Overview', in Öniş and Şenses, eds, *Turkey and the Global Economy*, 1–10.

Öniş, Ziya and Fikret Şenses, eds, *Turkey and the Global Economy: Neo-liberal Restructuring
in the Post-crisis Era*. Abingdon: Routledge, 2009.

Özbudun, Ergun. 'State Elites and Democratic Culture in Turkey', in Diamond, ed., *Political
Culture*, 247–68.

Öğüzlü, H. Tarik. 'Changing Dynamics of Turkey's US and EU Relations', *Middle East Policy*
11: 1 (Spring 2004), 98–105.

Pearson, John. 'Turkey's Gulf War Gamble May be Paying Off', *Businessweek* website (http://
www.businessweek.com/stories/1991-04-21/turkeys-gulf-war-gamble-may-be-paying-
off), 21 April 1991.

Pirim, Nurettin, ed. *Tanzimat'tan Bugüne Edebiyatçılar Ansiklopedisi*. Istanbul: Yapı Kredi
Yayınları, 2001.

Pope, Hugh. 'Erdoğan Can Win by Engaging Turkey's Park Protesters.' International Crisis Group website (www.crisisgroup.org), 7 June 2013.

Pope, Nicole. 'Breaking with the Past?', *Middle East International* 688 (22 November 2002), 18–20.

Pope, Nicole and Hugh Pope, *Turkey Unveiled: A History of Modern Turkey: Revised and Updated*. 1997; New York: Overlook, 2011.

Poulton, Hugh. *Top Hat, Grey Wolf and Crescent: Turkish Nationalism and the Turkish Republic*. London: Hurst, 1997.

Poyraz, Ergün. *Musa'nin Gül'ü*. Istanbul: Togan Yayınları, 2007.

Rice, Condoleezza. *No Higher Honour: A Memoir of My Years in Washington*. New York: Simon and Schuster, 2011.

Robins, Philip. *Suits and Uniforms: Turkish Foreign Policy since the Cold War*. London: Hurst, 2003.

Roos, Leslie, Noralou Roos and Gary R. Field. 'Students and Politics in Turkey', *Daedalus: Journal of the American Academy* 97: 1 (Winter 1968), 184–203.

Rubin, Barry and Metin Heper, eds. *Political Parties in Turkey*. London: Cass, 2002.

Rubin, Michael. 'A Comedy of Errors: American–Turkish Diplomacy and the Iraq War', *Turkish Policy Quarterly* 4: 1 (2005), at (www.turkishpolicy.com).

Rubin, Michael. 'Green Money, Islamist Politics in Turkey', *Middle East Quarterly* (Winter 2005), 13–23.

Sağlam, Süleyman. *Dağı Dağa Kavuşturan*. Istanbul: Can, 1999. English translation by Nancy F. Öztürk with Adnan Tonguç, *Embracing the Mountains*. Istanbul: Çitlembik, 2004.

Samim, Ahmet. 'The Left', in Schick and Tonak, eds, *Turkey in Transition*, 147–76.

Satoğlu, Abdullah interview (18 December 2009), online at *525-ci Gazet* website (old.525. az/view.php?lang=en&menu=12&id=23696&type=1).

Schick, Irvin C. and Ertuğrul Ahmet Tonak, eds. *Turkey in Transition: New Perspectives*. New York: Oxford University Press, 1987.

Selim, Yavuz. *Gül'ün Adı…* ['The Name of the Rose…']. Ankara: Kim Yayınları, 2002.

Sözen, Edibe. 'Gender Politics of the JDP', in Yavuz, ed., *Emergence*, 258–80.

Szyliowicz, Joseph. 'The Turkish Elections: 1965' *Middle East Journal* 20: 4 (Autumn, 1966), 473–94.

Szyliowicz, Joseph. 'Students and Politics in Turkey', *Middle Eastern Studies* 6: 2 (May 1970), 150–62.

Şen, Serdar. *Refah Partisi'nin Teori ve Pratiği*. Istanbul: Sarmal, 1995.

Taşkın, Hasan. *11 Başkomutan Abdullah Gül*. Istanbul: Neden, 2007.

Tezcür, Güneş Murat. *Muslim Reformers in Iran and Turkey: The Paradox of Moderation*. Austin, TX: University of Texas Press, 2010.

Timur, Taner. 'The Ottoman Heritage', in Schick and Tonak, eds, *Turkey in Transition*, 3–26.

Tokatli, Nebahat and Ömür Kızılgün. 'Upgrading in the Global Clothing Industry: Mavi Jeans and the Transformation of a Turkish Firm from Full-Package to Brand-Name Manufacturing and Retailing', *Economic Geography* 80: 3 (July 2004), 221–40.

Uncular, M. Hasan. 'Abdullah Gül's Unknown Sides/Exclusive', *World Bulletin* website (www.worldbulletin.net), 12 August 2007.

Vaner, Semih. 'The Army', in Schick and Tonak, eds, *Turkey in Transition*, 236–65.

van Velsen, Leo. *Peripheral Production in Kayseri, Turkey: A Study of Prospects for Industrialization Arising from Small- and Middle-Scale Enterprises in a Peripheral Growth Pole.* Trans. Donald Bloch. The Hague: NUFFIC/ IMWOO/ REMPLOD, 1977.

Webster, Donald Everett. *The Turkey of Atatürk: Social Process in the Turkish Reformation.* Philadelphia: American Academy of Political and Social Science, 1939.

White, Jenny. *Islamist Mobilization in Turkey: A Study in Vernacular Politics.* Seattle, WA: University of Washington Press, 2002.

Wiegers, Gerard. 'Dr Sayyid Mutwalli ad-Darsh's *fatwas* for Muslims in Britain: The Voice of Official Islam?', in MacLean, ed., *Britain and the Muslim World*, 179–92.

Wilson, Rodney. 'Capital Flight through Islamic Managed Funds', in Henry and Wilson, eds, *Politics of Islamic Finance*, 129–52.

Yavuz, M. Hakan. *Islamic Political Identity in Turkey.* Oxford: Oxford University Press, 2003.

Yavuz, M. Hakan. *Secularism and Muslim Democracy in Turkey.* Cambridge: Cambridge University Press, 2009.

Yavuz, M. Hakan, ed. *The Emergence of a New Turkey: Democracy and the AK Parti.* Salt Lake City, UT: University of Utah Press, 2006.

Yerli, Yusuf. 'Gül'ün Adı,' *Kayseri Haber* website (www.kayserihaber.com.tr/yazar-59), 5 December 2011.

Yeşilada, Birol and Barry Rubin, eds. *Islamization of Turkey under the AKP Rule.* London: Routledge, 2011.

Yıldırım, Engin. 'Labor Pains or Achilles' Heel: The Justice and Development Party and Labor in Turkey', in Yavuz, ed., *Emergence,* 235–57.

Yıldız, Ahmet. 'Problematizing the Intellectual and Political Vestiges', in Cizre, ed., *Secular and Islamic Politics*, 41–61.

Zaman, Amberin. 'The Looming Power Struggle Between Erdoğan and Gülenists', *Al-Monitor Turkey Pulse* (www.almonitor.com), 19 May 2013.

Zürcher, Eric. *Turkey: A Modern History.* 1993; 3rd revised edition, London: I. B. Tauris, 2004.

INDEX